THE GOOD NEWS NOBODY TALKS ABOUT

Christianity in Today's World

To Paugen & Sheila
With all good wishes
and Blessings.   *Lily*
               Lily Cloughley

First published in 2023 © Lily Cloughley 2023

Imprint: Independently published through Amazon

ISBN: 9798393191702

The Bible quoted throughout this book is the New Jerusalem Bible, Darton, Longman and Todd Limited. Standard edition published 1985.

©1985 by Darton, Longman and Todd Ltd and Doubleday & Company Inc. ISBN: 8459929493. All rights reserved. Used with permission

Extracts are not always literal quotes

Not written for financial gain, but to promote Christianity

Cover photograph: Marc Cloughley

To Mike

CONTENTS

Foreword		7
1	Some Reflections	13
2	What is this Good News?	48
3	The 10 Commandments	63
4	Christianity	68
5	The Coming of Jesus	106
6	Jesus' Mission Statement	117
7	Jesus Heals with a Word	120
8	The Cor et Lumen Christi Community	128
9	What Damian has to Say	136
10	Charismatic Renewal and The Holy Spirit	139
11	Jackie's Story	157
12	Multiplication of Loaves	163
13	The Power of the Eucharist	167
14	The Resurrection	175
15	Guardian Angels	181
16	Ghosts and Spirits	192

17	Satan and Exorcism	200
18	Heaven, Hell and Repentance	219
19	Apparitions of Mary	234
20	The Bible	251
21	Great Conversions	255
22	Finding Faith	269

Abbreviations for Books of The Bible	274
Notes	275

FOREWORD

Rising atheism in the western world, especially amongst the young, has been the driving force for writing this book. It seems that society is losing its way in a dark maze of a rapidly evolving technology, changing norms and novel ideas, akin to the pre-Christian era, when human life had little purpose and the prospect of hope was bleak. Humans cannot live without hope and yet all around we see signs of hopelessness and chaos, of crimes and despair.

I have written this book for people of all faiths and none who feel inspired to read it. I would like my readers to include parents and those who are educating the next generation, and all who were brought up in the Christian faith but during the course of their lives have renounced the Christian teaching as a lot of rubbish, untrue, irrelevant, or a story "we were told as children to keep us sweet."

In "The Good News Nobody Talks About", I will try to reconnect society with the centre of the maze, Jesus Christ, the Saviour of the world, who came to lead us out of this very darkness that the modern world seems to have plunged into and restore society to its rightful place in Christ's true light. Christ declared so often, "I am the light of the world, whoever follows me will not walk in darkness, but will have the light of life" (Jn 8:12).

My main source of inspiration is The Bible, this increasingly neglected tome. It is in the pages of the Old and New Testaments that we can trace who Jesus really was and the true purpose of his coming into the world. The Bible gives us hope that life is not an end in itself, but that it has a real meaning after all.

THE GOOD NEWS NOBODY TALKS ABOUT

During the three years of his public life in Galilee, Jesus restored the lives of the lame and the blind and of all those who were suffering from diseases of one kind or another. As impressive as miracles might be, they are not the essence of the Good News. Miracles are simply the means through which Jesus demonstrated that he has power over all creation, because as well as being totally human he is also totally divine.

Our own experience of evil, suffering and death often seems to contradict this Good News story. Is Jesus, who died 2000 years ago, still relevant in this age of atheism, reasoning, advanced technology, and scientific progress? Can we believe these ancient stories, and can they possibly make a difference to our present lifestyle, frequently of hedonism and instant gratification?

We will open the Book and page by page walk with Jesus through Galilee and see if he has left any footprints for us to follow which could change our lives for the better. Reading the Bible is like going on a treasure hunt: it contains so many precious pearls that we never knew or even dared to believe. "The kingdom of heaven is like treasure hidden in a field which someone has found; he hides it again, goes off in his joy, sells everything he owns and buys the field. Again, the kingdom of heaven is like a merchant looking for fine pearls ...." (Mt 13:44-45). St Augustine of Hippo urges us to "Dig deep in Christ for he is like a rich mine containing many treasures; however deep we dig, we will never find their limit. Indeed, in every pocket new seams of fresh richness will be discovered". And this is what we will do in this story, dig again for these pearls which have remained hidden for too long. Although we may not realise it, we have been sorely bereft without them, and we now stand by hopelessly watching our world descend into chaos and our youth into helplessness. The reality is that we have a spiritual nature, and we have the God-given power to revolutionize the world. This reality seems to have passed us by unnoticed.

FOREWORD

GK Chesterton, the great Christian writer, once said, "The trouble with Christianity is not that is has been tried and tested, it has never been tried". On the contrary, there are many who have tried and tested Christianity, and we will share the most amazing life changing conversions and healings they experienced following a personal encounter with Jesus, the risen Lord. We will compare contemporary experiences of believers and non-believers to the miracles Jesus performed which we read about in the gospels.

The lame, the deaf, the blind, the unloved, the drug addicts and the violent all have a story to tell when they dared to believe the promise Jesus made when he said, "I have come, so that you may have life, and have it to the full."

All good news needs to be shared, and that is exactly what the disciples did. Any recipient of good news is dying to share it like the disciples who could not contain themselves and forthwith obeyed Jesus' command, "Go out in the whole world and proclaim the Gospel to all creation" (Mk16:16). They set out immediately to proclaim far and wide this marvellous Good News of the love for all humanity of Jesus Christ. With this book I want to continue in this vein, sharing the Good News. I also want to share the good news I personally received with all who care to read it.

Throughout this book the word "Christianity" or the "Christian faith" refers to the teaching of Jesus Christ which he shared with his disciples and the people when he walked with them for three years through Judea and Galilee, and which was later recorded in the Gospels of the New Testament in the Bible.

As this book has been written over a period of five years, it has slowly taken on the shape of individual cameos. Each chapter could be an individual story in its own right. As such the reader will come across repetitions, for which I hope I will be forgiven. I have also tried, as best I can, to link each chapter to the golden thread of God's love running through the book.

It is my first attempt at writing a book, and it is not in my mother tongue. I realise I could have probably been more sparing with words and that I may not have adhered to the golden maxim, when writing, "less is more".

The main sources of inspiration are my love of history and a compilation of the numerous notes taken during the many courses and talks I have attended during the last decades, such as, at The Catholic Bible School, Oak Hill Extension College, the Prayer Group, The Alpha Course and especially the inspired teaching by the Cor et Lumen Christi Community. But my greatest inspiration is, of course, the Holy Spirit, the inspired word of God. The contributions of people's personal experiences and life stories were invaluable and contributed to the richness and veracity of The Good News Story. Without them the book would lose the objective for which it was written.

ACKNOWLEDGEMENTS

It would not have been possible to write this book without my husband Mike who, during these last five years stood patiently by me, and encouraged me with positive ideas and perceptive suggestions. I cannot find the right words to thank him enough for his loyal devotion and unwavering belief in me.

I wish to thank Fr Niven, my parish priest for his invaluable input, making sure what I wrote was theologically correct. And special thanks go to Richard Grey who, for many hours over the years, ploughed through the script, making useful corrections to the contents.

And a huge thanks goes to Alastair Emblem for his initial

FOREWORD

editing "The Good News Nobody Talks About". Alastair graciously accepted this onerous and time-consuming task, waving every offer of renumeration aside, regardless of being already actively involved in many areas of ministry in the Catholic Church. Having just published his own book, "Pray as you Can't," I could not have turned to a more experienced friend.

I am indebted and most grateful to my son Marc, who time and again came to my rescue when my computer ignorance let me down; and for the enormous task involved in publishing this labour of love and bringing the book into reality.

1

SOME REFLECTIONS

THE STORY OF THE BOY IN TROUBLE

In her book "The Word on the Wind" (a) Alison Morgan tells us the following story:

> Two Street Pastors were walking the streets at 2am, when the pubs close and young people leave. Seeing the logo on Anne's jacket a group of youngsters called out, "Are you Christians?" "Yes, we are," said Anne. Pointing to his left temple one said, "Do you see this scar?" This scar he had told his friends he got in a fight. "Yes, that's what I said, but I really got it when I had cancer aged nine. I was terrified. They were going to cut out the lump from my head and I might lose my sight and go blind. I was terrified but I prayed, 'God if you are really there, get me through this please.' I didn't lose my sight and I was cured of the cancer. I was so grateful to Jesus I went out and I bought this" and he pulled out a cross on a chain. His friends were staring in disbelief, "We didn't know you got that." "Yes, and I got this too." Opening his jacket, he revealed a T-shirt with a big black cross on it. "I don't know much about it, but I reckon there is someone up there looking out for me."

THE GOOD NEWS NOBODY TALKS ABOUT

The story of the boy did not appear in our newspapers. Such wonderful and heart- warming stories don't often feature in the media; gory stories or celebrity misdemeanours draw more sales. Yet deep down we all wish the boy's story could be true because we all love to hear good news. With the constant deluge in our media of disasters and corruption, we have become resistant to ungrounded stories of healings, or that God, if he exists at all, would intervene in anybody's life in the way the boy claimed.

The boy had no such thoughts. He cried for help to Jesus, and as far as he was concerned, he was healed. He did not lose his sight as the doctors had predicted and his operation was a complete success. He was sure there was someone up there who was looking after him. It would be great if we could all be just as trusting and believing as the boy was. Sadly though, along the way our nature has become inclined to dismiss divine interventions, and our acceptance of healings now rests only on solid medical evidence and there is no room for speculation. After all, the boy could have just been plain lucky, or he must have had excellent medical care.

With the enormous progress in science, technology and medicine, communications and exploring the universe, we have become somewhat cynical about supernatural interventions and the existence of God. It has become prevalent to challenge such reports and to ask questions. Blind belief, without irrefutable scientific evidence, has become a thing of the past and it is now evident that everything we want to know can be obtained from the internet or social media. We love to watch mysteries on TV, but we have little time for real life mysteries because they undermine the security gained through scientific knowledge, and it is important to be seen as people who are in touch with the latest fads and trends and news. It is all too true to say that miracles and religion are not on the agenda anymore, and if we take heed of them, we are labelled as gullible and scientifically ignorant. This is just not on. Worldwide, from the young to the old, many have fallen prey to the relentless call of their gadgets, resulting in loneliness that has grown at an alarming rate.

In Britain, according to a YouGov Poll (b): "Before 1982 when electronic gadgets did not exist, 76% of the population never felt lonely, but by 2010 this had fallen to 32%. People have more acquaintances online, but fewer close friends. Mother Theresa's remark that, "Loneliness is the disease of the West" appears to be true.

EXPLORING THE PURPOSE OF LIFE

Aristotle once said, "All men by nature desire to know." How true, as there will always be an urge to fulfil an innate desire for beauty in art, music, and literature, and to improve the quality of life. Yet, although the world has really become our oyster, surprisingly, we do not seem any happier than previous generations. A few decades ago, people would have given the world for the stable and secure existence we have achieved today. Looking back several decades, it appeared that people were content with their lot, and when lacking the material goods enjoyed today, they turned to religion for their material and spiritual needs. Friedrich Nietzsche, the German philosopher, hit the nail on the head when he said that "science has eliminated the need for God". Just as our spiritual wellbeing thrives on our close relationship with God, humans thrive on close contact with family and friends, parents, cousins, neighbours. Our happiness depends on these relationships expressed, not through gadgets, but through eye contact, facial expressions, love, and touch, but technology has cleverly managed to transform us into mere robots, who have lost the human and spiritual touch.

Technology is now progressing so fast that unless it is carefully managed it may soon get out of hand. And Nietzsche's remark, by all accounts, has become true; people are setting more store by the new-found truth of their material affluence and values than in their spiritual wellbeing. Their need and relationship with God, who is ultimately the source of all happiness, has all but disappeared. In her book "The Word on the Wind" (c), Alison Morgan asserts that 'Science can neither answer nor fulfil all our deepest desires since it is not interested in the purpose of life, only in the "How" and not in the "Why."

Sooner or later, I presume, most people will want to know the answer to questions such as, "Why did the universe come into being?" "What is the meaning of human existence?" "Is there life after death?" "What happens after we die?" These tend to relentlessly niggle at our subconscious and, as life progresses, they become more urgent by the day. Are we just a speck of dust in the universe, we wonder, aimlessly spinning around with no purpose? And how do we explain the restlessness within us, always searching beyond what we already have, and never being satisfied; or the outrage we feel at all the injustices in the world and the suffering of others. If we are just an accident of chemistry, why do we feel compassion and love? Are these questions not relevant, as some scientists make us believe, "for why should life have a meaning" some like to argue? The human body is not only made up of chemical elements like oxygen and hydrogen but, as Genesis the first book of the Bible tells us, it is created in the image and likeness of the creator God. Like him, we are sentient spiritual beings with emotions, feelings, and intelligence. It is doubtful that scientifically it will ever be possible to trace the origins of the human species within all the many chemical elements that make up the universe.

SOME REFLECTIONS

When all is said and done, we cannot ignore the fact that, despite our infinitely improved lifestyle and scientific progress, there is somehow a broken link in the chain of, on the one hand our material wellbeing, and on the other, the apparent breakdown in society. As much as modern society wants to advocate that after life there is void, and that we are just an accident of birth, people do not feel happy with this statement judging from the tremendous rise in the search for truth and for spiritual fulfilment. According to what we read in the media, more and more people turn to Eastern religions like Buddhism, Yoga, meditation, and gurus offering "Find Yourself" courses and must have personal shamans who for £300 an hour who will help you find your true self through mind reading, and information received from the other side. Yet without fully understanding what this "information from the other side' might mean, people readily fall for it. Such is the growing desire to get back in touch with our spiritual nature.

An interesting observation is that succumbing to prayer in the hour of need is not something a non-believer would readily turn to. Yet we have seen many times that through our human nature we instinctively grasp for any straw when danger is imminent and start to pray, desperately hoping that there might somehow be a higher power able to come to the rescue. The following story, to my mind, clearly shows that subconsciously, people know, that in the deepest recess of their being there is someone who will save them and protect them.

One day, during a journey by helicopter we were caught in an incredibly fierce thunderstorm. We were buffeted and tossed by the storm in all directions and the lightning was awesome. We feared for our lives but fortunately we touched down safely. No sooner had we set foot on solid ground when my friend, who is an atheist said, "I have never prayed in my life, but my goodness, this time I did".

Not so long ago there was a belief in God and an awareness of his love and protection. Visiting the First World War Cemeteries brought this vividly to bear. These heart-breaking memorials have become places of pilgrimage for tourists as well as for the relatives of the fallen soldiers. Great busloads of people from many countries arrive every year in the north of France and Flanders, to honour those who offered up their lives for their country and the world. And it was striking to see how, on nearly every soldier's grave, the epitaph carries a religious dedication. These religious quotations are a powerful witness of how people derived comfort and hope from their faith in remembering their loved ones, and faith and religion played a major role in all aspects of life, like families praying together before meals and at bedtime. These, and many more deeply ingrained religious practices have largely disappeared.

There is now a deep void in many peoples' lives of which they are acutely aware, but they see no way out. The maxim, "to believe in nothing is void, but to believe in something gives hope" is so true. And this is the great appeal of the Christian message: it is a message of hope and of love, expressed in Jesus dead on the cross. He did not wait until we were "good," he died for us anyway, so that he could fulfil his promise of eternal life for each of us. It is a love that will not let us go, because he desperately wants every individual on earth to enter the gates of Paradise which he opened by paying such an unbearable price.

Yes, the gates of the Garden of Eden are open, and all we need to do is to walk through them. Jesus cannot do this for us. Our problem, however, is that all too often we are not willing. Humans have an uncanny ability to cling to their anxieties, which are often of their own making. Although hope drives away the shadow of discouragement, we would rather rely on our own strength and resources even though this is a very negative way to tackle the ups and downs of life. It can lead to a debilitating state of despair, with not a glimmer of hope in sight, and soon depression sets in. Hope is so ingrained in the human psyche that nobody can live without constantly looking forward to the nice things in life - a holiday, a family visit, a seaside visit - longing to be healed, to be loved. This has been strongly evident in the recent Covid epidemic when people were forced to live in isolation, with no prospect of seeing family and friends. It had unprecedented negative effects on their mental and physical health.

We find so many comforting assertions from God that he can help us, but in how many homes is the Bible still present where one can dig for those precious pearls? "He is our strength and our and help, an ever-present help in trouble." (Psalm 46). "Perfect love casts out your fear" (1 Jn 4:18). Or "Come to me all who labour, and are overburdened, and I will give you rest. Shoulder my yoke and learn from me, for I am gentle and humble in heart, and you will find rest for your souls, for my yoke is easy and my burden light" (Mt 11:28-30). When in despair, we can cry for help and see if anybody is out there who can come to our aid. And not surprisingly, the innate presence of God in our souls, as he promises, does hear, and answer our pleas. If it were not so, prayer would be totally ineffective, meaningless, and powerless. And why is it so effective? It is because we are tapping into the dynamic power of the cosmos, into a creator God, for whom nothing is impossible.

There is a saying, "God governs the world, but prayer governs God", so we can be sure that He is forever listening and acting upon the pleas of those who pray, if what they ask is good for themselves, their neighbour, and the world. "If we know that He listens to whatever we ask of Him, we know that we already possess whatever we have asked" (1Jn:15).

Some people may be uncomfortable with a kind of God who intervenes and alters events, like in healing, but does not intervene in times of disaster. The truth is there are many examples when God intervened in the world during a crisis. Three examples I have heard of are first, the story of the so called "Angel of Mons", (d) which relates how angels came to the rescue of the English soldiers during the first World War in response to the prayer vigils that were taking place in London (c). Second, it is said that due to the many people praying for him, President FW de Klerk, who first was fiercely in favour of apartheid, relented and implemented the changes which brought apartheid to an end, because of a conversion experience. And third, the most famous example of God intervening in a war, is the "Battle of Lepanto. It was fought on 7th October 1571 between the combined Christian naval forces and the fleet of the Ottoman Empire, in the gulf of Patras in western Greece. Pope Pius V urged people in Rome to go to church and petition the intercession of the Virgin Mary through praying the rosary. Despite being in the minority, the combined Christian forces scored a resounding victory." (e)

We often stand powerless in the face of natural disasters and ask why God does not intervene. Unfortunately, natural disasters occur because, like the human race, our earth became imperfect when humanity separated itself from God and evil entered the world. Even today we see how our precious planet is being destroyed by our neglect. And wars, as well, are the result of man's greed and hatred. In Romans, St Paul writes, "We are well aware that the whole of creation has been groaning in labour pains, and even we are groaning inside ourselves, waiting with eagerness for our bodies to be set free. And the whole creation itself might be set free from corruption and be brought into the same glorious freedom as the children of God" (Rm 8:22-24). However, after all the anguish there is a promise, "God will wipe away all tears from your eyes and there will no more death, and no more mourning and sadness". As discussed previously, all His promises are not just empty words, for He says, "The word, that goes out from my mouth will not return to me unfulfilled before having carried out my good pleasure and having achieved what it was sent out to do" (Is 55:11). In Genesis, when God spoke a Word, things happened, but it is essential that we believe God's promises if we want to reap the full benefit from them.

Since stopping to believe "in all that religious rubbish", much has been forsaken of what could restore our mental and physical health, and the prospect of finding hope for many people trapped in desperation has become a fleeting hope.

A CRY FOR HELP AT AN ALPHA COURSE

Lucy (*name changed*) went through an incredibly harrowing experience when her sister died in an accident. She was extremely close to her sister, and it affected her deeply when she had to identify the body. It affected her so deeply that she blocked it from her mind for a while and went into denial, refusing to talk about it at all. She says, "I didn't know where or whom to turn to. I was crying all the time, getting to the point that I could not function anymore." One evening she found herself sobbing and crying to God: "If you are there, you have to do something to help me. I don't know what to do any more." The next day she walked past a church and saw a poster advertising the Alpha course, which is an interdenominational course explaining the Christian faith. She took this as a sign and enrolled to attend. "I wanted to find out what life was all about and if there could be a God who loves us," she said. At the end of the course, she started to go to church with her two daughters and became totally integrated and even started to help on Alpha herself.

When life dealt her another rough hand with hospital visits and the break-up of her marriage, she says, "I could not have got through all this without my faith, I now have a much greater understanding of why I am here and what my life is about. That gives me a far greater sense of purpose... I felt desperate when I went on Alpha, and I could have easily ended up completely depressed. I am a different person now and every day I ask the Holy Spirit to guide me and show me the right way to live. I have no doubts that my life is in his hands." It was also by inviting her parents on an Alpha Course that her parents received a new lease of life after the death of their daughter.

THE BREAKUP OF SOCIETY

Becoming a more rational, thinking society and getting hooked on gadgets are no doubt reasons why people have abandoned religion and belief in God. Material affluence and growing consumerism are also to blame. The period of austerity that people lived through during the war brought about a reaction, and morals relaxed as wealth grew. People started to live with abandon, as they had never had it so good. There was no more need for a God or religion.

It now seems that society is in the grip of selfishness and hedonism, with everybody making up their own rules as they go along. Soon marriage was the first victim of this looser way of living and divorce increased at an alarming rate. True, there are various reasons why it is better for both partners and even for the children that a couple should separate, nevertheless, I think that most can agree that the family is the happiest environment for a child to grow up in. Marriage is often called the knot that binds society together. Sadly, we see that the knot has become untangled, often because of the added stress of trying to juggle two jobs, career pressures, looking after children, and finding time for one's own needs. The added stress, coupled with the increasing focus on self, means that divorce has become more generally acceptable and commonplace, jeopardising the happiness of the children. It leaves in its wake young people wrenched away from their safe environment and creates an open wound of rejection, and as so often is the case, leading to mental and physical problems which then find an outlet in drugs and gang culture. The recent confession from a famous singer says it all: how she left her husband and child because she was putting herself first; if she stayed in the marriage, she would become unhappy. Contrary to expectation, the happiness she sought evaded her. As the lyric from her song explains, "I made him really unhappy, and this is a real wound for me that I don't know if I'll ever be able to heal." The latest statistics show that the main reason for a breakup between spouses is selfishness.

We can of course not stop humanity from progressing. It will inevitably bring about enormous changes for the better, but it may also have a sting in the tail. One step forward has been the emancipation of women in the western world. Finally, women have won the right to vote, to have a career, to become financially independent from their husbands, and to play an important role in society, in politics and in the arts and science. This advancement brought added pressure on the family with both spouses working, and at the same time caring for children and their own wellbeing. The triple bonus of being able to pursue a career, together with a double income, and now being able to regulate their biological clock, opened for them, as never before, a newfound vista of unfulfilled dreams come true.

These changes did not come one day too soon, and happily for the working woman the world has become her oyster, fulfilling a desire for self-realization and self-satisfaction on all levels. But in turn this has certainly led to a more individualistic approach. A double salary has encouraged consumerism and a focus on material possessions which resulted in an obsession with self, and the need for constant happiness, be it by amassing possessions, indulging in pleasure, or finding true love. However, self-seeking fulfilment has little or nothing to do with authentic love, which at its heart always has sacrifice, commitment and perseverance, ideals which generally have now been happily discarded. Love these days is more subject to the capriciousness of our ever-changing emotions and more bereft of the steadfast resolve to hang on in there.

"My rights, my free choice, he or she does not make me happy, so I am off" has become all too commonplace, and the consideration of "but do I make him or her happy" and "what will become of the children" does not in many cases enter the equation. All this has made the long-term commitment to marriage and fidelity a thing of the past. Motherhood as well has fallen to second class status, secondary to holding a career. Sometimes it was scorned upon not to have a job, and just staying at home to look after the kids was viewed as demeaning. The confession of a successful businesswoman in The Times Magazine of 29 January 2022 is all revealing, "the idea of being a mother and staying at home with the children was for her, and for most of her colleagues, an abhorrent idea."

Obviously, the world is filled with good people who do, or do not, hold a religious belief, and they lead happy and fulfilled lives, contributing liberally to multiple good causes and creating a happy family bond. But the abundance of free choices we now have in divorcing, in food and clothes, in travel, beliefs, sexual partners, gender, abortion, drugs, the right to die, etc. leaves the door wide open to do exactly as one pleases, rather than adhering to any religious norms, moral code, or just plainly doing one's duty. Governed by changing feelings, whims and wishes, and giving in without restraint to every desire and passion, with everybody claiming this as their entitlement; the moral compass has changed so dramatically that there is an alarming upward spiral in intolerance, violence, selfishness, ungratefulness, lack of respect and greed, rarely witnessed in the recent past, and the rapid rejection of God's laws.

Many people, and especially the older generations, feel powerless as they watch society crumble. A general feeling prevails that our past Christian history which made much of humanity compassionate, just, charitable, creative, loving, spiritual, forgiving, hopeful and tolerant has given way to the notion that we are just flesh and bones, easily fed by food and fun, and we might as well indulge in whatever we wish as the end will just be a box of bones or a jar of ashes. The point is reached that we have lost the ability to stem the rise in suicides and crime in the young which has risen at an alarming rate. According to the UK National Statistics male suicides are 75% higher than female suicides and have risen by 78% since 2013. The Samaritans' findings are equally dire: there are more deaths by suicide than by road accidents, many by men under the age of 35. Feelings of helplessness, desperation or living without hope all contribute to the rise in mental health issues and young people especially are a group most likely to be influenced by the media. And how do we make sense of 14-year-olds marauding the streets with knives, like feral animals out for the killing? How do we tackle poverty, rough sleeping, wars, and torture? How did everything get so out of hand, and do we just turn a blind eye and let all this wash over us and feel desperately helpless?

Dostoyevsky made a poignant remark, "If it were not for Christ's Church indeed there would be no restraint on the criminal in his evil doings and no punishment for it later" (f). And in a recent interview, even Professor Dawkins the great atheist, also expressed the same opinion saying, "If religion were to disappear people would indulge in all sorts of wrong behaviour." Are these two statements right and is this not what we see today in the knife crime in our streets, drug culture, the oversexualisation of the young and the rejection of what made society safe and responsible in the past?

We have highlighted some of the events, such as the scientific and economic progress and more recently the communications revolution and the emancipation of women. All secured enormous benefits for society, but also contributed in some way to the slow decline of the Christian faith, starting already with the Age of Reason. And who would not want to buy readily into a more comfortable and enjoyable life even at the expense of a providential loving God? But there are always two sides to a coin, and it has become apparent that freedom and material riches are not always synonymous with happiness.

CHRISTIAN EDUCATION IN CHILDHOOD

We remarked what a clear witness to the strong faith of past generations the Christian epitaphs on the war graves were, and how they demonstrate that the West was still adhering to Christian norms. This fidelity to belief in God was certainly due to the solid teaching practised by all Christian denominations.

Speaking from personal experience, this was certainly true in the Catholic faith. Religious education was very strict, and we had to learn by heart all the tenets of the faith listed in the "Catechism of Catholic Doctrine", which was a small handbook of all the dos and don'ts (Catechism literally means instruction by question and answer). We knew the Ten Commandments, the five commandments of the Church, the seven acts of charity and the seven deadly sins, the seven sacraments, the gifts, and fruits of the Holy Spirit. But it was not solely a question of learning things by heart; the great ideals for following Jesus were also imprinted on us.

The emphasis was often on sin and on a punishing God, not necessarily a bad thing as it did make us sit up and listen and put into practice what we had learnt. This thorough education gave the Church men and women with strong moral and ethical values, who in turn passed them on to their children, bringing forth many priests and nuns, many different religious orders, missionaries proclaiming the Good News world-wide, and thousands of saints who, through their perseverance and selflessness, made Christianity a vibrant world religion.

In recent times this strict upbringing has been replaced with a more lenient way and the emphasis is now more on "Jesus loves you" rather than on teaching the tenets of the faith. Happily, the Bible has finally found a central role in the Catholic faith. On the other hand, the Catechism of Catholic Doctrine, is no longer central to children's education, with the result that the younger generations have only a scant knowledge of what their religion is all about and are totally ignorant of the Ten Commandments. What is more, the whole vocabulary of Christian ideals has disappeared from use, such as the virtues of self-restraint, and chastity, tolerance, modesty, faith, hope and charity, joy, peace, and patience. And for all youngsters, religious or secular, the notion of right and wrong has become blurred, with behaviour increasingly influenced by peer pressure and social media, rather than by moral norms.

DISCOVERY

In the past, rigorous religious education stood us in good stead to navigate, without getting too bruised, the ups and downs of childhood, adolescence and adulthood, and helped form the important life choices everybody will make sooner or later. In other words, knowing exactly what we believed in helped us to make informed decisions on what course we wanted our life to take. And it is true to say that, as a rule, few children had mental health problems, if any, and suffered the anguish which is so common in young people today.

But this strict teaching, which was all in the head, omitted to address the spiritual side of the faith which was contemplation and meditation. Spiritual gems such as "The Practice of the Presence of God" which is often called the "Sacrament of the present Moment" were not mentioned, neither the possibility of having a personal relationship with Jesus - but that was the way religion was taught for many decades. The spiritual aspect of the faith was deemed only appropriate for the religious and the very holy, and many generations of ordinary people were sorely bereft without them. The teaching which spoke to the mind rather than to the heart was a reason for many to quit the faith with opinions such as: "Jesus is not God, he was just a wonderful teacher", "There is no God", "They told us all these stories to keep us quiet", "The Bible is not the Word of God", "Satan does not exist".

It is no wonder then that many now turn to the spirituality of the East, realising that at present we only function on half of our turbines by neglecting to feed and nurture our innate spiritual nature. Not only do we neglect that intrinsic part of our being, which is that still, inner voice of its creator, but we have also let that voice be stifled and dumbed down by the voices of the world and dissenting voices of the Christian faith. We are now very much lumbering through life with a disabled body, greatly surprised that society is failing to function properly.

Even though the emphasis of the teaching is now more on how Jesus loves us, and not on sin and punishment, I dare say that even many Christians are unaware that they can have a personal relationship with Jesus the living Christ, who rose from the dead, as he himself invites us, saying "If anyone loves me, he will keep my word, and my Father will love him, and we will come and make our home in you" (Jn14:15-24). There cannot be a more profound spiritual truth allowing a deep relationship with Jesus, whose presence can be felt in a real and powerful way. When we experience this, it brings a whole new dimension to one's faith and a gives a reason for why and what we believe. For what can be more satisfying that to have a meeting of the heart of man with the heart of God.

There are two implications, first, because God is in us, a truth he states himself, we can have a personal experience of his presence in our every-day comings and goings. We can find God in all things, and I have never felt his presence more closely than when I was ironing or cooking; it means that we do not need to feel lonely as he goes with us wherever we go, on a nature walk, shopping and yes, on holiday, on hospital visits and most acutely when facing illness. Second, it creates a desire to want to go to church, not out of a sense of duty or habit, or despite that we don't like the priest or for changes in the readings, but because there is a newly found love of a living person whose presence has become real. And prayer also took on a deeper meaning, it became more like 'a wine that gladdens the heart,' instead of a drudgery, as someone once put it. Prayer is 'the' way to get closer to God's heart and should never be given up for one single day.

The simple way is to ask him to come more deeply into our lives: I did just that and the response was overwhelming. I discovered why I went to church and in what I really believed. When later in life I discovered this truth, I felt horribly cheated and, like so many, that I had been short-changed of a wonderful and powerful reality which had been kept secret for far too long. If more people would understand this wonderful truth the churches might fill up again. And in fact, we already witness this in the evangelical churches where there is a great expression of joy and love.

One friend said to me, "Nobody ever told me to ask Jesus to come more deeply into my life, but when I did, it turned my faith from black to white to colour, and I have never looked back. It was such a powerful experience".

Yet still today spiritual pearls such as this are very rarely given an airing in church circles.

AWAKING TO MEDITATION

The recent departure from organised religion and the rise in secularism have given rise to a great cry for spiritual fulfilment that is now sweeping through the western world. "Our hearts are restless until they rest in God," says St Augustine and he spoke from experience after finally giving up his wayward lifestyle. This is exactly the restlessness that drives a great many people of all walks of life, religious or not, to turn to eastern religions in search of a meaning in life. They turn to the east because Christians in the west have for so long put this spiritual lamp under a table instead of "putting it on a lampstand for all to see. "You are the light of the world. No one lights a lamp to put it under a tub, they put it on the lampstand where it shines for everyone in the house. In the same way your light must shine in people's sight, that seeing your good works, they may give praise to your Father in heaven" (Mt5:15).

There is no doubt that meditation has tremendous value as it teaches to still the mind and focus on the "now" instead of harking back to the past or worrying about the future. And in our busy lifestyles its rediscovery has brought huge benefits to our mental, physical, and emotional health. Retreating into a quiet place and emptying the mind of all its ballast, anxieties and worries is very healing. The stress, which blights so many people's lives, physically ebbs away, and the whirling mind finally comes to rest. There is a difference between Christian meditation and secular meditation though. In Christian meditation we empty the mind to fill it with Christ, and this leads to a conversion of the heart. Secular meditation techniques, which are increasingly fashionable, encourage the emptying of the mind, which is then more readily left open to outward influences, for example, "getting in touch with the other side". Mindfulness, the latest popular version of meditation, is now widely available on the NHS. "A healthy mind in a healthy body" is the mantra, and meditation courses and yoga, paired with physical exercises, have sprung up everywhere, with huge benefits.

Yoga, which has become very popular, has its origins in 500-year-old Hindu texts but it is not without pitfalls. The danger is that westerners are unaware that Buddhist and Hindu spirituality contradict in many ways Christian spirituality and the message of salvation. There remains a fine line between practising yoga and meditation for the purpose of relaxation and de-stressing and practising them as a spiritual exercise. Some classes may introduce healing with crystal balls and promote occult practices, which are forbidden in Christianity. It is good to watch out for those differences and not just plunge headlong into a practice we know very little about.

There is no need for Christians to reach out to the religions of the East in the quest for spiritual fulfilment and peace. Instead, we can reach out to Christ. However, we cannot be Christian and Buddhist or Hindu at the same time, "You cannot serve two masters at the same time" (Mt 6:24). We can however learn from their wisdom and insight, such as the philosophy of living in the present rather than in the past. There are major differences between Christian spirituality and Eastern, and some western spirituality such as New Age philosophy and Reiki. The latter focus on trusting oneself and exploring the "inner reality." Christian spirituality, on the other hand, is a flight away from self and totally focuses on God. Jesus said, "I am the way, the truth and the life, no one can come to the Father, except through me" (Jn 14:6). This shows that he is the true way to reach union with God through Christian to meditation.

A friend recently went to India where she had her future foretold by a Guru. Not only did he read her future, but she was quite shaken by the fact he was able to tell so many accurate facts about her life. How could he possibly know all that, my friend wondered. This is a telling tale, that there is a power there which, as westerners, we don't understand, and it is wise to first question and explore where this power emanates from, before we plunge head over heels into a spirituality we don't understand.

WHO IS THE TRUE GOD?

In Genesis we read that humanity was created in the image and likeness of God. This means that the whole human race has God's life-giving breath in it that links each of us together by "one God, who is Father of all, over all, through all and within all" (Ep 4:6). Although man reflects the goodness and beauty of

SOME REFLECTIONS

God by being created in his image, there is one thing we cannot do. We cannot worship Him by any other name than the one revealed in Jesus Christ. People say, "Surely it is all the same God we worship, but by another name. Far from it: as Christians we have a distinctive experience of God who has certain properties. He is not a God who has to be put daily in a good mood by sacrifices before he will give us his love. The Christian God is a deeply personal God, whom Jesus reveals to us in the Lord's Prayer as Father and who, like a true father, is concerned with every little detail of our lives, from the very moment of conception until the end. Everything he gives is given as a pure gift; he doesn't want anything in return but our love. Other religions, and especially New Age philosophy, may claim that he is an impersonal energy force to be tapped into, commanded, channelled or manipulated for our personal use. He is none of those things, he is the one who created us, animates us and from whom we draw our very breath of life.

A big question remains in people's minds about who will be saved. Will people from other religions and none be saved? Lurid stories have done the rounds that people belonging to a certain religion will be damned. This is untrue. Many people, and worshippers of other religions, have never had the opportunity to hear about Jesus; the truth is that they will be saved if they fulfil the obligations of their faith, lead just and compassionate lives, and have an awareness of the wrong they may have committed and are sorry. Jesus has won salvation through his unconditional love for Hindus, Jews, Buddhists, Muslims, Christians and unbelievers alike. He is the universal saviour who sacrificed his life for all humanity. Peter makes this clear, "The truth I have now come to realise is that God has no favourites, but that anybody of any nationality who fears God and does what is right is acceptable to him" (Acts 10:35). This is called the baptism of desire.

THE GOOD NEWS NOBODY TALKS ABOUT

FINDING LASTING PEACE

In today's busy life we all thirst to get away from it all and find some peace and quiet away from the hustle and bustle of life. But where to find it? Numerous choices beckon in many travel catalogues with enticing photographs of the various options we can choose. All are promising to give just what restless souls are searching for. Often, we do not have to search far: absorbing the wonders of nature, being enrapt by a beautiful landscape, breathing in the scent of flowers and listening to birdsong are great sources of peace and wellbeing and soothe an overcrowded, over-burdened, over-strained life. Finding "lasting" peace is one of those pearls we can rediscover by digging more deeply into Jesus' many promises and taking him at his word. "Peace, I give you, my own peace I give you, a peace that the world cannot give. This is my gift to you" (Jn 14:27).

This is indeed a precious gift the world cannot offer. It is such a peace deep in the heart that nothing and nobody can take it away. All that is needed is to put our trust in that promise and hand over all our difficulties and hardships to him, and his consolation will flow like a soothing waterfall, permeating and diffusing the whirlwind and sadness of life. It is a peace that goes beyond all understanding as it sweeps away the waves of hardship, sickness, depression, and grief that threaten to overwhelm us and often lead to despair. Having this trust does not mean that we will be spared misfortunes and hardship, or that our mistakes are irrevocable; rather it means that they do not have a hold over our lives any longer, and it helps to weather any storm life throws at us and still feel that lasting peace deep inside us. It is a peace we all crave, a peace the world cannot understand. It is a peace the world can never give.

This peace can in turn also be passed on to others. They are not idle words when we say: "Peace be with you" but a sign of God's love. When we speak the words that Jesus spoke, he activates them with His peace which then descends on the people we want to bless. It shows that, by speaking a divine word, life here below is intertwined with the eternal life that awaits us. This truth we will explore in later chapters.

WHICH IS THE TRUE RELIGION?

This is a question that surprisingly few people ask, even churchgoing Christians. They assume that all religions are the same or that Christianity only started in the New Testament with the birth of Jesus. Jesus has always been present throughout the Old and the New Testaments as a person of the Trinity, one with the Father, the Son and the Holy Spirit. He is the cosmic Christ hidden in God as the WORD at the onset of creation, "and through him all things came into being" (Jn 1:3). Jesus affirms this later when he states, "In all truth I tell you, before Abraham ever was, I AM" (Jn 8:58). When in Exodus Moses asked God, "What shall I tell the Israelites your name is?" God answers "Say it is I AM who has sent me". By invoking the great "I AM," Jesus confirms that he has his origin in the Father since time began. From this statement we can deduce that Christianity transcends or overarches all cultures, all religions, all space and time. Jesus is not subject to the limitations of the material universe like humans are. He is Jesus Christ, Christ deriving from the Greek, "Christos," or anointed one, or king. He is the Messiah or Saviour, and it is he alone who, by shedding his blood on the cross, was able to atone for all the sins of the world, and offer salvation to every man, woman and child who ever lived and ever shall live, as he stretched out his arms, spanning the whole universe and the whole of human history from the beginning to the end of time. He is the King of the Universe, the Beginning and the End, "I am the Alpha, and the

Omega says the Lord, who is, who was and who is to come" and his kingdom will never end. (Re 1:8). It is the person of Jesus Christ who makes all the difference between Christianity and other religions.

If Christians are unaware of Christ's supremacy over all religions and cultures, no wonder that secular society is equally in the dark about it. This gap in awareness has greatly facilitated multiculturalism, which is a good thing, provided it is not to the detriment of our western culture. "A city built on a hilltop cannot be hidden. No one lights a lamp to put it under a tub, they put it on a lampstand where it shines for everyone in the house" (Mt5:14). Yet Christianity has been too afraid to put "The City of God" on the tall hill for all to see, and our religion has too readily conformed to the new trends and cultures, rather than shaping them.

There is a drive afoot which wants to abolish Christianity altogether. This drive chooses to forget that when Christianity reached the shores of Europe and the wider world, it brought respect for life, care for the poor and the sick, it brought learning, and especially it gave hope of eternal life, and abolished fear. If Christ has already won victory over death, what are we afraid of? We should let Christ's banner fly far and wide and give witness, instead of rolling the banner up and replacing it with a secular one. For example, "Happy Christmas" banners are changed to "Happy Festive Season" and the Christmas crib is no longer visible in shop windows. People are penalised for wearing a cross at work, or for praying, and preaching in public places. Some have even lost their job for offering to pray for a sick person, and freedom to quote the Bible becomes an offence. All this starts to smack more of the cruel persecutions of Christians by the Roman Emperors, and of history going full circle.

SOME REFLECTIONS

We presently witness a slow abandonment of the Code of Conduct enshrined in the Ten Commandments and, with it, the erosion of the witness to the victory of Christ's battle over evil. Not only faith, but the way life has become a pick-and-choose affair with people making up their own rules as they go along. "What is sin?" people ask, "that word has been out of use for a long time," and not only have we abolished the word, but the deed also. It is much more convenient to soften our vocabulary and make our wrong acts seem more acceptable and less grating on our conscience. Committing adultery is now called "having an affair", fornication is "having a sexual experience", and killing an infant in the womb is "having a free choice", while Euthanasia is "an act of compassion". How can an action which was immoral for thousands of years suddenly become moral in some countries, but not in others? It does not make sense! Something is either right or wrong. With the fear of offending God gone, His ways and laws are being changed with abandon.

With God there is no "but," and no "no" - with God, it is always "yes". His ways and laws remain unchangeable forever, and we do not have the authority to change them according to our desires. Regardless, morals have changed so drastically that what was previously frowned upon and impossible, has now become possible, and the possible is now becoming the norm.

It is not surprising that, with the uncertainty of what is right or wrong, our politicians have become painfully aware of a great need to introduce new laws to accommodate the so-called new wrongdoings, and that we see an alarming reversal of the meaning of traditional morality and legality. Sexual harassment, domestic violence, up-skirting, bullying, these before were immoral but not legally a crime. The really immoral acts prohibited by the Ten Commandments, like adultery and abortion, which were not so long ago punishable by law, are now tolerated. Everyone is expected to agree with the new laws even if they are contrary to their religious convictions, otherwise they risk being politically incorrect or even suffer harassment. "What we have done is thrown away thousands of years of Christian morality and replaced it with 'so-called secular morality', and that for Christians must ever remain a festering sore" (g).

With individual interpretation of what is right and wrong the order of the day, and the guidelines gone, everybody, and especially the young, has been abandoned to a turbulent sea of a permissive society, buffeted by ever-changing waves of new secular rules and laws. Often these laws lead to spiritual death, whereas living by the Spirit and laws of God is life-giving. "Let us not be tossed one way and another and carried hither and thither by every new gust of teaching, at the mercy of all the tricks people play and their unscrupulousness in deliberate deception" (Ep 4:14). How fitting is this exhortation from Paul for today's society!

Once, talking to a group of young people, many expressed a feeling of loneliness and a lack of identity, a malaise felt equally in the religious and the secular sectors of the population. Starting a conversation with the hippie-looking girl next to me on a plane journey certainly bore this out. She told me that she was a musician on her way to a music festival. And unprompted she suddenly said, "You know, the young generation feels lost. They hanker for some spiritual fulfilment which they find in Eastern meditation and music. They lack an identity, but through our music we feel we belong, that's why these festivals are so important to us." I was taken aback by her frankness as she had hit the nail on the head.

This same feeling of a lack of identity was again expressed by a member of my wider family. After the breakup of her relationship with a man who practiced New Age philosophy she confided, "I could not judge this man's beliefs and practices, because I feel a lack of identity, I don't know who I really am."

Recently we have seen an increasing number of people researching their family tree with the desire to know their origins and where they really belong. Adopted people go to great lengths to find their biological parents because people feel their identity is important to them. "Naming people and places seems all about becoming a whole person as it reveals something of the essence, the character or the reputation of the person" (h).

Judging from the confidences shared by the young people, knowledge of our spiritual identity and knowing where we truly belong in the large scale of things is primordial in boosting our self-esteem and confidence and marks out a vision for the future. We are all very good at disguising who we really are and very adept at showing our best face to friends and relatives, while on the other hand keeping one foot firmly in the camp where our ego has a sure footing. Practising a faith or not will obviously have a big impact on our life choices, but in the end our personal and only identity should really be selfless love, because it is only love that can make the world go round, and this is what we will all be judged on when our earthly life has run its course.

"Love is my true identity. Selflessness is my true self, love is my true character, love is my name" says Thomas Merton (i).

More and more, selfless love has been put on the back burner and in so doing we have forged many pitfalls and webs in which we get inextricably entangled, with disastrous consequences. Having granddaughters or friends in the teaching profession we are very aware how youngsters, especially girls, suffer from anxiety caused by bullying, peer pressure, body image, and likes and dislikes. And unlike their predecessors, they now have the added pressure of oversexualisation and gender issues. They suffer from mental health problems, they self-harm, and have panic attacks which keeps them off school. Why is this happening?

This epidemic can't be by chance! The shocking truth is that these woes and disasters are the result of the swiftly forgotten Christian teaching by so many over such a short time, as the modern mores and beliefs enticed them away from religion. Parents are left bereft with the spiritual and moral resources to combat the new moral and psychological trends their children are facing. If only they could share this simple truth that they are loved with the young musicians, the knife wielding youths, and the body-obsessed. It is Jesus who says to them "You are mine" (Is 43:1). The Christian message of love continually resounds if only we care to listen; I love you and I have offered up my life for you, and if you will follow my way, away from your self-obsession, destructive peer pressure, and media lies, it will lead you to the truth of a happy life. Sadly, we have thrown the baby out with the bathwater and rejected the offer of true happiness; for the 'real truth', we have exchanged the new-found truth of our self-sufficiency, material security, electronic gadgets, body obsessions and selfishness. And what is "good and right now" is what gives pleasure to the senses; any opposing ideas are taboo for the modern mind, and the modern mind makes sure that what it wants and feels becomes law.

Not following the "real way" will always be a cause for unhappiness, experiencing a void and a longing, but we don't know exactly what we are longing for. The French scientist and theologian, Pascal, so aptly called this "the God Hole". Until we rediscover our true identity and can refill this void in every human heart, with its rightful inhabitant our search for happiness will remain a fleeting quest.

A MORE FULFILLED LIFE

In answer to "Questions on life's issues" a lecturer sarcastically answered, "there is no time for dreaming, there is work to do or fun to be had." Below is the response of Giles, a participant at the lecture, sent to the organisers the next day:

> Thank you so much for giving your talk which I listened to earnestly. A church member had invited me and another friend to attend. On a number of occasions those friends had opened my sceptical eyes, and your talk also really helped. It has helped me making a large leap from atheism to becoming agnostic and now to the eye-opening and fulfilling warmth of God's embrace ...... almost.
>
> I have a lovely Christian wife and a wonderful four-year-old daughter, and I have been so fortunate that my wife is now expecting another child. I am a solicitor and I have loving parents and close relatives. As you referred to in your lecture, I have everything material and importantly I have more earthly love than I probably deserve. But then I sit there and feel a hole and something missing - but I don't know what. I do sometimes taste ashes in my mouth. I feel I am a nearly there. I have always read the Bible out of interest, but I am now beginning to read it with my eyes wide open. I desperately hope I can hold on to the faith to make that connection. (j)

Who has not been in that situation? I for one can completely identify with Giles. I too had all the love and comfort one can wish for, a loving husband and three lovely children. I had a lovely Christian family and a close bond with my siblings and wider family. But I vividly remember sitting on my bed after my husband had gone to work and the children to school, and a great void and a great longing for I didn't know what overwhelmed me. Something was missing, but what? Maybe I was being ungrateful. But then I realised that for some time I had not lived by my Christian principles. I decided to go to confession although I wondered what difference that would make, but somehow, I was compelled to go. People go to a psychiatrist and, for a vast amount of money, spill the beans. But God's forgiveness is free, and He alone can take our guilt away. No counsellor, no psychiatrist, or anyone or anything else can do this. And what an experience it was. The yearning was replaced with joy and a lightness filled me as if a ton of bricks had fallen from my shoulders. Since God was reinstated, life has never been the same again for there is nothing more powerful than repentance and forgiveness: they are the backbone of the Christian life; without them we stagnate in the same old habits and routines. It is by acknowledging that we have a need, that we give God the go-ahead to pour all his love into us and change a meaningless life into an incredible journey of peace and true happiness. Now the search is over, for I finally know what it was that I had been searching for all this time.

Later, I had a real experience of God being in the room. One evening with the kids in bed and my husband away, I was reading St Augustine's "Confessions" in which there is a lot of praising. Suddenly there was a huge luminous flash of light which filled the whole room, the book fell on the floor, and I just KNEW that God was in the room. It was an incredibly bright light lasting a couple of seconds and an amazing experience right out of the blue. I could never have dreamt that something like this could ever happen, and no one had ever prepared me for this. Many people might say that "it was all in my mind", but when it is God who is in the room, one KNOWS. It would certainly be very difficult to stage such a powerful light by simple brainpower and, as with all spiritual experiences, the proof was in the pudding. They are only authentic if they change one's life for the better and many people can testify that my life has never been the same again after this.

This experience is a vivid example of "Knowledge of God by personal experience", which together with "Revelation" and "Mysticism", which is knowing God beyond the intellectual understanding", are the three precepts of Christian spirituality.

"I KNOW" is a strong statement many find objectionable when we talk about religion, but there is no other way of expressing it: the truth of feelings and experiences cannot be denied as if they never happened. God's revelation to humanity runs like a live electric wire from the beginning of creation right through to each person here today, whoever we are and wherever we may be in the world. His still small voice is audible and that dramatic light is visible, no matter that anybody might want to make one believe they were a figment of the imagination. They are also confirmed by other people's testimonies of similar experiences, and what is more, they have been in conformity with all Christian experiences through the centuries, as they emanate from the same source, namely the power and love of God. These experiences entitle anybody to say, "I KNOW." God's revelations, as we will describe in the following stories, are like a dragnet, and all the countless men and women who have been caught in it, are unable to keep their experiences to themselves. They palpitate with impatience to share the wonders that God has wrought in their lives to all who care to listen.

Here is a friend's poignant testimony of finding God through personal experience:

THE GOOD NEWS NOBODY TALKS ABOUT

One sunny morning I read this beautiful text from Song of Songs 3:1:
"I sought him whom my heart loves. I sought but did not find him. The watchmen came upon me on their rounds. 'Have you seen him whom my heart loves?' Scarcely had I passed them than I found him whom my heart loves. I held him fast and would not let him go."

Reading this lovely passage brought back to me a dream I had, many years ago. This dream recurred every night for a very long time. I dreamt that I stood at the foot of a spiral staircase inside a huge, pointed seashell. The stairs wound up and up and with each step became narrower and narrower until they ended in a point. Ahead of me a person ran up the narrow stairs, a person I knew I loved and for whom I had longed for a very long time. I ran up the stairs in pursuit as fast as I could, in desperation wanting by every means to catch up with this enigmatic person. But getting closer and closer, and nearly catching him at the very top, the steps became so narrow that I could not go any further and I saw him vanish in a flurry of white robes, leaving me feeling utterly abandoned and forlorn. A feeling of loss of someone who was very dear engulfed me because I had failed to grasp him once again.

"Some years later I had a metanoia, a religious conversion, and suddenly the dream made sense. I found "whom my heart loves", and I knew immediately that it was him whom I had longed for all these years, Jesus, and that it was him whom I had tried to catch on those stairs in the dream, but never realised who it was, until I invited Jesus to come more deeply into my life, and it all fell into place. With that, the dream stopped, it had achieved its purpose."

SOME REFLECTIONS

We all long for something, but we do not know what that something is. When we find the truth of Jesus, we receive ultimate freedom and the fulfilment of our deepest desires and dreams because it is only Jesus who is the fulfilment of all human hope.

It is not only religious people who have spiritual experiences, and they do not necessarily involve the divine. Everybody can be enthralled at the sight of a powerful waterfall, the majesty of the mountains, or become mesmerised by another person. Being spiritual relates to who we are, what affects us, be it nature, music, the arts or other people or God. And it is true that people of all religions and none who meditate, experience a feeling of delight and peace in their innermost being, and that wellness and mindfulness really work. Nevertheless, non-religious people are often at pains to identify from where their spirituality emanates yet are not prepared to accept that the connectedness in all humans with this spiritual identity comes from the creator God.

The real proof of a spiritual experience is the joy it gives. It is a life-changing experience which cannot be hidden from friends and relatives and the people close by. When something incredible happens, like seeing the sun spin, we cannot deny what we have seen with our own eyes even though it is beyond all logical explanation or contrary to scientific evidence. The impossibility of it all is precisely the definition of a miracle, it is not the suspension of a natural law, but a higher power at work. When we enter places where such miracles take place we step, by definition, into the supernatural world where God, who is supernatural, is at work. This is the attraction which draws the crowds to such places.

God cannot be explained by mathematical formulae or through philosophical reasoning; it would be like trying to fit a cat in a matchbox. If we could get to know God with our intellect, how unjust would that be: it would deprive a whole category of people of ever getting to know Him in any way. God stands outside the realm of human reasoning. God's laws are constant, as God's nature is constant and unchanging. If God's laws were unreliable and would be different for one or other continent or different for another era in history, we would be at the mercy of a whimsical God and live in constant peril of our lives. Therefore, no government or worldly power, or church authority can change the Ten Commandments, they are written indelibly in stone and apply for all generations and all peoples. We will never grasp the mysteries of God, except by approaching them as "little children", as we are told to do in Mark chapter 10.

However much of a staunch atheist or agnostic we may be, when we come to the nadir of life, through illness or loss, rejection, or catastrophe we will automatically be drawn to ask the question, "what is it all for?" And looking at the wider world where wars, famine, torture, and poverty are a way of life, and pondering what catastrophe might befall us without warning, "Is this it?" And did we really build all those beautiful cathedrals and monasteries for a figment of our imagination, and were all those incredible painters inspired by a fable with no basis? We might as well not have been born: what is the point of it all? Surely there must be a different approach, equally valid, to make sense of it all. It cannot be that our only options are to believe that we are just an accident of evolution and that our search for the meaning of life is not legitimate as some scientists like us to believe, and that there is another explanation- the belief in God.

IN CONCLUSION

I have painted a very negative and disheartening picture of our

SOME REFLECTIONS

world at present. Global warming, decline of morals, wars, famine, increasing poverty, natural disasters, homelessness, and threats from different religions and states do not bear witness that the planet as a whole has reached a pinnacle of happiness. It may be that we are aware of those calamities because of social media and newspaper accounts. One thing is certain, though, the western world has forsaken God, and Christianity is no longer a subject for inquiry. Someone asked, "What is the present characteristic of the English nation? "The answer was, "A total ignorance of God, a total contempt of God, and we are caught in a vortex that is pulling us down to destruction because nobody knows what is right and wrong any longer". Frightening words but all too true. But is it all gloom and doom? Hopefully not. As the title of the book makes clear, there is still Good News at hand in the person of Jesus Christ our Saviour, an assertion we will explore in this book.

2

WHAT IS THIS GOOD NEWS?

The vast expanse of the universe is awesome. We marvel at the innumerable stars and planets that we can see like the Great Bear and Venus, and yet further afield invisible to the naked eye there are millions upon millions of other celestial bodies, impossible to count. Increasingly we are acquiring a staggering amount of knowledge about the makeup and properties of this wonderful world which has fascinated humanity since time immemorial. And we are regaled on our TV screens by mind-bending journeys into the cosmos. "There are an estimated two trillion galaxies in our universe, all containing billions of stars and countless planets, worlds that exist beyond our imagination. The universe is so vast, so incomprehensible, so terrifying that it is natural that we live our lives completely oblivious of it" (a).

Amidst staggering advances discovering more and more of this mysterious and awesome universe, one is tempted to doubt the existence of a God and where he would fit in if he did exist.

Each generation in turn may never know the full truth about the make-up of the universe despite all the progress that has been made; indeed, it may always remain a mystery. But generations of humans have felt that there must be an invisible being governing this vast impenetrable expanse, no matter what an impossible concept this appears to be. How can man ever be certain that this is true, or does he just carry on groping in the darkness, ordering his life in the hope that he is right?

Fear and uncertainty were undoubtedly the main drivers for looking up to something bigger than man himself. Was it in response to the presence of an as-yet "Unknown God," to whom the Greeks built an altar? (Ac 17:23) Or was it in response to a God who has always existed within the mind of man when He blew life into man at creation and made him in his image and likeness, as described in the Bible? Our present adulation of and obsession with pop stars and celebrities is very telling of an innate desire for hero worship, for a role model, for someone we can look up to and who can give us a sense of security and purpose in life.

Perhaps it is not such a far-fetched notion that man had always had a subconscious longing for a god and had an intuition that there was something out there that he could turn to in time of need. Around the globe we can visit numerous architectural wonders which, apart from the temples dedicated to Buddha, were dedicated to many gods, be they Borobudur in Indonesia, Angkor Wat in Cambodia, the Inca temples in Peru, or the pyramids in Egypt, the exquisite Greek and Roman temples, Stonehenge, and many more, and we are in awe at the vastness and refined craftsmanship of these structures. Closer to home, a plethora of magnificent churches and cathedrals rose in honour of the one true God. They give us glimpses into highly developed ancient civilizations.

The forces of nature too, the sun and the moon, had and still have a powerful hold over man's imagination, together with animism and ancestor worship. And we marvel at the imagination with which the arrays of gods were shaped in different materials and forms and the properties that were attributed to them. And not only objects, but also animals were and still are decreed to be holy creatures. Many gods had a continuous need to be placated with a variety of sacrifices, and the human sacrifices of the Incas and the Assyrians and Babylonians who offered up their children are legendary. These demands were often exploited by powerful and unscrupulous priests. Still today people are held in bondage by age old traditions, and by sorcerers and priests who wield real power instilling fear rather than love.

But there was also a monotheistic religion, Judaism, practised by the Jews. The essence of Judaism is contained in the early part of the Old Testament of the Bible, and it is here we encounter a God, not of fear, but a God of love, and it is with this God of love that the story of the 'Good News' for the whole world begins. He is not a God who needs to be placated with offerings, but a God who freely and personally interacts with the people he has chosen. He gives them, the Israelites, safe passage through the Red Sea from the pursuit of the Egyptian army (Ex 14), and "God spoke to all the people the words of the covenant, that is the Ten Commandments" (Ex 20). And he even promises in Genesis that in the course of time he will send one of their own to be their rescuer from oppression and sin.

What was this oppression and sin the Jewish people had to be delivered from? They had, during their long history been conquered by many nations and they aspired to be finally set free from foreign domination by the promised **Messiah**. This promise is fulfilled and is described in the New Testament.

This saviour as we know, for we have historical evidence that he lived in Israel, is none other than God's only Son, Jesus. With the coming of Jesus, no more animal sacrifices were necessary, as had been the custom in ancient times. Jesus accepted crucifixion wilfully to save humanity from the consequences of an act of rebellion against God by the very first people, Adam and Eve. God's Son will be the sacrificial lamb, so that no other sacrifice needs to be made ever again, anywhere in the world. Through this one sacrifice he has defeated Satan, "he has abolished death, and he has brought to light immortality and life through the Good News of the Gospel" for all peoples, past present and future (2 Tm 1:10). Indeed, the word "Gospel" simply means "Good News".

We get the full description of the act of rebellion by Adam and Eve in the allegorical account in the Bible, "God gave Adam this command, "you are free to eat from all the trees in the garden, but from the tree of the knowledge of good and evil, you are not to eat; for, the day you eat of that, you are doomed to die". (Gn2:16) By all accounts, God had created man with the aim for him to live in paradise, called the Garden of Eden, where hope, peace, love, and justice would reign, and every tree would bear continuous fruit, and man would live in harmony with God, with the rest of humanity and the animal world. This is called the "Kingdom of God". But Adam and Eve, who had been given free will to make their own decisions, spoiled God's plan. "The snake was the most subtle of all the animals God had created" and tempted the woman, Eve, saying, "God knows that if you eat some of the fruit your eyes will be opened and you will be like gods, knowing good and evil", and "She took some of the forbidden fruit, and she gave some to her husband, and he ate it. Their eyes were opened, and they realised that they were naked" (Gn 3:6-7). In the Chapter on "Satan and Evil Spirits", we shall read more about the snake, also called the "primeval or ancient serpent" in the Book of Revelation (12:9-20:2). He is Satan, the Devil, Christ's adversary.

We can assume that by the time man was able to assert his own free will he was already a fully developed "Homo Sapiens", capable of rejecting God's laws. We will never be able to verify what this rebellion consisted of exactly, but it very much sounded like an act of pride. In their pride, they wanted to be equal to God, but "Pride is hateful to God and the beginning of human pride is to desert the Lord and turn one's heart away from its maker" (Si 10:7). This huge act of defiance had dire consequences for the world, and it screams for punishment. God did not create us as his puppets to do with as he pleases. That would defy the purpose of the exercise. He created man with a free will to be stewards of a perfect paradisal, eternal world. The gravity of Adam and Eve's sin was in betraying the love and trust God had placed in them and in deriding the spiritual image and likeness to God in which they were created.

The Creation Story is no longer a much-loved story as it has generally been overridden by what we now know about the evolution of the universe. It is an error to read the opening story in Genesis as a literal account of how the world was made. We now have undeniable evidence from geology, palaeontology and physics about how creation evolved. Nevertheless, the Old and the New Testament of the Bible are accounts of facts which happened during the course of secular history. "The story of how God created the world is not a history lesson or a scientific report, rather it is a love story between God and man expressed as a narrative, a metaphysical story. Nor is the Bible just a document but a gateway into a spiritual reality. Its words are breathed by God himself through writers moved by his Holy Spirit, and these words offer a life-changing relationship with the creator of the universe" (b).

WHAT IS THIS GOOD NEWS

Yet even after being scorned, God does not stop loving his creation, and he will send his only Son Jesus, to restore this wrongdoing. It is not only in this show of extreme love after all that has happened but in the overriding evidence that God, in his love, continued to reveal himself to the Israeli people, as recorded in the subsequent account in the Bible of their history.

We can describe the Bible in its entirety, Old and New Testament, as the whole of the story of the "Good News", because it was in the Old Testament that God took pity on his people and promised to send a deliverer, and it is in the New Testament that this promise was fulfilled in the coming of the saviour, Jesus Christ (Jesus or 'Jeshuah' or 'Jahewh' means to save, and Christ, from the Greek 'Christos', means the Anointed One). Before Jesus' coming, the world lived in uncertainty of what the purpose of life was; all that people could see was oppression, injustice, sickness, war, and death, and they could not make head or tail of it. What was it all for, life? Was death the end or was there more? This is the question we still ask today. We still live in uncertainty of what the purpose of life is, and yet Jesus was born and died for us on the cross.

The very good news about the 'Good News' is that it comes in two parts, first that "God "loved the world so much that he gave his only Son, Jesus, (to be punished instead of us, by dying on a cross), so that everyone who believes in him may not perish but may have eternal life" (Jn 3:16). The Second Part of the Good News is that we also have God's power to heal people in mind, body, and spirit. This is the Good News story few believe in or talk much about any longer, yet it is one of hope and love, and it gives meaning to why we are here.

WHO WAS JESUS REALLY?

What is the God given power we have to heal, and how do we access it?

Genesis, the opening book of the Bible describes something quite amazing, which is that God's creative power took effect by speaking a "WORD". The Bible recounts: "In the beginning God created heaven and earth. Now the earth was a formless void, there was darkness over the deep, and the Spirit of God hovered over the waters. And God said, 'Let there be light, and there was light', and God said, 'Let there be a vault through the middle of the waters to divide the waters in two,' and it was so." (Gen1:1-8) And so, the story continues. The amazing thing is, that God only had to utter a WORD and things came into being. When God spoke, things started to happen, God's word creates. In the above passage we get a first mention of God's Spirit, who we now call the Holy Spirit and on whom we shall elaborate in chapter 10.

In the Chapter on "Miracles" we will see how Jesus also makes things happen by just uttering one WORD, people are then healed, and evil spirits are defeated. Today we can also perform many miracles by calling on Jesus' name who will give us the power to heal the sick in body, mind and spirit, and make this world a better place. It lies in the power of all those who are willing to bring The Second Part of the Good News to its realisation and give the world a foretaste of the Kingdom of God.

But how could Jesus' WORD produce such dramatic effects if he was just a human being like any of us. Two thousand years ago the Virgin Mary gave birth to a baby boy. She called him 'Jesus' and, like every baby born of women, Jesus had a normal human body of flesh and blood, and it is his human blood that will flow from the cross to redeem humanity.

But Jesus was also totally divine, for as Paul instructs "in his entire being, Jesus is the image of the invisible God"; in other words, he is also divine (2 Co:4). How can he be both, totally human and totally divine? He is totally divine as he is God incarnate. The word 'Incarnation' (from the Latin carno, 'flesh') refers to the moment when the divine nature of the second person of the Holy Trinity was united with the human nature of the Virgin Mary and became operative in Mary's womb. That moment was when the angel said to her, "you are to conceive in your womb and bear a son and you must name him Jesus" (Lk 1:31).

He existed since time immemorial, having his divine origin with God from the very beginning of time, and this truth Jesus shared many times with the Jewish people. Just like God, who told Moses "I am He who is" (Ex 3:14), Jesus tells the Jews "I am before Abraham ever was", so equating his divinity with God's (Jn 8:58).

And to God the Father he prays, "Father, you have given me power over all humanity, so that I may give them eternal life, which is to know you, the one true God". "Father, glorify me with that glory which I had with you before the world ever existed" (Jn 17:2-3/4-5). Again, when the Jews proclaim that his teaching is not from God, Jesus tells them, "You do not know God, but I know him, because I have my being from him, and it was He who sent me" (Jn 7:29).

Further, he asserts his divinity once more when he talks to the Samaritan woman. The woman said to Jesus "I know that the Messiah, that is the Christ, is coming, and when he comes, he will explain everything". Jesus replied, "That is who I am, I who speak to you" (Jn 4:4).

Paul writes "Christ is the head of all creation, he is the image of the unseen God, the first-born of all creation, for in him were created all things, in heaven and on earth, everything visible and invisible, thrones, ruling forces, sovereignties, powers, all things were created for him and through him. He exists before all things, and in him all things hold together, and he is the Head of the Body, that is the church. He is the beginning, the first born from the death, so that he should be supreme in every way, because God wanted all fullness to be found in him and through him to reconcile all things to him, everything in heaven and everything on earth by making peace through his death on the cross" (Co 1:15-20).

The above passages illustrate that Jesus is the Cosmic Christ who existed from the beginning of time, and this firmly establishes him as the "WORD" through whom God the Father created the world. Instead of "Word", the early Greek translation of the Bible referred to the 'logos'. Besides denoting a function or an utterance, 'logos' can also be associated with a "person". It was used in ancient philosophy and early Christian theology to imply the cosmos, its ordering and giving it form and meaning.

In the Holy Gospel according to John1:1-18 we read:
    In the beginning was the Word:
    the Word was with God,
    and the Word was God.
    He was with God in the beginning.
    Through him all things came into being,
    not one thing came into being except through him.
    What has come into being in him was life,
    life that was the light of men;

and light shines in darkness,
and darkness could not overpower it.

The Word was the real light
that gives light to everyone;
he was coming into the world.
He was in the world that had come into being through him,
and the world did not recognise him.
He came to his own,
and his own people did not accept him.
But to those who did accept him
he gave power to become children of God,
to those who believed in his name
who were born not from human stock,
or human desire, or human will
but from God himself.
The Word became flesh,
he lived among us, and we saw his glory,
the glory that he has from the Father,
as only Son of the Father,
full of grace and truth.

Indeed, from his fulness we have, all of us
received one gift replacing another,
for the law was given through Moses,
grace and truth came through Jesus Christ.
No one has seen God, it is the only Son,
Who is close to the Father's heart,
who has made him known."
(*Abbreviated version*)

We can no longer doubt that Jesus was God and that, through being the "Word" that became flesh, his spoken word has the power to heal the sick and drive out evil spirits, as we shall see in later chapters. And having his being with God from the very beginning, he spans all time, all nations and all cultures, and has power over all creation, the universe, and all it contains.

John describes Jesus as the creative "WORD" of the Old Testament. God said to let things come into being and they did, and Jesus said, "Be healed" and they were. Establishing the link between the Old and the New Testament and letting one story flow out of the other made an enormous difference to the way I could make sense of the Christian message. It made me see that there has never been another story which has impacted my life so much, and the life of every human being, as The Good News Story of the Bible. The best romantic love stories ever written are nothing compared to the historical love story between God and the human race, a story that continues today and is the thesis of this book.

THE LORD'S PRAYER

In the Lord's Prayer, Jesus as Son of the Father teaches us that God is our father, full of mercy and love, and not some frightening being ready to judge and to punish. Like Jesus, we can pray to Our Father, full of confidence that He will hear our prayer:

"Our Father, who art in heaven": this truly confirms that there really is such a place as heaven which was our original destiny, a place where we shall live forever in harmony with God.

"Hallowed be thy name": this is akin to the first commandment "Love God with all your might, with all your strength and with all your soul, and praise and glorify His name".

"Thy kingdom come": every time we are kind to others or help the poor and the marginalised, then a little of this ideal world, which is heaven, is being realized here on earth, and God's kingdom, where there shall be no more tears and suffering, is given to us.

"Thy will be done on earth as it is in heaven": when we have kept God's commandments here on earth and conformed to his desires, we know that we have made this world a better place and have given it a foretaste of what is to come. We will then be entitled to claim our rightful inheritance, which has been set aside for all humanity.

"Give us this day our daily bread": we pray that we will have daily bread to sustain not just our own bodies, but also those of the starving millions in the world. We also pray to be given spiritual bread to feed our spiritual nature, through the Eucharist, by praying and giving alms.

"And forgive us our trespasses as we forgive those who trespass against us": we find it very difficult to forgive others, yet unforgiveness can play havoc with our physical as well as our mental wellbeing and blocks the flow of God's grace and healing reaching us.

"And lead us not into temptation": help us not to be waylaid by the attractions of the world but keep our mind more focussed on our spiritual happiness.

"But deliver us from evil": we find it difficult to overcome temptation of any kind, but with God's help we will prevail.

CONCLUDING REMARKS

The Good News for the whole world and every human's destiny

is eternity after death, regardless of race or adherence to a religion or none. When humanity evolved into different cultures, each started to create its own perception of how, or what kind of god they wanted to worship, creating the divisions we see in the world today. But for God, we are all his creatures with the same value and worthiness of his love. The whole Bible is a story woven through with the golden thread of hope that God has for all his creatures to join Him in heaven. The story finds its high point in the birth of his promised saviour, the Cosmic Christ and the coming of the Holy Spirit. This is the good news that hardly anybody is talking about today.

SOME DATES WHICH PLACE THE HISTORY OF THE JEWISH PEOPLE IN THE SECULAR TIME FRAME (c)

The Bible Timeline places Genesis 1 -11 around 2000BC, which was close to the building of the great pyramids between 2589 BC and 2504 BC and the building of Stonehenge ca 2000 - 1500BC.

We have no historical record of who the Pharaoh was during Abraham's stay in Egypt to avoid the famine in Canaan, however historians agree "that Akhenaten was the Pharaoh of the oppression when the Israelis lived in slavery in Egypt. This was established through the fact that the city Akhenaten built was made from mud bricks and not from stone like the pyramids." This is confirmed in Exodus 5:6-18 when the Pharaoh said to the taskmaster, "Do not go on providing the people with straw for the brickmaking, let them go and find straw for themselves wherever they can find it but you will exact the same quantity of bricks as before, for these people are lazy and they cry that they want to go and sacrifice to Yahweh".

WHAT IS THIS GOOD NEWS

Historians think that Tutankhamun, Akhenaten's son was the pharaoh of Exodus and place this episode somewhere between 1720 and 1333BC. These dates fit well with the fall of the Wall of Jericho which the British excavator Kathryn Kenyon places in 1400 BC and similarly, with the Tanakh, or Hebrew Bible given to Moses by God on Mount Sinai in 1312 BC.

There are some details of history around the time of "the desert wanderings of the chosen people which occurred during the time of the Pharaohs Seti I and Rameses II around 1300 BC. Finally, the Jewish people settled in Palestine and appointed Judges and Kings, but soon the Kingdom was divided with Israel in the north and Judea in the south. With the fall of Israel to Assyria, once again the people are taken into exile for disobedience to God and for following pagan gods and customs. At the same time, in secular history, the first Olympic Games took place in Greece around 776 BC, Rome was founded in 753 BC, and Homer wrote the Iliad and Odyssey".

"In 538-444 BC the Jewish exile ended with the conquest of Babylonia, present day Iraq, by King Cyrus of Persia, now Iran. From this period until the birth of Christ much is happening in the secular world; in the Far East we see the birth of Gautama Buddha in India from 563-483 BC, and the birth of Confucius from 551-479 BC in China. Closer to home the Hellenist or Greek civilisation is flourishing under Alexander the Great (336-323 BC) who conquers the whole of the Persian Empire which included Palestine."

The empire was later divided, and Palestine fell into the hands of the Seleucids whose King Antiochus IV was keen to promote the Hellenist culture (163 BC). But the Hellenist culture was not in line with the chosen people of God, for to be Hellenised was akin to leading a licentious lifestyle. This lead, in 167 BC, to the

Maccabean Revolt, so named after its leader, but soon the Maccabees were beaten and fled, finding sanctuary with the Nabataeans in the Kingdom of Amman, present day Jordan.

Today more and more tourists flock to the incredible town of Petra. The region of Petra was a great trading post for the nomadic Nabataeans as early as 9000 BC, but the city of Petra was built around 50 BC by the Nabataeans, who finally settled there.

At this time, we see the prominence of the Roman Empire and the capture of the western world by Julius Caesar. The Roman leader Pompey is sent to Palestine to quell an unrest and captures Jerusalem in 63 BC. From then on Palestine suffers under Roman dominance and the people aspire towards the coming of a liberator, the promised Messiah.

Finally, in the reign of Herod the Great (37 BC- 4 AD), Jesus Christ is born.

3

THE TEN COMMANDMENTS

Chapter 20 in Exodus gives us the ten commandments that were spoken to Moses by God when He brought Moses and the Israelites out of Egypt:

> I am the Lord your God; you shall have no other gods to rival me.
>
> You shall not take the name of the Lord in vain.
>
> You shall not make yourself any carved images or any likeness in heaven above and on earth below or in the waters under the earth.
>
> Remember the Sabbath Day and keep it holy.
>
> Honour your father and your mother and you shall have a long life.
>
> You shall not kill.
>
> You shall not commit adultery.

You shall not steal.

You shall not bear false witness against your neighbour.

You shall not set your heart on your neighbour's house or possessions.

These commandments hold an unspoken list of all the evils humanity can commit. In the following passage, Jesus expands on these evils as follows: "Can you not see that nothing that goes into the mouth can make a person unclean because it passes through the stomach and is discarded into the sewer? But whatever comes out of the mouth comes from the heart, and it is this that makes someone unclean. For from the heart come evil intentions: murder, adultery, fornication, theft, perjury, slander, avarice, malice, deceit, indecency, envy, pride, folly. All these evil things come from within and make a person unclean" (Mk 7:18-23). And we can add some evils to this list too, like bullying, scorn, vengeance, hate, bearing grudges, unforgiveness and driving someone to suicide.

The Pharisees asked Jesus the following question, "Master which is the greatest commandment of the Law?" The answer he gave was: "You must love the Lord your God with all your heart, with all your soul and with all your mind and you must love your neighbour as yourself, on these two commandments hang the whole law and the prophets too" (Mt 22:40). It is obvious that by committing any of these evils, the commandments have not been kept. These acts are utterly selfish and harmful to us and to our fellow men. In Mt 5, by linking the Ten Commandments to the list of what makes a man unclean, Jesus explains that he has not come to abolish the law, but to complement it, because being God, he is the master of the law. "Do not imagine that I have come to abolish the Law or the prophets. I have come not to abolish but to complete them. In truth I tell you, till heaven and earth disappear, not one dot, not one little stroke, is to disappear from the Law until all its purpose is achieved. Therefore, anyone who infringes even one of the least of these commandments and teaches others to do the same will be considered the least in the kingdom of Heaven, but the person who teaches them will be considered great in the Kingdom of Heaven" (Mt 5:17-19).

In The Sermon of the Mount, Jesus gave a code of conduct which teaches ways in which his followers should behave in living an upright moral life:
How happy are the poor in spirit,
Theirs is the kingdom of heaven.
Blessed are the gentle,
They shall have the earth as inheritance.
Blessed are those who mourn,
They shall be comforted.
Blessed are those who hunger and thirst for justice,
They shall be satisfied.
Blessed are the merciful,
They shall have mercy shown them.
Blessed are the pure in heart,
They shall see God.
Blessed are the peacemakers,
They shall be called sons of God.
Blessed are those who are persecuted in the cause of uprightness,
The kingdom of heaven is theirs. (Mt 5:1-12)

And in Chapter 6 of Luke's gospel, we are told to be compassionate, to be of high integrity, to be generous and to love our enemies.

By giving these commandments, God established a moral code by which all humanity should live as a blueprint for a happy and holy life worthy of His promise of eternal life. Thus, He became the moral centre of the universe and of human existence and it is by His moral code that the standard of good and evil will always be measured. We often hear it said that these moral codes are "orthodox, traditional, fanatical or outmoded." This is mistaken as there is only one law by which we can live, a law which is unchanging and constant as God himself is constant.

When the world embraced Christianity, this moral code slowly permeated all life: religion, care for the sick, respect of life, the arts, and government - no more an eye for an eye. Today this moral code still permeates our lifestyle to a certain extent; believers and non-believers, maybe subconsciously, still live according to these precepts. More recently however, these tried and tested laws for 2000 years, and thousands of years before that, are being challenged in an unprecedented way, and are often declared less valid and even trampled over. A whole new set of rules is being prescribed which are more in line with the secular thinking of our modern age and brook no dissent.

In contrast to the modern misguided way, what better than Psalm 18 (7-10):
    The law of the Lord is perfect
    It revives the soul.
    The rule of the Lord is to be trusted,
    It gives wisdom to the simple.

    The Precepts of the Lord are right,
    They gladden the heart.
    The command of the Lord is clear
    It gives light to the eyes.
    The decrees of the Lord are truth,

THE TEN COMMANDMENTS

All of them just.

They are more to be desired than gold,
Than the purest gold.
And sweeter are they than honey,
Honey from the comb.

4

CHRISTIANITY

A SYNOPSIS OF JESUS' LIFE IN ISRAEL

Jesus came into the world, but the world did not recognise him, he came to his own, but his own people did not accept him. But to those who did accept him, he gave power to become children of God. (John1: 10-12)

After Jesus' most unusual birth that we celebrate on Christmas Day, his parents Mary and Joseph, a carpenter, take him home to Nazareth and there, we are told, he grows up "to maturity, he was filled with wisdom, and God's favour was on him" (Lk 2:39).

We can presume that Jesus, as he grew up, would become more and more aware of the mission he was to fulfil, and the kind of death he was to undergo, and it must have weighed heavily on him. Living with the increasing knowledge that he was to die by crucifixion must have increased his suffering a hundredfold as he went about healing and preaching. Already at the young age of twelve, his parents find him in the temple sitting among the teachers, listening, and asking them questions, and all those who heard him were astounded at his intelligence and his replies.

By his 30th birthday, the time has come for him to set out and start the mission he had been sent out to do by God the Father. Although without sin, he wants to abide by the law and goes to Galilee in Jordan where John the Baptist is baptising people for the forgiveness of sins. "And when he came out of the water after baptism, suddenly the heavens opened and he saw the Spirit of God descending on him like a dove, and a voice from heaven said, 'This is my Son the Beloved, my favour rests on him.'" (Mt 3:13)

With the Holy Spirit on him, who will instruct and empower him throughout his ministry, he is ready to preach and heal the sick. After just three short years of public ministry, Jesus is accused by the authorities of blasphemy for calling himself God: the ultimate blasphemy. He knew that such a claim would earn him the death penalty by crucifixion, but he could not deny the truth that he was God. There is no way he could have performed all these amazing miracles if he was just an ordinary person. Yet the Scribes and Pharisees, the religious establishment of the day, fearing that he was undermining their authority, closed their eyes to all the good that Jesus did. They were eaten up with jealousy because of his popularity with the people. He denounced their hypocrisy and vanity and their love of money. And he denounced the exploitation of the people by laying impossible burdens on them, including exorbitant taxes and laws.

There were some 600 laws the Jewish people had to obey; many a distortion of the original laws prescribed by Moses. Jesus reduced these 600 laws to just two, which are a summary of the Ten Commandments: "Love your God with all your heart and your neighbour as yourself." The Scribes and Pharisees repeatedly try to incriminate Jesus by asking him trick questions and relentlessly scrutinise his every move. Finally, their anger reaches boiling point when he calls them hypocrites, serpents, a brood of vipers, blind guides and murderers of prophets. "Everything you do is to draw attention, like wearing longer headbands and tassels and wanting to take pride of place at banquets and being greeted respectfully in the marketplace, and you lead people astray because your hearts are far from God" (Mt 23:1-18). And from that moment they look for a reason to do away with him. The chief priest Caiaphas and the elders of the people make plans to arrest him by some trickery and have him killed.

In the end it is one of his own disciples who betrays him, Judas Iscariot. Just before the Passover feast, when the Jewish people celebrate their exodus from exile in Egypt, he approaches the chief priest and discusses a way to hand Jesus over in return for thirty silver pieces. The Passover meal is the last meal Jesus will take with his disciples, on which occasion he will institute the holy Eucharist. "He took the bread, said the blessing, broke it and gave it to the disciples, saying. 'Take and eat it, this is my body.' Then he took the cup and when he had given thanks, handed it to them saying, 'Drink this all of you, for this is my blood of the covenant poured out for many for the forgiveness of sins'" (Mt 26:26-29). Jesus knew his arrest was imminent, he knew the stakes were high. He had come into the world to offer up his life on the cross to set humanity free from eternal death and restore the humanity's relationship with God which had been broken since the beginning of creation. Everything that will happen to him was foretold by the prophets. In the Garden of Olives, just before his arrest, his anguish was horrendous, and we are told that "his sweat fell to the ground like great drops of blood" (Lk 22:44).

Judas betrays him to the soldiers who have come to arrest him with a kiss, and as they take him away, they beat and mock him and hand him over to the chief priests and scribes. Anything they can find will do as a charge against him. They question him about being the Son of God. Jesus' reply is, "It is you who say so, yes I am." As far as the chief priest and scribes are concerned, this is the blasphemy that is going to seal Jesus' fate and, self-satisfied, they hand him over to Pilate, the Roman governor, because the Jews were not allowed to put someone to death. Their hypocrisy has no bounds, they just see fit to hand the deed to someone else.

Asked what charge they were bringing against Jesus, they claim that he has been inciting the people to revolt and that he is Christ, or king. Puzzled, Pilate asks Jesus, "Are you the king of the Jews?" to which Jesus replies "Mine is not a kingdom of this world, if it were of this world, my men would have prevented my arrest, but my kingdom does not belong here." "So, you are a king then," says Pilate. Jesus replies, "Yes I am a king, I was born for this, I came into the world to give witness to the truth and all who are on the side of truth listen to my voice." "Truth", says Pilate, "What is that?" (Jn 18: 33, 36-38)

Little did Pilate know that the one and only Truth was standing right in front of him, for Jesus had declared many times that he was the Way, the Truth and the Life and being God, he does not lie. Clearly, Pilate had not grappled with the truth and, indeed, many search for the truth all their lives but never find it. This is not surprising as every religion and political party is certain that what it proclaims is the truth. As Rudyard Kipling so astutely observed, "We are all islands shouting lies at each other across seas of misunderstandings." But there can be only one truth, God.

Pilate tells the people that he finds no case against Jesus that deserves death, but encouraged by the chief priests and the leaders, the people shout, "Crucify him, crucify him." And so, Jesus is taken away, first to be flogged then to be crowned with thorns and mocked by the soldiers.

"Roman scourging was cruel and designed to cause extreme suffering by hundreds of lashes. Carried out with a fulcrum or whip with several leather thongs, each end was weighted with lead balls or mutton bones. The thongs would cut the skin of the back, buttocks and legs, and the lead balls or mutton bones cause deep contusions." (a)

After all this immense suffering they load a great heavy crossbeam on his already raw shoulders and back. The blood loss is extreme, and he has barely enough strength to reach the place of execution, falling three times on the way. At the place of execution, called the place of the Skull, they throw him rudely on the ground causing even more suffering, and nail his wrists and feet to the wood, distorting them horribly, and leave him to die on this infamous gibbet.

"It was about the sixth hour and the sun's light failed, so that darkness came over the whole land until the night hour. The veil of the sanctuary was torn right down the middle and Jesus cried in a loud voice, 'Father into your hands I commit my spirit.' With these words He breathed his last. "The centurion together with the others guarding Jesus, had seen the earthquake and all that was taking place, and they were terrified and said, 'In truth, this man was the son of God' (Mt 27:54). And when all the crowds who had gathered for the spectacle saw what had happened, they went home beating their breasts" (Lk 23:44-48).

Jesus' friends receive permission from Pilate to take Jesus body down and, "wrapping it in a shroud, put it in a tomb which was hewn into a rock, and which had never held a body" (Lk 23:53).

But this is not the end of the story that the Pharisees and elders of the people had hoped for. Jesus will literally come back and haunt them, because "on the third day, at the first sign of dawn, the women who had been at the crucifixion went to the tomb with the spices they had prepared but they found that the stone had been rolled away from the tomb. On entering the tomb, they could not find Jesus' body. Suddenly two men in brilliant clothes appeared and said to the terrified women, 'Why look among the dead for someone who is alive, he is not here, he has risen. Remember what he told you when he was still with you in Galilee; that the Son of men was destined to be handed over into the hands of sinful men and be crucified and rise again on the third day' and they remembered his words." (Lk 24:1-8)

The gospel of Luke tells us that the disciples were dumbfounded when Jesus suddenly appeared in their midst. But he rebukes them "saying, 'Why are these doubts stirring in your hearts? See by my hands and my feet, it is I. Touch me and see for yourselves, a ghost has not flesh and bones as you see I have.' They were overjoyed, they did not know what to say. He said, 'have you anything here to eat?' And they offered him a piece of grilled fish which he ate in front of their eyes. He then opened their minds to understand the scriptures. 'Everything written about me in the Law of Moses and the Prophets and the Psalms was destined to be fulfilled. It is written that the Christ would suffer and on the third day rise from the dead and that in his name, repentance for the forgiveness of sins would be preached to the whole world beginning from Jerusalem. But stay in the city until you will be clothed with power from on high. You are witnesses to this.' He then took them out as far as the outskirts of Bethany and raising his hands he blessed them. Now as he blessed them, he withdrew from them and was carried up to heaven" (Lk 24:38-51).

They go back to Jerusalem full of joy and they are continually in the temple praising God. Full of anticipation and wondering what this "clothed from on high" would be like, they meet regularly for prayer and for the breaking of the bread as Jesus had told them to do. He had promised them that "I will not leave you orphans" and that he would send the Holy Spirit, the Spirit of Truth, to be with them forever. He "will teach you everything and remind you of all I have said to you" (Jn 14:18, 26).

As they meet once more for prayer in the upper room, "... suddenly there came from heaven a sound as of a violent wind which filled the whole room and there appeared to them tongues as of fire who came to rest on the head of each of them. They were all filled with the Holy Spirit and began to speak different languages as the Spirit gave them POWER to express themselves" (Acts 2:2-4). And all who lived in the city were amazed at hearing the disciples talk in their own language, "Parthians, Medes and Elamites, people from Mesopotamia, Cappadocia, Asia, Egypt, Judea and Rome, Cretans, and Arabs .... they heard them preaching in their own language about the marvels of God" (Acts 2: 11-13). What a wonderful sound it must have been when the Spirit of God turned those poor frightened fishermen into language gurus. No doubt all those present at this amazing spectacle would have recounted their experience of that incredible day in their own countries and talked about those marvels of God that they witnessed in Jerusalem. In so doing they were already spreading this new teaching far and wide.

Just as Jesus had been filled with all the gifts of the Holy Spirit and with POWER at the start of his public life, so also were the apostles transformed from frightened men into bold proclaimers of the Good News "that God so loved the world that He gave his only son, so that everyone who believes in him may not perish but may have eternal life" (Jn 3:16). They were the eyewitnesses of all that Jesus had said and done and now that they were equipped with the same POWER, Jesus "sent them out" (apostle literally means "he who is sent out") to bear their testimony to the world and spread the message. Jesus affirmed that "All authority in heaven and on earth has been given to me, go therefore to make disciples of all the nations; baptise them in the name of the Father and of the Son and of the Holy Spirit, and teach them to observe all the commands I gave you. And look, I am with you always, yes to the end of time" (Mt 28:18-20).

When the disciples lived with Jesus, they must hardly have had any understanding of what he was all about. When he told them that he had to die a grievous death but would be resurrected, it must have sounded like nonsense; how could they ever make sense of such an outrageous statement and of the many other things Jesus told them. Nor could they have had an inkling that the precepts Jesus preached, would pan out into a world religion and that they would be the ones who would spread it worldwide at the expense of their lives. Like good citizens they would no doubt have heard the Torah preached in the synagogue and shared the longing of the Israeli people for a Messiah, or deliverer, to free them from foreign oppression, but like the people around them, they did not link this deliverer with Jesus, the son of a carpenter. And yet they followed him, why? They left everything, just like that, even their bread-winning and families, all to lead the uncomfortable lives of itinerant preachers. What was the magnetic attraction of Jesus? Like all the people who saw Jesus operate, they were bowled over at the power he had to give sight to the blind, make the deaf hear and the lame walk. Who was this man who had such power? Such amazing miracles had never been seen in their midst before, and the news spread like wildfire through the countryside and beyond.

No doubt the disciples, like all the people around them, could see that Jesus was an extraordinary human being. Not only did they see the miracles, but they experienced at first hand the incredible love and compassion for the sick and the downtrodden which emanated from Jesus' whole being. God's nature is love, that is his very essence, and through the miracles, Jesus manifested the love that God has for every human being, a love that is beyond compare. It was for love's sake that Jesus came into the world to die so that he could draw humankind back to himself after we wounded his love for us so deeply by our pride.

It was the powerful love of Jesus, no doubt emanating from his glance, that the disciples were unable to resist, and which helped them to follow him without preamble. Moreover, we witness to this very day that this super-human love of Jesus does not fail to find resonance in an open heart and create a powerful response. Once anyone experiences the magnet of Jesus' love, it is impossible to resist its power; responding to it with the whole person becomes a must, and he can never be disowned. But this was not true for the Pharisees because their malice, self-righteousness and closed hearts prevented them from responding to his love; and they could not acknowledge even the miracles they saw Jesus perform in front of their own eyes. Just as some people are tone deaf to music, so they were tone deaf and spiritually blind. (This spiritual blindness also afflicts many people today.) It was only after the apostles had received the Holy Spirit, that their original ignorance as to whom Jesus really was swiftly disappeared. They were led by the Holy Spirit to accept that he was the Son of God so that they finally came to understand the importance of his mission and for what purpose he had chosen them. The Spirit of Truth further revealed to them the things to come, as Jesus had promised.

Peter's first sermon after Pentecost is called the "first apostolic preaching," or the "Kerygma", and it contains the essence of the Christian faith: "Jesus the Nazarene was a man commended by God by the miracles and signs that God worked through him ..... You put him to death, but God raised him to life" (Acts 2:22-24). "To be saved you must repent, you must be baptised in the name of Jesus Christ for the forgiveness of sins, and you will receive the gifts of the Holy Spirit. The promise was made for you and your children and for all those who are far away, for all those whom the Lord our God is calling to himself" (Acts 2: 38-49). This first sermon of Peter has become the building block on which the Creed was formulated, and which is said every Sunday at Mass.

When the disciples started their mission of spreading Jesus' message worldwide, the Holy Spirit was guiding them step by step and reminding them about Scripture and of all that Jesus had told them. There are numerous sources supporting this, such as Eusebius, who was bishop of Caesarea in Palestine around, 260-341 AD; and the Jewish historian Josephus a first century Jewish scholar and Saint Hippolytus of Rome (170-235 AD) who was born in Jerusalem, then part of Roman Judea; and the Bible, describing the travels the apostles undertook, which makes arresting reading. But the biggest evidence of their travels is the fact that all the countries they visited have to this day retained a vestige of the Christian faith as preached by the disciples.

What a providential start the spreading of the message had! The people who experienced the incredible miracle on Pentecost day and heard Peter's address were certainly bubbling over with excitement and eager to relate to friends and family what they had witnessed. The message in this way spread like lightning in many countries situated around the Mediterranean and as far as Mesopotamia, present day Iraq, parts of Iran and Syria, and later also to parts of the Roman Empire, North Africa and Western Europe and far-away India.

Considering the dangers travellers faced in the past, it is awe inspiring how those brave men weathered storms, hostile tribes, delays, sickness, and persecutions. Paul's account in 2 Corinthians gives us a vivid description of these risks: "I have been in prison, I have been flogged severely, many times exposed to death, five times have I been given thirty nine lashes, three times have I been beaten with sticks, once I was stoned, three times have I been shipwrecked, I have been in danger from brigands and from my own people and from gentiles, in danger at sea and in danger from people who were masquerading as brothers" (2 Cor 11: 23-26). And what courage missionaries still have as they face some of the same perils today. The list of missionaries who have been martyred in the last 2000 years for proclaiming the faith is endless. And in the present day we are experiencing an ever-rising persecution of Christians.

In those early days there was obviously no written "manual" of what to preach, and the apostles spreading the Good News would only have had access to the written word of the Torah and to the other books of the Old Testament, as they were read in the synagogue on the Sabbath. According to the New Jerusalem Bible, "The first five books of the Bible are known to the Jewish people as the Torah, or the Law. The Greeks called it the Pentateuch, or the Book in Five Volumes and it was Moses who was credited with having written this vast volume of literature, but most ancient traditions never claimed this. However, Moses was the central figure who dominated the "Yahwistic" religion, so called because the Jewish people called God "Yahweh". It was Moses who from the start initiated the people into that religion, as he was their first lawgiver. Moses inscribed the "Ten Words", or the Decalogue, on the tablets at Sinai, laying down the fundamental law which at once was moral and religious. It was a sacred law as it was dictated to Moses by God.

Although some of Paul's written letters date from as early as 53-54 AD, people would have heard the Message mostly from oral accounts, as was the case in Macedonia and Achaia, "because it was from you that the word of the Lord spread and not only there but everywhere," Paul tells the Thessalonians. Given the fact that there was no established formal way of worshipping nor a set liturgy, it is amazing that each disciple was able to teach the undiluted "kerygma" wherever they went in the world.

"What I wanted to make quite clear to you, brothers, what the message of the gospel I preached to you is; you accepted it and took your stand on it, and you are saved by it" (1Cor15:1). What Paul is saying here is what matters most to him is, that he preached what all the other apostles preach. This statement is very important as it will reverberate through the centuries, firstly because all the apostles, being inspired by the Holy Spirit, including Paul, be it at a later date, were all able to preach the same message. And secondly it clearly stated that to be saved, every human, past, present, and future should obey the "same Ten Commandments" given by God to Moses and adhere to the same principles and rules set out in the Kerygma. However, some exceptions can apply as described in the chapter "Reflections". It was to be expected that disagreements would arise, like the ones we read in Acts 11 and 15 about clean and unclean food, or about circumcision, but these do not apply to the conditions needed to be saved.

St Paul did not receive the Holy Spirit at Pentecost like the other disciples. However, as we read in his testimony, he did receive the Spirit when he was baptised. As a Pharisee Paul would have had a thorough knowledge of the Jewish scriptures, but his profound knowledge of "The Way," as Christianity was then called, came as a direct result of his personal meeting with Jesus on the road to Damascus when Jesus commissioned him with his specific task. All through his ministry he was directly taught by Jesus as is clear from his many letters. In the prophets it is written, "They will all be taught by God" (Jn 6:45 quoting Isaiah 54:13). After having been a fierce persecutor of The Way, he had a vision of the risen Christ on the road to Damascus which changed his whole life, and ours also. We still talk about having a "Damascus experience" as an experience that changes our lives.

This is Paul's personal account to King Agrippa of what precisely happened on that famous road:

> I once thought that it was my duty to use every means to oppose the name of Jesus of Nazareth and I even pursued his followers into foreign cities. On such an expedition I was going to Damascus, armed with full powers and a commission from the chief priest, and in the middle of the day as I was on my way, Your Majesty, I saw a light from heaven shining more brilliantly than the sun round me and my fellow travellers. We all fell to the ground, and I heard a voice saying to me in Hebrew, "Saul, Saul, why are you persecuting me. It is hard for you kicking against the goad." Then I said, "Who are you, Lord?" And the Lord answered, "I am Jesus whom you are persecuting. But get up and stand on your feet, for I have appeared to you for this reason; to appoint you as my servant and as a witness of this vision in which you have seen me, and of others, in which I shall appear to you. I shall rescue you from the people and from the nations to whom I send you to open their eyes, so that they may turn from darkness to light, from the dominion of Satan to God, and receive, through faith in me, forgiveness of their sins and a share of the inheritance of the sanctified."

Paul continued "After that, King Agrippa, I could not disobey the vision and I started preaching" (Ac26:12-20).

Paul further said: "The Good news I preached is not something that I was given by men, but something I learnt only through the revelation of Christ" (Gal. 1:11-12). With this direct revelation, Paul threw himself head over heels into his new task. "I did not stop to discuss this with any human being, nor did I go up to Jerusalem to see those who were already apostles before me, but I went off to Arabia and later straight to Damascus. Only after three years did I go to Jerusalem to meet Cephas. After that I went to Syria and Cilicia and was still not known by sight to the churches of Christ in Judea. They simply kept hearing it said, "The man once so eager to persecute us is now preaching the faith that he used to try to destroy" (Gal:1: 16-24).

His zeal and dynamism, his enormous knowledge of this new faith as yet not written down and which we read about in his numerous Letters, points to the unquestionable fact that his work and the whole message of the Gospel handed down to us by the apostles is truly the 'inspired work of the Holy Spirit.' He, together with Peter, are the two great pillars of the faith.

PETER'S SPECIFIC ROLE

It was not only at Pentecost that Simon Peter received the light of his mission, but also when he was walking the roads of Israel with the Lord who asked him "Who do you say I am?" Peter spoke up "You are the Christ, the Son of the living God." Jesus replied, "Simon, son of Jonah, you are a happy man, because it is not flesh and blood which has revealed this to you but my Father in heaven, so now I say to you: you are Peter, on this Rock, (from the Aramaic word Cephas or Peter, meaning rock), I will build my church, and the gates of the underworld can never hold against it. I will give you the keys of the kingdom of heaven:

whatever you bind on earth will be bound in heaven and whatever you loose on earth shall be considered loosed in heaven" (Mt 16:15-19).

With these words it is Jesus himself who established the Church and chose Peter as the founding stone on which to start building it, not with bricks and mortar but with the Word of God: Jesus' teaching. Jesus first ascertained that Peter knows that he is the Son of God, and he can now rest assured that he can leave the building of his church in safe hands. He knows that Peter will proclaim everything he has taught him - the whole message of the Good News in its entirety, nothing added, nothing taken away - to the whole world and to all generations to come. It was not by chance that Jesus chose Peter, whose name means Rock, for building his church on. The indestructible qualities of rock are a symbol of the indestructible everlasting existence of the Church as founded by Jesus.

As we saw earlier, it is not God who creates division but humans, who are very good at creating strife and enmity. Through the course of the centuries many Christian denominations evolved due to disagreements, misunderstanding, excesses, and political strife. Nobody is in control of where they are born or what their religious education would be, but all are united in the service and love of our Lord Jesus Christ. And what is more, we can be sure that whoever we are, believer or not, if we seek earnestly for God, we will find him.

Peter preached in Asia, Galatia, Pontus and Italy and it was in Rome that he died a martyrs' death. Subsequently the seat of the church became Rome. With the many popes, good or bad, succeeding Peter, it became the official central seat for establishing Doctrine and maintaining the purity of the message. Right from the outset the Church endured many calumnies, persecutions and has known corruption, scandal and deserved criticisms. People point the finger at religious people when they make mistakes, wrongly judging them as being holier than the rest, but this is far from the truth. Religious or not, everyone is fallible and prone to succumb to temptations and church leaders are no different. Like any other establishment the Roman Catholic Church is run by fallible humans, but it is not, like some assume, run like a propaganda machine trying to get everyone to join the "club" of the Roman Church. Its aim is first and foremost to help every human to reach their eternal destiny, namely eternal life gained for all through Jesus' sacrifice on the cross.

Regardless of the mistakes the Church made in the past and still makes now, the popes are the direct followers of the Apostles in an unbroken line, and accordingly are directly inspired by the Holy Spirit, just like all of us can be as well. Peter's imperfections are so highly visible in the gospels and yet Jesus chose Peter as head of his church.

Throughout Christian history we can trace how the followers of Peter and the apostles have, to the best of their abilities, endeavoured to fulfil their divine mission to bring the whole human race to the salvation promised by God, and to safeguard the purity of Jesus' teaching. The evidence of this endeavour is shown in the long list of holy men and women who, despite the Church's imperfections, have protected the purity of the core message in its entirety and unchanged. Such scholars and saints include:

St Jerome, (AD 347-420) who translated the Bible into Latin from both Greek and Hebrew and resolved theological controversies.

Saint Gregory Nazianzen, (AD 329-390) who countered the Arian heresy that denied the divinity of Christ and helped formulate the definitive teaching on the Holy Spirit. He was a prolific writer in prose and verse.

Pope Saint Gregory the Great (AD 540-AD 604), who deserved this title in more than one regard. He fought tirelessly against corruption in the church, safeguarded the sacraments and wrote many commentaries on the Bible, and influenced the Liturgy as we know it today. He also promoted the church music still today known as the "Gregorian Chants."

St John Damascene (AD 676-754) who was a famous theologian of the Eastern Church in the 7th century. In his many writings he vehemently defended the veneration of sacred statues to which the Iconoclasts were opposed. They were so enraged by his opposition that they cut off John's right hand, which miraculously was restored to him. In 787 AD, the council of Nicaea finally supported John's stand.

Saint Thomas Aquinas, (AD 1225-1274), renowned for his superhuman intellect is recognized as the greatest scholastic philosopher and Christian theologian, whose writings have influenced Roman Catholic doctrines to this very day.

St Thomas More, (AD 1478-1535), close friend of Henry VIII and chancellor of England, who was beheaded for upholding the indissolubility of Henry's marriage to his wife Catharine of Aragon.

Through good times and bad, through reformations, heresies and persecutions, Jesus' teaching to his disciples and the doctrines of the Roman church handed down unaltered will withstand the test of time, for "The gates of the underworld can never hold out against her" (Mt 16:18).

Jesus had a wonderful and varied way to communicate the essence of his message; through his miracles and using parables. His parables seem to be simple stories, but all teach a profound lesson for daily life. They convey a deep and central teaching, and this is especially visible in his teaching on the sacraments, most of which we can trace directly to the four Gospels, and they have become the mainstay of the Christian life.

SACRAMENTS

Sacraments are in essence the grace, or power given by the Holy Spirit to execute a particular state or role in life; they are conferred either by a bishop or a priest. Let me address four of these sacraments:

Baptism
Baptism is the first sacrament required to enter the Christian life, although as we shall discuss later, there is also a baptism of desire, for those who have never heard about Jesus. The very first tenet Jesus gave his disciples is, "Go and spread the message to the whole world. Whoever believes and is baptised will be saved; whoever does not believe will be condemned" (Mk 16: 15-16). Although Jesus was sinless and needed no baptism, at the start of his public life the first thing he did was to be baptised by John the Baptist in the river Jordan (Mt 3:13-17).

It is also the first revelation that Peter receives in the Holy Spirit in the Kerygma, that to enter the kingdom of heaven people must be baptised for the forgiveness of sin and thus the Sacrament of Baptism is instituted. In Baptism we are born again, we receive the gift of faith and eternal salvation and become children of God. We are justified and made righteous.

(Rom 6)

Confirmation
Today the bishop administers the Sacrament of Confirmation to adults who wish to make a personal commitment to the promises made on their behalf when they were baptised as infants. The gift of the Holy Spirit, received at Baptism, is activated so that the confirmand can benefit from Jesus' assurance that he will not leave the disciples without help: "The Holy Spirit, whom the Father will send in my name will teach you everything, and remind you of all I have said." (Jn 14:26).

Jesus himself received the Holy Spirit when he was baptised, "and as he came out of the water, the heavens suddenly opened, and he saw the spirit of God descending on him like a dove" (Lk 3:22). Jesus implies that both baptism and confirmation are necessary to enter the kingdom of heaven, "for unless a man is born again of water and the Holy Spirit, he cannot enter the Kingdom of heaven" (Jn 3:5).

Marriage
Some pharisees asked Jesus if it was against the law to divorce one's wife on any pretext whatever? But he replied, "Have you not read that the Creator from the beginning made them male and female ...... this is why a man leaves his father and mother and becomes attached to his wife, and the two become one flesh..... I say this to you: anyone who divorces his wife, except for the case of an illicit marriage, and marries another is guilty of adultery" (Mt 19: 4-5, 9).

Confession
Peter's, and St John the Baptist's messages of repentance were not the only ones we read about in the Bible. In numerous stories people are exhorted to repent of their evil ways or fear

God's retribution. The feeling of guilt and regret is a most debilitating state to be in. It affects our physical and mental health and eats away at our conscience. An article I recently read in a newspaper, found that people who felt shame and guilt, felt small, worthless, and suffered from tension. We are quite appalled at the lack of remorse shown by convicted criminals, yet the feeling of unacknowledged guilt has become part of many people's lives and all too often they do not know how to rid themselves of this crippling feeling.

The sacrament of confession is at the heart of the gospel as it is a meeting point with the God of forgiveness and mercy. It is the most liberating feeling we can avail ourselves of. No psychiatrist can reach into the deepest recesses of our souls and free us from our guilt like God's forgiveness can. Jesus knew our need and instituted the sacrament of confession with these words to his disciples when he was sending them out into the world. "Receive the Holy Spirit, if you forgive anyone's sins they are forgiven; if you retain anyone's sins they are retained" (Jn20:23). The priest speaks the WORD of God which has power to grant forgiveness, as we discussed in our reflection on Genesis, and wipes our sins clear away as if they have never been committed.

There is a lot of misunderstanding about this sacrament and a feeling prevails that it is a meaningless exercise. People perceive it to be just rattling off a list of sins, get absolution and then feel free to carry on sinning to their hearts content. This attitude smacks of self-delusion and lack of intent to become a better person. To make a valid confession three conditions are required: true repentance, a firm intent to change one's ways, and penance. This can either be saying a prayer suggested by the priest or doing some work of charity or a kind act.

At birth humans immediately start walking on the road that

leads to our ultimate destiny, eternal life. It is a road full of pitfalls and the Christian life is a constant endeavour to avoid them. Anger and frustration often occur when the same mistakes are made time and again or we have an addiction that cannot be mastered. Often these mistakes, or sins, gnaw at our conscience and guilt sets in. Repenting, or feeling sorry, often called metanoia, literally means changing direction from the darkness of sin towards the light of life that is Jesus. He is "The Lamb of God who takes away the sins of the world" and, with confession, he reveals a way for our sins to be removed. Having the humility to confess shows our dependence on God. It frees us from this feeling of guilt and literally helps us make a U-turn away from those bad habits, provided only that there is a firm resolve to do better next time.

A valuable habit we were told as children was to search our conscience daily to see where we went wrong that day, and firmly try to get rid of bad habits, so that we would become more and more worthy to gain our prize at the end of the race. Bad habits will be cropping up all through life; but it is the firm resolve to do better, and of throwing ourselves on God's mercy, that lies at the heart of sincerely wanting to change our lives for the better. With the grace the sacrament gives, there is no doubt that slowly we become better people. Religious discussions often lead to the question, is bringing up one's children in a certain religion not a kind of indoctrination? It is generally the norm to teach children from an early age to be "good girls and boys" and to impart one's own strong held faith, which parents believe is for the child's benefit.

Tragically this lifegiving sacrament of Confession has fallen by the wayside in many Roman churches and has never been prominent in other Christian denominations even though, interestingly, Luther saw the need to go to confession all his life.

No one raises an eyebrow when people have counselling or consult a psychiatrist, and yet they skirt away from going to confession. Fewer people would be suffering from depression and mental illness if they availed themselves of this marvellous opportunity to unburden themselves of lifelong guilt and oppression, and this is free of charge! Forgiveness is the biggest treasure Christianity can offer. In fact, it is essential, for without saying sorry to God and forgiving ourselves and others, we cannot enter the Promised Land.

THE APOSTLES' RESOLVE

On the day they are sent out by Jesus to preach to the world, he presses upon them to teach the people to "observe all the commandments I gave you" (Mt 28:20). And after having received the Holy Spirit at Pentecost Peter addresses the people with The Kerygma, or first revelations about the truth of the Gospel, "You must repent, and everyone must be baptised in the name of Jesus Christ for the forgiveness of their sins, and you will receive the gift of the Holy Spirit" (Ac 2:38).

When following Jesus so spontaneously, the disciples were certainly totally unaware what hardship the future would hold for them. But Jesus did not leave them in the dark and prophesied the price the Apostles would have to pay for following him and preaching the Good News. "Be prepared for people to hand you over to the Sanhedrin and scourge you in their synagogues.... You will be universally hated on account of my name, but anyone who stands firm to the end will be saved" (Mt 10:17, 22). These terrifying predictions must have scared the living daylight out of them, and yet they stood firm and did not abandon him. They had experienced his love and knew that there was no true love without sacrifice, as Jesus himself was to show them when he was crucified. Apart from St John, they all followed in Jesus' footsteps and suffered martyrs' deaths.

WHERE DID THE APOSTLES PREACH?

PETER preached in Galatia, which is modern day Turkey, Cappadocia, Bethania, which is situated in western Madagascar, Italy and Asia Minor.

PAUL, the last appointed apostle, set out from Jerusalem and advanced as far as Illyricum, a Roman province that stretched along the Adriatic coast as far as Dalmatia, Albania, Bosnia, Croatia, Montenegro and Serbia. After their extensive travels Paul and Peter both suffered martyrdom in Rome under Emperor Nero. Paul was beheaded and Peter was crucified head down at his own request as he felt unworthy to suffer the same death as Jesus.

ANDREW preached to the Scythians and Thracians, and eastern European and Indo-European people and was crucified on an X-formed olive tree in Patras in Greece. The head of "the first disciple" as he is called now rests in St Peter's Basilica in Rome.

JAMES seems to have stayed in Judea and was the first to be martyred by the sword under Herod the Tetrarch. (Ac12:1-2) He may have travelled to Compostela in Spain where he is revered to this day.

PHILIP preached in Phrygia and was also crucified head down under Emperor Domitian in Hierapolis, an ancient Greek city, and was buried there.

JOHN preached in Asia Minor, was banished by Domitian to the Isle of Patmos in Greece, where he wrote the gospel and saw the Apocalyptic vision. He fell asleep in Ephesus where he is buried.

JAMES, the son of Alphaeus, was stoned to death by the Jews when preaching in Jerusalem and was buried there beside the temple.

JUDE, who was also called Thaddaeus, preached to the people of Edessa and Mesopotamia and was beheaded and buried in Berytus.

BARTHOLOMEW preached to the Indians, to whom he gave the gospel according to Matthew, and was crucified with his head downward and buried in a town called Allanum in Parthia, modern day Iran.

MATTHIAS, mentioned in Acts 1:21-26, was the replacement for Judas Iscariot. He preached in Jerusalem, fell asleep and is buried there. There are however some conflicting tales as he is also associated with Armenia on the Black Sea, and he is thought to have been stoned there by an angry mob in AD 51 and buried there.

SIMON and Jude were martyred on the same day. They seem to have ministered together in Iran and Babylon where we are told they converted 60,000 to Christianity. Simon was sawn in two by an angry mob.

THOMAS preached to the Parthians, Medes, Persians, Hyrcanians (peoples of a region in present day Iran), the Bactrians (peoples in an ancient country in Central Asia) and the Margians. Thomas was a very active missionary and went further than all the other disciples. He established the oldest Christian community in India when the sea trade with the Persian Gulf made it possible for him to introduce Jesus Christ at Cranagore in Kerala, south India, in AD 52. He may even have gone as far as Afghanistan. He was stabbed in the four members of his body with a pine spear in Calamene. His tomb is situated in Mylapore, India.

"Where Did the Apostles Preach," Article attributed to the 2nd-3rd century Church Father St. Hippolytus in very early Christian traditions, by Mark de Bolt, schizophrenic writer and poet, USA. (b)

CHRISTIANITY'S JOURNEY

Thanks to the intrepid zeal of the apostles the faith took a foothold in all the above- mentioned countries. But as we can deduce from the deaths that the apostles suffered, much opposition was encountered to this new way of thinking from the Jewish, Roman and local leaders alike, who felt their authority being undermined as more and more people turned away from state religions. In Rome especially, Christians started to endure horrendous persecutions imposed by various Roman Emperors. Although Christians were not required to give up their beliefs, they found it impossible to pay respect to the divinity of the emperor. When they refused to do so they were seen as rebelling against the State and paid a heavy price. Under Emperor Nero, the covering with tar and setting alight of Christians to illuminate his parties, stands out as one of cruellest persecutions of all centuries. The reign of Emperor Diocletian rivalled that of Emperor Nero in its cruelty towards Christians.

"Finally, the persecution of Christians came to an end when Emperor Constantine published the 'Edict of Milan' in AD 313 granting freedom of religion for Christians and all religions, after he defeated his rival Maxentius in the battle of the Milvian bridge in 312AD." (c) The story I remember from the history lesson, is that Constantine most probably converted to Christianity because of the many prayers of his mother St Helen, and it is said that soon after, he had a vision of Jesus before going into battle. Constantine together with his whole army saw a cross of light in the sky with the words 'By this sign you will conquer.' After this, Constantine put the sign of the cross on the shield of his army.

"This heralded the end of the persecution of Christians, and missionaries could freely go to the ends of the earth, as Jesus had commanded, baptising all nations in the name of the Father and of the Son and of the Holy Spirit. It was then that Europe as we know it was born." (d)

Once the prohibition on practising Christianity was lifted, the faith spread like wild-fire throughout the western world and beyond. The numbers of Christians increased at an amazing rate, but it goes without saying that it was not all plain sailing. As soon as Christianity became associated with the powerful, many jumped on the band wagon, joining to gain political status and hoping to curry favour with the Church and authority. But through the centuries, Christianity also encountered heresies, schisms and strings of oppositions and further persecutions.

In1099 the first crusades started with the re-capture of Jerusalem which had been under Muslim domination for 450 years, by the Duke of Loraine, Godfrey of Bouillon (which is a town in the Ardennes, Belgium, where he still has his statue). However, in 1187 Jerusalem was wrested back by a Muslim army led by Saladin, the Sultan of Egypt and Syria. Christian Europe united its armies against Saladin and the crusades continued with victories and defeats and lasted until 1271 and beyond. Art, commerce, literature, music and scholarship were budding during the Middle Ages with many universities created and many of Europe's glorious cathedrals built. Since Europe was still divided into small kingdoms which seemed to be forever at war with each other vying for supremacy, it was also a violent time with many calamities, such as the plague, famines, and religious schisms.

By the 16th century the Church had become politically very powerful and corrupt with popes and bishops amassing power and wealth. Many unsavoury practices flourished like the buying of indulgencies to save one's soul. This caused the rise of the Protestant Reformation in Germany by Martin Luther. In England we saw the separation of the Church of England from Rome, establishing Anglicanism, and many new movements followed, such as Calvinism, The Scottish Reformed Church, Puritanism, and a score of others.

With the advent of different Christian denominations horrific violence was perpetrated by Christians against Christians. Legendary is the cruel persecution of Catholics by Anglicans, and vice versa during the reformation in England. In the St Bartholomew's Day Massacre in France in 1572, more than 5000 Huguenots were killed by Catholics in less than 24 hours. We also witness the cruel Inquisition by Spain against Jews, Muslims and against Protestantism which was spreading throughout the Empire. The Roman Inquisition by the Church itself targeted witchcraft, sorcery, and heretics. All this violence was engendered by different interpretations of the Gospel, and sadly deviated in a big way from its true message of forgiveness, justice, peace, and love.

With The Age of Reason or the Enlightenment as the 16th and 17th centuries are known, a whole new era starts with fascinating scientific discoveries in many fields such as technology, medicine, communications and especially mathematics. One of the great minds of the time is undoubtedly Isaac Newton, who demonstrated that there was a natural explanation for many things such as gravity, whereas before it was believed that natural phenomena had a supernatural explanation. Other great minds of the time were in England John Locke, philosopher and physician and the philosopher Francis Bacon, and in France, René Descartes, mathematician, scientist, and philosopher. With the scientific revolution emphasising rationalism, logic and reason, the supernatural became obsolete. Religious tolerance was promoted, and individualism became the order of the day. Slowly, secularism started gnawing away at centuries long-held religious beliefs and practices.

But "not everybody was caught up by the Enlightenment and in the 18th century a huge spiritual revival swept through the American colonies, England, and Wales. One of the leading motivators in England and Wales was John Wesley, while in America Jonathan Edwards spearheaded the "Great Awakening." In the following century in America, others with powerful healing ministries were Aimée Semple McPherson, (1890) and Kathryn Kuhlman, the woman who believed in miracles (1907), while the revival in Wales was led by Evan Roberts (1878) and others." (e)

"They started what is called an Evangelical movement with the emphasis on the power of the Holy Spirit, but some of them still belonged to an established religion like the Methodists. In Wales, the most famous revivalist was Smith Wigglesworth born in 1859. He did not want to be part of any denomination, but wanted everybody to have access to the power of the Spirit. The dramatic and amazing healings performed in the name of Jesus by Smith Wigglesworth are described at length in his book "Greater Works, Experiencing the Power of God." (f)

THE DIFFERENCE THE COMING OF JESUS MADE IN THE WORLD

Re-examining the beginning of the Christian era in Europe and the wider world, we question what difference the coming of Jesus Christ and his teaching made on the world stage? How could Christians, in any era, choose those horrendous tortures rather than renounce Jesus? How did the son of a carpenter born in Israel 2000 ago revolutionize the way in which the Western world and eventually the world at large, thought and behaved? We can safely assume that there has never been a king, or a leader, emperor, philosopher, or holy man who has impacted the history of humanity in such a powerful way as Jesus did. He brought about a revolution and a whole new way of thinking. His extraordinary teaching went against the grain of all logical ideas and norms; never and nowhere had such controversial ideas been advocated anywhere in the world before.

In the following passage, it is clear why Jesus' teaching was so earth-shattering and controversial:
I say this to you, who are listening, love your enemies. Do good to those who hate you, bless those who curse you, pray for those who treat you badly. To the man who slaps you on one cheek, present the other cheek too, to the man who takes your cloak from you, do not refuse your tunic. Give to everyone who asks you and do not ask for your property back from the man who robs you. Treat others as you would like them to treat you. If you love those who love you, what thanks can you expect. Be compassionate as your Father in heaven is compassionate. Do not judge and you will not be judged yourselves; do not condemn and you will not be condemned yourselves; grant pardon and you will be pardoned. Give and there will be gifts for you: a full measure,

pressed down, shaken together, and overflowing will be poured into your lap; because the amount you measure out is the amount you will be given back. (Lk 6:27-38)

This was a totally different way to that lived by people all over the world. And once this message reached the wider world, something slowly changed in the human mindset and "Slowly, slowly, into dull and muddled-headed man came the idea that power was manifest in meekness, strength in love, and life in the death and resurrection of Jesus". (g)

THE RAPID SPREAD OF CHRISTIANITY

In the paragraphs below, my source of information is the writing of Dr J Uytterhoeven which I have translated and paraphrased.

From the 1st century AD onwards, Christianity spread through the evangelizing apostles with St Matthias converting the Gothic tribes in Eastern Europe, Armenia and other regions on the Black Sea. The cruel persecutions of Christians around AD 303, by Emperor Diocletian in countries like Croatia and along the Dalmatian coast, shows that there was already a strong Christian presence in this part of Europe. Although St Martin, bishop or Tours, had already in AD 360 established the first monastery in Gaul, it was not until AD 496 that the Gallic tribes became Christian, with the baptism of the Frankish King Clovis I in Reims together with his whole retinue. All the regions he had conquered became Christian with him. He unified these states into one country with Paris as the capital, and since then France has been called the cradle of Christianity.
Opposed to the sophisticated, civilised regions of the Mediterranean South, which was the seat of learning and progress at the time, we find Gaul still entrenched in the Iron Age. The Gaelic as well as the Germanic world was dominated

by violence and the sword. There was no unified state, but people were divided into clans who were at the mercy of the two governing classes, the nobles and the Druids. The Druids, selected from among the nobles, were all powerful. They had a say in education, science, justice and religion, and were helped by soothsayers and bards. They were the ones who held sway over the people, a situation strongly resented by the Romans, who did everything possible to break their power. Nature was worshipped and represented by different gods who excelled in cruelty and often demanded human sacrifice. In their honour the poor victims were tied to monstrous effigies made of hay and burned alive.

It was to this uncivilized country, Britain, that St Augustine was sent in AD 597 by Pope Gregory the Great, together with 40 Benedictine monks. They came ashore, in procession, singing and praying, to share the Christian faith with the Anglo-Saxon population, so the story books tell us. The difficulties were enormous, but in a peaceful way they were able to instil a new way of thinking into the bellicose tribes whose way had been dominated by violence. On 26th May, 604, Augustine became Archbishop of Canterbury and was venerated as a saint immediately upon his death.

Christianity had emanated from the Middle East, the cradle of learning and civilization for thousands of years. When it reached Europe, it salvaged the Roman civilization left behind by the retreating Roman armies and complemented it with the values and precepts of the new religion. It brought with it a new learning and a new way of thinking, not only in religious matters but also in other aspects of life.
The newly established Christian church functioned through bishops, priests, and monks who, because of their knowledge and dedication, improved and softened in no small measure the still

raw and often cruel lives of the people. They cared for the sick, who until then were often at the mercy of witchdoctors, they taught the people to read and write and developed more efficient ways of agriculture. Towns were created and courts of justice came into being. The clergy were often called upon to be councillors as mediators for the local authority, especially giving advice during attacks from neighbouring tribes, and for the first time the people found in them defenders against the injustices they suffered from the domineering classes. Convents and abbeys, originating in the Middle East, were established and became the centres of knowledge and learning independent from the state. Not only did they preach the precepts of the faith, but they especially instilled respect for human life and the person, a whole new concept never heard of in those early days. (h)

The directors of the new Dracula film, two self-professed atheists proclaimed: "they could absolutely not leave out the scene with Sister Agatha holding the cross towards Dracula, because the cross has power to start a civilization". This statement really hits the nail on the head because never has there been one who has revolutionised the mindset of the whole world and impacted history in such a powerful way as Jesus did. Christian values have imbued our way of life and influenced our beliefs, our morals, our architecture and art, our culture, and the way we have interacted with each other for the last 2000 years.

The call of Jesus is a universal call because it speaks to the heart of all peoples. It is a call to show compassion and mercy, healing, forgiveness of sin, justice, and peace. This call exhorts us to love our neighbour as ourselves and even to love our enemy. It is a controversial message, in the extreme creating a revolution by requesting extreme love and giving the promise of paradise where death is not the end, where injustice and pain do not exist as "The Lord will wipe away the tears from every cheek" says

Psalm 64. This was, and still is, the message of hope everyone subconsciously thirsts for.

The other extremely controversial story about Jesus was that he rose from the dead. Many a time he had declared, "I am the resurrection" (Jn 11:26). It was only after his resurrection that the disciples realised what he meant.

> When Mary of Magdala went to the tomb of Jesus, she saw that the stone had been rolled away and that the tomb was empty. She ran to Peter and John and said, "They have taken my Lord away, and we don't know where they have put him" (Jn 20:1-2).

> The two disciples went into the tomb and found the linen cloths on the ground, but the tomb was empty: they saw, and they believed. "Till this moment they still had not understood the scripture, that he must rise from the dead" (Jn 20: 9).

Jesus, by his resurrection witnessed that he was the Lord of the living and the dead, and by conquering death his promise to us could be fulfilled that after death our souls will be immortal. What would be the reason for life on earth, for living in this vale of tears with all its calamities, poverty, sickness, crimes, and wars, if there were not to be a silver lining at the end of it all. It would be totally pointless and hopeless. Sadly, many people see it this way.

St Paul, in 1 Corinthians, emphasises that the resurrection is the core message of the Good News, "If Christ had not been raised (from the dead), then our preaching is without substance and so is your faith. What is more we have proved to be false witnesses to God. …….. If our hope in Christ has been for this life only, we are of all people the most pitiable" (1 Cor 15:14-19).

Jesus being raised from the dead is the primordial difference between Christianity and all other religions as it means that he is alive and has the power, not of a dead man, but of the living Christ, to carry on influencing and transforming all of humanity from the darkness of sin into the light of his universal love.

OVER TO US!

Jesus' resurrection story sounds more like a science fiction story, so remarkable that many have difficulty in accepting it. Likewise, believing that Jesus was not only human, but also God, is an enigma to most people. Yet he declared very openly that he was God. Why would he do such an extraordinary thing, knowing that he would die a horrible death. Was he deluded or a fool to say such a thing? The fact was, that he deliberately accepted a death sentence to fulfil his mission, which was to commute humanity's death sentence into eternal life. This argument, to demonstrate that Jesus is God, has been used by many preachers and writers such as CS Lewis who says, "Jesus is neither a lunatic nor a fiend, and consequently I have to accept that he was and is God. God has landed on this enemy-occupied world in human form". (i)

Pope St John Paul II described it in a similar way, "Jesus Christ is the centre of history. God entered the history of humanity. Through the incarnation, God who is spirit, became flesh in the person of Jesus, and gave human life the dimension that he intended man to have from his first beginning".

Forty days after his resurrection Jesus ascended to heaven in this human body witnessed by his disciples. This leads us to the amazing concept that if we believe this, we "know," that there is a heaven and equally that there is a God, for Jesus said, "to have seen me is to have seen the Father" (Jn 14:9). I will be reprimanded for using the word 'KNOW', as I so often am: "You do not know, you believe, because if there is evidence then it is not a belief," is the objection. First, religious "knowing," rests on the historical evidence by Roman and Jewish historians that Jesus existed, and it is said that there is more evidence about Jesus' existence than about Julius Caesar's. Second, it rests on the testimony of the disciples and of all the saints who had a first-hand experience of the risen Lord. And third, it rests on our own personal experience and by all the experiences and testimonies of millions of believers through the centuries who were caught in the dragnet of God's transforming power. We do not believe blindly: it is these testimonies and experiences which inform our beliefs, our intellect, and our faith. With our own testimonies and those of millions, we cannot delude ourselves any longer and hide behind the excuse that "there is no evidence, only belief".

Jesus said, "I am the way, the truth and the life" (Jn14:7). What does it mean? Many religious leaders have shown a way towards 'enlightenment' through their teaching, but none can testify that they themselves are the way towards it. Jesus is the true and only way we can follow if we want to earn salvation. One sermon expressed this so succinctly; "without the Way, there is no going, without the Truth there is no knowing and without the Life, there is no living." Without Jesus we are left in limbo.

Finding God's love is a truth which begs to be heard, because Jesus' Mission Statement offers "good news to the afflicted, liberty to captives, sight to the blind and freedom for the oppressed" (Lk 4:18). He has come to restore our brokenness, heal our sickness and remove our physical and mental pain. "If the Son of man sets you free, you will be free indeed" (Jn 8:36). If we believe this, we will be really free! This is the reason why the apostles, the saints, the missionaries, and all those who have experienced this overwhelming love of Jesus at a personal level, want to shout from the roof tops: "Do not despair, there is someone out there who loves you to bits." This Good News needs to be bandied around the world, now more than ever before, as true love is in short supply in our sad world with divorce on the rise, children being told they are useless or bullied on social media and worse. Every human is entitled to find true love; it is the most invaluable treasure which makes us capable of moving mountains and sends our self-confidence rocketing sky high. To be truly loved, unconditionally and valued for just who we are, sets us on the road to reaching our true potential and to finding our true identity and the happiness we crave.

But unconditional love is always love with a sting; like all true love it demands sacrifice as it is always geared towards the other, away from self, and this is what makes it so immeasurably powerful. "Anyone who wants to save his life will lose it; but anyone who loses his life for my sake will find it" (Mt16:25). This is a controversial message and difficult to grasp, but then may not be so puzzling, as often we feel more joy in giving than in receiving, or from compromising rather than from sticking stubbornly to our own guns.

Jesus shedding his blood for love on the cross was love with a tremendous sting. We have not often fully grasped the implications of his sacrifice: that it was done wilfully, that it was done for our benefit, and that through his earth-shattering resurrection, he gained victory over death, sin, suffering and Satan. This implies that there is now absolutely nothing in our lives, and throughout the whole universe that cannot be made whole, even the animal world will be restored when the time comes, and "the wolf and the young lamb will feed together, the lion eat hay like the ox, and dust will be the serpent's food" (Is.65:25).

Although we still live in the valley of tears and in the shadow of death with all the difficulties this entails, it means that all the calamities which befall us do not have a hold over our lives anymore. People are weighed down through life by their past misdemeanours, sins, and guilt. As an example of the point I am making, two people, one a successful businessman and the other an elderly lady, confided in me that in their youth they did something very wrong, and it still haunted them in old age and had led to bouts of depression ever since. If only they would have turned to the certainty of being forgiven by having been washed clean by his blood. We do not need to give in to despair and commit suicide when we have been bullied or when life turns against us. The reason for God taking on flesh and coming on earth was so that "we could have life and have it to the full" (Jn10:10).

Life often passes in a utopian bubble of light, blinding us to see the darkness in and around us. The darkness around is all too visible: wars, famine, torture, sickness, poverty, injustice, prostitution. Closer to home it is more difficult to pinpoint, for surely, we do not do anything wrong!? Adultery, sexual immorality, unforgiveness, slander, gossip, lying, stealing, breaking one's promise, abortion, and despair might ring a bell, and we know that their consequences spread a blanket of darkness over us and over those we have wronged. "For the wage paid by sin is death, the present given by God is eternal life" (Rom 6:23). The secret for healing lies in our acknowledging that we need help, letting go of our pride and reaching for the true light that is "Jesus the light of the world" in order to burst the bubble of our delusion and see where the true darkness lies. "Whoever follows him will not be walking in darkness but will have the light of life" (Jn 8:12).

What an incredible message of hope and joy we have now that there is light at the end of the tunnel of life. As the boy in our opening chapter assumed "There is someone out there who is looking after us." By all the physical healings, Jesus showed that he did not just want to set us free spiritually, but also to set our bodies free from suffering and give us a foretaste of heaven. These two intrinsically linked components of the Good News of the Kingdom, hope and wholeness in body, mind and spirit, are accessible here on earth by the healing presence of Christ.

He paid the price for the good and the bad alike, the criminal and the addict, the rich and the poor, the downtrodden, the pauper and the untouchable, from all nations, races, and time. All are included and all are loved by God. One preacher put it this way, "His love is a magnet drawing us ever beyond our present situation".

CONCLUSION

In a nutshell, Jesus' law of love unified Jews and Gentiles first and then a divided world of many nationalities, cultures, ideologies, and religions. He defeated the fear of death and the sense of hopelessness in the face of mortality, he offered hope and new possibilities in life, and even of an everlasting life for our souls; for death has no more hold over us. Thus, he gave all a place in a unified and transformed universe.

5

THE COMING OF JESUS

For three years Jesus crisscrossed the paths of Galilee, preaching and healing all those who came to him with one disease or another. He also performed incredible feats: he calmed the sea, raised people from the dead and cast out evil spirits. "Astonishment seized them, and they said to one another, 'What is it in his WORDS? He gives orders to unclean spirits with authority and power, and they come out.' And the news of him travelled all through the surrounding countryside" (Lk 4:36).

Not only did this news spread through the local countryside, but it also spread far and wide during the following centuries and once it reached Europe, Europe became known as the cradle of Christianity. The Holy Roman Empire was formed in AD 800 by Charlemagne and stretched across Europe from west to east and was ruled under the banner of Christianity. But it is said that the name of Jesus may have reached England as early as the conquest of Britain in AD 43. The soldiers would no doubt have recounted the stories they had heard from their friends, about the incredible things that had happened in Jerusalem on the day of Pentecost; how the followers of this man Jesus were preaching, and how "each one was bewildered to hear these men speaking their language. ….. 'Surely', they said, 'all these men speaking are Galileans. How does it happen that each one of us hears them in his own native tongue, Parthians, Medes and Elamites, people from ….. Egypt, Libya and Asia, Arabs and Cretans alike, we hear them preaching in our own language about the marvels of God'" (Acts 2:7-12).

For more than 2000 years the name of Jesus was a household name in most of Europe and beyond with people faithfully keeping religious festivities like Easter, Pentecost and Christmas. In many European countries children receive presents on 6th December from St Nicholas of Myra who lived in the 4th century. There are many stories of St Nicholas having restored children's lives, and so he became the patron saint of children. Christmas was solely a religious festival, celebrated with the whole family with a lovely meal often followed with singing carols round the crib with the Christmas tree baubles scintillating in the background, and despite the lack of presents, it was a magical day. I remember how exciting it was to go to midnight Mass in the dark, way past our bedtime, to celebrate Jesus' birthday. The bells were tolling joyfully, the carols were enrapturing, and the white snow crunching under our footsteps sparkled in the dazzling light of our torches. It was like a fairy tale. But now many years later we hear a different story. Jesus' name does not hold as much fascination as it once did and many "like the boy in trouble" are not quite sure any more who Jesus is. The familiar knowledge we have of him is that he was a holy man, a great teacher or a great prophet; but who Jesus really was and is remains an enigma, and the idea that he might be God is rejected outright.

Around Christmas, a young woman approached the priest asking if he would baptise her baby. "What do you know about baptism?" asked the priest, "Nothing really" was the reply. "And what do you know about Jesus?" was the next question. "Not much" she answered. "But surely you know that we have only just celebrated his birthday?" asked the priest again. "Oh really, well I suppose so" was the astonishing answer.

My friend went to the supermarket, wearing a cross with the figure of Jesus on it. A woman approached her full of surprise, saying, "You have a little man on your cross, who on earth is it?" "Do you not know it is Jesus?" asked my friend. "I had no idea - who is this Jesus anyway?" was the surprising reply.

Yet on 25th December the old and the young celebrate Christmas Day with abandon. It is a day which is universally spent in a frenzy of extravaganza, present giving, lavish decorations, and stunning light displays - a must on this very special day. Jesus described himself, as being, "the light of the world" (Jn. 8:12). But with the passing of time, this symbolism has largely been forgotten, and lights have become part of the general decorations. It is a day for family and friends to get together and celebrate with a tasty meal. Children especially are excited about the favourite present they have just received. It is a wonderful family day, but what is actually being celebrated? And where we wonder is the "The Birthday Boy"? - has he not been invited? His very existence seems to have fled from our memories as well as many traditions like singing Christmas carols around the crib. Such is the absence of the true Christmas spirit that Pope Francis felt moved to encourage people "to return again to this lovely habit and also to the devotion of this irresistible little baby who is God born small, so that he could be one of us and be like us, so that we might start to love him once again."

Sadly, what is being generally ignored now in education, is that the Christmas story is not a fairy tale with angels and shepherds and kings and a baby born in a stable, but that it is part of our Christian history, culture, and inheritance. The evidence is staring us in the face in the many marvellous paintings of Christmas scenes by great painters in our museums and churches, in the art of foreign nations, in our literature and architecture, in ancient tales, in plays like Joseph and his multicoloured cloak, and in the names of the many saints given to important buildings, roads and towns. These names slip so easily from our tongue, St Pancras, St George, Saint Patrick, St Paul's Cathedral. Who are these people who were worthy to have a town or building named after them? The history of the saints throughout Christianity merits several volumes on its own, yet so little is generally known about the saints. Without an in-depth knowledge of Christianity children today remain ignorant about a large part of the make-up and history of their country and their own identity. Many do not know what happens on Good Friday or Easter Sunday, or know about the crucifixion or that Jesus was a Jew.

The birth of a baby is such a wonderous event that all the discomfort and weariness are soon forgotten. And on 25th December every year, the whole world has more than reason to be joyful, for on this day something truly marvellous happened 2000 years ago. It is the day when God came on earth as a baby. He came for all of us, and he came to change humanity's destiny from despair to hope. Jesus' birth heralded the day that the saviour long promised by God was finally born. He came to atone for our rejection of God's original plan which was for all humanity to live with God in harmony forever. God created us out of love and for love and to free us from eternal death. Pope Saint Leo (440-461 AD) writes, "Being at once like unto us and equal with God the Father, he lowered his divinity to the human state and lifted humanity up to the divine".

Having wilfully accepted death on the cross, Jesus' suffering was not only physical but mental and spiritual. His Word only ever spoke love, yet his heart was broken by the indescribable suffering of man's rejection. Innocent as he was, all the darkness and evil humanity ever committed was heaped on his bloodstained body on the cross. He was branded a criminal, a murderer, a thief, a paedophile, a liar, a traitor, an adulterer, and condemned to die on a cross. His most horrendous death, being nailed naked on the cross, expiated all our sins and took our shame away while he was being plunged into the deepest pit of degradation. His sacrifice is a love without telling. It defines every Christian's existence in the world by giving each one of us a new identity and baptism initiating us into his fellowship with the sure knowledge that the future holds eternal life.

Thomas Merton, an American Trappist monk, writes: "The secret of my identity is hidden in the love and mercy of God. We have been made clean by the blood he shed for us on the cross and been made children of God". This is the fullness of the Gospel, or The Good News that we are talking about. (a)

In the fulness of time, as the Bible tells us, Jesus the Christ was born in a stable in Bethlehem. The Christmas story is full of mysteries. Why was Jesus born in Bethlehem and laid in a manger and why in a field of shepherds tending their sheep and lambs? Mary and Joseph had to travel to Bethlehem to enlist in the census that King Herod was holding, for Joseph descended from the line of King David. Bethlehem means "House of bread," significant in that Jesus would eventually become "the bread of life" in the Eucharist. That he was laid in a feeding trough, or manger, foreshadowed that one day, Jesus would be feeding humanity with his own flesh and blood and in future, on the cross, he would become the sacrificial lamb, without spot or stain. Hence the meaning of being born among the precious lambs which were also without spot or stain as they were destined to be sacrificed in the temple.

It was the custom in Israel at that time to give the child a name with meaning, thus when the angel Gabriel announced to Mary that she was going to have a child, he commanded her to name him Jesus, for Jesus means, "Deliverer" or "Saviour," "because he will save people from their sin, and he will be called "the Son of God" (Lk 1:26) and "For all the names given to men, this is the only one by which we can be saved" (Acts 4:12).

On Christmas day

> We celebrate the birth,
> Of that sweet little baby sleeping in a crib
> Its swaddled little body
> Will soon be red with streaks of blood,
> Frail flesh pierced by nails, thorns, lance.
> The Christ Child born for this,
> To pay our ransom price?

He did this for all humanity, and sometimes it is good to stand still and ponder the enormity of it all. To die wilfully in such a horrendous way for someone else is a sacrifice beyond our comprehension, but nevertheless true. Some remark that it was utterly cruel of God to let His son suffer like that. But as well as being fully human Jesus was also God as the second member of the Holy Trinity, Father, Son and Holy Spirit, three persons in one God. And there cannot be a more closely linked loving relationship than the Trinity. We may therefore be quite certain that God the Father, being a sentient being, suffered as much in his Spirit as Jesus suffered in his physical body on the cross. Jesus knew that when he declared that he was also divine, he would be blaspheming in the eyes of the Jewish people and would be punishable by crucifixion. What incredible courage, and what is more he accepts this horrible death without us deserving it. He tells Pilate, "I have my origin in God" (Jn 8:42), and he tells the people, "I am Son of God" (Jn 10:36). The whole point was that this was his destiny, this was the reason why he had to come into the world to save humanity from eternal death.

For many people the Christmas story still enthrals Yet the origin of this controversial and complex story is not often explored in depth, and there is little awareness that it already started in the Old Testament. St Augustine tells us that, "The Old Testament is pregnant with Christ." Jesus' birth was predicted by the prophets hundreds of years previously, and In the following psalms which date from 1050-930 BC, we find many references describing the advent of the Messiah or deliverer:

> He shall endure like the sun and the moon from age to age.
> May he defend the poor of the people and save the children of the needy....
> The kings of Sheba and Seba shall bring him gifts.
> Before him all kings shall fall prostrate, all nations shall serve him.
> (Psalm 72: 5, 10-11.)

> They tear holes in my hands and my feet,
> And lay me in the dust of death.
> These people stare at me and gloat,
> They divide my clothing among them.
> They cast lots for my robe.
> (Psalm 21:16-18)

In the Prophet Isaiah, who lived 700 years before Christ, we find many graphic descriptions of the kind of death Jesus was to undergo: "I have offered my back to those who struck me, my cheeks to those who plucked my beard. I have not turned my face away from insult and spittle" (Is 50:6). This is just one example to describe accurately how Jesus was mocked and tortured, before being led away to Calvary.

And here Isaiah describes why Jesus had to suffer, "He was a man of sorrows familiar with suffering …… yet ours were the sufferings he was bearing, ours the sorrows he was carrying ……. he was wounded for our rebellion, crushed because of our guilt, the punishment reconciling us fell on him, and we have been healed by his bruises" (Is 53:3-5). We had all gone astray like sheep, and by his wounds we have been healed. Paul tells us in Ephesians the Good News which flowed to us of Christ's suffering: "In Christ we have redemption through his blood, for the forgiveness of our sins, according to the richness of God's grace, which he lavished on us."

Jesus himself clarifies to his disciples that what they read in Moses and the prophets is all about him, and he chides them for being slow-minded when he meets them on the road to Emmaus after his resurrection, "You foolish men! So slow to believe the full message of the prophets. Then starting with Moses and going through all the prophets, he explained to them the passages throughout the scriptures that were about himself" (Lk 24:25-27).

For thousands of years the Jewish people were expecting a great warrior, who would free the people from the yoke of foreign domination. Throughout the centuries Israel had endured many invasions and suffered the humiliation of her people being exiled first to Egypt and later to Babylon. But throughout this history of oppression and domination there runs a common theme of hope for the people, namely God's promise through the prophets that he would send a Messiah, a deliverer, who will rid them of all foreign intervention so that they will finally be able to govern their own country.

"It is wrong to think that the people were just expecting a political Messiah to free them from foreign yoke. After they returned from exile in Babylon they were also looking for their freedom as a nation to worship Jahweh and to follow his laws under the rule of their own Messiah. The rule of the Messiah would be both political and religious in the Kingdom of Yahweh". (b)

Isaiah's description of Jesus, however, does not portray a picture of a great warrior who at the head of an army could defeat the invader. It is easy to understand that the Jewish people could not accept that this baby born in a stable in Bethlehem and brought up by a carpenter and a virgin no less could have anything to do with the mighty warrior promised by God throughout their history. Jesus did not come up to scratch, for how could a man dying on a cross, the most ignoble of all deaths, free them from foreign domination? "To the Jewish people, the cross is an obstacle they cannot get over, to the gentiles it is foolishness, but to those who have been called, it is Christ who is both the power and the wisdom of God" (1Cor.1:18). For the Christian it is a sign of salvation.

At the time Jesus was born and died the most humiliating of all deaths. the Jewish people had forgotten the aspiration of their forbears who on return from exile hoped, not so much for a physical deliverer, but for the fulfilment of their aspirations that, free from foreign meddling in their religious affairs, they would be able to worship God as his chosen people and live by the Ten Commandments they had received from Moses. In the course of time, they came to overlook their need for spiritual reform. They misinterpreted God's promise, which was not to send a man of arms, but a spiritual leader, who would heal the rift between God and man created by man's disobedience. He would pay the ransom price, not only to set the Jewish people free, but the whole of creation as well.

What the Jewish people could not anticipate was that it was God who would himself take on flesh in the person of Jesus Christ to finally deliver them, not so much from their physical oppressors but from their own iniquities. Jesus' death is, to say the least, a notion difficult to grasp for all nations, but for the Jewish people it was impossible to accept even to this day.

In Genesis we saw Jesus as the Word, "through whom all things came into being." It was only Jesus as the great "Alpha and the Omega, the First and the Last, the Beginning and the End" (Rv 8:13-14) who had the power, as God, to make good the mess man made with his creation. As creator of it all he pre-existed time as he made clear in John 8:58, "In all truth I tell you, before Abraham ever was, I am", so only Jesus as God can span time and space and atone for all the sins of all peoples, and all races past, present and future. No ordinary human being could have fulfilled this task even by suffering a thousand grievous deaths on a cross. It was only the divine purity and the whiteness of the eternal light, Jesus, who could blot out the darkness of sin. Only God could fulfil this task ….. and did.

This clarifies that it is not Mohamed, or Buddha or Confucius or a Hindu God, or any other holy person, who is the saviour of every man, woman and child who ever lived. None of them existed from the beginning or are the author of life with power over all creation, life, and death, as Jesus demonstrated by his resurrection. Through conquering death Jesus is the only one who can give us eternal life. All other religious leaders were humans destined to die like ordinary people. To be sure, they were great holy people belonging to their own time and culture and bringing their own vision for leading a good life. Their teachings were praiseworthy but none of them could heal the blind or the deaf, make cancers go away, heal past hurts, and forgive sins, like we witness Jesus doing in the Bible and as we will, in the following chapters, still witness to the present day.

He is the only saviour of the whole world, there is no other, and no other religion can lay claim to this truth. The essential property of the Christian God is love, which transpires most clearly in the way God sent his only son into the world to die. Christ has never killed anyone, on the contrary, he himself was the victim who died for his followers. Nor has he asked his followers to kill those who did not follow him, he is always ready to give them another chance and restore them to eternity, the very reason for which they were created. In response to the question of the High Priest, whether he was the Christ, the Son of the Most High God, Jesus responded "Yes I am, and at the end of time all peoples of the earth will see the Son of man seated at the right hand of the Power and coming on the clouds of heaven with power and great glory" (Mk 14:62).

One question remains: why would we believe what those prophets told, who lived so long ago? For the simple reason that they related to the whole world, the covenant, or deal that God made with Abraham, in Genesis 12:1-3, "You will become the father of many nations. I shall maintain my covenant with you and your descendants, generation after generation, a covenant in perpetuity to be your God and the descendants after you". This is the message that has travelled through the centuries to the present day and will travel through time and for ever.

6

JESUS' MISSION STATEMENT

You are worthy to take the scroll and to break its seals because you were sacrificed and with your blood you bought people for God of every race, language, people and nation and made them a line of kings and priests for God to rule the world (Revelation 5: 9-10)

Luke's gospel tells us that Jesus started his public life at the age of 30 and that it lasted for only 3 years. After he was baptised in the Jordan by John the Baptist he retired to the desert where he fasted for 40 days. And then with the Holy Spirit in him he crossed Galilee and Judea many times, on foot, teaching, and healing people of all sorts of diseases. He made the cripple walk and the blind see and raised people from the dead. He taught in their synagogues, and everyone glorified him. And after his death, his resurrection and his ascension to heaven he unleashed a world revolution lasting to this day.

"One day he went to Nazara where he had been brought up and went to the synagogue, as he usually did on the Sabbath. Immediately they handed him the scroll of Isaiah. Unrolling the scroll, he found the place where his mission statement is written:

> The spirit of the Lord is on me
> For he has anointed me
> To bring good news to the afflicted
> He has sent me to bring liberty to the captives,
> To give sight to the blind
> To let the oppressed go free,
> To proclaim a year of favour from the Lord.

He sat down and handed the scroll back to the assistant and all eyes were fixed on him. Then he began to speak, 'This text is being fulfilled today even while you are listening.' And he won the approval of them all and they were astonished at the gracious words that came from his lips. They said, surely this is Joseph's son" (Lk 4: 16-22).

By reading this scroll, which was written 700 years previously, Jesus was in effect telling them that it was he who was the long-awaited Messiah, who had finally come to set the Jewish people free. It is not surprising that they were astonished at this knowledge. The people of this poor village of Nazara found it impossible to believe that this long-awaited Messiah could be one of their own: no, the Messiah would be a mighty warrior and not the son of carpenter, and they would not accept him. And because of the rejection by his own people Jesus could not work any miracles among them.

But Jesus did not waste any time to demonstrate that it was truly to him that this text referred and "he went to Capernaum, a town in Galilee and there he delivered a man from an evil spirit, cured the mother-in law of Simon and a man with a virulent skin disease, and he healed all those they brought to him with one illness or another. All the people were astonished for he also spoke with authority, and they said, this is a new teaching which we have never heard before. And his fame spread through the whole countryside of Judea" (Lk 4:31-37).

For three years Jesus' ministry was a plethora of healing as Mark's gospel tells us, "He withdrew with his disciples to the lakeside, and great crowds from Galilee followed him. From Judaea, Jerusalem, Idumaea, Transjordania, and the region Tyre and Sidon, great numbers who had heard of all he was doing came to him. And he asked his disciples to have a boat ready for him because of all the crowd, to keep him from being crushed. For he had cured so many that all who were afflicted in any way were crowding forward to touch him. And the unclean spirits, whenever they saw him, would fall down before him and shout, 'You are the Son of God.'" (Mk 3:7-12).

What a testament!

7

JESUS HEALS WITH A WORD

Showing his deep compassion for the sick and the needy, Jesus travelled throughout Galilee so that all could hear the message of the Good News that the Kingdom of God was close at hand, and people would be set free from their oppressors and infirmities.

Now we are stepping into the realm of true miracles, miracles being events which suspend the law of nature. They can only happen through God's intervention since only He is the Lord of life.

Curing of a man with a virulent skin disease: (Lk 5:12-14)
> It happened that Jesus was in one of the towns when suddenly a man appeared, covered with skin disease. Seeing Jesus, he fell on his face and implored him saying, "Sir if you are willing you can cleanse me." Jesus stretched out his hand and touched him, saying "I am willing, BE CLEANSED". At once the skin disease left him. He ordered him not to tell anyone, "But go and show yourself to the priest and make the offering for your cleansing just as Moses prescribed, as evidence to them".

JESUS HEALS WITH A WORD

Curing of the man with the withered hand: (Lk 6: 10.)
On a Sabbath he was teaching in the synagogue and a man was present with a withered right hand. The scribes and Pharisees were watching him to see if he would cure someone on the Sabbath, hoping to find something against him, but he knew their thoughts. He said to the man, "Come and stand in the middle". Then he said to them, "Is it permitted on the Sabbath to do good or to do evil, to save life or to destroy it?" Then he said to the man, "STRETCH OUT YOUR HAND." He did so and his hand was restored. But they were furious and began to discuss the best way of dealing with him.

Curing of the centurion's servant. (Lk 7:8-10)
Jesus went with the Jewish elders who had been sent by the centurion to ask him to come and heal his servant, and he was not far from the house when the centurion sent word to him by some friends with the message, "Sir, do not put yourself to any trouble, because I am not worthy to have you under my roof, but let my boy be cured by you giving the WORD". When Jesus heard these words, he was astonished at him, and turning round said to the crowds following him, "I tell you, not even in Israel I have found faith as great as this." And when the messengers got back to the house, they found the servant in perfect health.

In Mark 2:1-12 Jesus heals a paralytic when his friends lower him through the roof of the house because there were so many people that they could not get him through the door. Jesus seeing their faith said to the paralytic, "My child your sins are forgiven, and I order you to pick up your stretcher, and go home." And the man got up, picked up his stretcher and walked out in front of everyone, so that they were all astonished and praised God saying, "We have never seen anything like this."

These are incredible miracles that the people of Israel witnessed 2000 years ago. Jesus healed in many ways, with spittle, by touch and most amazingly by speaking a WORD of command. That WORD reverberates or reflects what we read in the beginning of John's Gospel: "In the beginning was the Word, the Word was with God and the Word was God …and the Word became flesh and lived among us, and we saw his glory, full of grace and truth" (John 1:1,14).

God has only ever been intent on our salvation and for this purpose He sent Jesus his son in human flesh and blood to atone on the cross for humanity's sin. And, as the cosmic Christ, the WORD, the creator, - who was like God from the beginning, a member of the Holy Trinity, Father, Son and Holy Spirit - Jesus has power over all physical creation. We see this not only in healing the sick and raising the dead, but in calming the storm as recounted in Matthew's Gospel: "Suddenly a storm broke over the lake so violent that the boat was being swamped by the waves. 'Save us Lord' the disciples cried 'we are lost.' And he said to them, 'Why are you so frightened, where is your faith?' And he stood up and rebuked the wind and the sea, and there was great calm. They were astounded, and said, 'What kind of man is this, that even the winds and the sea obey him?'" (Mt 8:24-27). Little did the disciples know that Jesus spoke the Creative Word to calm the elements and quieten their hearts.

And this is what he does in our lives when the going is rough and we shout, "Save us Lord, for we are lost!" Like the storm in the lake, he will calm the storm in our hearts. He came into the world precisely for this, to set us free from the turmoil of sin which causes us to drown. The miracles he performed were twofold, he still heals us physically and he sets us free of the burden of guilt weighing us down, for to whom else can we turn to be delivered from our guilt? And to show this and that he can forgive sins, he says to the paralytic, "My child your sins are forgiven." By healing him physically and then by forgiving his sin, he makes the paralytic a whole person, fully alive in body mind and spirit worthy to enter the kingdom of heaven.

Miracles give us a message of hope and vividly demonstrate that his words are not idle words, but that he is telling the truth, that he can free us from evil spirits, from depression, from all the mistakes we make in life, from all the evil committed in the world and from our guilt which weighs so many people down today until they lose all hope and want to opt out.

But Jesus' miracles also led to the onset of the battle between himself and the cause of all evil, Satan. Nowhere is this more visible than in the following examples where Jesus casts out evil spirits. He is publicly recognized by these forces of evil as being the Son of God, who realise that their time is up, and by being cast out of the unfortunate people whom they have tortured without mercy, they know they are defeated. They have lost the battle, because Jesus' battle to win souls for heaven will always triumph and bring "the Kingdom of God ever nearer" (Mt 10:8).

Demoniacs of Gadara: (Mt 8: 28-34)
> When he reached the territory of the Gadarenes, two demoniacs came towards him out of the tombs, they were so dangerously violent that nobody could use that path. Suddenly they shouted, "What do you want with us Son of God? Have you come here to torture us before it is time?" Now some distance away there was a large herd of pigs feeding, and the devil pleaded with Jesus, "If you drive us out, send us into the herd of pigs." And he said to them, "Go then" and they came out and made for the pigs; and at that the whole herd of pigs charged down the cliff and into the lake and perished in the water. The herdsmen ran off and

made for the city where they told the whole town what had happened to the demoniacs. Suddenly the whole city went out to meet Jesus and as soon as they saw him they implored him to leave their neighbourhood.

In the following two miracles we see that Jesus not only healed with a word but used other ways as well: in the first he lays hands on the blind man and in the other he used spittle.

Curing of the blind man at Bethsaida: (Mk 8: 22-26)
Jesus came to Bethsaida, and they brought a blind man whom they begged him to touch. He took the blind man and led him outside the village. Then putting spittle on his eyes and laying his hand on him he asked, "Can you see anything?" The man who was beginning to see said, "I can see people, they look like trees as they walk around." Then he laid his hands on the blind man's eyes again and he saw clearly: he was cured, and he could see everything plainly and distinctly. And Jesus sent him home.

Healing of the deaf man: (Mk 7: 31-35)
Jesus went to Lake of Galilee, and they brought to him a deaf man who had a speech impediment; and they asked him to lay his hands on him. He took him aside away from the crowd and put his fingers into the deaf man's ears and touched his tongue with spittle. Then looking up to heaven, he sighed and said 'Ephatha,' which means, be opened, and his ears were opened, and the impediment of his tongue was loosened, and he spoke clearly.

Despite Jesus telling him not to tell anyone about his healing the healed man declared it with a loud voice and the onlookers' admiration was unbounded and they said, "Everything he does is good." It is not surprising, "that they were all astonished at what they saw, for never had anybody done anything like this before and his reputation spread through all the surrounding Galilean countryside.

MIRACLES AFTER THE ASCENSION OF JESUS

After his resurrection Jesus showed himself to the eleven and he said to them, "Go out into the whole world; proclaim the gospel to all creation. Whoever believes and is baptised will be saved; whoever does not believe will be condemned. These are the signs which will be associated with believers, in my name they will cast out devils, they will have the gifts of tongues, they will pick up snakes in their hands and be unharmed should they drink deadly poison, they will lay their hands on the sick who will recover" (Mk 16: 15-18).

After Jesus' ascension into heaven, the apostles, having been filled with the Holy Spirit at Pentecost, worked extraordinary miracles:

> To the lame man, Peter said, "I have neither silver nor gold, but I will give you what I have: in the name of Jesus the Nazarene, Walk!" Peter then took him by the hand and helped him to stand up. Instantly his ankles and feet became firm, he jumped up, stood, and began to walk, and he went with them to the temple, walking and jumping and praising God. Everyone could see him, and they recognized him as the man who used to sit begging at the Beautiful Gate of the Temple. They were all astonished and unable to explain what had happened to him. (Ac 3: 6-10)

> A man sat listening to Paul preaching. He had never walked in his life because his feet were crippled from birth. He managed to catch Paul's eye and, as Paul saw that he had the

faith to be healed, he said in a loud voice, "Get to your feet, stand up." and the cripple jumped up and began to walk. After this the people from Lycaonia said, "These are gods who have come down disguised as men" and they proposed that all the people should offer sacrifices to them. But Paul said, "Friends, what are you doing? We are only human, and we have come to give you the good news, to turn away from these empty idols and turn to the living God who made heaven and earth and the sea and all that these hold". (Ac 14: 8-15)

After Pentecost, full of the Holy Spirit, the apostles started to preach the message far and wide. Soon, what we call the Apostolic Church became established and from the onset, the message was strengthened with many miracles which became part and parcel of the Church as we know it today. Over the centuries, a great lapse in miracles occurred, for various reasons; but thank goodness the Holy Spirit is powerfully at work again today, and miracles are happening in many Christian denominations.

Why is there so much scepticism about the possibility that miracles are manifested, here and now in our midst? Contrary to general belief, miracles are still a wonderful reality in the twenty-first century, if only we care to look in the right direction.

According to research amassed over decades we know that the healing work of God shows especially in the lives of those who believe. They seem to have better mental health, have better immune systems, and are less depressed. This stands to reason when a true believer puts his full trust in God, full of confidence that Christ will keep his promise when he says, "I am the Lord who heals". The wonderful work of the Cor et Lumen Christi Community will shed more light on the subject as we shall see in the next chapter.

8

THE COR ET LUMEN CHRISTI COMMUNITY

Miracles are still happening in the twenty-first century and always will, and no more so than through the intercession for healing by the members of the Cor et Lumen Christi community.

If miracles had stopped happening over the centuries, it would be difficult believing in a loving God. For God, being the essence of love, can never stop loving and caring, as he cannot deny his true self. His only care is to get all humanity back to the Garden of Eden, heaven. To realise his plan, He has demonstrated the greatest possible love and has given us his only Son to save us from perdition. What greater proof of love do we need? How can we ever doubt that He would stop performing miracles, they are part and parcel of salvation history. God is constant, and his love is constant, and it has never stopped flowing in a continuous healing stream down to humanity from the beginning of time and forever. The truth on much of humanity's part is that it has stopped taking notice of a loving God and has gone its own way. But as we shall see, this cannot be said of the members of The Cor et Lumen Christi

Community. They have taken God at his word and have put his assurance, of being a healing God, into practice. But who are the members of this community and how can their claim that they can perform the same miracles as Jesus be justified?

Their name identifies exactly what they stand for and who they proclaim to be, for the Latin phrase "Cor et Lumen Christi" literally means the "Heart and Light of Christ". This is what their mission is all about; to bring the loving heart and light of Christ as the source of all healing and conversion into our needy world. They are a 100% bone fide Roman Catholic community who received the official backing of the Pope on the evidence of the many miracles that have been happening worldwide through their dedication and zeal (some 40,000 over the years).

The community was founded near London in 1990 by Damian Stayne and has as its members young people and married couples with their children, who have dedicated their lives to prayer, poverty and teaching the faith. They organise conferences and Miracle Healing Rallies in London and all over the world, from Asia to Africa and beyond. These rallies are free, open to all people of all faiths and none, and are attended by thousands.

Offering miracle healings is an audacious undertaking and one may rightfully wonder how many people have been left disappointed. But the facts point to the opposite. God has brought healing to thousands through Damian and the team. In the name of Jesus Christ he has commanded cancers to disappear, blind eyes to see and the lame to walk, and many have also been emotionally healed. Damian firmly believes that something always happens when we pray in Jesus' name for healing. His aim is to proclaim Jesus the WORD with the same signs and wonders which happened at Pentecost and to equip Christian churches to move into the supernatural. There is no doubt, and I have seen it with my own eyes, that extraordinary healings really do happen at the healing rallies which parallel the many miracles Jesus performed.

Here is an example in Damian's own words of the healing powers he is blessed with:

> Recently a mother was testifying on stage at one of our Miracle Healing Services, of the healing of her young son. He was born with a twisted spine, and because of this, his shoulders were hunched over. At the beginning of the prayer, she put her hand on his spine and clearly felt the twist in it. Then she removed her hand. From the stage I gave a WORD of command for healing of spines, and to her utter amazement she could feel that his spine was completely straight, and his shoulders were no longer hunched over – for the first time in his life. Her tears of love, gratitude and joy as she testified the healing moved the whole crowd, and they all praised and thanked God like in the days of Jesus.

On a Miracle Healing Rally in India, Damian was asked by a Bishop who was present, to pray for a Hindu man. He had suffered two strokes and was unable to stand or walk unaided or raise his left hand, and he had been carried into the meeting by his sons. Damian, confident that God was going to act, laid his hands on the man and after a short prayer he invited the man to stand, which he did, and then commanded: "In the name of Jesus, walk!" and he began walking freely and waving his previously paralysed arm, to the wonder of all present.

Like Jesus who healed the centurion's servant with a WORD, Damian healed the Hindu man by speaking a WORD of command in Jesus' name. When Jesus spoke, something happened. He healed, he restored Lazarus to life, and calmed the storm with one word of command. As a result, the darkness in people's lives became light, they received hope for a better life free from sickness and oppression. Cor et Lumen Christi, by speaking Jesus' word, bring healing and light to our needy world, and the people will say, "We have never seen anything like this before", because as God says, "The word that goes forth from my mouth does not return empty, without carrying out my will and succeeding in what is was sent to do" (Is 55:11).

Apart from our scepticism of healing in general, there is even bigger unbelief attached to healing by using objects, such as handkerchiefs, although there are many such examples of people being healed by just touching the hem of Jesus' cloak (Lk 8:40-48), and by the Apostle Paul: "so remarkable were the miracles worked by God at Paul's hands that handkerchiefs or aprons which had touched him were taken to the sick and they were cured of their illness, and the evil spirits came out of them" (Ac 19:11-12).

Materials used in Christian ministry also include holy water for baptism and blessed oil used in the anointment of the sick, in the healing ministry, during baptism, and in the ordination of priests. In the following testimony by Damian we see that handkerchiefs, as in Paul's case, have been used as channels of God's power:

> A nun asked me to pray over a hanky for an absent sick person. That night she laid the hanky upon a fourteen-year-old girl who was so lame that she was hardly able to drag herself across the floor to the shower. The morning following the prayer, the girl woke up and found that she could stand and walk. I must say, I had never expected to see this. God is great!

The following two powerful healings by Damian are unrelated to material things but occurred from a distance as the people lived abroad and were being prayed for in London as God's power is omnipresent:

Miracle 1
In Hungary, a woman had acute leukaemia. The doctors said, if you don't have a blood transfusion, you will be dead in a year. She had had many tests during the week before the healing service and went back the week after the service for more tests. Before the Miracle Rally her medical document showed that she was blood type AB negative. After the service many more blood samples were taken and tested in several medical facilities. All of them showed that she had now a completely new blood type, type "0". Her medical document now states that there is "No medical explanation" for this change. The Lord had given her a blood transfusion and she was completely healed.

Miracle 2
At the end of the healing service people were asked to hold up before the Lord the names of their loved ones who could not attend the service. A woman in London held up the name of her father in India who for two weeks had been in a coma. When the crowd prayed the healing prayer the Lord's power reached the hospital bed in India and he instantly woke from the coma and was healed.

Damian says:
When I stand in front of the physically sick, I stand with the authority of Christ, exercising my kingly anointing in him. As I speak to the various conditions – "Ears hear – eyes see – legs be strong – cancers be gone," and so forth, I do not simply

speak with hope. I speak with faith and authority, knowing that if I am acting in the Holy Spirit, people's bodies will resonate to the CREATIVE WORD of Christ on my lips, not to my voice but to the words of Jesus from me.

When we command healing, we do so as people exercising Christ the King's authority over what he has made. When Scripture says, "For the creation waits with eager longing for the revealing of the sons of God" (Rm 8:19), this is because the children of God hold the material world's healing in their hands. As co-heirs with Christ, we are the kings and queens of God's creation; we are called to govern his kingdom in love, turning back the effects of the fall, man's rebellion against God, and establishing his kingdom.

Here are some more testimonies from Damian:

Miracle 3

A woman flew in from another country to attend one of our events in England. She was deaf in one ear. She tried to get her husband to come, but he refused saying, "I'll only come if your deaf ear is healed. At the event she was filled with the Holy Spirit and - you guessed it - her deaf ear was healed. Later her husband finally agreed to attend the next event, and despite all his former reservation, he was converted. Praise God! Now many in their family are on fire for Jesus. A person who receives a powerful healing becomes a sign and wonder to all who know him or her.

Miracle 4

A young nurse was working in a hospital when a man who was intoxicated attacked her. He broke her spine and severely damaged her spinal column. As a result, she underwent a total of forty medical interventions, during which several metal plates and bolts were inserted into her spine, but none of the treatments helped. The damage to her spine was so severe that for six years she could not get out of bed. Standing was completely impossible and although she was on very high doses of morphine, the doctors were unable to manage her pain. Her speech had also been affected as was the use of her arms. Neither could she cope with light, so she had to always be in the dark or wear sunglasses. For 6 long years she lay bedridden in pain in a dark room. In desperation her mother brought her in a wheelchair to one of our healing services. I preached, and then we heard a joint testimony of healing from a woman and her physician husband. At one of our previous healing services in France a year before, this woman had been healed of an incurable degenerative condition that had kept her bound to a wheelchair.

Damian describes further miracles:

> As I led the healing, I asked the Christians in the auditorium to place their hands on the sick near them and pray. As God prompted me, I COMMANDED conditions to be healed in Jesus' name. I concluded, "Be freed from your crutches, be freed from you sticks, be freed from your paralysis, be freed from your wheelchairs, in Jesus' holy name." Then I told the people, "Now in Jesus name, do what you could not do before." All over the room hundreds demonstrated their healings.

> Suddenly we heard a big cheer from the centre of the crowd. I jumped off the stage and approached the area where the excitement was. There was the young woman standing next to her wheelchair, hugging her mother. I asked her what had happened, and they explained that she just stood up with no pain. All the strength had returned to her legs. I could see

that she was completely stunned.

I walked her to the stage. With her empty wheelchair next to her she gave a brief explanation of her incredible healing. She walked up and down the platform freely and then jogging back and forth with tears in her eyes. The people were cheering and shouting the praises of God. A year later she was still completely healed.

It was reported to me afterwards that some of the male members of the security staff for the facility in which we were meeting were moved to tears. Through witnessing such a beautiful act of God, they were convinced of the Lordship of Jesus, and there and then asked for his mercy and invited him into their hearts as their Lord and saviour. Glory to God!

I have attended many Healing Rallies and can attest that many of these miracles happened in front of my eyes. I am utterly surprised that people, when asked to attend, refuse to do so, I presume because of a lack of faith. I find this distressing and truly heart-breaking. So many missed opportunities!

# 9

WHAT DAMIAN HAS TO SAY

Below in his own words, we can read what Damian had to say in an interview a few years ago:

> We have truly seen blind eyes opened and deaf mutes from birth healed and cancers instantly disappear. These are things I never thought I would ever see - even after years one still feels somehow stunned that God is doing this through us. Over the last 12 years more than 40.000 people have raised their hands at our monthly Miracle Healing Services around the world to say they have been instantly physically healed. Even if half of these have been over enthusiastic, it is still a vast number, and we have personally interviewed thousands of people who have been able to demonstrate that they have been healed.
>
> Why God has chosen me I don't know. All our community have prayed every day for the last 25 years and all fasted once a week that God's anointing and the miraculous would accompany our proclamation of the word. So maybe these things have made a difference. I have been greatly helped by the anointed lives of many people from many streams of the

Church, but it was at a conference led by John Wimber, an American evangelist, that the penny dropped, and I became convinced that supernatural ministry was for the whole Church and that I could be used in miraculous healing.

In the services where most of the healings take place, we first have a time of praise and worship. Then I preach and include a short film of miracles from previous services to build up faith. Next, I get people to repent and to forgive. We saw a woman get out of a wheelchair after she forgave her sister having not spoken to her for 40 years. Following the service, not knowing where she lived, she tracked her down and they were instantaneously reconciled.

When there are poorer people present there are more miracles. The poor know their need and somehow change the faith atmosphere. In the same way people from ethnic minorities in this country, whatever their financial situation, seem to have more faith when it comes to miracles. These groups are a special gift in those services and act as a kind of lever for us poor westerners who have got a bit bogged down in our rationalism. The discovery of the gift of faith has been such a liberation to me. I understand that faith is not essentially a feeling but an act. I do not have to feel a surge of faith when using a word of command for healing. When I speak those words of commands I do so out of obedience because Jesus said these signs will follow those who believe (Mk 16:16-17) and I keep my eyes on the Lord.

People have been taught poorly about dynamic faith. The charism or gift of faith is not just believing it can happen but believing in the power of God in us to make it happen. This is a gift we can pray for. God has so much for us all to do, so many privileges to unpack and live out. To be a Christian is to be 'supernaturalised'. A non-supernatural Christian is a contradiction in terms. Supernatural ministry is whatever God calls us to do; is just part of being ourselves in Christ."

Interview by Christine Zwart for Recourse UK, used with permission.

Damien has ministered to hundreds of thousands in five continents. The Lord confirms his preaching with wonderful physical healing miracles and powerful encounters with the Lord's love and glory in the Power of the Holy Spirit.

10

CHARISMATIC RENEWAL AND THE HOLY SPIRIT

All peoples clap your hands, cry to God with shouts of joy, praise him with dancing and the sound of the trumpet, and the cymbals, lift up your hands in prayer as a fragrant offering and with loud cries of joy and thanksgiving, may we sing a canticle of praise. Psalm 47

Since the beginning of the world when "The Spirit hovered over the waters" (Gn 1:8) and life was created, God's Spirit has been visibly active in human history. And this was never made more evident to a group of people than when the Spirit of God, who brought the material world into being, baptised the Apostles, Mary, and other believers with tongues of fire on the day of Pentecost. In the Creed we call the Holy Spirit, "The Lord the giver of life" and that is who He is; this is his role, right from the start, giving new life to all who desire it. These days, the words "renewal," "charismatic" and "gifts" have been prominent in church language but have been little understood. Congregations are repeatedly told that, "Yes they have the Holy Spirit." Yet many question why we speak about "renewal" when the Spirit has been active in the world since creation, and we were meant to receive him at baptism and at confirmation. And what is this about "charismatic" and "gifts"? And all this clapping, and arm-waving and speaking in tongues that feels like mumbo jumbo?

In 1 Corinthians 12, Paul speaks in no uncertain terms about the many different gifts given by the Spirit which can be used in different ways for building up the Church and supporting the community. They are called the servicing gifts and are wisdom, knowledge, healing, miracles, prophecy, discernment of spirits, tongues and interpretation of tongues. Later he goes on to say, "I thank God that I speak in tongues more than any of you" (1 Cor 14:18) and "I wished you all spoke in tongues" (1 Cor 14:5), though he added that "If I speak without love I am no more than a gong booming or a cymbal clashing." (1 Cor 13:1) We see that in Isaiah 11:1-2 slightly different gifts are mentioned: "That on him will rest the Spirit of wisdom and insight, the Spirit of counsel and power, the Spirit of knowledge and fear of the Lord". These are often called sanctifying gifts for they give strength in adversity and help in leading a good life. Today we speak of the charismatic gifts of the Holy Spirit, the word charisma deriving from the Greek word "Charis" meaning favour or grace. The dictionary explains "Charis" as a "divinely conferred power or talent to inspire followers with devotion and enthusiasm". These are impressive lists of gifts on paper, but they have not been practised in present-day congregations for a long time.

For centuries, the proclamation of the Gospel in general, has almost solely concentrated on teaching doctrine and on the sacraments. The main emphasis was very much, "God so loved the world that He sent His only Son to die for us on the cross to give us eternal life". God's love and Jesus' Sacrifice are no doubt the core messages of the Christian faith, but these focus solely on the saving of our souls. There has always been a general appreciation of the Holy Spirit, the third person of the Holy Trinity, but no great importance has been attached to the "Gifts" of the Holy Spirit mentioned in Paul and Isaiah. These were often just enumerated with no further explanation as to their usefulness in evangelising and leading a Christian life.

Because of this lack of instruction about what both Paul and Isiah obviously found so important, I have always felt that the message of the Good News was not handed down in its entirety. When we see that Jesus, soon after receiving the Holy Spirit at baptism in the Jordan, was able to go out and perform miracles; and that the apostles also were able to start preaching without fear and perform miracles after Pentecost, it is apparent that Christians also are in need of the Holy Spirit and his gifts, to be able to powerfully execute their ministry. God gives his gifts for specific reasons. Without them, we are unable to effectively put into practice the doctrine of the Good News of the Gospel. Why were these gifts neglected for so long?

When Jesus started his public life, he did not start by preaching and teaching; his very first acts were acts of physical healing. Jesus was passionate, not only about spiritual healing but also about physical healing because he came into the world to fulfil a threefold mission; to heal, to free and to save; and thereby make us whole people, worthy to receive eternal life.

Put in today's terms we would say that Jesus was a "holistic healer" who healed the whole person, body, mind, and spirit and so transformed the whole of flawed humanity that had lived in a world burdened under a yoke of violence, injustice and oppression, and transformed it into a kingdom of justice, peace, love. This is the Kingdom he speaks about in Mark 1:15, when he tells the people, "The Kingdom is close at hand" and he puts it into practice by healing the sick and forgiving sins. A prime example that I have quoted earlier is found in Mark 2: 1-12 when he takes the paralytic by the hand saying, "My child, your sins are forgiven", and to prove that the Son of man has the authority to forgive sins on earth "I say, get up, pick up your stretcher and walk home". In making the man whole physically as well as spiritually by forgiving his sins, he helped him to believe in God, healed his body and restored him to the perfection God had intended for him and all humanity. In this way, Jesus revealed that he was God and Saviour, who had come to turn the world on its head, and transform it from evil into good, from sickness into health, and from oppression into justice.

By this dramatic healing, the Kingdom of God entered the world, and all those whom Jesus had healed from one sickness or another received a foretaste of this marvellous Kingdom too, where suffering and death are no more. Their physical healing engendered a spiritual healing when their 'spiritual' eyes and 'spiritual' ears and heart were opened, and they experienced a transformation of the heart. They had a 'conversion' and were suddenly able to 'see' and 'believe' that Jesus was the Son of God, and they all praised and thanked God for their wonderful healing" (Lk 5:25). Jesus did not convince the people that he was God by any philosophical reasoning but by overruling the laws of nature by the power of the Holy Spirit. He showed that the Kingdom of God is not just for when we are dead, it is here already. It is by doing the same acts as Jesus, with the Holy Spirit in us, that we can and must bring the Kingdom to the world. So far, we have not made a very good job of it.

THE IMPORTANCE OF THE GIFTS OF THE HOLY SPIRIT

Shortly before he ascended to heaven, Jesus told his disciples "John baptised with water, but not many days from now you will be baptised with the Holy Spirit" (Ac 1:5), and "I will send a helper, the Holy Spirit, he will teach you everything. He is the Spirit of truth, and he will be with you for ever" (Jn 14:17). When Jesus was baptised with water and the Holy Spirit "he came out of the water and the heavens suddenly opened and he saw the Spirit of God descending on him like a dove and a voice came from heaven, saying "This is my Son the beloved, my favour rests on him" (Mt 3:16-17). It was God the Father who "conferred sovereignty and kingship over all created things", and on Jesus and his followers, as prophesied in the book of Daniel "and his Kingdom will never pass away" (Dn 7: 27). Since God is spirit, his kingdom is a supernatural kingdom which does not obey the natural laws, and it stands to reason that we need to expect spiritual actions such as miracles to happen. We also need to refrain from denying that miracles still happen today, like some would believe.

In all miracles Jesus defied the natural laws of physics through the power of the Holy Spirit; in stilling the storm in Mark 4, in feeding the five thousand in Mark 6 and Luke 9 and in walking on the water in Matthew 14. These supernatural events continue today in the Eucharist, where the bread and the wine change into the body and blood of Christ; in forgiving of sins in the confessional; in engraving the indelible seal of the Holy Spirit at confirmation, baptism and the priesthood; in the spinning of the sun as at Fatima in Portugal and Medjugorje in Bosnia; in the lives of the saints and in the many miracles we will discuss later. One could say that miracles are God's way, by hook or by crook, to save us from ourselves and give us a glimpse of his wonderful Kingdom, which is our inheritance and which we can claim by collaborating with him. But fear and pride prevent us from throwing ourselves head over heels into such a dicey adventure. Christianity is de facto a belief in the supernatural, as much today as it was in the past.

In Jesus' baptism with both water and Spirit we cannot find a more compelling example that we too need to be baptised with both water and with all gifts of the Holy Spirit. Only then will we be able to speak with power and authority the words of healing in Jesus' name to bring the Kingdom closer to home. "It is written in the Prophets, 'They will all be taught by God, and to hear the teaching of the Father you have to come to me" (Jn 6:45). When on earth, it was Jesus who taught his disciples; but now, through the Holy Spirit and his gifts, he communicates his designs, his will, and his plans to our spirit by revelation, by personal experience, through reading the Bible, through other people, through prayer and through his miracles. As a result we can embrace his work of evangelising and help redeem humanity.

Although the most frequent depiction of the Holy Spirit is in the form of a dove, the most apt description is "Ruah" meaning wind in Hebrew, which we find in the Old Testament. Referring to the Holy Spirit, Jesus says: "You must be born from above, the wind blows where it pleases, you cannot tell where it comes from or where it is going, so it is with everyone who is born of the Spirit" (Jn 3: 6-8). The third person of the Holy Trinity, The Holy Spirit is the 'moving' member who, like a wind, blows where he pleases and settles on all who desire him, irrespective of who or what they are.

There are many reasons why the desire to practise the Gospel in the power of the Spirit, including miracles as Jesus commanded his disciples, faded away with time. In his book, "The Nearly Perfect Crime," Francis MacNutt, the great pioneer of the Catholic Charismatic Renewal says, "When the first Christians were baptised, they expected to receive some of the gifts of the Holy Spirit, but once great numbers of people were baptised, this expectation fell away." In the Middle Ages, the clergy forbade the laity to use the gifts of the Spirit. The gift of healing was solely in the hands of the clergy who used a combination of herbs and prayer to heal the sick. Often sickness had to be accepted as a way to holiness and should be suffered in silence, and any lay person who dared dabble in healing was soon suspected of being a witch and was burnt at the stake. The Church, becoming more institutionalised and authoritarian for fear of heresies, neglected the spiritual gifts, especially healing. Interestingly, if we read through history, we find that many kings in England, France and Spain such as Henry VIII and Louis XIV of France, had healing powers, which was called the Royal Touch, but again it was only for a select few and not for everybody.

Another reason why putting to use the Gifts of the Spirit faded, was that many believed that they were only necessary for the apostles to establish the Church. Once their task was accomplished, they were not needed anymore and even as recently as 1961 at the meeting of cardinals and bishops, (Vatican II), some were of the same opinion.

Receiving the sacrament of Confirmation is the moment that, as a responsible youngster, one is meant to 'affirm' one's belief in the faith. But it is also the moment that one is conferred by the bishop with the indelible stamp of the Holy Spirit with his gifts. However, I am sure that many had the same experience as I did, when the gifts of the Spirit were only mentioned fleetingly, or in some cases they are not mentioned at all for fear of confusing the youngsters. For most confirmands, the gifts have not left a lasting impression in their lives or fostered a desire to have them. A conference leader asked a group of around thirty adults if they had ever received an in-depth teaching on the gifts: only two hands went up. But whether they are mentioned or not, the Spirit does confer his gifts at confirmation and also when we pray to receive them, as he is inseparable from his gifts.

I heard the following story on a course I attended on the Holy

Spirit. An American bishop actually saw tongues of fire descend on a group of youngsters at confirmation, which overjoyed him. But when he told this amazing experience to some of his fellow bishops, they would not believe him. After that he never mentioned it again." Like some of the presents we receive on our birthday, they are left unopened, and as soon as the party is over, we don't bother unpacking them but stack them away in the far corner of our memories, never to be revisited again.

With this lack of in-depth teaching not only at confirmation but also from the pulpit, it is not surprising that the spiritual gifts remain a mystery for most people and that many devout churchgoers do not believe Jesus' exhortation to "Lay your hands on the sick and they shall be healed", yet they believe everything else Jesus said. Even Jesus' conviction that, "No one can enter the kingdom of heaven without being born through water AND the Spirit" (Jn 3:6-8) does not sound convincing to many. It is now only too evident in the decline of many churches that something is missing, and that is the living, moving, working reality of the Holy Spirit. On the other hand, the Spirit is very much alive in many Evangelical churches where the Spirit is given full rein. Pope Francis says "We need a new language to evangelise and a new mindset to minister. We need more of the language of the Spirit." We need to equip people with the desire and tools necessary to bring the church and Christianity back from the brink.

John Wesley, the 18th century revivalist said: "God does nothing, except in response to believing prayer" and we can only get as much out of God as we put in ourselves, so what are we waiting for? "Pursue love and earnestly desire the spiritual gifts" (1 Cor:14-1), and that is what we need to do if we are serious about changing this world for the better. All we need to do is ask. "Would a father give his child a stone when he asks for bread, or give him a snake when he asks for a fish? The more will your heavenly Father give the Holy Spirit to those who ask him" (Lk 11:11-13). As Christians we are all too ignorant of the power that we have to transform the evil around us. We need to release all this God-given pent-up power and then, like the apostles, we will be able to step out with boldness, "for God does not give us a spirit of timidity but of boldness, power, love and self- control" (2 Tm 1: 7). And with this boldness and with faith we have enough dynamite to transform the world and bring the Kingdom of God closer by, step by step.

We saw at the start that Jesus was the WORD and, activated by the Spirit, when he spoke things happened. When he performed miracles, it was by speaking a WORD that healed, created, forgave sins and changed lives. Our words have no power at all, but if we speak the word "Be healed in Jesus' name," something will happen because we use it with his authority and our command will have the same power as Jesus' because his words "are Spirit and they are life" (Jn 6: 63) - he has the message of eternal life. There is no other name under the sun we can use to heal but the name of Jesus.

Smith Wigglesworth, the great Pentecostal evangelist, was very adamant that we must take Jesus at his WORD and claim his promises which are always fulfilled as free gifts. We cannot pick and choose, we either believe everything he says, or we don't; there is no optional extra. We are so keen to stick to the familiar and the comfortable, which limits the Spirit but "The power of God is beyond our conception. The trouble is that we do not have his power in a full manifestation because of our finite thought." (a) (Smith Wigglesworth, Greater Works.)

Living in Nigeria, I went with the driver to buy some charcoal at a local market. It was necessary there to have a driver as driving oneself as a visitor carried too many risks. Arriving at the market, the driver told me to wait in the car while he went into the shop to buy the charcoal. Looking through the window I could see a group of people on the otherwise empty square, and it looked as if they were beating someone, as great shrieks of pain echoed across the empty square. Curious as to what was happening, I decided to investigate. Slowly I approached the group of men who were wielding large sticks, but the driver who had emerged from the shop, told me in no uncertain terms to get back into the car. He knew his countrymen only too well, realising that things could easily get out of hand if a foreigner tried to intervene. But I would have none of it, and fearlessly carried on walking towards the commotion. Where did I get my courage from (usually I am quite a fearful person)? I suddenly remembered the words of Scripture, "I do not give you a spirit of timidity, but of boldness."? That must be it I thought, the Spirit is working. Getting to the group they explained that they were beating this woman because she had stolen a papaya, which belonged to one of the salesmen. When I asked her if this was true, she vehemently denied the charge; I said to the men, "are you absolutely sure it was her"? but to this they had no reply. And suddenly they all turned on their heels and left. The woman scurried away to safety as fast as she could. She was saved.

THE RENEWAL OF THE GIFTS

Despite the fire of the Holy Spirit being silenced for centuries, thankfully the embers have kept smouldering through time and have recently been fanned into a new and powerful flame. Finally, we have let the Spirit go free and blow where he wills and revolutionise the world, rather than keep him trapped in the cage of our conventional lives. After having laid dormant for many decades, God has seen the world's need and has answered the prayer of many, "O, Holy Spirit, renew your wonders in this our day as by a new Pentecost", by giving a new and enormous outpouring of his many charisms all over the world. Hence, we speak of the Charismatic Renewal, a renewal that applies to all

CHARISMATIC RENEWAL AND THE HOLY SPIRIT

Christian denominations.

'Renewing' means that we accept, desire and are willing to exercise God's gifts for our own benefit and for the community and to renew the face of the world for the better. In the mid-20th century, like a dormant volcano, the power of the Holy Spirit suddenly erupted with supernatural manifestations just like on the day of Pentecost. This happened in various parts of the world in different Christian denominations. In 1967 there was as a powerful "Catholic Charismatic Renewal" and in 1991 "The Toronto Blessing" erupted at the Toronto Airport Vineyard Church and made headlines worldwide. In both the Catholic Renewal and the Toronto Blessing people started praying in tongues, there were physical healings, and healings from emotional hurt from childhood, and many people had a new awareness of God's love. It was obvious that the Spirit of God had not left us but was starting the much needed "renewing of the face of the world, as of a new Pentecost." The events leading to this renewal had in fact already started as far back as 1986 in the Vineyard Church. "We invited a team to come and minister at our church. They prayed before the meeting and the Lord gave them a vision of a map of the world with fire breaking out in Toronto and then consuming the whole map. Since then, people have come from all over the world to our church and millions have been healed and their lives changed." (b)

Closer to home, the renewed outpouring of the Holy Spirit was not always well received by the established churches as they were not familiar with the outward manifestations such as clapping, hand-waving, falling in the Spirit and speaking in tongues. More than once have I heard a sermon denouncing the "charismatic revival" as over excitable, mass-hysteria nonsense. All these demonstrative feelings go so against the grain of our demure upbringing and put fear into our hearts. Having concentrated their teaching on the sacraments and the liturgy, unlike

THE GOOD NEWS NOBODY TALKS ABOUT

Pentecostalism which is in touch with the Holy Spirit, Catholics and Anglicans and others, including priests, bishops as well as laity, stayed well clear of it fearing that it was not truly universal Christian teaching.

Priests especially testify that when they have received the Baptism of the Holy Spirit their ministry is transformed beyond recognition. It becomes more powerful, more meaningful and efficient. Sadly, not all respond in this way and come forward to receive Baptism in the Holy Spirit. My friend, a priest and a missionary in Nigeria, ran a mile when he heard that he might be prayed with to receive Baptism in the Spirit as he did not want to be "slayed in the Spirit" and fall down in front of his congregation.

Reading the Psalm quoted at the head of this chapter, it could not be more apparent that worshipping in this exuberant way is nothing new. "Praise the Lord with shouts of joy, lift up your hands in prayer like a fragrant offering" beseeches the psalmist. Did the Apostles not look as if they were drunk when the Spirit came over them at Pentecost? Why are we not shocked when we see a rave where hundreds of young people, high on drugs, dance and wave their arms chanting, yet we are surprised, even shocked, when we see people in church behaving in the same way when the Holy Spirit comes? The Holy Spirit is after all the Lord, the giver of Life, who created thunderous waterfalls, roaring oceans, snowy peaks, human life; is it any wonder then, that when he comes with that same power, we explode with laughter, with tears of joy, with clapping hands, with waving arms and with falling in the Spirit. Receiving the same power as the creator of the universe can be no less dramatic than an explosion within, a surge of power not containable in our physical being but finding expression in exuberant joy, in looking drunk and being totally bowled over by it, and yes, starting to speak in strange tongues and foreign languages, and healing the sick and prophesying, and being filled with miracle-working ability. It is the Spirit setting us free from our hang-ups and inhibitions and freeing us to do the impossible!

Speaking in tongues, the first gift which is usually manifested when we are Baptised in the Spirit, is the most misunderstood of all the gifts and remains a stumbling block for most people, but St Paul says, "I wish you would all speak in tongues" (1Cor 14:5) and "do not suppress the gift of tongues" (1Cor 14:39-40). The truth is we are fearful because we don't really understand what it's all about as it has never been properly explained. Who wants to make a fool of himself talking a lot of gibberish?

What is so special about it? First, because there comes a moment in our prayer when we run out of words, our natural speech is left behind, and we enter upon the language of the Spirit. The Spirit takes over praying in us. This language given by the Spirit is the vehicle for God to release his power in us. It is often likened to charging one's batteries which sets in motion our boldness and power which we never knew we had, and we become ready to act. It is said that in our lives we only fulfil about 20% of our full potential. This is very true on the spiritual level because as Christians we have been unaware for far too long of the power we really have. With God's power in us we cannot but be powerful. Knowing that we are not the healers, but that God can do all these amazing healings through us, we can safely leave our comfort zone and leave the familiar behind and step out into the unknown. Seeing the lame walk and the deaf hear is bound to give us an indescribable feeling of euphoria beyond belief. In comparison, any secular daredevil feat pales into insignificance. Our fear often limits God's power, but "His perfect love casts out our fear" (1 Jn 4:18) and we "can let God have His way, as there is no limit to what our limitless God will do in response to a limitless faith" (a).

It takes courage to start to speak in tongues because it feels that we utter nonsensical words that we ourselves don't understand; but this language is given for our benefit. It does wonders when we face any challenge in life, it controls our anger and temptations and impatience. It is a great protector, and we can use it in healing, for defending the faith, or to defend people in trouble. It is a marvellous gift which we can use at any moment of day or night, wherever we are: in the car, at home doing our daily chores, or on our daily walks. It is a powerful weapon that we can always have at hand for use when difficult situations arise.

Paul speaks of tongues and "interpretation" of tongues, of speaking a language which we have never learnt before, or even understanding a language we have never studied. These are gifts which not only build us up personally but the community as well. Somebody in a group may be given the gift of being able to interpret what the Spirit is saying when somebody speaks in tongues, and this message may be for the benefit of the whole group or one specific person. This is what happened at Pentecost when the Apostles started to speak and all the people present heard them speaking each in their own language and they said, "All these men speaking are Galileans. How does it happen that each of us hears them in our own native language? Parthians, Medes and Elamites; people from Judea and Cappadocia, Pontus and Asia, Egypt and Libya, Jews and Arabs" (Ac 2:8-11).

The following are testimonies of a friend who has this gift in abundance.

> I did not know what it was like to be filled with the Holy Spirit until I had received the Baptism of the Spirit. I am an ordained Evangelist and Fellowship Worker. Praying for people when asked is just natural for us. One day we went to Kings College Hospital in London to pray for the husband and father of a family friend who had had an operation.

While praying for the patient, a nurse came in to see how he was, so I stopped praying. But she said, "Don't stop praying, I am a Christian", so I carried on praying and the Holy Spirit took over big time. I started to pray in the nurse's language which was Spanish, a language I have never studied, and I had no idea that she came from the Philippines. Suddenly she started to cry and said, "I must phone my mother in the Philippines, this message is for her." The Spirit had given me a message for her mother in her own language.

And ….

One day I prayed for a lady from Ghana, and as I was praying the Holy Spirit took over and I started to pray in her own language and mentioned all sorts of funny names concerning her family in her language. After the prayer, the lady experienced a deep conversion. And I can vouch that I cannot speak a word of Ghanaian even if you paid me to do so.

In both cases the messages received were for the benefit of the recipient.

The clapping, arm waving and falling in the Spirit, which are but the outward manifestations of the Spirit, do send fear into our hearts because we do not want to make fools of ourselves. But any consideration for our mundane feelings and emotions soon evaporates when the power of God descends on us like a thunderclap, more powerful than 100 shots of heroin as the drug addict likened it to, or when we receive a joy so glorious that it is impossible to describe. What we receive is infinitely more valuable than gold, overriding any feeling of discomfort and doubt: it is after all an earth-shattering experience. Perfect love casts out fear, and we know that the Christian message is one of love. Love and compassion are at the heart of healing, for us as it was for Jesus. Christianity is not about religion, but it is about making humanity as God intended. Like the disciples we are sent out to "restore the Kingdom of God, with power and authority over all unclean spirits and to cure all sorts of physical diseases" (Mt 10:1), and especially the diseases of the soul. I heard of one man who complained that he was no better for having seen a psychiatrist for many years; expert medical help was good, but not sufficient to make him totally better. Maybe there was an area in his life, like unforgiveness, which a psychiatrist cannot reach but only the Spirit.

Without the gifts of the Spirit we stand by helpless, not knowing what to say and do despite the compassion we feel for a sick person. Jesus said, "Cut off from me, you can do nothing" (Jn 15:5), for it is the Spirit who gives us that something extra. Now we don't need to walk blindly on our busy shopping trip oblivious of the people around us who may need help, such as a downcast person who needs cheering up, a homeless who needs an encouraging word or healing, or a harassed person who needs defending. Full of the Spirit's confidence we can step out with a WORD, and in faith, knowing that God will act in us, and all we need to do is obey the impulse or the still, small voice.

It is quite an eye opener how readily people consent to prayer if it is being suggested to them. This kind act could make all the difference in their lives and help them to discover something about the healing love of God. There is no mistaking the promise is for all; we don't all need to be arm waving, hand clapping, falling in the Spirit believers. All that is needed is to be open to the Spirit, desire His gifts, have faith and trust, and the Spirit will do the rest.

It is vital that we become truly aware of the incredible power we have as Christians. We are not the run-of-the-mill people, because "Jesus, the Way, the Truth and the Life" created a revolution and as Christians we are part of that revolution. From the Spirit we receive energy which is not of our own making, a faith that can move mountains and a love that can set the world on fire. We witness this revolution in the many marvellous stories and in my own experiences recounted in this book.

One of these incredible experiences was when a bright light suddenly filled our living room, and I just knew that it was God in the room. After this, I wanted to do something for God, but I didn't know what I could do. Standing on a soap box preaching was definitely not my scene. We were living in a confined environment at the time where gossiping was rife, and who does not like a good gossip? So, I decided that this was one thing I could stop, it was not much but it was a step in the right direction. Then a friend decided to clean out her books and brought me an armful wondering if I would be interested in having them. I took them all and started to read, and amazingly they were all on the healing ministry. Like most Christians and Catholics especially, I had never heard of the gift of healing or certainly didn't know anybody who had such a gift. Maybe it had been mentioned when I got confirmed but none of it had made a lasting impression on me. One of the books told how a nun who was permanently paralysed, was healed through people praying with her. There was my answer, this is something I could do for God.

I went on my knees and prayed for the gift of healing. That same night my whole body felt as if an electric current was passing through it, starting from my feet and all the way up to my head. First, I thought I might be having a heart attack, but I felt no fear, just perfect peace. Thankfully, I had read in one of the books that this could be a manifestation of the Holy Spirit, and after a sound night's sleep I decided that my prayers must have been answered. But how does one check the veracity of such an incredible experience. Maybe I had been dreaming after all. There was only one thing to do and that was test it out. On my return to Nigeria after some home leave, I asked my parish priest who was suffering from recurrent bouts of malaria, if I could pray with him. He readily agreed and knelt on the floor before me, which was quite a humbling experience. But after the prayer his malaria never returned. There was my answer.

Give the Holy Spirit a chance by saying yes. Then see what happens and be amazed!

11

JACKIE'S STORY

Lord, I have heard of your fame, I stand in awe at your deeds. Do them again in our days, in our days make them known.... Lord, your splendour covers the sky, and your glory fills the earth. Your brilliance is like the light, rays flash from your hands; there your power is hidden. (Hab 3: 2-4)

I first heard about the marvellous work Jackie Pullinger was doing when we lived in the Far East. Two young girls from Hong Kong visited the region and began to teach in the local Anglican Church about the gifts of the Holy Spirit and how famous drug addicts and gangsters in Hong Kong were converted and set free from their drug addiction through praying with them "in tongues." Most people hearing this "rubbish" were obviously very sceptical and thought this did not belong to the established teaching of Christianity.

My second encounter with this teaching was when I met Jackie when she came to talk of her work in Hong Kong at a meeting in Wintershall in Surrey. This was many years later and by this time I had myself started to pray in this way. Jackie told us her incredible story: how she came to be in Hong Kong and how she had felt the hand of God leading her there all the way. It is a remarkable story of God's victory over the powers of darkness in the vice and drug dens of the Walled City of Hong Kong. It is the truly uplifting tale of a young girl seeking to do God's will in her life. In a prayer meeting the message she receives is, "Go. Trust, and I will lead you, I will instruct you and teach you in the way you shall go." She does just that, she trusts God's promise that her "name is written in the palm of his hand" (Is 49:16). With such a promise she can only be safe. Through her obedience to this message, she gave God the opportunity to overthrow the powers of darkness which kept people in bondage through drug abuse, violence and prostitution. He was able to perform the most amazing miracles of healing and released seasoned drug addicts from their addiction without the dreaded withdrawal symptoms.

Jackie's story is a perfect example of when a person is willing, God is more than willing to reveal, to communicate and to guide that person towards the purpose He has had in mind for that life all along. He is not a God who sits in the clouds far removed from us, but the God who is interested in every aspect of our lives and of the state of the world in general. All he wants is our willingness and trust, because without those God will not act. He has given us free will which he will never override, and he would never force his own will upon us. It is up to us to accept or to refuse to be his collaborators in bringing his kingdom of peace and light and righteousness to the world. If we say "no" he is powerless to act. They say: "God governs the world, but prayer governs God."

The history of the Walled City is little known. It is an enclave situated in Kowloon City, one of the eighteen districts of Hong Kong. According to "Urban Sociology" an enclave is defined as a territory whose geographical boundaries lie entirely within the boundaries of another territory. "It was originally a Chinese fort built around 960 BC measuring only 6.4 acres. It was still inhabited by the mandarin of the Qing dynasty until 1899 when the British attacked it. Expecting to find soldiers there, they found it empty, apart from the mandarin and 150 inhabitants who handed it over to the British who left it untouched for a long time" (a). As the population in Hong Kong grew, people started to occupy the Walled City, which grew at an alarming rate with buildings going up on to top of each other. Apparently by 1990 this rather small area was inhabited by no less than 50,000 people.

When Jackie arrived in the Walled City in 1966 it had become a notorious, lawless, sprawling warren of slums, rats, gangsters and drug addicts and was truly one of the most dangerous places on earth. Drug smuggling and heroin addiction flourished, as did prostitution and pornography, extortion and fear. Strangers were not welcome and even the police dreaded entering it. This is where Jackie started a Youth Club and began telling all who wanted to hear about the incredible love Jesus has for everybody: the poor, the needy and even the prostitutes and the drug addicts. This message did not fall on deaf ears of the youth who slowly ventured into her club, because most had never experienced real love in their lives. Jesus said, "I am the light of the world; anyone who follows me will not walk in darkness, he will have the light of life" (Jn 8:12). This promise of Jesus became a visible reality when the most amazing things started to happen and brutal Triad gangsters converted, prostitutes quit, and Jackie discovered a new treatment for drug addiction without withdrawal symptoms, which was baptism in the Holy Spirit and speaking in tongues. The Walled City was indeed one of the darkest places on earth, but nothing is impenetrable for the all-encompassing love of God's Holy Spirit.

Christopher's story, told here by Jackie, is a perfect example of how The Bible is truly the inspired word of God, a fact so many disbelieve.

> Christopher refused to go ahead with his Triad initiation as he had become a Christian. The change in Christopher was remarkable. As I continued praying in tongues, the results became apparent when boys like Christopher became Christians. We met for Bible study and prayed anywhere we could, in teahouses, the street or in my home. One evening, at a church service, one of the boys had a message in tongues and Christopher began to sing the interpretation. Astonishingly it came in a beautiful English song, a language he hardly spoke. "Oh God who saves me in the darkness, give me the strength and the power, so I can walk in the Holy Spirit, fight against the devil with the Bible, talk to sinners in the world, make them belong to Christ." (b)

Coming off drugs without withdrawal symptoms through praying in tongues, Winston's story below is a truly amazing story of the power of speaking in tongues, still very much feared and misunderstood.

> Winston's rank in the 14K Triad was number 426, which means that he was the fight fixer. He was a very tough Triad indeed and he was under orders to guard our club. I began to tell him about Jesus; he didn't want to know, but as he was on duty he could not escape. Suddenly though, he began to talk about his friend who had an opium problem, but I soon realised that it was Winston who had the problem. I told him that it is only Jesus the Lord of life, who can settle a man's heart, and take the craving away. Winston would never come inside but one night when the club was empty, I said, "How

about coming inside and praising God." "Okay" he said without hesitation. While keeping guard outside, he had heard the boys inside praising God, and suddenly there he was standing inside my club praising God himself and I have never listened to such a joyous prayer. Suddenly he began praising God in tongues, this was extraordinary as he had never heard anyone speak in tongues before. After half an hour he stopped. The miracle had taken place: he and I knew that he was completely cured of his drug addiction. He had come through withdrawal as he prayed. (c)

Jackie's joy was immeasurable when she experienced this incredible miracle. This story again shows how ignorant we are as Christians about the power that is given to us to combat evil. Even today we denigrate speaking in tongues, one of the great gifts of the Holy Spirit. It is high time we cast fear aside and had a change of heart about this concept of speaking in tongues.

In the next excerpt, Jackie tries to persuade the gang leader to let go of his girlfriend who has decided to become a Christian, but will have none of it:

I sat in the café with a gang leader, who was a brutal figure, and six of his cohorts armed with knives, negotiating the release of Angel who wanted to start a new life as a Christian. He was furious that I had not brought Angel with me. We are not going to stand on any ceremony, he said banging the table, because you are a Jesus lady. You have to produce the girl. I was terrified and asked if I could make a phone call. As there were more armed men standing outside, I whispered to Willie, a friend, "Call the police." Back in my seat I told them that Angel was not coming; thank God, at that time the police arrived, and all the knives slid silently under the table. Afterwards I heard that one of the gang present in the café, asked, "Who is this Jesus lady? Did you see her eyes, we were frightened, we did not dare to look into her eyes, she had some kind supernatural power. (d)

What incredibly powerful testimonies these stories are! We have a lot to learn.

12

MULTIPLICATION OF THE LOAVES

First miracle of the loaves, Matthew 15:15-21:
> When Jesus stepped ashore, he saw a large crowd, and he took pity on them and healed their sick. When evening came his disciples said to him, "This is a lonely place and time has slipped by. So, send the people away and they can go to the towns and villages and buy themselves some food." Jesus replied, "There is no need for them to go, give them something to eat yourselves." But they answered, "All we have is five loaves and two fish." So he said, "Bring them here to me", and he gave orders that the people were to sit down on the grass; then he took the five loaves and the two fish, raised his eyes to heaven and said the blessing. And breaking the loaves he handed them to his disciples, who gave them to the crowds. They all ate as much as they wanted, and they collected the scraps left over twelve baskets full. Now about five thousand men had eaten, to say nothing of women and children."

Second miracle of the loaves. Matthew, 15:32-39:
> Jesus reached the shores of the Lake of Galilee, and he went up to the mountain. He took his seat and a large crowd came

to him, bringing the lame, the dumb and many others. These they put down at his feet, and he cured them. The crowds were astonished to see the dumb speaking, the crippled whole again, the lame walking and the blind with their sight restored and they praised the God of Israel.

But Jesus called the disciples to him and said, "I feel sorry for all these people, they have been with me for three days now and have nothing to eat. I do not want to send them off hungry, or they may collapse on the way." The disciples said to him "Where in a deserted place like this could we get sufficient bread for such a large crowd to have enough to eat?" Jesus said, "How many loaves have you?" They said, "Seven and a few small fish." Then he instructed the crowd to sit down on the ground and he took the seven loaves of bread and the fish, and after giving thanks he broke them and gave them to his disciples who gave them to the crowds. They all ate as much as they wanted and they collected what was left of the scraps, seven baskets full. Now four thousand men had eaten, and that is without the women and children.

Who other than God can work such miracles as these, in which only five or seven loaves and a few fish can feed thousands? The baskets of food left over point to the biggest miracle of all: the miracle of the Eucharist, where Jesus offers his body in the bread and the wine as his blood to feed the bodies and souls of the whole human race. In the Eucharist, His one body fragmented into millions of hosts will feed millions upon millions with his true flesh and his true blood which become for us the bread of life.

But, do such miracles still happen today?

MULTIPLICATION OF THE LOAVES

THE MIRACLE AT THE GARBAGE DUMP IN EL PASO, MEXICO

Fr Richard Thomas was an American Jesuit priest who worked for the poor and destitute who inhabited cardboard shacks, gleaning a living from the scraps they collected from the garbage heaps in El Paso, Juarez.

> One day members of his prayer group were reading the passage in Luke 14 where Jesus tells the crowds, "When you give a lunch or a dinner, do not invite your friends or your brothers, or your rich neighbours, or your relatives, in case they invite you back, and so can repay you. No, when you have a party, invite, the poor, the crippled, the blind and the lame, then you will be blessed, for they have no means to repay you and so you will be repaid when the upright rise again" (Lk 14:12-14). When they discussed the passage, someone queried whether anyone in the prayer group had ever done that, but nobody had. However, Fr Rick and his helpers believed that miracles still happen today, and they decided that, as a surprise, they would give the workers on the dump a Christmas meal.

> On Christmas Day 1972 Fr Rick and his team approached the dump, where they were met by the two rival groups who worked on different sides of the dump and who were deadly enemies, as this was their livelihood. One leader stepped forward and said, "Right, I have lined my people up to be fed first and when we have finished you can feed these others." But Fr Rick refused saying, "What food we have brought we will share equally as Christian brothers and sisters". They agreed and both factions met on neutral ground.

A piece of plywood was laid on top of a drum for a table and a sheet served as a tablecloth. Then the food was put on top: tamales, burritos, cookies, sandwiches, baloney and Christmas candy and ham. Fr Rick apologised that there may be not enough as they had brought food for 150 people but there seemed to be well in excess of 300 and an even larger number drifted in from all around. Then the food was served. Children lined up for the candy, then joined the queue again for more. The helpers knew that the bag would not last, but it did.

Someone had brought a guitar and people started to dance. The helpers kept giving and giving and giving. A woman had started to slice the ham, and she sliced and sliced, and they all received a generous portion. She continued to slice until she got tired and then asked a young man to take over and the ham did not run out. There was more than enough for everyone and afterwards there was enough left over to share with two orphanages on the way home. Some people even took food bags home with them. It was not until the prayer group had assembled later in the day that they could take in the scale of what had really happened that day. In his generosity God showed that he did not want anybody to be left out and go hungry by also providing food for the poor orphans down the road. Who says miracles do not happen anymore today?

Fr Rick said afterwards "Many people across the world attend communion services, read Bible stories, but they walk away and live their lives as if none of this makes any difference. We need to take God at his word and act upon what we read in the Bible; it is the inspired word of God." (a)

13

THE POWER OF THE EUCHARIST

These are the words the priest speaks when he consecrates the wine and the bread:

> It was the time to celebrate the Passover and Jesus was at table with his disciples and as they were eating, he took the bread, and when he had said the blessing, he broke it and gave it to his disciples saying, "Take it and eat, this is my body given for you, do this in remembrance of me". Then he took the cup, and when he had given thanks, he handed it to them saying, "Drink from this all of you, for this is my blood of the covenant poured out for many for the forgiveness of sins." (Mt 26:26)

Every time these words spoken by Jesus 2000 ago are repeated on our altars at the Consecration, they represent the unchanged doctrine of the Catholic faith, which is, that Jesus is truly present in the Eucharist. When the priest speaks these words, a miracle occurs as the power of the Holy Spirit descends and changes the bread and the wine into the body and blood of Jesus.

The Roman Catholic Church has always interpreted Jesus' words for what they are meant to be, that at consecration the bread becomes his real body and the wine his real blood, a transubstantiation. Jesus states clearly in John 6, "I am the bread of life, anyone who eats this bread will have eternal life ……. for my flesh is real food and my blood real drink that I gave for the life of the world. Whoever eats my flesh and drinks my blood lives in me and I in him" (Jn 6:51,55-56). As Jesus has promised, the Eucharist is real nourishment for our souls and our bodies when the bread and the wine become part of our bodies. It is difficult to see how one can give any other meaning to these words. Some Christians do not interpret these words literally but give them more of a symbolic meaning.

Jesus instituted the Eucharist in the Upper Room the night before he was to die, when he was celebrating the Passover feast with his disciples. The Israeli people were saved from being killed when the exterminating angel passed over them by painting the lintels of their houses with the blood of an unblemished lamb; the angel did not kill them, but instead the Egyptians. Jesus' real body and blood became everlasting food for our souls in the Eucharist, as he became the unblemished lamb himself, being killed for us the very next day on the cross of Calvary. Deuteronomy 12:23 tells us "The life of a creature is in the blood", and this was 2000 years before we found out about the circulation of the blood. Blood gives life-giving oxygen to the body; with loss of blood the body fails. So it is with the spiritual body, our soul. If we do not replenish our spiritual nourishment through prayer, for example, or receiving the sacraments, our spiritual life slowly dies. It is said that we are leaky spiritual vessels who constantly need refuelling. Jesus, knowing we cannot survive without spiritual nourishment, offers us this wonderful provision; he gives us his own blood and body to feed on to make sure that we will have the strength to reach our goal, in this life and beyond. And it is in the eucharist that he perpetuates his presence with us.

Like the people who heard Jesus' statement so many years ago, that his flesh was real food, and his blood was real drink, we too find it difficult today to envisage how this could be possible. It requires enormous faith to accept it. What kind of teaching is this, how can a man give us his flesh and his blood to eat and drink? It really sounds like cannibalism. No wonder many of Jesus' followers fell away when they heard this message, and many have stopped listening to it today. But his disciples reacted differently saying, "Lord, who shall we go to?" They had lived with Jesus for three years and by then they realised that he was not only a man but that he was also God; and because of all they had seen Jesus do in those three years, they knew that for God nothing is impossible and that he has the message of eternal life.

The real presence of Jesus in the Eucharist brings us the closest we can come in this life to the living God abiding in the host with all his power to heal, to change and perform many miracles. Every time we receive Communion, we become transformed into better people. It has often been called the greatest work of God and the mirror of Divine perfection. Which God could have devised such an act of love as to let his followers feed on his very body? It is through the creative power of the Holy Trinity, Father, Son and Holy Spirit, creator, redeemer and sanctifier that the miracle which changes bread into flesh and wine into blood takes place on our altars every time the priest speaks the WORD that Jesus spoke; and we saw that when this word is spoken, things come into being. He is a God who loves us so much that he will stop at nothing to get closer to his people. This is what the apostles witnessed in Jesus, and they embraced wholeheartedly what he told them. They proclaimed the truth of the "Real Presence" of Jesus in the Eucharist right from the start wherever they went to preach, and it has reverberated through the centuries, unchanged on every altar of the world wherever Mass has been said.

> "Foolish men, why do you keep pondering your unworthiness preventing you from receiving me in Holy Communion? Of course, you are unworthy and always will be. But you are compounding the sin of pride upon sin of pride depriving yourself of my grace to overcome your shortcomings and evil feelings. My power is greater than your sin. Cast away your pride and put on the sackcloth of humility and bring your burden to me in the Eucharist to let me transform you, step by step into the whole person I want you to be and have created for the Glory of my name. Too many hide behind this false humility of not being worthy and hold it as an excuse for not offering themselves for service in the community or for not receiving me in Holy Communion and deprive themselves of getting to know me better by stagnating their spiritual growth." (*Anonymous*)

MIRACLE OF THE EUCHARIST AT EL PASO, MEXICO

If Jesus could feed 5000 people with five loaves and two fish, and if at the refuse dump in El Paso uncountable people were fed with food destined for only 150 people (Chapter 12), then maybe Jesus knows what he is talking about. Furthermore, we need to take him at his word, that his flesh is real food and his blood real drink and, when we feed on it often, we will have his life in us and be able to perform even greater miracles than he did.

THE POWER OF THE EUCHARIST

Here we are again at the garbage dump in El Paso, Juarez, Mexico where the following extraordinary miracle happened. Sr Briege McKenna is an Irish sister who was healed of crippling arthritis and since then has had an extraordinary healing ministry which has taken her all over the world. I met her briefly probably thirty years ago at a conference at Westminster Cathedral, and I cannot remember if I heard the following story there or somewhere else, but it has always stayed with me and, for the sake of accuracy, I will use an excerpt from "The Curate's Diary" by Fr. T Doyle.

On one of her visits to the US, Briege was invited by Fr Rick Thomas to meet him across the border at the garbage dump in El Paso, where he had a special ministry. On arrival, Briege was horrified at the incredible squalor everywhere and when Fr Rick told her he was going to say Mass she could not quite figure out where he was going to do this. She was also wondering if these poor people were going to understand what was going to happen. Fr Rick set out a small table and all the Mass requirements. Already about 1000 were gathered and more were coming from all directions. These people did not have a church, they had nothing and lived from the bits they collected from this scrap heap. She looked across this crowd of miserable people and not more than fifteen minutes walk away she could see smart houses and a big Mexican seminary.

Before Mass, an old woman carrying a bundle approached and when the woman opened the cloth, she saw a small child completely burned from head to foot, skinless, dirty and screaming. The woman said to Fr Rick, please pray for him, I found him on the way here. Sr Briege and Fr Rick both prayed for him and then Fr Rick suggested to put the child under the table on which Mass would be said.

Once Mass was being celebrated, Briege said that she felt and saw the presence of Jesus and when Fr Rick said, "Let us pray the Gloria," the people praised God at the top of their voices. These poor people praised God with all their hearts. Jesus said, if the people don't praise me, the stones will cry out. But there was no such a danger here. When the very large Host was being raised at consecration everybody was prostrate on the ground and Briege could see the most beautiful image of Jesus with his arms outstretched, smiling, and she heard the words of the gospel, "Come to me all who are burdened, and I will refresh you". Then she saw that the people lifted their faces and were shouting, "Viva Christo Rei – long live Christ the King." At that moment she knew that Christ was in the Host, it was not just a piece of bread, but truly Jesus. These people had a king, the Kings of Kings. They clapped and cheered and cried, "Viva Christo Rei." And she found herself weeping when she saw the great faith of these people.

Mass ended and the burnt little boy had long since stopped crying. She went to look for him and was overwhelmed when she saw him. He had crawled from under the table, he was totally healed and playing in the sand. When the bread and the wine were being changed, so was the little boy being changed, he had been given a new skin. Also, before mass a young mother had brought her baby with Downs Syndrome asking Fr Rick and Sister Briege to pray with him. Suddenly, at the end of Mass the child's mother came running to her, shouting "Look at my baby, he is completely healed.

After this incredible experience she could not sleep, she got up and heard the Lord say "People go looking for healers and for something to help them, they will go to anybody. Yet I am on their altars all over the world and in their tabernacles, yet they pass me by. I have a mission for you, this is why I brought you here. I want you to go in the world and speak of the power of the Eucharist. Needless to say, Sister Briege's ministry today is totally centred on the Eucharist. (a)

SECOND MIRACLE OF THE EUCHARIST

In 1247 in the small town of Santorem in Portugal an unknown woman was extremely unhappy in her marriage and suspected her husband of being unfaithful. At the end of her wits, not knowing what to do about it, she approached a sorceress. The sorceress advised her that if she stole a host from the church of St Stephen next time she went to communion and brought it to the sorceress, her husband would return to her. The woman agreed and the next day after going to communion she did not swallow the host but kept it in her mouth and left the church straight away. Once outside she took the host out of her mouth and went straight to the sorceress, but on the way there, people saw her with blood on her clothes as if she had been wounded. Suddenly the woman herself noticed the blood. She realised then that the host was bleeding and changing her mind she went home and buried the host and her stained clothes in a wooden trunk without telling her husband what she had done. In the middle of the night husband and wife were woken up by a very bright light that shone through the wood of the trunk illuminating the whole room. The woman told her husband the story, they got up and went on their knees in adoration all night. In the morning they took the still bleeding host to the priest confessing what had happened. The host by then had turned into real flesh with veins running through it from top to bottom. It was then quickly encased in some wax and put in the ciborium. Many years later it was encased in a resin compound and put back in the tabernacle of St. Stephen's

Church where to this day the still bleeding host, still flesh, and defying all natural laws, is visited by thousands of visitors from all over the world. (b)

Over the centuries many miracles have happened concerning the consecrated host, but I think that these two examples summarise nicely the power of the Eucharist and the Holy Spirit.

14

THE RESURRECTION

When Paul visited Athens he started to preach saying: "God has fixed a day when the whole world will be judged in uprightness by a man he has appointed. And God has publicly proved this by raising this man from the dead. At this mention of raising from the dead, some of the men burst out laughing ......" (Acts 17:31-32).

The reaction of the Greeks is totally logical. How can anybody believe such nonsense? This has never happened anywhere in the world! And we would be the first to have the same reaction if a street preacher told us that we would be resurrected after we died. We would take this preacher for a nut case.

The Resurrection of Jesus is the most earth-shattering event in human history and the universe has never been the same since. It is a unique event in the history of the world and manifested only in the Christian faith. Coming back to life breaks through all the barriers and norms of science and common sense. But the disciples' testimony about this story, the speaking and eating with Jesus for forty days after his resurrection, and the consequences this had worldwide, leaves us in no doubt that this event really took place. In fact, without the resurrection of Jesus the whole of the Christian faith is meaningless because it is through his death and resurrection that Jesus wilfully paid the ransom price for our souls which had been doomed to eternal death. Jesus conquered the death of our souls so that we might have life.

It was not only Jesus who was resurrected. One of the best-known stories in the Bible is the resurrection of Lazarus:

> There was a man named Lazarus who lived with his two sisters, Martha and Mary in a village called Bethany. Now Lazarus became ill, and Martha his sister sent a message to Jesus saying, "Lord the man you love is ill". On receiving the message Jesus said, "This sickness will not end in death, but it is for the glory of God so that through it the Son of God may be glorified". Jesus stayed two more days where he was and then said to his disciples "Come let us go back to Judea, Lazarus is dead but for your sake I am glad I was not there because now you will believe". When Martha heard that Jesus was coming, she went to meet him and said to Jesus "Lord if you had been here my brother would not have died". Jesus replied, "Your brother will rise again". Martha said, "I know he will rise again at the resurrection on the last day". Jesus replied, "I am the resurrection, anyone who believes in me will never die. Even though that person dies, he will live. Do you believe this?" "Yes Lord, I believe that you are the Christ, the son of God, the one who was to come into the world." Then Mary also went out to meet Jesus and she threw herself at his feet saying, "Lord, if you had been here my brother would not have died".
>
> At the sight of her tears and those of the Jews who had come to be with Martha and Mary, Jesus was greatly distressed and asked, "Where have you put him?" "Come and see" they said, and they took him to the place where Lazarus was buried. It was a cave with a stone to close the opening. Jesus wept and

some of the Jews said, "See how he loved him!" Jesus commanded that they take the stone away, but Martha said, "Lord this is the fourth day, by now he will smell". Jesus replied, "Have I not told you that if you believe you will see the glory of God". So, they took the stone away and Jesus lifted his eyes to heaven saying, "Father, I thank you for hearing my prayer, I know that you hear me always, but I speak for the sake of all these who are standing around me, so that they may believe that it was you who sent me". Then he cried in a loud voice, "Lazarus come out". The dead man came out, his feet and hands bound with strips of material, and a cloth over his face. Jesus said, "Unbind him and let him go free". (Jn 11:1-44)

Sadly, there was no sequel as to how Lazarus felt and what happened next, but I am sure they had a great celebration.

Since the resurrection of Jesus and the advent of Christianity there have been numerous instances of people being raised from the dead. A man with a tremendous ministry in this field was Smith Wigglesworth.

"Smith Wigglesworth is part of this group of men and women who brought about the Great Revival at the turn of the 20th century. They were dynamically empowered by the Holy Spirit to bring a revival of God's miraculous presence worldwide. The majority belonged to various Christian denominations, but Smith Wigglesworth preferred to remain unattached to any denomination throughout his ministry. It was in his heart to reach all people regardless of their doctrine. Smith knew how to draw the Spirit of God and always ministered with deep compassion.

"Raising the dead was only one facet of the ministry of Smith

Wigglesworth. This great apostle of faith walked in such an amazing measure of God's anointing that the miracles following his ministry were only secondary to it. In his lifetime this one-time plumber would give new meaning to the word 'adventure.' Adventure's only requirement? – Only believe'! To Wigglesworth, simple obedience to what one believed was not an extraordinary feat, it was simply the fruit of it. His own faith was said to be unflinching and sometimes ruthless. But he was also said to possess an unusual teaching, anointing and a keen sense of compassion, the fruit of which produced countless salvations and miracles in his ministry every day." (a)

A resurrection miracle:
"My friend said, 'she is dead.' He was scared. I have never seen a man so frightened in his life. 'What shall I do?' he asked. You may think that what I did is absurd, but I reached into the bed and pulled her out. I carried her across the room, stood her against the wall and held her up, because she was absolutely dead. I looked into her face and said, 'In the name of Jesus, I rebuke this death.' From the crown of her head to the soles of her feet her whole body began to tremble. 'In the name of Jesus, I command you to walk,' I said. I repeated, 'In the name of Jesus, in the name of Jesus, walk!' and she walked." (b)

Let me quote a second miracle:
A boy was seriously ill, and the family sent for Smith, but when he arrived the mother came to the door saying, "You are too late, there is nothing that can be done for him." Smith replied, "God has never sent me anywhere too late." The boy's condition was so bad that if he was moved his heart would give in and he would die. Before he could pray with the boy Smith had to leave for an engagement at a local church. But before he left, he told the family he would return

and then he instructed them to lay out the boy's clothes, because The Lord would raise him up. When he returned the family, who had no faith, had not put the boy's clothes out as Smith had asked them.

On seeing Smith's faith, they were very embarrassed and immediately began setting out the boys' clothes, but Smith asked them to put socks on his feet. Once inside the boy's room, Smith closed the door and told the lifeless boy that something would happen that would be different from anything he had ever experienced before. "When I place my hands on you the glory of the Lord will fill this room till I shall not be able to stand. I shall be helpless on the floor." The moment Smith touched the boy, the Power of God filled the room and was so strong that Smith fell to the floor. Suddenly the boy began to yell, "This is for your Glory Lord." Smith was still on the floor when the boy jumped out of bed and began to dress himself. Opening the door, the boy yelled, "Dad, God has healed me, I am healed."

Smith says he has a living faith, and the living faith is the Word. The Word is life, and the Word is equipment, and the Lord is the same yesterday, today and forever, and we have to take Him at his word. (c)

The following well-known resurrection story happened in 2001. A Nigerian pastor Daniel Ekechukwu died after a road accident and was pronounced dead on arrival at the hospital in Owerri. His body was partially embalmed but, as there was no cold storage in the mortuary, he was taken at his wife's insistence, to the Grace of God Mission Church in Onista where that afternoon, as people prayed for him, Daniel was raised from the dead. The event was partly captured on video.

In another story, an Australian, Ian McCormack, tells audiences around the world how he was laid out as dead in a hospital in Mauritius after being stung by a notoriously lethal box jellyfish. He was restored to life fifteen minutes later to the terror of the medical staff attending him. The stories of both Ian and Pastor Daniel are available on the internet with all the details.

The amazing fact about Pastor Daniel's story is that, in his own words, when he had died, he was led by an angel to see heaven and hell. And on seeing hell, the angel told him that he would end up there. But Daniel protested saying that he was a man of God, and he served God with all his heart. But at the time of the accident Daniel was holding a grudge against his wife because she had slapped him, and he would not forgive her. The moral of this resurrection story is, that if we do not forgive those who have hurt us then God cannot forgive us either. This brings into focus why we say in the Lord's Prayer, "Forgive us our sins, as we forgive those who have sinned against us".

"Saints who Raised the Dead" by Fr Albert J. Herbert, S.M. states that the raising of the dead has been performed hundreds of times since the day of Christ. Our Lord, in Matthew 10:8, told his apostles to raise the dead, and over the Christian centuries, many saints have done so, particularly St Francis Xavier, St Patrick, St Vincent Ferrer, St Catherine of Sienna. St Theresa of Avila, St Elisabeth of Hungary and more. Yes, "Why should it be a thing incredible that God should raise the dead?" (Ac 26:8.4).

Through Jesus' own resurrection, the resurrection of Lazarus and many other resurrection miracles we witness the power of God revealed in all its glory, for he is truly the Lord of the living and of the dead.

15

GUARDIAN ANGELS

The angel of the Lord is encamped around those who revere him and rescues them from all their distress. …… Blessed are those who take refuge in him. (Psalm 34:7)

Angels have always held a big fascination. There has been quite a craze of late trying to get in touch with one's guardian angel and the spirit world, a trend encouraged by The New Age movement and the Occult. We see angels celebrated in the arts in different shapes and sizes and portrayed as other-worldly beings, powerful and luminous, mostly wearing white robes, with huge wings and beautiful faces speaking to our imagination. Baroque artists favoured painting them as endearing chubby cherubs adorning the heavens. They certainly are enigmatic beings belonging to another world altogether. Many religions believe in supernatural beings which are generally malevolent especially in the polytheistic religions of the East. Religions in other parts of the world believe in supernatural beings who can either be malevolent or benevolent. But the concept of angels as we envisage them to be in Christianity belongs only to the four monotheistic religions of Judaism, Islam, Christianity and

Zoroastrianism, which also believe in the existence of demons and Satan.

The good news that angels bring is only a small part of the wider picture of the Good News, but it is nevertheless yet another example of God's caring and concern for us. In the Bible we encounter many vivid images of angels which go as far back as the story of Abraham, whose arm was stayed by an angel to stop him from sacrificing his son Isaac. The most familiar angel story must be the Christmas story of the angel Gabriel telling Mary that she was to become the mother of Jesus. At his birth, we read that a great multitude of angels announced his birth to the shepherds and sang praises to God. And later that the angel of the Lord appeared to Joseph in a dream to warn him to flee to Egypt to prevent Herod killing the baby Jesus. In all these stories, angels are messengers of good news, and they are true to their Greek name "Angelos" meaning bringer of good news.

Angels are superior beings to humans in power and intellect and are sent by God to watch over us, protect, comfort, and strengthen us. They are loyal to God and obey His commands to promote his kingdom on earth. This is so clearly portrayed in Luke 15:10 where Jesus says, "There will be more rejoicing in heaven by God's angels over one repentant sinner than over ten who do not need conversion." Angels ultimately always point us to God whose design it is that they keep us safe from spiritual and physical harm. The fact that angels have been given a responsibility towards men tells us something of the way God values us humans. Angels are pure spirit, but humans are of a composite nature, made up of both flesh and spirit, and yet the angels perform services for human beings. According to Revelations 5:11, there is an immense number of angels gathered round God's throne, "there are ten thousand times ten thousand of them and thousands upon thousands loudly chanting praises."

This great number of angels is divided into quite a complex hierarchy with familiar names such as seraphim, cherubim, powers, archangels, just angels and many more.

Many can recall I am sure that when they were young, they were told they had a guardian angel on their right shoulder and a little devil on their left shoulder. It is a shame that we do not make our children aware of the presence of their angel anymore, because guardian angels are always at the ready to protect us, not only from bodily harm but also from spiritual harm. Young people would be more protected against the vicious onslaught of their electronic gadgets and not fall victim to mental illness so readily. This is not wishful thinking: Jesus himself said, "See that you never despise any of these little ones, for I tell you that their angels in heaven are continually in the presence of my Father in heaven" (Mt 18:10).

Many books have been written about angels and many people worldwide have reported to have been the happy recipients of protection and help from their guardian angels. In my own case, I believed I had never had an experience concerning my guardian angel until one day, reminiscing about the past, I came to realise that an experience I once had was so unreal, it could only have been an angel who gave me a warning. One cold winter's evening I was heading for home after a 6 pm church service. Exiting the car park and looking both ways to see if the road was clear, I drove out, crossed the road and was already on my way when suddenly out of nowhere a man in a short-sleeved shirt appeared on the left side of the car signalling me to stop. Naturally, I wound down the left window asking what he wanted, and he said, "Be very careful tonight as you drive home, because there is black ice on the road." Greatly surprised to see him there, in a short-sleeved shirt on this cold winter's evening and wondering where he had suddenly appeared from, I thanked him and drove on at a snail's pace, over what by then were very icy roads, arriving home safely.

I thought how kind of this man to warn me, as I had no idea that it had been freezing so hard, but I never dwelt on the incident any further. It was only after reading stories from other people who had similar experiences, that the penny dropped. Because, like most people, I was certain that guardian angels would appear dressed in white robes, the garment we are so used to seeing them represented in, and of course with wings. The thought had never occurred to me that angels can appear in any guise they want, and they can also suddenly appear as quick as a flash of light and disappear in the same way, before one can even thank them. A striking example of this is in Acts 12 when Peter is being freed out of Herod's prison by an angel. "After having passed through two guard posts one after the other they reached the iron gate leading to the city. The gate opened of its own accord and after having walked the whole length of one street, suddenly the angel left him." (Acts 12:10)

On another occasion, my gardener Henry, a parishioner at my church, had decided it was time for him to get confirmed, something he had been postponing for years. Mary, a good friend of both of us kindly offered to drive him to Worth Abbey in West Sussex where the ceremony was to take place which was about a 2-hour drive away. About one and a half hours into the journey, Mary realised that she had lost the way. Time was running out and they did not want to be late for the ceremony. Relieved, they soon came to a petrol station where they could stop and ask for the way to the abbey. No sooner had they stopped when a motorbike carrying TWO men dressed all in black, drew up beside them and asked if they could help. My friends explained they were heading for Worth Abbey but were hopelessly lost. The motor cyclists assured them that they knew the place well and why not follow them and they would get them there in good time. My friends were delighted with the offer and followed the motorbike for quite some time. Suddenly however, Henry shouted, "Mary, you are following the wrong motorbike, there is only ONE man on it, there is nobody on the pillion seat." Mary protested that she had followed the same bike all the way and that there was no way the passenger could have got off as the bike had never stopped. Both were very perplexed by this strange occurrence, and they continued to follow the bike, now with only one man on it. Soon the abbey loomed up before them and they had arrived in good time for the ceremony. But before they could even wave goodbye, the motorbike had disappeared into thin air. (*Names changed*)

DISTANCE IS NO OBSTACLE FOR AN ANGEL

An American missionary told the following story while visiting his home church in Michigan.

> While serving on leave at a small field hospital in Africa, every two weeks I travelled by bicycle through the jungle to a nearby city for supplies. This was a journey of two days and requires camping overnight at the halfway point. On one of these journeys, I arrived to collect money from a bank and purchase medicine and supplies. Upon arrival, I observed two men fighting, one of whom had been previously injured. I treated him for his injuries and at the same time witnessed to him about the Lord Jesus Christ. I then travelled two days, camping overnight, and arrived home without incident.
>
> Two weeks later I repeated my journey. Upon arriving in the city, I was approached by the young man I had treated. He told me that he had known I carried money and medicines. He said, "Some friends and I followed you into the jungle,

knowing you would camp overnight. We planned to kill you and take your money and drugs. But just as we were about to move into your camp, we saw that 26 armed guards surrounded you." At this I laughed and said that I was certainly all alone out in the jungle campsite. The young man pressed the point, however, and said "No sir, I was not the only person to see the guards. My friends also saw them, and we all counted them. It was because of those guards that we were afraid and left you alone.

At this point in the sermon, one of the men in the congregation jumped to his feet and interrupted the missionary. and asked if he could tell him the exact day that this happened. The missionary told the congregation the date, and the man who interrupted told him his story. "On the night of your incident in Africa, it was morning here and I was preparing to play golf. I was about to putt when I felt the urge to pray for you. In fact, the urging of the Lord was so strong that I called men in this church to meet with me here in the sanctuary to pray for you. Would all those men who met with me on that day stand up?" The men who had met together on that day stood up. The missionary wasn't concerned with who they were – he was too busy counting how many men he saw. There were 26. (a)

Don't we all wish we had friends like those 26 praying "soldiers of Christ" because that is what they are. Through their faithfulness to prayer, they were able to respond to God's voice to go and do battle against far-away evil.

ARCHANGELS

In the book of Enoch in the Apocrypha, an ancient text, there appear to be seven Archangels. This is confirmed in the Book of

Tobit, where the Archangel Raphael tells Tobit that he is one of the seven angels ever ready to enter the presence of the glory of God. The three archangels commonly known as Michael, Gabriel, and Raphael have a special role in bringing important messages to humans often when they are in danger. The prefix "arch" means that they are heading another group of angels. The name of the Archangel Gabriel means, "Man of God" or "God is my strength" and he is also "The Protector." He brought good news to Mary that she was to have a child, but also in a way he brought God's assurance that she would be protected from being stoned to death for expecting a child out of wedlock.

Archangels often have a majestic appearance as in the book of Daniel, where we get a glimpse of the awe-inspiring attire in which the Archangel Gabriel appeared on the second occasion that he showed himself to Daniel. On the first occasion he had been dressed like any ordinary man. "Standing on the bank of the great river, the Tigris, this is what I saw. A man dressed in linen with a belt of pure gold around his waist, his body was like beryl, his face looked like lightning, his eyes were like fiery torches, his arms and his face had the gleam of burnished bronze, the sound of his voice was like the roar of a multitude." (Dan.10:6)

In this instance he is sent to Daniel to interpret Daniel's dream about the impending disaster which was to befall King Belshazzar. Here again he was protecting Daniel against being thrown to the lions if he were unable to interpret the dream.

Few references in the Bible are made to the Archangel Raphael. His name means, "God heals," and therefore he is generally accepted to be the protector of healers. He features in the story of Tobit 12:14-15 where after having healed Tobit of his blindness, and his daughter-in-law Sarah, "Raphael took both

Tobit and his son Tobias apart and said, 'I was sent to test your faith and at the same time heal you and your daughter-in-law Sarah. I am Raphael, one of the seven angels who stand ever ready to enter the presence of the glory of God.'"

The Archangel Michael, whose name means, "One who is like God," is a warrior angel and we will find him always depicted holding a shield, a sword and a lance to crush Satan under his feet. He is the one who with his angels will defeat Satan at the end of time (Rv 12:7-9). When I grew up a special prayer to St Michael was always said at the end of mass, but this was stopped in 1964. Recently some churches have reinstated it:

> St Michael the Archangel, defend us in the day of battle, be our safeguard against the snares of the devil. May God rebuke him, we humble pray, and may you, prince of the heavens, by the power of God cast into hell Satan and all evil spirits who wander the earth for the ruin of souls.

A YOUNG MARINE SAVED FROM ATTACK IN KOREA

This is the true story of a marine wounded in Korea in 1950. Writing to his mother, he told her of a fascinating encounter he experienced in the war. Father Walter Muldy, a US Navy Chaplain who spoke to the young marine and to his mother as well as to the outfit commander, affirmed the veracity of the account. The story is told in the first person to better convey some of the impact it must have had when it was first told by the son to his mother.

> Dear Mom, I am writing to you from hospital. Do not worry, I am fine, the doctor says I will be up in no time. But what I really wanted to tell you is that something happened that I

don't dare to tell anyone else for fear of their disbelief. You are the only one I can confide in, though even you might find it hard to believe. You remember the prayer to St Michael you told me to pray when I was little? Before I left home for Korea, you urged me to remember this prayer before confrontation with the enemy; I always prayed it, and when I got to Korea, I sometimes said it a couple of times a day while marching or resting.

Well one day we were told to move forward to scout for commies. It was a very cold day. As I was walking along, I saw another fellow walking beside me, and I looked to see who it was. It was a big fellow, a Marine about 6'4" and built proportionally. Funny I did not know him, and I thought I knew everyone in my unit. I was glad to have the company and I broke the silence between us. "Chilly today, isn't it?" then I chuckled, because it seemed absurd to talk about the weather when we were advancing to meet the enemy. "I thought I knew everyone in my unit, but I have never seen you before," I continued. "No, you haven't as I have just joined. The name is Michael," he said. "Really, that's mine too." "I know" the marine," said, "Michael, Michael of the morning......." I was really surprised that he knew about my prayer, although I had taught it to many of the other guys, so I supposed that the newcomer had picked it up from some of the other guys. As a matter of fact, it had gotten around to the extent that some of the fellows were calling me Saint Michael. Then out of the blue, Michael said, "There is going to be trouble!" I wondered how he could know that.

I was breathing hard from the march, and my breath hit the cold air like a dense cloud of fog. Michael seemed to be in top shape because I couldn't see his breath at all. Just then it started to snow heavily, and soon it was so dense that I could no longer hear or see the rest of my unit. I got a little scared, and I yelled, "Michael"! Then I felt his strong hand on my shoulder and heard a voice in my ear, "It's going to clear up soon." It did clear up suddenly and then a short distance ahead of us, like so many dreadful realities, were seven commies, looking quite comical in their funny hats. But there was nothing funny about them now; their guns were steady and pointed straight at us. "Down Michael!" I yelled as I dived for cover. Even as I was hitting the ground I looked up and saw Michael still standing as if paralysed by fear, or so I thought at the time. Bullets were flying in all directions, and Mom, there was no way these commies could have missed us at this short distance. I jumped up to pull him down, and then I was hit. The pain was like a hot fire in my chest, my head swooned and I remember thinking, "I must be dying." Someone's strong arms were holding me gently in the snow. Through a daze I opened my eyes, and the sun seemed to blaze in my eyes. Michael was standing still and there was a terrible splendour in his face. Suddenly he seemed to grow, like the sun, the splendour increasing steadily around him like the wings of an angel. As I slipped into unconsciousness, I saw that Michael held a sword in his hand, and it flashed like a million lights.

Later on, when I woke up, the rest of the guys came to see me with the sergeant. "How did you do it son?" he asked me. "Where is Michael?" I asked in reply. "Michael who?" The sergeant seemed puzzled. "Michael the big marine walking with me right up to the last moment. I saw him there as I fell." "Son" the sergeant said gravely, "You are the only Michael in the unit, I handpicked all you fellows, and there is only one Michael, you. And you weren't walking with anyone. I was watching you because you were too far behind us, and I was worried. Now tell me son" he repeated, "How did you do it?" It was the second time he asked me that, and I was irritated. "How did I do what?" I asked. "How did you kill those seven commies? There wasn't a single bullet fired from your rifle." "What?" "Come on son, they were strewn all around you, each one killed by a sword stroke." And that Mom, is the end of the story. It may have been the pain, or the blazing sun, or the chilling cold, but there is one thing I am sure about, it did happen: how else could they account for the sword strokes? (b)

Yes, angels are for real!

Volumes have been written about fascinating interventions of angels in all sorts of dangerous situations. Two I would recommend are, first, the story of "The Angel of Mons," Belgium, and how they protected the allied forces on the front, during the first world war. The second is a story of a remarkable man in India, Sadhu Sundar Singh, and how, three times, he was rescued by an angel. (c)

16

GHOSTS AND SPIRITS

Put God's armour on to be able to resist the devil's tactics. For our battle is not against flesh and blood, but against the Sovereignties and Powers who originate the darkness in the world, the spiritual army of evil in the heavens. (Eph 6:11-12)

What are we to make of the paranormal, of ghosts, witchcraft, the existence of evil spirits, haunted houses, contacting the dead and the like? It does not make sense to our scientific understanding of how things work or exist. Creepy though they may be, guided tours to haunted houses are a big money spinner, and it is wise to book well in advance if you don't want to miss the fear of your life. Ghosts are often called unenlightened or earthbound spirits. This may not be the right definition, but it certainly seems an adequate one for describing ghosts such as ladies dressed in white or the moaning of prisoners in ancient buildings. Is all this not pure fantasy and projection on our part? Does witchcraft not belong to the realm of uncivilised tribes whose leaders use them as scaremongering means to dominate their subjects? Most people shrug their shoulders in disbelief and scepticism on hearing of ghost stories. Our modern world has stopped believing in irrational fairy tales, and showing any symptoms of irrational behaviour is often classed as "mental illness."

The following story, told to me by a friend, was met with different reactions: some people present believed it outright, but most were silent, not knowing what to make of it.

> I was visiting a friend in Somerset who lives in a medieval farmhouse. I was awoken in the middle of the night by a faint noise and sitting up in bed, I peacefully watched the figure of a young woman who had mysteriously appeared and made her way through the large bedroom. She was dressed very simply in medieval clothes, with a white veil over her hair and carrying a pile of folded linen on her outstretched arms. I watched in fascination as she slowly crossed the room from one end to the other and then disappeared through the wall at the other end of the room. I assure you I was fully awake and saw everything quite clearly as it was dawn by then, and I was not frightened at all. It was an unbelievable experience.

On the one hand, in the west we live in our civilized bubble of facts proven to be true by scientific investigation. There is enormous scepticism about the existence of ghosts and the power of witchcraft, but on the other hand, tales of haunted houses, Ouija Board activity, ghosts, and films like "The Exorcist" have never stopped holding a strange fascination. Despite the scepticism, interest in astrology has risen tremendously with popular magazines displaying the monthly Zodiac signs. Spiritism, Tarot Cards, and fortune telling, healing with crystals, Reiki, interest in Angels, contacting the dead and more, have all become very popular. Information on all these subjects is now widely available at large fairs which have sprung up in many towns. It is all at our fingertips with bookshelves full of literature on the various subjects and, of course, also the internet.

Many people, Christians, and non-religious people alike, are overlooking the fact that they are dangerously exposing themselves to uncertain and damaging forces at work in these practices, by either practising or subjecting themselves to Reiki healing and other New Age therapies. Not believing them does not mean that they are not real.

> Some time ago a lengthy investigation was carried by the Catholic Church at the request of greatly concerned priests after they received enquiries and complaints regarding New Age spirituality and Reiki healing. Some New Age courses promote "Mind, Body, and Spirit" courses which contain pagan philosophies, rebirthing, Silva mind control, crystal healing, Chakra balancing, bio-energy therapy, aura healing, psychic healing, astrology, dream analysis, palm reading, horoscopes, and tarot cards. Also can be added to the list Yoga meditation containing yogic spirituality, Eastern mantra meditation techniques, transcendental meditation, communing with angels and connecting with Spirit Guides such as in using the Ouija board, the Enneagram course, psychics, mediums, clairvoyants, shamans and Feng Shui - all involve methods connected with occult beliefs and are diametrically opposed to the Christian faith. They appeal to forces outside God and can be damaging to our physical and spiritual health and lead to oppression and even possession. These occult techniques are designed to manipulate occult energies drawn from Tantric Buddhism and Tantric Hinduism which are supposed to open the chakras, important in Reiki, and are based on the Kundalini Shakti which is a dormant energy or serpent power, and is conceived in Yogic Spirituality or Hinduism, as a goddess or coiled serpent. (a)

GHOSTS AND SPIRITS

Psychic healers, mediums and channelers get their power and guidance by dabbling with unknown forces, such as spirit guides and so-called higher power or spirits, or 'from the other side' as discussed earlier. The Apostle St John warns us, "It is not every spirit that you can trust. Test them and see if they come from God" (1 Jn 4:1). We should be aware that God condemns channelling as a heinous sin. "Let no one be found among you, who is a medium or a spiritist, or who consults the dead. Anyone who does these things is detestable to the Lord" (Dt 18:11). "Satan masquerades as an angel of light seeking to deceive people" (2 Cor 11:14).

Here is another story relating to spirits:

> Mozambique is well known for its witchdoctors and because there is little if any medical care, many people go to witchdoctors to be healed. Mary and Sandra went to church, but they found that they could not pray. When they opened their mouths to pray or sing, no words would come out. Something was blocking their speech and they could not understand why this was. There was nothing wrong with them physically, so we asked them if they had been to a witchdoctor. Both women had been to a "Curandeiro" who consults spirits and prepares herbal medicine, and who they believe has spiritual power to heal. Mary who seemed tormented, had often taken her husband there when he was sick, but he had died. Sandra said she had been twice with her son. They could not look at me and their eyes flickered violently when they tried. We invited them to answer the baptismal questions, "Do you turn to Christ? Do you repent of your sins? Do you renounce evil?", and then we prayed for them to be filled with the Holy Spirit. Suddenly they were able to pray aloud, they left singing and the next morning they appeared with a spring in their step and a glow of confidence in their step. (b)

THE GOOD NEWS NOBODY TALKS ABOUT

The magic of the unknown drives people, either through curiosity or a need for spiritual fulfilment, to explore the unknown. Often, and when it is too late, curiosity has been to the detriment of the curious with disastrous effects. According to a Christian Ministry the number of people who have suffered from the adverse effects of the occult such as hallucinations, nightmares, cold patches in the houses or compulsive addictions has increased to alarming numbers.

All this is nothing new; those supernatural tales that we are so keen to discard out of hand as pure fantasy have always been with us. As far as the human mind can hark back, most religions and civilizations practised witchcraft, sorcery and superstition and are still practising it today, as we commented earlier. However, the rising trend in paranormal activity in our western society is very worrying and according to opinion polls, an increasing number of people said that they have had personal awareness of an evil presence or have experienced a personified evil and they were at a loss to its provenance.

When I lived for many years in the Far East, I heard several stories:

One day the husband of our very good local friends had to go to London on business. They happened to live quite close to the jungle which made for a very noisy neighbourhood with all the cacophony one would expect to hear in a jungle, the noise of birds, crickets chirping, and monkeys barking. Their amah said to my friend, "Now that you will be alone for some time would it not be a good idea to have a guard at the front door to protect us?" "Whatever do you mean?" our friend asked. "I can arrange for a local man to come and be your guard" said the amah but did not explain what she had in mind. Our friend totally rejected the idea, saying that it was not necessary and not to do anything of the sort.

On his return the husband settled happily back into his home, until a few days later things did not feel quite right. "What has happened, why is there no noise outside coming from the trees?" he asked his wife. "Everything is so eerie silent." Then the wife told her husband that she had also noticed the silence. Perplexed as to why the jungle could suddenly have fallen so silent, they started to investigate, and when evening came, opening the front door they saw a man standing, dressed as a warrior from the past in mail and holding a sword, giving them a terrible fright. They slammed the door shut as fast as they could. Then she told her husband what the amah had suggested and that she had forbidden her to go ahead with it. She had not linked the silence to the amah's suggestion to get a guard, not knowing that she had gone ahead and done just that. Confronting the amah, it was revealed that the warrior was the ghost of a man who had been unjustly condemned for murder and whose skull she had somehow obtained and buried in their garden. Being able to obtain a skull is very plausible in a country where witchcraft is still widely practised. With the strict order to get rid of the skull, the am ah was dismissed, and the spell broken.

A tall story? It was experienced by intelligent normal people, in fact he is now a high ranking official, and they would not see the need to invent a story like that.

Exploring the markets in Africa is a fascinating but also daunting excursion. In a market selling absolutely everything you can imagine, you will most certainly come across an area offering what to us westerners are the most bizarre objects imaginable. The most striking articles no doubt are the vast collections of dried animal parts, claws, hoofs, horns, feathers, skulls. The whole atmosphere exudes a feeling of eeriness and evil and the hostile stares of the sellers, all dressed in their local garb, leaves one in no doubt that foreigners are not welcome here. It is said, that if you would ever need a baby skull for some witchcraft, this is the place to go. This puts into perspective the discovery of the skull in the above story and makes it very feasible.

The same friend in the Far East lived through another very unpleasant experience: She decided to open an art gallery in the capital city and chose a large first floor room in a shopping centre. Below her gallery there was already a large shop, run by a lady whose business was doing very well. After a while, our friend's business was really thriving too, which of course was very satisfying. A year or so went by when one day she noticed that the shop below wasn't doing as well as before.

Then one day the owner came to visit her in a fury and started to threaten our friend because her business was going downhill, whereas our friend's shop was doing extremely well. "If you do not move out of here in a couple of weeks, I am going to put a curse on you." Although shaken at the violent threat, our friend could not take this too seriously; the last thing she wanted to do was pack up her business and leave, so she stayed put. Amazingly though, slowly, slowly the customers stopped coming to her gallery, and in the end her business totally floundered, and very reluctantly she had no option, but to close.

Another story from the Far East. My parish priest told me that when he was a boy, he used to go to school accompanied by a friend who, at the time he told me the story, was my husband's secretary. In the morning they would follow a path which ran close to the jungle, and on several occasions, to their amazement, they watched as large crystal balls travelled through the air, high above the jungle trees. These balls would then fall and spill their poisonous content over the designated area, and either destroy the crops, or house, or cattle of the enemy. Again, these two people were of sane mind and not given to fantasies of this sort, in fact he is now a bishop. This goes to show that we know very little about the supernatural world, if anything, and if we want to destroy these forces, we cannot discard them out of hand, but have to take them very seriously.

The following story happened in England and was told by our local vicar: One day he was called by a distressed landlady of a local pub, who claimed that the place was haunted. Already for some time her young son could not eat and was constantly sick. They had noticed a wet puddle that would appear for no reason on the landing, although there was no leak to be seen in the ceiling, and there had been unexplained noises coming from the first floor. All very frightening and mysterious.

Mounting the stairs, the vicar indeed noticed the wet stain, and suddenly he became aware of what looked like some human shaped shadow disappear around the corner. Edging slowly forward he saw a medieval soldier dressed ready for battle, but again disappearing fast from sight. Shocked but not put out, he made the sign of the cross with holy water, prayed the prayers of exorcism and forever banned this tortured soul from haunting the place ever again. The true story of the ghost was never resolved but most probably something dreadful had happened in that place many years previously.

We need to ask the question, where does the power of the paranormal, the occult, spiritism, the Ouija board, contacting the dead and the supernatural emanate from, because it is evident that real power is manifest in all these extraordinary stories. If not from God, from where? We will explore this in the next chapter.

17

SATAN AND EXORCISM

The seventy-two came back rejoicing, "Lord," they said, "even the devils submit to us when we use your name." He said to them, "I saw Satan fall like lightening from heaven. Look, I have given you power to tread down serpents and scorpions and the whole strength of the enemy; nothing shall ever hurt you". (Lk10:17-19)

Jesus demonstrated the existence of a spirit-world and he continually highlighted the clash between two kingdoms, the Kingdom of God and the Kingdom of Satan, in his preaching. There is a large array of stories in the Gospels of people being possessed in various ways by the devil or Satan and being delivered by Jesus of this terrible curse. Some spirits recognised Jesus as being the Son of God and were aware that only he had the authority and power over them to drive them out of the unfortunate people they had taken possession of.

The cure of a dumb demoniac:

> A man was brought to Jesus, a dumb demoniac. And when the devil was driven out, the man spoke and the people were

amazed and said, "Nothing like this has ever been seen in Israel" (Mt 9:32-33).

The epileptic demoniac:

> As Jesus and his disciples were joining the crowd, a man came up to Jesus and went down on his knees before him, "Lord please take pity on my son, he is demented and in a wretched state, he is always falling into the fire and into the water. I took him to your disciples, but they were unable to cure him." "Bring him here to me," said Jesus. Then Jesus rebuked the spirit, the devil came out of the boy, and he was cured from that moment (Mt 17:14-18).

The Gerasene demoniac:

> They reached Gerasene, on the other side of the lake, and when he disembarked a man with an unclean spirit at once came out from the tombs towards him. The man lived in the tombs, and no one could secure him anymore, even with a chain. Every time the chain snapped and broke the fetters, and no one had the strength to control him. All night and all day he would howl among the tombs and in the mountains and gash himself with stones. Catching sight of Jesus from a distance, he ran up to him and fell at his feet and shouted at the top of his voice, "What do you want with me, Jesus, son of the Most High? In God's name, do not torture me!" Jesus had been saying to him, "Come out of the man, unclean spirit".

> Then Jesus asked, "What is your name?" He answered, "My name is Legion, for there are many of us." And he begged him earnestly not to send him out of the district. Now on the mountain side there was a great herd of pigs feeding and the unclean spirit begged him, "Send us to the pigs, let us go into them." So, Jesus gave them leave and with that the unclean

spirits came out of the man and went into the pigs, and the herd of about two thousand charged down the cliff and into the lake, and there they were drowned. Then the people from the country around came to Jesus to see what was happening, and they saw the demoniac sitting there - the man who had had the legion in him - properly dressed and in his full senses, and they were afraid, and they began to implore Jesus to leave their neighbourhood. The man who had been possessed, begged Jesus to let him come into the boat with him, but Jesus said, "Go home to your people and tell them all that the Lord in his mercy has done for you." So, the man went off and proceeded to proclaim in the Decapolis all that Jesus had done for him. And everyone one was amazed. (Lk 8:26-39)

After having demonstrated his power over evil spirits, Jesus' reputation spread far and wide, all the way across the Decapolis that comprised the 10 cities on the Eastern frontier of the Roman Empire, stretching through Syria, Jordan, and Israel. By giving his disciples "the power to drive out devils" ahead of healing the sick, Jesus demonstrated that he came into the world first and foremost to overthrow Satan's reign and, by exorcising so many who were possessed, he showed that "the Kingdom of God was close at hand" (Mk 3:15).

The many years of anxious waiting for the promised Messiah were over: the havoc the primeval serpent or Satan wreaked over the world since the beginning of time has been expiated by Jesus' sacrifice and humanity has received a new lease of life; we have been saved from eternal perdition by an act of unsurpassed love.

The tragedy of today is that we have stopped believing in Satan's existence. If he does not exist, what do all these stories of Jesus casting out evil spirits relate to? Where does all the evil in this world emanate from? The human mind is certainly capable of conjuring up the vilest of evil deeds. But to be able to take possession of a person's personality, as described in the above stories, is a totally different dimension of evil, and even the most astute and clever person in the world could not achieve and elevate it to such power and depravity. We cannot brush aside all those stories in which Jesus freed those poor people oppressed by demons in favour of a more modern interpretation of evil and we can never fully understand the saving power of Jesus if we do not believe in Satan's existence.

WHO IS SATAN?

> War broke out in heaven when Michael with his angels attacked the dragon. The dragon fought back with his angels, but they were defeated and driven out of heaven. The great dragon, the primeval serpent, known as the devil or Satan, who had deceived all the world, was hurled down to earth and his angels were hurled down with him. Then I heard a voice shout from heaven, "Victory and power and empire for ever has been won by our God, and all authority for his Christ, now that the persecutor, who accused our brothers, day and night before our God, has been brought down. And they have triumphed over him by the blood of the Lamb." (Rv 12:7-12)

We are familiar with the description here of the "primeval serpent" who tempted Eve to eat from the tree of life, described in the Book of Genesis. Since the moment that Eve sided with Satan when he told her she would be "like God" and, out of pride, she ate from the forbidden fruit, she disobeyed God and condemned the whole human race to be separated from God, and irretrievably closed off heaven which was our original birth right. We can trace back to this one act of disobedience all the calamities under the sun that have afflicted humanity, from the murder of Abel to all the horrors raging on our planet today. From this schism, God suffered as much from unrequited love as any of us would, because He loves us to excess. Everything He did for us was excess, coming into the world like a baby, living like an itinerant preacher with not a pillow to rest his head on, and dying like a criminal on Calvary.

Satan was at first a good angel, but he was driven out of heaven because of a war of words that broke out: he wanted to be as great as God. Michael and his legions of angels drove Satan and his legions of angels out of heaven who from then on have not stopped to make "hell for mankind." "From the very beginning the Bible and the Church have always given witness to the reality of a realm of evil inhabited by Satan and his demons." The Council of Lateran in 1215 said "The devil and other demons were created naturally good, but they became evil by their own doing". (a)

The world has always been divided into two camps, one good, personified by Jesus, the Light of the world, and the other bad, personified by Satan, the creator of all darkness. Every form of evil under the sun, we can lay at his door. This dualistic reign, one being the Spirit of God living in us when we were created in His image and likeness, the other a spirit of evil, which we inherited through Eve's sin, are the two camps we must choose between, because we cannot belong to both though we often wish we could. But there is a warning: "for who is not for me is against me and who does not sow with me scatters" (Mt 12:30). Choosing which camp we want to belong to has been the perpetual struggle facing everyone, every day of our lives. The choice is between honesty and dishonesty, between fidelity and infidelity, between selfishness and altruism, between good and evil.

To fully understand why Jesus needed to come and save us, and what we need to be saved from, we first need to acknowledge that we need salvation, because none of us is perfect. But before we can do this, we need to be conscious of what we consider to be sin, such an unpopular word, and in how far we have consciously contravened the original commandments, the universal laws of "Thou shall not steal, Thou shall not kill, Thou shall not commit adultery or give false witness," and "there must not even be a mention of sexual vice or impurity in any of its forms, or greed among you.... and take no part in the futile works of darkness" says Paul in Ephesians 5:3 &11.

It is now very fashionable to think that religion is a matter of personal opinion and need not be based solely on rules and regulations as revealed by God in the Ten Commandments. It is so easy for our sense of right and wrong to become atrophied and give the false impression that we have the freedom to go beyond God's laws by making our own rules and regulations to accommodate our modern way of approaching what we think is right and wrong and appease our conscience in this way. But in so doing the reality of sin is rejected. This modern approach to sin stunts our conscience in such a way that we think we don't do anything wrong; and we are not conscious of disobeying any commandments, as we do not put them in the realm of religion but only see them in a secular context. Jesus did not come to offer us a lifestyle choice or a differently packaged way of doing things, but to show a way of life which engages our whole commitment and integrity and is not just an optional extra. We can never compromise God's words and we can never dissent from any of the commandments. All commandments must be believed in and be obeyed, or we will forfeit the power we are given to combat the rampant evil raging in the world. Jesus is the only Way away from evil and can be the only way open for us to follow if we wish to achieve all our dreams; the alternative leads to misery.

To live as a true Christian is certainly a hard graft. The temptations are many and very appealing. It is so much easier to put our heads in the sand and go for the easier option by believing that two masters can be served at the same time, and then collude with evil whether wilfully or unwittingly. On the one hand, one good act done, makes this world a better place but by the same token disobeying one commandment neutralises all the benefits from our one good act, and the state of our soul and the world is unchanged from the status quo. "Who is not with me is against me" we are warned in Luke 11:213. The major stumbling block we so easily trip over is no doubt obedience because we want to do it all "our way"! It was the first trespass of our ancestors and since then we hate obeying our parents and teachers, traffic rules, safety warnings, etiquette on how to dress and speak and eat. But unpleasant consequences soon follow on the heels of disobedience; havoc and disorder ensue and put in jeopardy our safety and our health. It creates pain, deep unhappiness, and division.

God gave the commandments for our wellbeing and for the smooth running of the world and society. We need to take stock again of what sin means to our modern way of thinking. It is now so easily explained away as a psychological weakness or a flaw in our genes, or the fault of society or education. The advanced psychological and medical knowledge has made us believe that there is no personified evil and that it emanates from within us or from a sick mind which can be put right with proper psychotic drugs and has absolutely nothing to do with the personal failures and wrong acts committed with our free will. This argument destroys a willingness to acknowledge that we have gone wrong and that we are in great need of repentance. But whatever the case may be, we will always be asked to make choices and the choices can only be between good and evil, between Jesus and Satan. In our heart of hearts, we know that we do not want to be part of all the evil in the world.

Today's denial of Satan's existence is to our own detriment and only plunges the world into yet more misery and horror. Satan thrives on hearing that his existence is being denied, as this gives him a clear playing field to turn good into bad and vice versa. But Jesus affirms clearly that Satan does exist by branding him a "liar and the father of lies," and further calls him "a murderer from the start, and he is the father of lies, there is no truth in him at all" (Jn.8:44). The following stories and the previous accounts of Jesus delivering people from evil spirits cannot make it clearer that Satan really does exist. The horrors of Nazism and Apartheid cannot be given a rational explanation other than that there was an inexplicably powerful force at work that did not just emanate from within the human heart but rather from an outside source of enticement.

Satan is master at appealing to our weaker points, our compassion, our sexuality. Unwittingly we fall for his wiles and lies which he so cleverly disguises by making wrong appear as right. It did not take society long to be deluded into thinking that adultery does not harm anybody as long as the spouse does not know; that we have a right to pleasure, and that sex for the young is permissible provided there is consent. Cohabiting is now a way of life and even abortion, pornography and threesomes are now generally acceptable and lust, one of the deadly sins, is no longer frowned upon.

In 1 Corinthians, Paul says, "Keep away from sexual immorality, all other sins one commits are done outside the body, but the sexually immoral person sins against his own body. Do you not realize that your body is the Temple of the Holy Spirit, who is in you and whom you received from God? You are not your own property, you have been bought at a price, namely the death on the cross of Jesus Christ" (1 Cor.6:18-20). "Do you not realise that people who do evil will never inherit the kingdom of God? Make no mistake, the sexually immoral, idolaters, adulterers, the self-indulgent, sodomites, thieves, misers, drunkards, slanderers, and swindlers - none of these will inherit the kingdom of heaven" (1 Cor 6:9-10). It appears that we have strayed a long way away from these exhortations.

Never, in any century, has there been such a relentless, brazen, and open attack on Christian values as we see today. All these lies have been so slowly and imperceptibly woven into the fabric of everyday life and are now generally accepted as being the norm.

Europe, and the west in general, and many parts of the world embraced Jesus' teaching because people had a personal experience of how he turned their lives upside down and brought them the peace, happiness, and protection they craved for. They discovered that his way of life made sense as it gave them hope and security. Several centuries have elapsed since the gradual breaking away from Christianity in the 16th to 18th centuries due to the relentless anti-Christian opinions promulgated by non-believing scientists and philosophers, and it seems that in the 21st century its apotheosis has been reached. This relentless attack has come about by forces who obey the dictates of the father of lies, Satan, whose purpose it is to destroy the Christian faith and everything that is good and true.

Slowly the western world has reverted to paganism and jettisoned the Christian faith with its message of hope, love and compassion so dearly won by the blood and sweat of many missionaries and martyrs over the past 2000 years. In many parts of the world religions are thriving such as Hinduism, Islam, the Jewish faith, and many other kinds of worship of gods and spirits, yet western nations have gone back to atheism and abolished worshipping God and His laws and instead have embraced the worship of the body and its pleasures, taking the broad road to perdition. Paul in Ephesian 6 writes, "Put on the full armour of Christ to be able to resist the devil's tactics. For it is not against human enemies that we must struggle, but against the principalities and the ruling forces who are masters of the darkness in this world. That is why you must take up all God's armour or you will not be able to put up resistance against evil. So, stand your ground with the belt of "truth' around your waist and righteousness as a breastplate. On your feet wear the shoes of eagerness to spread the gospel of 'peace" and always carry the shield of faith so that you can quench the burning arrows of the Evil One" (Ep 6:11-16). In this passage the shield is Jesus our truth and peace, and our faith is in him.

By discarding the weapons which the Christian faith offers to enable us to withstand the onslaught of the enemy - like prayer, worshipping in church, the sacraments, the Eucharist, obeying God's law, welcoming strangers, and practising virtues - the way was left wide open for the devil's tactics and for denying Satan's existence, which gave him free rein to cleverly disguise evil for good and attack humanity's vulnerable nature.

In the stories we read earlier in this book, it was evident that miracles could only have happened through people who are full of the Holy Spirit, who have lived their lives according to the rules. This is the only option open to the Christian to enable him to annihilate evil in the world.

This liberalism has plunged the western world, without it being aware, into an immoral impasse that casts a blanket of darkness over it. It also brings us into conflict with Islam and Judaism and even with other religions who have adhered more rigorously to the same mores as the west once did. So called fundamental Christianity often gets a bad press, but this is the wrong notion, as there is no such stance as "fundamental Christianity." There is only one God-given law which we cannot compromise, for it is a matter of life and death. And so it is for the Muslim religion: western governments continually try to persuade Muslims to embrace our more "lenient values", but how can they forsake their religious doctrine, which for them is also a way of achieving eternal life, when they find our so-called "values" a threat to their religion?

Not being grounded in the Holy Spirit, the Church and society have lacked the powerful arguments to counter the false ploys of the evil one, who is constantly enticing us to commit evil instead of good. His brainwashing soon took root in society's feeble mind and grew to the extent that evil has been redefined and many practices previously forbidden have become fully acceptable.

A fresh approach is needed to be able to appraise truthfully the full scope and horrors of evil; we cannot pick and choose by putting our own stamp on what we think is right and wrong. The only way we can approach personified evil is not by denial but by praying to have our spiritual eyes and ears and heart opened so that we can "see" and fully acknowledge that Satan is real. Then can we move on and embrace the love and the hope for real happiness we are offered by repenting, and accept our salvation so dearly won on the cross.

According to "The Society in the Defence of Tradition, Faith and Property," Satanism is taking hold in the Unites States at an alarming rate. Satanists are now demanding the same rights as other religions, they want to erect statues of Satan in public squares, or hold Black Masses in Municipal buildings, "inviting people to the ancient ritual where the Dark Lord is summoned through Satanic invocations." If we can equate Satanism to Nazism, then it is like publicly giving the right to grant Nazism equal rights. Events like these can only bring more disaster to the world which is already shrouded in more than enough darkness.

"Satanists are very active in most countries of the world. All kinds of people are Satanists, from nurses, to teachers, bankers, shopkeepers and lawyers and they promote Satan by all the means they can think of and infiltrate all strata of society. Powerful witches' covens also exist and at initiation ceremonies many perverted sexual acts are committed, as sex is very important in Satanism and Witchcraft." (b)

The film "The Exorcist" made quite an impact when it was first shown in 1973. It recounts the exorcism or freeing by prayer of a person who is demon-possessed. Possession by demons are rare occurrences, yet the Catholic Church in Italy recounts that more and more people are coming forward to receive prayer, to receive exorcism. The film had a very disturbing effect on many viewers. Some scenes in the film were so gruesome that they caused many theatre goers to throw up, while others fainted. One man leaving the theatre said it best: "I believe! I believe!"

The following case is the only documented exorcism in the United States and important because one of the biggest lies of the devil is to convince mankind that he does not exist. This perhaps explains the stunned reactions of audiences to the dramatized version of the real exorcism from a teenager known by the pseudonym "Robbie Mannheim" or "Roland Doe." While the movie showed the horror and repugnance of demonic possession, it left out the most important part of the true story of this possessed boy. He was freed from the devil's clutches through the intercession of our Lady and St Michael. The details of these extraordinary real events at this exorcism in 1949 were meticulously recorded in the book "Possessed" by Thomas Allen.

> As an only child Robbie would only play with adults, and it was his aunt, a spiritualist who taught her thirteen-year-old nephew how to use a Ouija board. Soon the parents noticed strange things happening to their son. They heard strange noises in his room such as the noise of a dripping tap and scratching noise like claws scraping wool. When his aunt died

Robbie started to use the Ouija board as a means of contacting her. He would use it for hours until it became a possession both figuratively and literally.

Soon they started to notice alarming physical abnormalities, such as scratch marks, welts and bruises. More disturbing was the personality change. Her normally quiet boy became aggressive, angry and had violent temper tantrums directed at them. He began to speak Latin, a language he had no means of knowing. It was time to look for help and they tried everything, from doctors to a psychologist, psychiatrist and even a psychic before turning to Revd Luther Schultze. Whilst the parents had already considered diabolical possession, Revd Schultze was sceptical. He decided possession was a medieval relic, something that had been left to Catholics when the Luther-led reformation split the Christian world.

Revd Schultze decided to find out for himself what was really going on by inviting Robbie to spend the night at his home. That night he watched with his own eye as Robbie's bed moved back and forth then jumped up and down. When he asked the boy to sleep in a chair, it moved across the room then fell on its side leaving Bobbie sprawled on the floor. When Schultze could not stand the chair upright, he realised he was in the presence of a colossal force and had a change of heart. He told the parents, "You have to see a Catholic priest, the Catholics know how to do these things." Fr E. Albert was chosen but he saw the boy's violence as a threat and ordered him to be put under hospital restraint. As the priest began the ritual prayers, the boy managed to free his arm, reach underneath the bed and remove one of the bedsprings. He then used it as a weapon and slashed the priest's forearm from wrist to elbow. It took one hundred stitches to close the wound.

The Mannheims moved to St Louis to be close to their relatives and through Robbie's cousin, Elizabeth, contacted Fr R Bishop one of her professors, who handed the case over to Fr William Bowden a Jesuit priest described by fellow Jesuits to be absolutely fearless. Fr Bowden was then officially assigned by Archbishop J. Ritter to perform the exorcism.

From the very beginning Fr Bowden placed "Our Lady of Fatima" at the centre of the fight. On his first visit to the boy at his home on March 11, 1949, they heard terrible screams coming from the room upstairs. On entering they realised that the boy was visibly frightened by what he sensed was an evil spirit in the room. The priest boldly placed his rosary beads around the boy's neck and began to pray. Then he told Robbie about three children of about his age who had seen something that other people had not seen. He then explained the Fatima Apparitions and how those children received the special privilege of seeing Mary the mother of God. This helped to explain the Hail Mary when he prayed the rosary to the boy, who was not a Catholic. The boy was fascinated by the Fatima story, and Fr Bowden repeated it several times over the next thirty-eight days. This led Robbie to inquire more about the Catholic Faith and ultimately led to his conversion and that of his parents. On March 23 he began to study the faith and on April 1 he was baptized and received his first holy communion the next day.

On 10 April, Palm Sunday, Robbie was taken to a psychiatric hospital which provided privacy for the exorcist Fr Bowden and his assistant Canon Cornelius to deal with the boy over the next weeks. After Robbie's baptism, the devils which possessed him became more violent and the priests brought a statue of our Lady of Fatima and placed it in the main ground floor corridor. The two men endured unspeakable insults, blasphemies, filthy language and even violence from the devils. At one point, another priest who was also present had his nose broken when Robbie hit him with a precise blow with his eyes closed. Through the process, Fr Bowden pondered something the devil had uttered in the beginning. "I will not go," the guttural voice said, "until a certain word is pronounced, and I will not allow this boy to say it."

On Holy Saturday Brother Cornelius brought a statue of St Michael into Robbie's room. Easter Sunday came and went but the next day something truly extraordinary happened. Robbie awoke in a fury and the same foul voice taunted the priests. "He has to say one more word, one little word, I mean one BIG word. He will never say it. I am always in him. I may not have much power always, but I am in him. He will never say that word." When the spirit manifested himself, Robbie would go into what appeared like a seizure. The boy's voice on these occasions was cynical, harsh, and diabolical. Throughout the day the priests heard that voice but that night however something changed. At 10.45pm Robbie became very calm and entered a trancelike state. Those in the room were surprised when they heard an entirely different voice come from Robbie. The voice did not provoke fear or disgust but rather confidence and hope. In clear and commanding tones an august personage said: "Satan! Satan! I am Saint Michael, And I command you, Satan, and the other evil spirits, to leave the boy in the name of "Dominus," immediately, now! Now, Now"! Robbie then went into the most violent convulsions of the entire exorcism. Finally, he became calm and said to those surrounding the bed, "He is Gone!" Robbie explained then what he had seen. "St Michael appeared as a very beautiful man with flowing wavy hair that blew in the breeze as he stood in the midst of a brilliant white light. In his right hand he held a wavy fiery sword in front of him. With his left hand he pointed down to a pit." The boy described how he felt heat come forth, but also he saw the devil laughingly resist St Michael.

What happened clearly showed that the devil was outmatched by the abrupt appearance of his Angelic nemesis on this spiritual battlefield. St Michael turned towards Robbie, smiled, and then spoke. However, the only word that Robbie heard while he was in the trance was the one which his tormentor had sworn he would not allow him to say, Dominus, Lord. With that one word, Robbie was free. After these horrific events, Robbie went on to lead a normal life. He married and named his first son Michael after the warrior angel who came to his rescue in the time of urgent need. While it seemed that Fr William Bowden's life also went on as normal, the opposite is true. Relatives say that, until his death in 1983 at the age of 86, this heroic priest suffered mentally and physically from what he had endured during the exorcism. This stunning victory of St Michael over the devil is merely the continuation of a war that started in the beginning of creation. The fact that this particular episode between the angel of light and his eternal enemy centred on one word, Dominus, is not surprising; it is truly linked to the "Fatima Message." (c)

Not all occult practices lead to full possession. There can also be infestation and oppression or a spirit of trauma. With the increased denial of Satan's existence which has led to the growth of psychiatric treatment for mental illness, less help has become available for people who find themselves in the same or similar situation as Robbie Mannheim. Even the clergy has become sceptical because very few seminaries that offer courses in Christian spiritual healing are equipped to deal with this increasing scourge. The following testimonies from professional people who have a world of experience in the field can shed more light on this complex subject.

THE GOOD NEWS NOBODY TALKS ABOUT

TWO POWERFUL TESTIMONIES

In his book, "Deliver us from Evil Spirits" Francis McNutt writes:

"Because of the rise in the number of cases of Satanic Ritual Abuse which they have witnessed, many psychiatrists and physiotherapists have taken a more serious look at the demonic world. It is no longer true that mental illness is only curable by the medical approach. Some psychiatrists have started to pray with their patients and by discussion and learning from one another, have started to discover the existence of satanism.

"The best known example of this increasing openness is the celebrated author and psychiatrist, Dr Scott Peck. In "People of the Lie," Peck states that he has come to see that some people are truly evil. In the beginning Peck did not believe in the devil or in exorcism, but now he believes in Satan because of his own experience; he has seen the face of evil. Peck agrees that believing in Satan, or having a conversion to God, requires personal experience. For him that experience came by participating in an exorcism, and I quote his narrative as follows:

> As a hard-headed scientist, I can explain 95% of what went on in these two cases by traditional psychiatric dynamics, but I am left with a critical 5 percent I cannot explain in such a way. I am left with the supernatural or, better, the sub-natural.
>
> When the demonic finally spoke, clearly in one case, an expression appeared on the patient's face that could be described only as Satanic. It was an incredibly contemptuous grin of utter hostile malevolence. I have spent many hours before a mirror trying to imitate it without the slightest success. I have seen that expression one other time in my life – for a few fleeting seconds on the face of another patient.

The patient suddenly resembled a writhing snake of great strength. Viciously attempting to bite the team members. More frightening than the writhing body however was the face. The eyes were hooded with lazy reptilian torpor – except when the reptile darted out in attack. At which moment, the eyes would open wide with blazing hatred. Despite these frequent darting moments, what upset me most was the extraordinary sense of a fifty-million-year-old heaviness I received from this serpentine being. It caused me to despair of the exorcism. Almost all the team members at both exorcisms were convinced that they were in the presence of something absolutely alien and inhuman. The end of each exorcism proper was signalled by the departure of this Presence from the patient and the room.

Another remarkable case of deliverance was written up in, "The Archives of Sexual Behaviour" and entitled "Gender Identity Change in a Transsexual." The authors described the change of a transsexual, whom they call John, through exorcism. The remarkable part of this case was that John suffered from a psychological disorder that normally resists all treatment. They had tested John thoroughly and decided that the best thing was to encourage him in his determination to have a sex-change operation. In preparation for the surgery, John changed his name to Judy, had his facial hair removed through electrolysis and his breasts enlarged through oestrogen. The date for the operation was set.

But on the insistence of a Christian friend of his, John visited another doctor, who told him his real problem was possession by evil spirits. John consented to a three-hour exorcism session during which 22 evil spirits purportedly left him. After this session John was confirmed in his masculine identity and discarded his female clothing. At a subsequent prayer session, the enlargement of John's breasts subsided almost immediately.

The doctors tested John for the next two and a half years and were amazed that he showed a clear reversal of his gender identity- something they had never seen in their own practice or heard about it in psychological literature. They concluded their report by stating: What cannot be denied, is that the patient was clearly a transsexual by the most conservative criterion and assumed a long- lasting masculine gender identity in a remarkably short period of time following an apparent exorcism. "(d)

Satanism is something we need to take very seriously and, in our ignorance, we must prevent at all costs giving it the power it demands by its claim to being equal to theistic religions. It is in fact totally anti-religion and destructive to the world.

In disbelieving the existence of Satan, society will slowly crumble away leading to its eventual downfall. Unless we stand up for what is good and right, our children will be the victims.

18

HEAVEN, HELL AND REPENTANCE

Who shall climb the mountain of the Lord? Who shall stand in this holy place? The man with clean hands and pure heart, who desires not worthless things, who has not sworn to deceive his neighbour. He shall receive reward from the God who saved him. (Ps 23:3-5)

I, John, saw a door open in heaven ...and I saw a throne standing in the heaven, and the One sitting on the throne looked like a diamond and a ruby. There was a rainbow encircling the throne and this looked like an emerald. Round the throne, in a circle were twenty-four thrones and on them I saw twenty-four elders dressed in white robes with golden crowns on their heads. Flashes of lightning were coming from the throne, and the sounds of peals of thunder.... The twenty-four elders prostrated themselves before him to worship the One who lives for ever and ever, and they threw down their crowns in front of the throne, saying, "You are worthy, our Lord, our God, to receive of glory and honour and power because you made the whole universe by your will, when it did not exist, it was created. (Rv 4:1-5, 10-11)

THE BEATIFIC VISION

Paul tells us that, "we have all fallen short of the glory of God" (Rom 3:23) - what does this mean? The word glory may sound antiquated; it is not a word we use daily. The dictionary describes glory as an exclamation of delight or surprise, and that is exactly what it is when we say, "What a glorious sunset" or "I have had a glorious day." It also means unearthly beauty, magnificence, splendour, bliss, heavenly light, radiance, or halo. The above allegorical story from Revelation describes the greatness, magnificence, majesty, power and awesomeness of God, and this glory also reflects God's omnipotence, omnipresence, omniscience, and his love, mercy, and justice. Mark's Gospel paints a picture of Jesus' transfiguration which is no less glorious and luminous in its dazzling light than that described in Revelation:

> Jesus took with him Peter and James and John and led them up a high mountain on their own. There in their presence he was transfigured, his clothes became brilliantly white, whiter than any earthly bleacher could make them.... and a cloud came covering them in shadow and from the cloud came a voice, "This is my Son, the well Beloved, listen to him". (Mk 9:2-3,7)

God dwells in inaccessible bright light, much brighter than sunlight and obviously impossible to look at. This is the glory of God called "The Beatific Vision" that blinds our sight because we have fallen short by not keeping the commandments. The joy of heaven will be seeing God's beauty and splendour, a vision unparalleled on earth, and it is this beauty we have pursued in life but never found because we were looking for it in the gold mines rather than in the desert. "It is the final end, the ultimate goal for all human life, which so satisfies man's appetite that nothing is left for him to desire" (Pope John Paul II).

It is through our good deeds and our faith in Jesus as our Saviour that we give glory to God. Falling short of God's glory literally means that, when we die and come face to face with God, his amazing, brilliant splendour will blind us because of the rubbish we bring with us. At that moment, we will come to realise the magnitude of sin, its ugliness, repulsiveness and darkness that we read about in exorcisms, wars, famine and corruption, in marked contrast to God's majesty and blinding light.

The rubbish of greed, lust, and injustice blocks the windows of our souls. None of us, bar the saints, have reached that degree of perfection which Jesus talks about when he says, "Be perfect as my heavenly Father is perfect" (Mt 5:48). And who is perfect? Who has strictly obeyed God's commands and has said sorry for all the wrong he or she has done. This is bound to obliterate the vision of that dazzling light, like the dirt and sleet that stick to our car windscreens on a stormy night and which we are desperate to clear away, because it prevents clear vision of the road ahead.

HEAVEN AND PURGATORY ARE FOR THE SAVED

Repentance grants forgiveness. Just as a criminal in prison is expected to make good for his crime, there will be for each soul a period of purification in Purgatory before it is cleansed from all its imperfections, even though we have said sorry and repented. Only then will the soul be worthy and able to enjoy God's glory. We would not expect a criminal to be invited to the King's banquet unless he had expunged his crime in prison and been forgiven, or for anyone to appear at a wedding without wearing the prescribed dress code. Purgatory then is a temporary state of purification by fire of those who have obeyed the commandments but need to be cleansed from their habitual or lesser faults before they can see the Beatific Vision.

Once I listened to a street preacher who selected a young man from the attentive bystanders and proceeded to ask him all sorts of personal questions. "Have you ever slept with a married woman? Have you ever stolen something? Have you ever broken the speed limit? Have you kept a grudge against someone or failed to pay a parking ticket and hoped to get away with it? Have you been envious of your friends' success in his job? Have you ever lied to your employer, saying you were sick, when you weren't?" To my amazement the young man replied with total honesty. Most of the questions were answered with a "yes."

They didn't seem like great crimes to me, something most of us might do. The street preacher then said, "For some of these offences you had to pay a fine, or if the speeding was excessive, you may even have had to face jail, and if you are caught stealing that could bear serious consequences like a prison sentence too. As for sleeping with a married woman, it is called adultery in God's eye, it is not punishable by secular law, but it is punishable by God's law, "Thou shall not covet they neighbour's wife nor his goods." The law has no choice but to punish you, and so it is with God and although he is perfectly merciful, he is also perfectly just. The point I am trying to make is that most people commit one or more of these offences, but never consider what the ultimate consequences of their acts might be and think they will get away with them. However, all our actions bear consequences and, whether people believe it or not, there is a God to whom we ultimately will have to give account for the way we have lived. "Those who did good, will come forth to life, those who did evil will go forth to judgement" states the Bible (Jn 5:29). "If you were to die now," the preacher asked the young man, "where do you think you might end up going, to heaven, to hell or to purgatory?" There was quite a stunned silence among the listeners after this.

WE ALL HAVE A FEAR OF DYING

The fear of dying gripped many during the recent pandemic which ravaged the world's population and led to greatly increased mental health issues and loneliness. With so many uncertainties about loss of job, health and losing loved ones at an alarming rate, people's focus on the good things in life was taken away, with no light in sight and the fear of dying suddenly become a reality. Humans spend their lives looking towards something agreeable, and pleasing to the senses - this is what keeps us going because hope gives life. When all this is taken away, including our material and physical security, we feel hopelessly trapped and the fear of death stares us in the face like a big gaping hole with no hope left except the inevitable end. Many are driven to suicide. This is the moment when our inner resources like self-control, selflessness, not giving in to depression, and trust and hope should be at hand. And Jesus assures us that his perfect love for all casts out fear (Jn4:18). But when we have not taken hold of this anchor at the time of great need and life is focussed solely on material things, we find that the storeroom of the spiritual treasures with all its promises is pitifully empty, and we are left totally in the dark. Sadly, this is the situation many find themselves in at such a difficult time. If only we would listen to the message God gives for our spiritual welfare we would be so much better off: "Stay awake. Stand ready because the Son of man is coming at an hour you do not expect" (Mt 24: 44). It seems that only a very small percentage of the population these days can safely say that they are ready to die at any time without fear.

Only the other day did I hear of a good friend's friend who could not cope with the uncertainty of the pandemic virus any longer and took his own life by hanging. He had a good job and leaves a wife and two small children. This need not be, because life is not as the Japanese proverb would have us believe: "Man's life on earth? Boats rowed out at dawn, and no trace left"!

WHAT IS THE REQUIREMENT TO ATTAIN HEAVEN?

Different religions and some Christians believe that we have a second chance to be redeemed by reincarnation, but this goes against all Christian teaching. Every human by virtue of being created in God's image and likeness, has received one life only. There is only one God, the God of the cosmos, who reigns over all ruling forces, sovereignties and powers", meaning the devil". (Co1:15-20). To think we can be reincarnated is to ignore Jesus' death on the cross. There is one life and death, one heaven, purgatory and hell, one eternal life, and one judgement and resurrection for all.

Yet today there is still a general belief and a fundamental misunderstanding that everybody will go straight to heaven and be saved by what is called "Sola fide," "by God's grace alone," no matter what state of sinfulness they find themselves in when they die. Yes, "It is by grace that you have been saved, through faith; not by anything of your own, but by a gift from God" (Eph. 2:8.) The grace, meaning "pure gift," is that Jesus died willingly for all humanity out of pure love, regardless of whether people are religious or not, and it is not something that men can deserve by their own good actions. With our free will we can either reject this pure gift or accept it by keeping the Ten Commandments. Without our free will, God could have just lorded it over us and made us his puppets.

It is wishful thinking that we will go direct to heaven when we die regardless of what state of sinfulness we find ourselves in. The conditions for being saved are that you must be baptised in the name of our Lord Jesus Christ, repent of your sins, and forgive those who have sinned against you. Forgiveness is dependent on repentance, and those who hang on to grudges obviously find it impossible to forgive. We cannot expect to be forgiven if we are not sorry and do not repent.

Jesus commands clearly: "You have to forgive your brother not seven times, I tell you, but seventy-seven times" (Mt 18:22). And a harsh sentence befalls the unforgiving debtor who had been forgiven but who would not forgive the servant who owed him money: "I had pity on you and cancelled all your debt. Were you not bound to have pity on your fellow servant and cancel his debt?" said the king, and "in his anger he handed him over to the torturers till he should pay all his debt." (Mt 18:32-34)

"Believe in the Lord Jesus Christ and you will be saved", says Paul in Acts16:31. "I tell you, every human sin and blasphemy will be forgiven, but blasphemy against the Holy Spirit will not be forgiven. And anyone who says a word against the Son of man will be forgiven; but no one who speaks against the Holy Spirit, will be forgiven either in this world or in the next" (Mt12:31). What we are saying to God through our refusal to believe in his existence is that He is a nobody, and we reject all his love and goodness. Believing in him, but not in all the supernatural wonders He works, is an act of pride. It is basically telling God that even He cannot change the natural laws of physics.

For God nothing is impossible, He is infinite in his power, infinite in his wisdom, infinite in his mercy, infinite in his love for us, and infinite in his zeal for our salvation. Believing in God is "de facto" believing in the supernatural realm because God is not only a supernatural being but also a person, our Heavenly Father as Jesus affirms in "The Lord's Prayer." Only humility rather than pride will stand us in good stead on the way to salvation.

Forgiveness is the most precious gift Christianity has to offer. God is slow to anger, full of mercy, and ready to forgive and redeem even at the very last moment of our lives. This we call the "extravagant" mercy of God which is best explained in the following parable:

> The kingdom of Heaven is like a landowner who at daybreak made an agreement with some workers for one denarius a day to go and work in his vineyard. But going out about the third hour he saw some others standing idle in the marketplace, and said to them, "You go to my vineyard too and I will pay you a fair wage." And at about the sixth hour and again at the ninth hour, he went out and did the same. At the eleventh hour he went out and found some more standing around and said, "Why have you been standing around idle all day?" "Because no one hired us" they answered. "You go into my vineyard too" he said.
>
> In the evening, the landlord told the bailiff, "Call the workers and pay them their wages, starting with the last arrivals and ending with the first". So those hired at the eleventh hour came forward and received one denarius. When the first came they expected to get more, but they too got one denarius each. They took it but grumbled at the landowner saying, "The men who came last have only done one hour's work though we have done a heavy day's work in all the heat, yet you treat them the same as us." He answered, "My friend, I am not being unjust to you; did we not agree on one denarius for a day? Take your earnings and go. I choose to pay the latecomer as much as I pay you. Have I no right to do what I

like with my own? Why should you be envious because I am generous? Because the last will be first and the first last." (Mt 20:1-16)

This all sounds incredibly unfair and, if we were the early workers, we would certainly protest the injustice of it all. What the story is doing is relating that his mercy and justice are all encompassing and immeasurable. All who have tried so hard all their lives to be faithful to God in all things, often with sweat and tears and many ups and downs, have done what has been expected of them and they will certainly get their just reward. But those who have not bothered to keep the commandments or believed in Him as the Son of God and rejected him outright will also be rewarded with eternal life, provided that at the end, they will find in their hearts the will and humility to say sorry, ask for pardon and cry out for mercy, even if they are motivated by fear. They will be rewarded because God never spurns a humble and contrite heart - anyone who admits that they were wrong and finally accepts Jesus' sacrifice for them on the cross, acknowledging the existence of God and saying sorry, will be rewarded.

This "extravagant mercy of God" that gives all of us hope and a chance to be redeemed at the last minute, is the grace we need to pray for sooner rather than later. We can of course never presume what happens to a person at the end of their lives: we don't know what goes on in the human heart and mind of even the most staunch unbeliever or the greatest sinner, and we have the consolation that just whispering sorry will be embraced by God's extravagant mercy, which is so deep-reaching and beyond recall. And added to this, we have Jesus' comforting words, "In my Father's house there are many mansions" (Jn14:1-6). There is redemption for all. But why wait until it might be too late: we never know when the great reaper will come and knock on our door. The day of decision is the day to repent and to act is the maxim.

Our other redeeming grace will be our compassion and love for the poor and the needy, for the immigrant, and the prisoner. When we have loved much, we will be forgiven much. The parable explains:

> When the Son of Man comes in his glory, escorted by all the angels, then he will take his seat on the throne of glory. All the nations will be assembled before him, and he will separate men from one another as the shepherd separates sheep from goats. Then the King will say to the ones on his right, "Come, you whom my Father has blessed, take for your heritage the kingdom prepared for you since the foundation of the world. For I was hungry, and you gave me food; I was thirsty, and you gave me drink; I was a stranger and you made me welcome; naked and you clothed me; sick and you visited me; in prison and you came to see me." And they will ask, "Lord when did we do all these things for you?" And the King will answer, "I tell you solemnly, in as far as you did this to one of the least brothers of mine, you did it to me". Next, he will say to those on his left hand, "Go away from me with your curse upon you, to the eternal fire prepared for the devil and his angels. For I was hungry, and thirsty and naked and a stranger and in prison and you totally neglected to look after any of the least of these brothers of mine, you neglected me." And they will go away to eternal punishment, and the virtuous to eternal life. (Mt 25:31-46)

HELL

"Do not be afraid of those who kill the body but cannot kill the soul, fear him rather who can destroy both body and soul in hell"

HEAVEN HELL AND REPENTANCE

(Mt 10:28-29).

"If your right eye should be your downfall, tear it out and throw it away; for it will do you less harm to lose one part of yourself than to have your whole body thrown into hell" (Mt 5:29).

The existence of hell is a difficult and fearful truth nobody wants to share, and no one wants to hear about, and the very idea of it has been greatly denied and repulsed. The above quotes are of just two of the many occasions Jesus mentioned hell, so we cannot just dismiss it as fantasy. It remains an abhorrent notion, nevertheless. Not only in the New Testament, but also in the Old, do we find hell mentioned. Hell is not so much a punishment as a choice, as we saw above; if we side with Satan we will go where Satan is, if we side with God, we will go where God is. The Catechism of the Catholic Church affirms the existence of hell clearly: "Immediately after death the souls of those who die in a state of mortal sin descend into hell ... The chief punishment of hell is eternal separation from God, in whom alone man can possess the life and happiness for which he was created and for which he longs." (CCC#1035)

The film, "The Seven Deadly Sins" springs to mind when we read about mortal or deadly sin, but it is not something we hear a lot of these days. There is a mention of deadly sin in 1 John 5:16, "There is sin that leads to death, every kind of wickedness is sin, but not all sin leads to death". The Catechism of Christian Doctrine states, "What are the deadly sins and why are they called deadly? They are called deadly because they are the source from which all other sins originate, and they merit hell when not confessed and atoned for before dying. They are pride, covetousness, lust, anger, gluttony, envy and sloth." These form the wellspring for all the evil that comes from the human heart enumerated by Jesus in the chapter on the Ten Commandments.

(Mt 15:19). However, "sloth" as a deadly sin causes confusion. It is usually associated with laziness, but it manifests other aspects too. It can be defined as an aversion to spiritual things and uses the excuse of being too busy to take the time to explore the reality of God, to pray, to go to church and study their faith.

Mirjana, one of the visionaries of Medjugorje, asked Our Lady, "Why is God so merciless in sending sinners to Hell?" Her reply was: "Men who go to hell no longer want to receive any benefit from God, they do not repent, nor do they cease to swear and blaspheme. They make up their mind to live in hell and do not at all contemplate leaving." By this reply was meant that if we refuse to believe in the message of the Good News of The Bible, refuse to repent of all our bad deeds, and reject God outright, ignore our neighbour, and are impenitent to the very end, then we have made our choice.

Various saints have received visions of hell, such as St Don Bosco, St Theresa of Avilla, and St Faustina Kowalska, who in her diary tells us that some of the punishments are "the loss of God, a perpetual remorse of conscience, continued darkness, despair and hatred of God. But she said, "I noticed one thing, that most of the souls there are of those who did not believe that there is a hell."

Its existence was also one of the important messages of Fatima. The young visionaries were given a glimpse of what it was like. Sr Lucia writes, "First Our Lady showed us purgatory and then hell. We saw it as a vast sea of fire, terrifying to behold. Plunged in the fire we saw demons and the souls of the damned. The latter were in human form. The demons were distinguished from the souls by their repellent likeness to unnamed animals, black and transparent."

How can a loving God, who created us for love, let us perish if all He ever wanted for humanity was eternal life? The question is not "why is there such a punishment as hell?" The question is, "why do we reject a loving God?" And though we are guilty of a thousand hideous sins, his infinite mercy is always ready to forgive and stop us from being separated from Him forever. So, we all stand a chance to claim our reward; as He is perfect, his mercy and judgement are also perfect.

Consideration of the horrors perpetrated in the world that horrify and demand justice puts into perspective again the enormity of sin and evil We can envisage that rejecting this wilful sacrifice brings God's perfect judgement over us. The question often arises why the Christian faith is the most persecuted faith of all faiths; it is because it is the constant spiritual battle of two armies, headed by two powers, one personified by all that is good, one personified by all that is evil; the battlefield is the world and the price, the human soul.

THE WALK OF THE PILGRIM

> "Follow right to the end the way that I mark out for you, and you will prosper says the Lord" (Jeremiah 7:23).

Our walk through life is like that of a pilgrim who walks with one aim in mind, to reach unscathed the purpose he set out to achieve, regardless of all the dangers he will encounter on the way. He does not take the highway, but rather a dangerous mountain path that clings to the side of a rock with steep precipices at the outer edge. He resolves to walk this path as a challenge, with purpose and tenacity to reach his goal unhurt and unscathed. This requires the cunning of a fox and the wisdom of an owl to avoid the constant pitfalls and dangers of rock falls, slippery slopes, narrow gullies, wild animals, aggressive birds, waiting reptiles, narrow passages and, in the valleys, tempting oases. At the end of each day, he views his progress, bandages his bruised feet, blisters and bumps and sets out the next day full of courage resolving not to get battered as before. Each day the going gets better as he becomes astute in avoiding a rockfall, a snake blocking the path, a hole in the road, or an enticing mirage. Ploughing on, he perseveres no matter what, because like any athlete, he is determined to gain that trophy, that gold medal which at the end he will be able to claim as rightfully his. This trophy for the believer is the Beatific Vision.

We frail humans rather opt for the highway on which the going appears smooth but, to our sorrow, we discover it is rather treacherous, that it has no specific destination and has many possibilities for taking wrong turns. As children we were taught to do some "Ritual Cleansing:" not of our bodies, but of our hearts and inspect "our bruised feet and blisters" every day. In other words, we searched our conscience and said sorry for the times we had failed and firmly resolved to do better the next day. "Never go to sleep in mortal sin, not even for a single night," we were told. If we don't keep a tag on where we go wrong, it is easy to slip into situations which have no redress.

Late in the day, if at all, people wonder how they can repent and make good the adverse circumstances and their consequences, created by all the wrong choices they made in their lives. A broken marriage, ruining our health by excesses, hurting our children, parents, neighbours; all have negative consequences. The remedy is to have the courage to examine where they went wrong, accept the responsibility for the hurt caused, say sorry, ask for forgiveness and move on. Many tend to carry a rucksack of guilt throughout life and bear its debilitating effect on their mental and physical wellbeing. Forgiveness of self or of others helps to achieve better health and an inner peace with others and with God. Unforgiveness can lead to self-loathing and guilt and create a distance from self and others: it leads to anxiety and depression. And evil done on a social scale will destroy peace between the injured parties or nations unless they can forgive each other.

Saying sorry frees the conscience and the mind and restores peace within and without. It is important to own up to the mistakes made, rather than blaming others for the disaster they wreak. How many parents ask their children for forgiveness for messing up their lives and depriving them of the family bond and the security it offers? Or how many people say sorry to a separated spouse or a hurt friend or parent? And most importantly, we cannot keep grudges and be unforgiving. These are great blocks to our physical and mental health. The hurt festers on both sides, guilt builds up, ruins our health and often leads to depression. People cannot be forgiven by God if they do not forgive others. It is to Him we need to cry out for forgiveness, for it is He alone who can set us free.

There is not a single person who does not desire love, justice, peace, happiness, long life, food and drink, warmth and good health, and no one desires sickness, war, persecution, starvation, greed; the list goes on. Now we know the stakes, now we can make a choice. "God left us free to make our own decisions. He has set fire and water before you, put out your hand to whichever you prefer. Man has death or life before him, which ever a man likes better he will be given" Deuteronomy 30:19.

19

APPARITIONS OF MARY

Near the cross of Jesus stood his mother and his mother's sister, Mary the wife of Clopas and Mary of Magdala. Seeing his mother and the disciple he loved standing near her, Jesus said to his mother, "Woman this is your son." Then to the disciple he said, "Woman this is your mother." And from that moment the disciple made a place for her in his home. (Jn 19:25-27)

Jesus is Mary's only son, but her spiritual motherhood extends to all men and women whom he came to save, states the Catechism of the Catholic Church.

Our Salvation story would not be complete without the mention of Our Lady, who was so intrinsically linked with it. She gave Jesus his human DNA and his human blood which was poured out on the cross for our salvation. All through her life she must have been agonizing about what would ultimately happen to this child she conceived in such an unusual way. Simeon's prophecy in Luke 2:35, that a sword would pierce her heart too, must have shocked her to the core, pondering what it all meant. This prophecy was fulfilled all through her life, but never more so than on Calvary at the foot of the cross, seeing her son dying in the most excruciating of agonies. Her suffering must have been all the more agonising as she realised that he had wilfully chosen to die in this way. Through this intense suffering, as only a mother can suffer, she became intimately and painfully united to his suffering and she cooperated with her son in a unique way in his redemption of all humanity. In her numerous apparitions throughout the Christian era, she became God's messenger and intercessor for us, and, like a true mother, she is constantly warning, chastising, and consoling humankind, while always leading us to her son Jesus.

The front page of the National Geographic Magazine of Friday, 11th December 2015, dubs "Mary the most Powerful Woman in the World". The article goes on to say that Mary has inspired countless works of art and millions have visited the shrines of the 2000 reported sightings of her worldwide since AD 40.

The enormous interest of millions of people in one woman would certainly make her worthy of the title "The most popular woman in the world." This popularity however does not make Mary the most powerful woman in the world, for the tangible power at apparition sites is the power of Jesus, her son, which is manifested through her intercession. Her role is always to draw us to Jesus, not to herself.

St Bernard says, "She is the advocate of humanity, so quick to do good to mortals that, so far, no one has ever come before her who has not been heard, helped, and remedied." St Augustine confirmed this praise, adding, "She is so powerful that whatever she says happens."

Over the centuries, the United Kingdom has been blessed with numerous apparitions of Our Lady. Glastonbury is the oldest recorded site of pilgrimage in England associated with a miraculous statue of the Virgin Mary dating back to the 7th century. "The actual miracle only happened around 1234 when the new Abbey Church was burnt to the ground together with the 7th century church which housed the statue. The statue however miraculously survived and was placed in the newly built church. From then, Glastonbury became a place of pilgrimage until the reformation around 1538" (a).

The next in line must be Walsingham in Norfolk. In 1061 a noblewoman Richeldis Faverches, wanting to do something special for Our Lady, asked her what favour she could give her as a present. Our Lady led her in the spirit to the house in Nazareth where the annunciation had taken place and asked her to build a replica in Walsingham. The story goes, that after many mishaps the house was finally built overnight, by angels in the right materials and on the right site stipulated by Mary. Because of the many crusades which took place in the 11th century, pilgrims were unable to visit Jerusalem, and the house of Nazareth in Walsingham became instead a great place of pilgrimage. King Henry III came many times and it became one of the centres of his devotion, and King Henry VIII came twice. Walsingham became the foremost shrine of pilgrimage in Europe, after Rome and Compostela. (b)

Belgium has been favoured with several apparitions from Our Lady, the most famous being Banneux, and Beauraign from November 1932 to January 1933. Banneux escaped the destruction of WW1 after the people promised in 1914 to consecrate the village to Our Lady. Our Lady appeared to Mariette Beco in this poor part of the country and said that she had come to console the sick and the suffering and called herself the Virgin of the Poor. She said: "I am the Mother of the Redeemer, the Mother of God. Pray hard." Many miracles have been reported at the spring since then, in which she asked

Mariette to put her hand. "This spring is reserved for "Me" this source is reserved for "All The Nations" she declared to Mariette. (c)

Interestingly, many years later Mary declared again that she was the "Lady of all Nations" when on 20 March 1953 she appeared in Amsterdam to Ida Peerdeman. She appeared 56 times to Ida and requested Ida to pay great attention to what she was about to say. Our Lady requested the official recognition of her vocation as "Co-Redemptrix, Mediatrix and Advocate and that as Lady of All Nations she would give peace, true peace to the world. This is the new and final Marian dogma which will be greatly disputed but it will pull through." (d)

Our Lady also appeared in Japan, this time with many miraculous phenomena which we will not recount here. Suffice to say that on 12 June 1973 Sister Agnes Sasagawa saw a brilliant mysterious light coming from the tabernacle which was repeated the next two days. On 28 June a cross-shaped wound appeared on the inside of her left hand which bled profusely and was very painful. On 6 July Sr Agnes heard a voice coming from the statue of Mary which was made from one block of wood, and which would bleed human tears on many occasions. Our Lady asked Sr Agnes to pray with her to her Son who is truly present in the Eucharist and said that the heavenly Father is preparing to inflict a great chastisement on ungrateful mankind if they do not mend their ways. "Pray, do penance and courageous sacrifices to soften the Father's anger. (e)

Lourdes in the French Pyrenees must be the most well known and most popular of all pilgrim sites in the world. When I grew up it was this story that was talked about most at home as well as at school. Each year the sick and disabled travel in their thousands to Lourdes in the hope of a cure after immersion in the spring endowed with miraculous powers. Many people, especially the young, go as volunteers to help the sick and report receiving a great blessing from the experience.

On 11th February 1858 Our Lady appeared to a poor fourteen-year-old girl, Bernadette Soubirous, in the village of Lourdes. This was the first of eighteen apparitions to Bernadette. As in many of her apparitions, Our Lady requested Bernadette to pray for sinners, to do much penance. She also requested for a chapel to be built and for people to come in procession, meaning that she wanted people to worship united with one another. But it was the spring with the miraculous healing powers which was such a great draw for pilgrims. The stream was at first silted up and no longer flowing, but Our Lady asked Bernadette to clear it and the next day it produced a staggering 5000 litres of water. After bathing in the spring miraculous healings started immediately and have continued to this day. She also told Bernadette her special name which was of great significance, she said, "I am the Immaculate Conception." With this name, she gave, as it were, a divine verdict meaning that she was without sin from birth, that she was a virgin who conceived Jesus through the Holy Spirit and thus, that Jesus was God, and she was the Mother of God. Bernadette being illiterate at the time of the apparitions, would never have heard this name for our Lady, or have understood it. Since the Dogma of the Immaculate Conception had been declared by Pope Pius IX in 1854, it authenticated Bernadette's claim that it was really the Virgin who had appeared to her. (f)

Hundreds of pages could be written about Marian apparitions worldwide. She appeared in La Sallette in the French Alps on 19th September 1846 and asked for respect for the name of God, to abstain from work on Sundays, to pray daily and to receive the sacrament of penance and the Eucharist often. After this incredible revelation, the whole region took to heart the message and experienced a profound Christian revival. She also appeared again in France, in the Rue du Bac to a nun, Catherine Laboure. She appeared with rays shining from her hands symbolising the graces she gives to those who ask for them. She asked for a special medal to be made with the words, "O, Mary, conceived without sin, pray for us who have recourse to thee". After 141 years Catherine's body is still totally intact. She lies encased in a glass coffin at the altar of the Chapel of the Miraculous Medal, in de Rue du Bac. and many visitors are drawn to it each year. (g) Some other famous apparitions occurred in Guadaloupe, Mexico, in Garabandal, Spain, on top of Mount St Michel in Gargano, in Ampullia in Italy, in Unterflossing in Bavaria, to Simon Stock in Kent, and in Knock in Ireland. There is a shrine dedicated to Mary in Westminster Abbey called our Lady of Pewe, which originally may have meant, "Our Lady of the Poor" and there are other numerous Shrines of Our Lady across England. (h)

The apparitions in Fatima, Portugal, deserve a special mention for their predictions, for their messages and especially for the world-famous miracle of the sun and for the vision of hell which the children received.

> The apparitions of the Virgin Mary in Fatima, Portugal, were gospel-like in their seriousness, simplicity and credibility. All the events she prophesied were fulfilled, the conversion of Russia, the end of the first World War, and a new war coming, and so was Our Lady's promise of a sign at the 6th and last apparition. She appeared to three shepherd children, Lucia, Francisco and Jacinta as a lady dressed in white, shining brighter than the sun, and giving out rays of a bright and intensive light. The chosen seers were young, Francisco and Lucia were eight and Jacinta was seven. They were

innocent and incapable of conjuring or embellishing what they had seen. Our Lady spoke like a messenger, plainly and objectively and listened attentively to the questions the children asked. The same theme as in all apparitions, ran through all 6 visits: pray for sinners or they will go to hell because they have nobody to pray for them. Pray the rosary every day for peace in the world, do a lot of penance, and people must convert or there would be terrible consequences. And she promised a portentous sign, so that all might believe.

It was a bad time for such an apparition and such a promise. In 1908 King Carlos and his heir Prince Louis Felipe were assassinated, and a Republic was installed. The new government were adamantly anticlerical and aimed at secularising centuries-old Catholic Portugal. The apparition deeply disturbed the status quo which went as far as to imprison the children. But God was at work and the sign that Our Lady had promised happened.

On October 13 maybe as many as 70.000 thousand spectators filled the Cova da Iria, among them journalists, the curious and the incredulous. The day was rainy but suddenly the seers saw a bright light after which our Lady appeared atop the usual holm oak. Mary asked for a chapel to be built and revealed that she was "The Lady of the Rosary". She predicted that World War One would soon end and the soldiers would soon come home. Lucia asked for a cure for some sick people to which Our Lady responded, "Some yes, some no. They must amend their lives and ask forgiveness for their sins." On saying this she opened her hands projecting the light coming from the children unto the sun. Lucia cried, "Look at the sun." The heavy clouds parted revealing a huge silver disc. Though it shone intensely it did not blind. The sphere began to dance, then spin rapidly like a giant circle of fire. It stopped momentarily then spun vertiginously again, its rim scarlet, scattering flames through the sky. The changing lights were reflected onto the faces of the spectators, on the trees, on the ground in fantastic hues. After performing this incredible pattern twice, the fiery globe trembled, shook and plunged towards the earth in a zigzag. People screamed. All this lasted a few minutes. The sun then zigzagged back to its place and resumed its normal appearance. People noticed that their rain-soaked clothes were dry and so were the pools of water that had formed in the fields. Engineers later confirmed that an enormous amount of energy was necessary to dry those pools in a few minutes. Numerous people who were 25 miles away also saw the miracle of the sun. To the chagrin of the secularists but the support of the faithful, newspapermen present reported the miracle throughout the world. The miracle of the sun sealed the authenticity of the Fatima message, a crucial message for the sinful troubled times. (i)

The one apparition site I have visited, is the most recent one in Medjugorje, Croatia, formerly Yugoslavia. This small village was totally unknown until, on June 25, 1981, Our Lady appeared to six young persons, Mirjana Dragijevic, Ivanka and Vicka Ivankovic, Ivan Dragijevic, Maria Pavlovic and Jacov Colo. In 1981 Yugoslavia was still governed by a strict communist regime, and religious practice was very limited. But the news of the apparition spread quickly through the country and within days of the first apparition, thousands of people were accompanying the children up the hill for their apparition. The authorities reacted quickly and barricaded the entrance to the hill with barbed wire and soldiers. However, Fr Jozo, the then local priest, protected the children and allowed them to have the apparition in the local church. This act of kindness was to earn him a three-year jail sentence and torture. After this, the church was closed by the authorities and, in an attempt to stop the children from receiving the apparition at the appointed time, they were driven away to some unknown destination. On this journey, the cars suddenly came to an abrupt halt and the children rushed out and Mary appeared there and then, on the side of the road. This experience had such a shocking effect on the three drivers of the cars that they immediately believed. After this, Mary promised the children that she would appear to them wherever in the world they were. Even if they were separated in different countries, she would appear to them at the same time, and this has been so until now.

Mary revealed herself to be "Mother of God," and "Queen of Peace." The group of six met with her every day and to this day four still see her daily, one sees her once a year, two see her on a daily basis and the other on her birthday. She said, "I have come to tell you that God exists. He is fullness of life, and to enjoy this fullness and obtain peace you must return to God." As at Fatima, she repeats the conditions for peace in the world – peace through prayer, fasting and repentance. Mankind must be reconciled to God and with one another." The message is for the entire world.

The visionaries underwent exhaustive investigations by doctors and scientists. These investigations concluded that the young people were seeing a person who is external to themselves and whom they can hear as well as touch. One can observe the children during the apparition, and there is no mistaking that they all lift their heads and eyes in the same direction, at the same level, and at the same time, and their eyes do not blink once for the whole duration. Our Lady comes surrounded by a brilliant light out of which she emerges. "They describe her as being no more than 19-20 years old, beautiful beyond words, radiant with holiness and, as a rule, smiling. She is overflowing with tenderness and love just like a real mother and they describe her as being slender, with dark hair and blue eyes, wearing a translucent silver-grey robe with a white veil reaching down to her feet, and wearing a crown of 12 stars" (j).

A fascinating story has emerged very recently relating that, during the communist regime, Catholics were only allowed to say Mass once a year. To do so they were to congregate in a small unknown tucked-away village in the hills; this village, it was discovered, was Medjugorje! God works in mysterious ways. Many supernatural phenomena appear there on the hills and in the sky, people have seen burning crosses and had the silver chain of their rosary turn to gold. Many who had their rosary examined by a jeweller received confirmation that it is real old gold. Just as in Fatima, seeing the sun spin and pulsate is another incredible experience. With God being the creator of the universe, as Christians we expect there to be supernatural activity, because the whole notion of there being a God pertains to the supernatural, and it is not a static God, but a God constantly at work in the world and in the human soul and mind. One predominant experience of Medjugorje is the feeling of peace that surrounds one as soon as one sets foot on the soil.

It is estimated that 40 million people of all religious persuasions and none, have visited Medjugorje since the first apparition in 1981 and, as with all supernatural experiences, we can only ascertain their authenticity by the fruit they bear. Such fruit is evident in the story of Wintershall, a country estate tucked away in the Surrey hills.

THE STORY OF WINTERSHALL

The story of Wintershall starts with Charlotte, Anne and Peter Hutley's daughter, telling her mother how she met a priest at a wedding reception who had just returned from a small village in Croatia where the Virgin was appearing to six young children and giving them messages for the world. The priest had been so struck by the messages and what they contained, that it had profoundly changed his life; and that for the first time in thirty years, he knew for sure why he had become a priest.

Anne says, "When she told me this, I immediately knew that I had to go there." This was quite a strange impulse seeing that Anne had been brought up an Anglican, but then maybe not so unusual as she had attended a Catholic school as a child. There she had been strongly influenced by the film, The "Song of Bernadette" which tells the story of the Virgin Mary appearing to Bernadette Soubirous in Lourdes. "I had believed that, like the child Bernadette, I too one day would see the Virgin Mary, but my mother would not hear of this nonsense and took me away from the convent of St Mary, but I never forgot the Virgin Mary nor the rosary, and later I was to recall the Stations of the Cross which had been such a big part of convent life".

Anne's story

Of the many consequent visits Anne and Peter made to Medjugorje, two stand out and are recounted by Anne in the following paragraphs. One was the wonderful healing of their grandson and the other the message Anne received which, like a seed once planted, became the miracle of Wintershall that has grown over the years into a great vigorous life-giving tree, including such events as the Nativity Play, the Passion Play and the Life of Christ. These are now yearly events attracting thousands of visitors from all over the country. In Anne's own words:

> On one of our earlier visits in 1989, Charlotte's eldest son, Kyle, was healed at the tenth Station of the Cross in Medjugorje. Rupert and family were going to Australia for a

time, and were packed and ready to leave, except their little boy was suddenly suffering a great pain. Eventually the diagnosis was made at Great Ormond Street Hospital that Kyle had a condition known as Perthes disease. It is an incurable disease of the hip joint, rendering the boy unable to walk and he faced a boyhood with callipers and severe limitations for years to come. Kyle was examined by various other doctors and after more X-rays they all came to the same conclusion. Kyle was four and a half at the time. It seemed that there was nothing the doctors could do so Charlotte started to search for alternative help. I had also done myself some frantic praying and I mentally handed him over to the Lord. My love for him could not cure him but His love could if He willed. I decided to take him to Medjugorje (I am not a Catholic), I really wanted Kyle to be blessed there, and especially by one very saintly monk Fr Jozo.

-Charlotte and Rupert would not leave for Australia before taking their children to Medjugorje for a blessing from Father Jozo. Rupert had walked the Hill of the Cross, known as Krisivac, with Kyle on his shoulders as he was unable to walk. But it was at the 10th Station of the Cross that Kyle said to his dad, "Daddy put me down, I am alright now" and when Rupert put him down on the ground, apparently he threw his stick away, and ran up the hill, never to complain of pain again. Later when Charlotte and Rupert took Kyle to Ormond Street Hospital again, after their return for the last X-ray before he was to be transferred to the Sydney Orthopaedic Hospital, they admitted that there must have been a mistake. The X rays were perfectly normal; Kyle had been healed. Kyle had further X-rays at Harley Street, these X rays also showed a totally normal hip joint.

The second story that Anne Hutley told me is this:

THE GOOD NEWS NOBODY TALKS ABOUT

I was persuaded by our second son Edward to accept an invitation to go on a retreat in Medjugorje given by Fr Jozo. Seeing that Fr Jozo was so holy, Edward reckoned that it would be like going on a retreat with Jesus himself. I decided to go but before I left, I received a book to take with me, from my local vicar with the inscription, "To Anne, don't let the saints get you down." This is exactly what happened. As I was the only Anglican in a party of twenty or so I felt totally out of my depth, unhappy and unsure of myself. Everything we did, the services we went to, the meals we took together, was beyond me and I longed to go home. Father Jozo was a delightful person, but I was soon nicknamed Anglican Annie, as Anglicans were beyond him. It was very puzzling to him that I had been both baptised and confirmed.

The day I was due to leave, I attended a healing service in the Church and my companion encouraged me to go forward to the altar for healing. As I went, the priest who conducted the service threw holy water over me as he passed through the congregation, whereupon I lost consciousness or so I thought, as I had never heard of "falling in the Spirit." As I came to, lying on the floor, I looked straight up to the statue of the Virgin Mary which was above me, and I was filled with peace and joy. It was all very strange, and as I lay there, the words I had heard in the sermon kept repeating, "Build a monument." When it was time to say goodbye to Father Jozo, I handed him my rosary which had turned to gold. Then he said, "Go home and next time bring your husband".

When I returned to England apparently looking quite ill, the words "Build a monument, so that the world, and your greatgrandchildren will know that the Blessed Mother came here, at this time, asking the world to repent and to pray within the family" were reverberating in my mind. I started to discuss this extraordinary message with Edward, wondering what monument this was supposed to be, and both of us suddenly fell upon the idea of the Stations of the Cross, which is a devotion always close to my heart. I had in fact painted fourteen tiny Stations for St Francis chapel by the lakeside, and then found to my amazement that there were seven beams on each side of the chapel and that they just fitted. It was easy then to envisage a bigger and expanded version around the garden, starting by the Lake and going right up the hill to Holly Barn with its staggering views over the countryside. After applying to famous international sculptors for ideas, from whom we got no reply at all, we decided to contact schools and colleges and try to find unknown students who might be interested in such a project. Before long, the phone began to ring, and the requests came in. My only stipulation was that they should meditate on the stations, pray a little and then come back to me with the station of their choice. Operation "Mustard Seed" had started. Before long, these talented and thoughtful young people "came all the way with me" and soon they knew exactly what they wanted to create.

Soon we had to decide where we were going to place the stations, so one evening, Henri, Nic and myself walked up the hill with fifteen white sticks. This was an important evening, for we were going to mark out where the Stations were to be placed. Would they fit and how would they be gently melting into the background and where on earth was the Tomb station going to be? It was raining softly as we placed our markers in the ground trying to envisage how it would all look. At last the project was taking shape, but it was while we were at the 12th Station, the Crucifixion, that the sky changed completely. When we placed the stake into the ground and rounded the corner of the hill into the open, we all three gasped at the sun. It had suddenly come out through the rain – brilliant and unexpected. It was bouncing and pulsating and moving up and down in the sky. Nic gasped with astonishment, as we all did, and a white disc in the centre of the sun made it possible to look at it. The rain had stopped, and as we approached the top of the hill, we looked back. To our amazement, the most beautiful little rainbow encircled the way of the cross from where we had just come. The rainbow was so near that one could almost touch it. We could hardly speak. When we reached the barn itself and looked back, another rainbow encircled the first. We went home shaking with what we had seen. Later that night, Henrietta and Nic phoned to tell us that the moon was bright pink, so we all felt that we had received a sign of affirmation that the Stations of the Cross were right for Wintershall after all. Later each of the young sculptors wrote to me testifying how their lives had been touched in some way, changed by being involved in "Operation Mustard Seed". (k)

Now at 7 am on every first Friday of the month, people gather from all the surrounding villages to walk The Stations of the Cross.

Peter's story

Wintershall has seen the plays, "The Life of Christ," "The Nativity" and "The Passion of Christ" (all written by Peter Hutley), enacted in its glorious grounds for many years now. The Nativity started in 1989 and the Passion Play in 1993. This was then expanded into the Life of Christ in 1999. The Passion play is also enacted on Guildford's High Street on Good Friday. And since 2010 The Passion of Christ is performed twice every Good Friday in Trafalgar Square in London, visible from enormous screens to an estimated audience of twenty thousand shoppers, tourists and passers-by who happen to saunter past, leaving a deep impression on all who watch it. But we shall let Peter Hutley, the author of the plays, relate how all this came about:

> Although always wanting to be a writer, the driving force in my life was to provide a safe home for my wife, children, and grandchildren, but it all changed in 1998. That year I read somewhere that the Pope had said that we should prepare for the Millennium, and it flashed into my mind that there would be no millennium without Jesus. He had started the beginning of our new centuries.
>
> I instantly thought that I should write a play on the Life of Christ (to mark the Millenium), produce it, get people to act in it and obtain directors and do all the things that are necessary to make it known. I didn't appreciate everything that I would have to do at the time. I was gifted to own Wintershall, perhaps that is why I was able to buy it and expand the lands. I knew immediately where I would put Mary's house and where to act out the crucifixion and then the resurrection. What a wonderful memento I would make of all that.

Peter spent the rest of 1998 and the beginning of 1999 writing the play and realised that a few performances should be undertaken that same year before going into full production in 2000. He obtained the services of a National Trust director skilled in organising outside events. After using three actors to perform the crucially important role of Jesus, he chose James Burke-Dunsmore whom he had met earlier, and he has performed the part ever since.

Peter continues:

THE GOOD NEWS NOBODY TALKS ABOUT

Performances and extracts have been performed in Australia and South Africa and in this country, in Staines, where all denominations have collaborated and used the Wintershall script. Other towns have done the same and we are looking to branch out to many more great towns and cities in UK. Scripts and advice on how to perform the play are available to all who are eager to spread the name of Jesus. In the meantime, thousands flock to Wintershall for the six days each year that we perform.

I am always delighted that hundreds of children are regularly coming to the performances in school parties and that the public demonstration of Jesus' public life becomes known to them. I prayed regularly that the truth as to who Jesus really was, and the fact that he came to Palestine over 2000 ago as the Son of God, was being truly represented by our play.

I am overwhelmed with emotion when strangers tell me how their lives have benefitted so much from seeing the Life of Christ at Wintershall, and often they did not know I had anything to do with it. The Passion of Christ in Trafalgar Square every Good Friday, I pray will continue for ever despite its great cost. So many people realise they want to know about Jesus, but they don't know how to do it. (l)

20

THE BIBLE

Man cannot live by bread alone but by every word which comes from the mouth of God. (Matthew 4:4.)

"I don't believe in the Bible," "The Bible is not the word of God?" "Why are we not allowed to see the other scrolls which have been discovered recently?" These are some opinions people express about the Bible. One way to address these questions is to consider the quote under the chapter heading, which is the response of Jesus to Satan who had told him to "turn these stones into loaves" after Jesus had fasted for 40 days. The response intimates that God not only provides for our bread to feed our bodies, like the manna He gave to the Israelites in the desert, but that His word feeds our souls. And this is the Word that we read in the Bible.

The Bible was not written for God. It was written by people inspired by the Holy Spirit to convey God's dreams and desires for humanity. In 2 Timothy 3:16 it says that all scripture is inspired by God, and Jesus confirms this when he quotes from Isaiah, "All will be thought by God" (Is 54:13). To read the

Bible as any ordinary piece of literature totally misses the purpose of the exercise. "The word of the Lord is something alive and active, it cuts more incisively than a two-edged sword, it can seek out the place where the soul is divided from the spirit or joints from the marrow. It can pass judgement on secret emotions and thoughts" (Heb 4:12). This is the desired effect it should have if we care to read it with reverence and ask the Holy Spirit to open our minds with his formidable power to activate our zeal, our faith and our love.

Gandhi had a great admiration for Jesus' teaching, but not so much for how we Christians put the Word into practice. He said, "You Christians have in your keeping a document with enough dynamite in it to blow civilization to bits, to turn society upside down, to bring peace to this war-torn world, yet you treat it like an ordinary piece of literature." (a) And long before Gandhi was born, St Jerome warned us that "ignorance of the Bible is ignorance of Jesus."

Yes, Gandhi was right, we have great trouble taking God's word seriously and fail to put it to good use. Throughout the previous pages it has been evident that those who followed God's ways revealed in the Word of The Bible have blown preconceived ideas, unbelief, scorn and scepticism to bits when they spoke the words that Jesus spoke – like Damian and Jackie and Dr Scott Peck, and Fr William Bowden who exorcised Robbie Mannheim, and the people of El Paso. These people have without doubt transformed people's lives from suffering wrecks into men and women fully alive in body, mind and spirit.

In this lovely gospel story, Jesus, by pointing to the prophesies about himself in the Old Testament, reiterates the validity and the truth of the whole of the Bible:

Two of the disciples were talking about all that had happened in Jerusalem, and how this Jesus of Nazareth proved he was a great prophet by the things he said and did, and how the chief priests and leaders had him crucified. And how some women of their group had seen a vision of an angel who declared that he was alive and how they had hoped that he would be the one who would set Israel free. But Jesus had walked up behind them, and something prevented them from recognising him. He asked what they were talking about. When they told him what they had been discussing, Jesus said, "You foolish men, so slow to believe the message of the prophets! Was it not ordained that the Christ would suffer and so enter into his glory?" Then, starting from Moses and going through all the prophets, he explained to them the passages throughout the scriptures that were about himself.

As it was late, they invited him to come and stay with them. So, he came in and when they were at table, he took the bread, said the blessing, and handed it them. And their eyes were opened, and they recognised him, but he had vanished from their sight. Then they said to each other, "Did not our hearts burn within us as he talked to us on the road, and explained the scriptures to us?" (Lk 24 13:35)

And here is the crunch: their hearts burned within them as they heard the scriptures. This is the effect the word of God has on us, or rather is meant to have: if we read it with reverence and wonder, then our hearts will also burn within us.

More life-transforming miracles on the world stage could be enacted if more exposed themselves to the graphic description in Hebrews of a "two-edged sword." This sword is meant to convict us. And this word does not lie, it cuts us to the quick. It makes us sit upright and take stock of our spiritual shortcomings and sinfulness. The dictionary defines "convict" "to make a person admit he is guilty of sin," or "declare guilty by verdict." Such conviction hits between the eyes and does not let go, it goes to bed with you, and you get up with it. It is telling us that all is not well with the way we live, and it challenges us to a change of heart, to repentance and a returning back to God who is always waiting with open arms. "Blessed are those who hear the Word of God and keep it" (Lk 11:27-28). "For the prayer of a righteous man is powerful and effective" (James 5:16).

In the chapter about conversions that follows, I hope to show how the double-edged sword in the Bible has cut to the quick three persons who have whole-heartedly responded and have never looked back.

21

GREAT CONVERSIONS

Your new birth was not from any mortal seed but from the everlasting Word of the living and eternal God. (1 Peter 1:23)

"Knowing God through personal experience", Mysticism, and Revelation are the properties of Christian spirituality. As we have seen and contrary to general belief, God still reveals himself today to the most unlikely of people. From criminal to saint, to the everyday man and woman in the street, He shares his desires for that person's wellbeing and is always waiting for us to turn to him because "all are loved by God."

The desire or conviction for people that their lives need changing can be triggered by many factors; through books, through other people's prayer, by a feeling of emptiness and longing, by remorse, by misfortune or by a sentence in The Bible which cuts them to the heart. In most stories, we find recurring patterns in people's experiences, which they can only describe as having an irresistible desire to confess, to be drawn to go to church frequently, to start praying, to want to receive communion and to be drawn to reading the Bible. One experience, however, that is common to all, is being overwhelmed by an incredible feeling of love and the knowledge that God loves them. The following stories will show abundantly, how Jesus still has something to offer and which, sadly, our present world is so eager to deny.

CONVERSION STORY FROM A PRISON CELL

I told the Methodist preacher that when I take the bread and the wine at communion, I feel a warm feeling. He told me how much Jesus loves me and that I should read the Bible. In my cell I tore a page from my Bible to roll a cigarette, but an inner voice said, "Read it." It was the Gospel of John. The more I read the more I wanted to know about this Jesus. The only image of Jesus I had seen came powerfully to mind. Outside the police station a cross with Jesus on it stood in front of a Catholic church. I stood with my eyes shut tight and that image of Jesus became visibly alive, I saw His wounds and the blood, then Jesus lifted His head and looked at me and his eyes were piercing my soul. He said, "Richard, I did this for you". I just broke down with tears flowing. I said, "Lord, I give you my life". Then all the years of crime, drugs and aggression were rolled away! But I thought I still needed my regular fix from my drugs, or I would be in a mess. Several days went but I did not experience any withdrawal. It came as a beautiful dawn, mentally and physically, I was free! (a) (*Name withheld*)

FROM DRUG ADDICTION TO FAITH IN GOD

I really never thought it would come to this, but here was I with my friend listening to an ex-Hell's Angel talk about Jesus! I was down to nine stone, as white as a ghost with eyes protruding and hair meticulously spiked for aggression, the effect of four years of drug abuse. We were both desperate as

GREAT CONVERSIONS

I had tried everything I knew to get out of the hell of addiction and self-loathing, but nothing had worked. The very last and most uncool thing on the list was religion. How had it all gone so wrong? I grew up as a good Catholic kid in a middle-class family, with mum, dad, brother and sister. I went to a good school where I did very well.

But at the age of fourteen somehow everything started to change, and I began to go off the rails. I started experiencing a deep emptiness and tried to find something that would give me a sense of importance. I began to smoke behind the bike shed, shoplifting and petty vandalism, fights and always looking for thrills. Next came alcohol, drugs and girls. And at the age of fifteen I started sleeping around. My parents were furious when they learnt from the school everything I had been up to. They put me in another school where I did not fit at all. I was really looking for an identity. And one day I found it when I followed some long-haired kids into the basement underneath the swimming pool at the school. Opening the door, I was hit by a strange world of psychedelic music and a green sweet-smelling fog. I literally threw myself into this new identity, I became "Dave the Druggie" and grew my hair long. I started to listen to Black Sabbath, the Doors and Led Zeppelin. This new scene was something I could do very well, I did not have to be super fit or super intelligent, I just had to have a bit of a death wish. For a fifteen-year-old I began to take a lot of drugs. With money I stole from my parents I bought drugs from a place which was like a supermarket with people selling you anything and everything very cheaply. And so, I took a lot of speed, loads of acid, smoked vast amounts of dope and began messing about with much older guys, often sleeping in rat infested squats.

Surprisingly, I crawled through my 'O' levels. I began hating school, work, my parents and rebelled against all authority. Amazingly I scraped through the sixth form. One day I got totally stoned on a drug called Mandrax, which was a very powerful sedative. I stumbled home in a terrible state. Finally, my poor parents had to face the terrible truth that their blue-eyed boy was taking drugs. They went ballistic and locked me away to protect me, but my friends carried on sending me drugs through the post. I went to a local college to take my "A" levels and convinced my parents that I had changed, but soon I was back on the slippery slope. I got swept up in Punk Rock, my hair got shorter, the music got louder and the drugs harder.

And then in the middle of it all I met a young woman called Ruth, she was very beautiful and although everybody fancied her, she seemed to like me. Love came pounding into my life. It seemed the real thing and soon we got involved in a deep passionately sexual relationship which soon became like an addiction. I wanted to keep this girl, but of course she didn't want a stoned punk rocker for a boyfriend. So gradually with the power of this new-found love, slowly I came off the dope. Now I needed a new identity again, for how was I going to keep her.

I tried several jobs which failed. I knew I had several gifts, one of which was being a bit of a con man and being a good poker player, skills that would be handy in the business world, and I was proved right. Working hard, at the age of twenty-one I had built my empire, an employment agency in the City. I drove a very fast red car and was living with Ruth in a posh Hampstead flat. I had money, power and influence. And my parents were very happy that I had made something of my life. But my empire crashed down after two years as the relationship with Ruth was difficult, we were jealous, possessive and hating and loving each other at the same time. We were spending too much money and soon I was under tremendous pressure for a twenty-two-year-old of a failing relationship and bankruptcy looming. And what was more, the emptiness was still there.

One day I came home and found Ruth in bed with my best friend. After having built six years of my life around this relationship, it all came crashing down and I was devastated and crushed. The depression was extreme and all enveloping. My life was a failure. I moved into a bedsit and with the money I made I turned back to drugs. I just wanted to kill the physical, mental and emotional torment. With a real death wish this time I turned to methadone, a heroin substitute which is very clever as it makes you feel alive and makes you feel like a hero, and that's where the name heroin comes from. It numbed the pain for a while but soon I was totally addicted to it and could not function anymore. It was a living hell, trying to come off the drugs on my own and I experienced "cold turkey," with stomach cramps and depression. I became a "speed freak," I took it every day, pumping myself full of cheap impure amphetamine sulphate which dehumanises you. At 4am I took very strong sleeping pills with cheap whisky and LSD for entertainment - a drug that destroys the mind. As part of the empty life I was sleeping around with women, and I didn't even know their names. I caught diseases and the darkness started to snuff out any life at the end of the tunnel. My mind was in pieces and my kidneys were burning from the abuse, and the speed was crippling my body making me extremely thin. If I carried on doing this, I knew that I would be dead in no time at all, at twenty-five.

While all this was happening, my mother, who was a

Catholic, had been through a kind of weird religious experience. She had always been to church, but I did not know what this new thing was. When I would phone her, she would tell me that she had "experienced the power of God." Then she would tell me that Jesus could "set me free" from the prison I was in, and she wanted me to go to church. I thought she was utterly crazy. I had left the church at the age of fifteen because I found it utterly boring and totally hypocritical. God, if he existed at all, was utterly irrelevant. What had he ever done for me? But my mother kept telling me that Jesus is alive and wanted a relationship with me, and I thought she must be on LSD too. Every time I went home to get some food or to borrow money, she would give me another Christian book to read.

One day, out of boredom I started to read one of those books. The front cover attracted me as it had a flick knife on it like the one I carried with me everywhere in my drug-induced paranoia. It was called, "Run Baby, Run" by an American gangster named Nicky Cruz. This was a true story of New York street gangs. They were doing harder drugs than me, they were more violent and more into crime. Then a preacher, David Wilkerson, told them that "Jesus could set them free." The gangsters were going to cut him into pieces and throw him in the Hudson River. But shaking with fear he said to them, "you can kill me, but God's love is going to get you." Amazingly, one by one these hard men experienced a powerful conversion which set them free from drugs and gave them a fresh start in life. As I read this, hope started to tingle deep inside me. "Maybe there is a God after all who can get me out of this tortuous life I am in" I thought. Then I read "Chasing the Dragon," which means, smoking heroin - something I was doing all the time. This girl goes to Hong Kong and prays with the drug addicts, and they come off drugs as she prays "in the power of the Holy spirit" whatever that is, and they have no withdrawal symptoms. That is amazing; maybe there is a way out for me too.

Then fear set in not many weeks after reading these books. We started on Friday morning at a party doing loads of speed and LSD and magic mushrooms. It was normal, we did this every week. The drugs and the hallucinogenic power were flowing nicely in my body. But soon, I started to sense something very evil. I had a few bad trips before but nothing so serious like this. Now I began to experience a "presence" in my room and in the people around me, a presence of intense evil. I started to smell it, feel it, hear it and it frightened me deeply. I grabbed the sleeping pills, enough to knock out an elephant, but they did not help, and I could not sleep for forty-eight hours, I was trapped. It was as if the devil himself was in the room and there was no escape. Now I was certain that I believed in the devil. It was as if I had a "revelation" of life and death. Death for me was going to be like the "big sleep", I would never wake up and all my disappointment, pain, anger and fear would be finished. That nightmare weekend I saw very clearly, like a deep reality deep inside me, and I just knew that it was true, that death was not the end and all that religious stuff I had been taught in school came flooding back. This hell I was living now at the age of twenty-five, of emotional torture and pain, was going to continue after death and last for a very long time and get worse. And that scared me more than anything had ever scared me in my whole life.

I went home to my mother and said, "You have been telling me about this God of power, where is He? I need to try him out." I was not full of faith, but I was desperate as nothing so far had helped, drugs, sex, even crime. Very relieved, my mother said, "It just so happens that next week in town an ex-Hell's Angel from America is giving a talk. Would you go to that?" I nervously agreed, at least it wasn't as bad as going to church. I only knew one Christian guy as most people I knew were into the occult and on drugs and many were ex-Catholic school boys. When I asked him, he happily agreed to go with me. We went for a beer and then stumbled into the meeting in our old tatty clothes feeling very self-conscious.

The Hell's Angel stood at the front, he was huge, with a huge beard and wearing an old bearskin waistcoat, thank goodness he seemed like my kind of guy. His life story almost looked like a set up job, it was identical to mine. He was brought up in a good Christian home, but as a teenager, things had gone wrong. Just like me, his girlfriend had betrayed him, the drugs followed to still the pain, then the gangs and the violence. Driving along one day he was desperate as his whole life was in a mess and he decided to commit suicide. In desperation he flicked on a cassette his mother had given him, thinking, "why not, I have tried everything else." Then he heard a preacher telling him about the Son of God coming 2000 years ago in order to die for mankind and rise from the dead to offer new life to all. He thought, "Well, big deal, what has that old story got to do with me?" But the preacher went on to say that through the power of God this event could affect lives now. Whatever the problem, drugs, depression, despair, this violent murder on a cross of this man who was God could change any life, no matter how messed up it was.

At this the Hell's angel pulled up, got out of his car and knelt on the tarmac and cried out, "God, I don't know if you exist, but I am at an end of my tether. If you are real, come now and show yourself." God came into his life there and then on the side of the road. He experienced power and forgiveness. His drug addiction was broken, the depression lifted, and his life was irrevocably changed.

I was transfixed, I am at an end of my own tether, and here is a man in flesh and blood, a cool looking guy, telling me that God is real and had moved in his life. This wasn't distant or in a book, this was here and now. Hope was beginning to stir in me. Then he said, "There is someone in this room who needs to meet with God tonight, don't leave it or it may be too late." He said that if we reject this message and go our own away from God, it would ultimately lead to destruction, and that place is called hell. I knew he was talking about me; I knew this was it, I had to try God. Then he said, "You have got to stand up now." Can you imagine, there are a hundred businessmen sitting there, and my mother is there, and I have to stand up in front of all of them and in my tatty clothes. I gripped my chair and thought "No Way," but then I found myself slowly standing up. It was the most courageous thing I have ever done in my life. Here I was standing in front of God and saying, "I need You; I do not want to make it on my own anymore." He led me through a prayer saying, "God I ask that you forgive my sin." and I cried out to God in my heart, "God you have got to forgive the things I have done wrong, resentment, lack of forgiveness, bitterness and jealousy. I am sorry, I want to change." Then the Hell's Angel said, "Now pray that you'll believe in Jesus, pray and declare that Jesus is the Son of God." It was as if I had a little speck of faith inside me, enough to say, "Jesus, I think I believe in you, that the cross you died on was for me, and that you rose from the dead which is enough to free me now." Then I begged Him to come into my heart, take control of my burnt-out life, to be my boss and to forgive me.

Looking back, I can see that those few mumbled prayers in a stuffy banqueting hall would forever change my life. It was as if I had opened a door into my heart that would never again be shut, and the light came flooding in. Something changed inside me there and then, hope started to flow, and I felt a weight lift off my shoulders, the heaviness of despair and guilt was gone after all those long harsh years. After the meeting, my friend and I rushed to the pub and drank lots of beer, but something crazy was happening inside me. My body was still gripped by the drugs, yet I was starting to believe in God and feel powerful hope inside me and experienced love and forgiveness, but I needed physical change too. I went back to my mother and said, I need more." She said, "You need the Holy spirit, you need to go to a prayer meeting. That sounded really boring, but I agreed to go. I just hoped that the God of New York and Hong Kong was waiting for me in leafy old Hertfordshire.

It seemed like a room full of old Irish ladies when my friend and I got there. They started to sing, and it was terrible and of course we started to snigger. But something started to change, they suddenly started to sound like angels. They were singing in this new language, called singing in tongues. I read about it when they prayed with junkies in Hong Kong. It was the language of the Holy Spirit. In the following weeks we loved going to those ladies and there were also a few men present. On the third week, they said to John, "You don't have to smoke any more you know, God can set you free." He was a 40-a-day man and he had tried to give up many times, but he just laughed. But they persisted and he finally gave in. They took him away to another room and five minutes later he burst out with a huge grin on his face, he said, "I don't need to smoke anymore," but I would not believe him. But to my amazement, he started to throw all his cigarettes away which took about 10 minutes as he always carried lots of packets in his car. After three days phoning him every day, he still had not lit a cigarette, it was a "miracle," he had been set free!

The next week it was my turn. I went with fear and trepidation, almost not going at all. Maybe God would not come at all because of all the bad things I had done. My mother and sister had been praying for me for years and through their prayer, I am sure, I found the inner strength to go. After the singing, we sat in small groups praying for the power of the Holy Spirit to come, or a "personal Pentecost," as it is sometimes called. The lovely ladies laid their hands on my still spiky head and began to pray. The result was almost instantaneous. It was as if God just started to flow into me, like he was pouring in a precious liquid, and I began to feel all warm inside. All the emptiness that had haunted me since I was fourteen fell away, and I prayed, "God please give me everything. Come Holy Spirit and give me all your gifts." And amazingly I started to pray in this new gift of tongues. The same happened to my friend and we left buzzing, floating out as happy as we had ever been.

Over the coming days, I felt that it was really true. It was the 18th February that I felt I had been set free from all my addiction, drugs, sleeping around and many other problems. I had no need to take drugs anymore, there was no "cold turkey" and no withdrawal symptoms. I had been born again, as they say, and as the weeks rolled on, I began to know through prayer my new friend Jesus the Lord and I even heard his voice gently leading and encouraging me. It was a miracle of God's healing love. (b)

(Since 1996, with encouragement from the Vatican, David has

been running CaFE (Catholic Faith Exploration) producing a wide variety of modern and attractive DVD resources. CaFE courses help people of all ages to learn, share and pray together in a relaxed, welcoming 'café' style atmosphere. Courses cover Faith Formation, Sacraments, Youth and General Resources. More information online at faithcafe.org)

A MOST POWERFUL ENCOUNTER WITH THE WORD OF GOD

I reached my early 30s with a reasonably sound intellectual understanding of what Christianity was about, having been brought up as a Catholic in the 1950s. Looking back now, I would say that I had no real commitment. I was doing the bare minimum of going to Mass on Sundays and holy days and was feeling very dissatisfied with the lack of any connection between religion and everyday life.

My brother had a powerful renewal of his faith and started lending me books and tapes about renewal, but I admit that I was initially sceptical. It did not sound very Catholic at all, this was just not the way Catholics do things surely, I found myself thinking, it can't be right. I was in two moods about what I was finding out. On the one hand I was attracted by the testimonies of people's life-changing experiences of finding a deeper relationship with God. It was a real revelation that God can help us in every part of our lives. On the other hand, I was reluctant to step away from the security of the familiar, however unsatisfactory this was.

In 1983, my brother invited me to go with him to a dinner meeting of an inter-denominational Christian group where there were a couple of speakers giving their testimonies. I remember being impressed but I can't remember any details of what was said apart from one sentence. At one point the speaker quoted from the gospel where in Matthew 12:30 Jesus says, "Whoever is not with me is against me." The words went straight to my heart, and I knew God was speaking to me. I realised I had been sitting on the fence about making any proper commitment and, although I wasn't entirely sure I was ready, or able to be with Jesus, I knew for certain that I didn't want to be against him. I had absorbed so much teaching about Jesus over the years, so I knew "about" who he was, I just didn't know him personally and had not made an adult acceptance of him as my personal Savour. At the end of the talk, they said if anyone wanted to make a commitment to Jesus as their personal Lord and Saviour, they could silently repeat a prayer, which I did. They then invited anyone who wished to receive personal prayer to go to the people who could pray with them. I was nervous, as I had never received personal prayer like this before, but I felt an inner confidence which compelled me to go forward. I felt nothing special at the time or immediately afterwards; maybe slightly foolish, slightly relieved that at last I had taken this step which people seemed to think was so important. I had read testimonies where people had dramatic physical or spiritual experiences when they made this prayer and I felt perhaps a little disappointed or maybe relieved that nothing dramatic had happened. I realised later that God is of course very wise and gentle, and only gives us the experiences He knows are best for us.

Although there were no outer signs, inwardly things began to change almost immediately. First of all, I had the intense desire to go to the Sacrament of Confession, which was most unusual as I normally went somewhat reluctantly before Easter and Christmas. When I went, I was able to speak deeply from the heart in a way I had never done before, and the same when it came to make an "Act of contrition". Instead of reciting the usual set of prayers like a parrot, I was able to express my sorrow and my acceptance of Christ's forgiveness in my own words. Afterwards I wept as I realised how much Jesus had suffered for me personally to take away my sins and bring me into a new loving relationship with God my heavenly Father. I already knew in my head that Jesus was Saviour of the world and had died for the forgiveness of mankind's sins, but I felt this was the first time I really began to understand that Jesus had died for me personally. I also had a desire to start reading the Bible every day and the words began to come alive. It was as if God was speaking directly to me, and I just knew that He loved me. I began to understand that prayer is a two-way communication which begins with listening to God and responding from the heart.

This was the start of a journey which has continued, with many ups and downs, for almost 40 years now, and is still continuing. God has blessed me in so many ways and inspired me and enabled me to do many things in His service as an active layperson in the Catholic church as well as in many inter-church activities. My appreciation of the Catholic faith has progressively deepened but at the same time I have also developed a strong appreciation and fellowship with other Christian denominations. What sounds like an impossible paradox has been made possible by the Holy Spirit. (c)

These stories, and many more like them, are each quite amazing. But so is the love we can derive from a relationship with God.

22

FINDING FAITH

It is well-known that trying to convert people by reasoning or by waving the Bible at them only puts them off. As soon as religion is mentioned the shutters come down in defence because nobody wants to be preached at with words that speak to the mind rather than to the heart. The gift of faith is a personal experience which touches deep down in the heart and makes us sit up and reflect. And it comes in many guises, and often strikes unawares like a flash of lightning, or a gentle spark may be ignited through literature, or a beautiful sunset, a special person, a sudden awareness of the presence of God, or a realisation of one's unworthiness, guilt or despair when we are at our lowest ebb. These are all powerful means for God to reveal Himself, and for us to take a first tentative step towards seeing things in a different way and having "a change of heart", which is what conversion literally means. Conversion could also be considered as a suddenness of seeing the truth and wanting to conform one's life to it.

Christianity is not solely for the righteous, it is also meant for the unrighteous, and that means everybody. No one is perfect, and we are all a long way from Jesus' exhortation, "Be perfect as your heavenly father is perfect" (Mt 5:48). Recognition that we are in need of God's forgiveness is the most powerful act of humility. It does not fail to attract His forgiveness and healing grace.

Grace is a free gift from God that leads to repentance and a changed and improved life. We do not earn grace through our good deeds, but by having the will to accept the presence of God in our lives.

Many people will be familiar with the lovely hymn Amazing Grace (a) since it is often sung at funerals. They must wonder what the sentences allude to when they sing, "I once was lost, but now I am found, was blind, but now I see", and "How precious did that grace appear, the hour I first believed". It is not the blindness of our physical eyes that makes it impossible to make sense of God's mysteries, but the blindness of the spiritual eyes of our hearts. Sadly, this spiritual blindness has been a curse for the human mind from the outset. It was the pharisees' problem, not wanting to acknowledge Jesus' miracles, and it is still ours because it is inflicted by the evil one, Satan, who delights in preventing us from seeing the way ahead and from being able to say, "Yes, I see."

We can sympathize with John Newton, who wrote the words for Amazing Grace, when he says, "I was lost", because John was at first a slave trader, and like him, we too are lost because of our sinfulness and our spiritual blindness that renders us unable to acknowledge and believe in God's past and present miracles.

Later in life, John became an Anglican Minister after he "saw the light" that he was a sinful man. Through God's saving grace, he penned the words for the hymn when he was able to see that it was God that had saved him from almost certain death on a sinking ship. In the moment of fear, he called out to God for help. And the help did not only come in the form of saving his physical life, but also in saving his spiritual life from eternal death. And how precious was the grace he received, to be able to see finally that his life was in a mess and that he had been given the opportunity to make amends.

On our own it may be impossible to have an awareness of our inner spiritual state. We need help from the Holy Spirit, and we can have this help if we pray for the grace to see the truth and for the gift of faith, as the apostles did. They said to Jesus, "Lord, increase our faith" (Lk17:5), and the Spirit opened their hard hearts and opened their spiritually blind eyes and deaf ears. We just need to ask. it is that simple. Nothing can stop God's power to help us to believe if we cry out, "Lord, help my unbelief".

The response to such an "ask" will be that the darkness in our hearts will be illuminated. This can be a fearful and unsettling experience as the enormity of our wrongdoings is suddenly revealed to us in all its horror; we who thought we had never done anything wrong! (Thinking that we don't do anything wrong is of course the first shortcoming we have, the sin of pride.) Now, with God's grace we can finally "see" the truth about ourselves. This may trigger a deep feeling of repentance and the desire to own up to all that was mistaken, and in all humility ask for forgiveness. Admitting our mistakes has often a softening effect on people, and it surely has a softening effect on God who will not delay in granting his forgiveness.

The feeling of guilt can have a debilitating effect, but there is nothing like the feeling of joy at being forgiven. The darkness of sin can never consume the light of Jesus' forgiveness, for "anyone who follows me, will not be walking in darkness but will have the light of life" (Jn 14:6). In life after death, we will finally reach the true inheritance, to sit at the banquet of eternal life and enjoy the awe-inspiring beauty of God's majesty and power enthroned. All the deep desires in the human heart, to live in peace, to have hope and to be loved will be fulfilled now and for ever. This is the irrefutable destiny we need to believe in, it is the only true faith, according to Paul, "The faith which we preach is, that if you declare with your mouth that Jesus is Lord, and if you believe with your heart that God raised him from the dead, then you will be saved" (Rm 10:9).

Sooner or later, we need to make a choice, we cannot sit forever on the fence, we either reject or accept God's supremacy in all things. We cannot forever confine God to the limitations of our narrow world. God is the creator of all things and NOTHING is impossible for Him.

God "is" the Christian religion, which has a beauty all of its own. It is reflected in the love and creative power of God, in the immense variety and intricacy of nature, in the astonishing complexity of the human body, in the wonder of animal life, in history, in its wonderful cathedrals, in the lives of all who laboured ceaselessly to bring the Good News to the world, in the lives of the saints who sacrificed their comforts, health and safety to make this world a better place, by founding abbeys, schools and hospitals. It is in the suffering of martyrs who died rather than renounce Christ, it is reflected in art and civilizations, and in the acts of kindness shown by millions to their fellow men through the ages, all done for the love of God, for that is where the real power is hidden for maximum effect. Most of all, the beauty of the Christian religion shines through the sublime self-giving act of love by Jesus voluntarily laying down his life for mankind. No other religion can surpass such love.

In the end, only one small word is needed: sorry. Then we will feel the joy of forgiveness, as pride has been buried and the fetters of the 'I know better than God' attitude loosened. We will be enveloped, like children, in the arms of a loving God, and the feeling of love and ecstasy will surpass all understanding. We will KNOW that we are loved by God, beyond belief. This is the message of the |Good News of the Gospel, which has been kept silent for far too long.

THE GOOD NEWS NOBODY TALKS ABOUT

Ac	Acts	Lk	Luke
Am	Amos	Lm	Lamentations
Ba	Baruch	Lv	Leviticus
1 Ch	1 Chronicles	1 M	1 Maccabees
2 Ch	2 Chronicles	2 M	2 Maccabees
1 Co	1 Corinthians	Mi	Micah
2 Co	2 Corinthians	Mk	Mark
Col	Colossians	Ml	Malachi
Dn	Daniel	Mt	Matthew
Dt	Deuteronomy	Na	Nahum
Ep	Ephesians	Nb	Numbers
Est	Esther	Ne	Nehemiah
Ex	Exodus	Ob	Obadiah
Ezk	Ezekiel	1 P	1 Peter
Ezr	Ezra	2 P	2 Peter
Ga	Galatians	Ph	Philippians
Gn	Genesis	Phm	Philemon
Hab	Habakkuk	Pr	Proverbs
Heb	Hebrews	Ps	Psalms
Hg	Haggai	Qo	Ecclesiastes/Qoheleth
Ho	Hosea	Rm	Romans
Is	Isaiah	Rt	Ruth
Jb	Job	Rv	Revelation
Jdt	Judith	1 S	1 Samuel
Jg	Judges	2 S	2 Samuel
Jl	Joel	Sg	Song of Songs
Jm	James	Si	Ecclesiasticus/ Ben Sira
Jn	John	Tb	Tobit
1 Jn	1 John	1 Th	1 Thessalonians
2 Jn	2 John	2 Th	2 Thessalonians
3 Jn	3 John	1 Tm	1 Timothy
Jon	Jonah	2 Tm	2 Timothy
Jos	Joshua	Tt	Titus
Jr	Jeremiah	Ws	Wisdom
Jude	Jude	Zc	Zechariah
1 K	1 Kings	Zp	Zephaniah
2 K	2 Kings		

NOTES

1 SOME REFLECTIONS

(a) Alison Morgan, The Story of the Boy in Trouble, "TheWord on the Wind", published by Lion Hudson plc. .Copyright 2011. Wilkinson House, Jordan Hill Road OX2 8DR. ISBN97800857210159. Reproduced ....with permission of Lion Hudson plc through PLS clear.
(b) You/Gov/Poll, www.uk.coop/model/7. Fair Use.
(c) Alison Morgan, "Word on the Wind". With permission from the author.
(d) Hope Price, "The Angel of Mons, Angels and how they touch our lives." Copyright. Fair Use.
(e) "Battle of Lepanto", Wikipedia
(f) Fyodor Dostoevsky, "Ten Quotes of Dostoevsky, About God, Faith and Christianity". Fair Use.
(g) What we have done is throwing away the key...., Monsignor Lorenzo Albacete, Author Theologian and former Scientist. Magnificat. www.magnificat.co.uk, ...Fair Use.
(h) Resource Magazine, Venerable Kevin Roberts, Director. With permission.
(i) Thomas Merton, American Trappist monk, writer, theologian, social activist, mystic, poet and scholar of Comparative Religion (1915-1968). Seeds of Contemplation, 1949. Universe Books. Fair Use.
(j) Alison Morgan, Giles Story, "The Word on the Wind". With permission.
(k) Alison Morgan, "The Word on the Wind". With permission from the author.

2 WHAT IS THIS GOOD NEWS?

   (a) Professor Brian Cox, Programme, BBC iPlayer 2022.

   (b) Alison Morgan, Although the Bible and the Gospels are.accounts of facts, The "Word on the Wind". With permission.

   (c) "The Bible Timeline", Ascension Press, POB Ox 1990, West Chester, PA, 199380   US. ISBN 978 – 1-9934217-11-5. Authors; Jeff Cavins, Sarah Christymer and Tim Gray. Reproduced with permission from Ascension Press.

3 THE TEN COMMANDMENTS

4 CHRISTIANITY

   (a) David McClister, "Truth of God, Restoring Original Christianity– For Today". www.cbcg.org. Article by . Fair Use.

   (b) Article attributed to the 2ndc Church Father St Hippolytus in very early Christian Tradition, by Marc de Bolt, Schizophrenic writer and poet, USA. With Permission from the author.

   (c) Wikipedia, the free encyclopaedia, Battle of the Milvian Bridge Article "Talk", Paraphrased. Fair Use.

   (d) This heralded the end of the persecution, Quote by Professor Anthony Esolen, writer in Residence at Magdalen College of Liberal Arts in New Hampshire, US. Magnificat, www.magnificat.co.uk, Fair Use.

   (e) Roberts Liardon, "God's Generals", © 1196 by ISBN-13: 978-0-88368-944- 8 Whitaker House, 1030, Hunt Valley Circle, New Kensington, PA, 15068. ISBN-10:0-88368-944-8 15068. With Permission.

   (f) Smith Wigglesworth, "Greater Works", ISBN-13:978-

NOTES

0-88368-584-1, Printed in the USA, © 2000 by Whitaker House, 1030 Hunt Valley Circle, New Kensington, PA 15068. With Permission.

(g) Professor Esolen, "But once this message reached the wider world", Fair Use.

(h) "The Rapid Spread of Christianity over the Whole World, A Compilation of Geschiedenis der Middeleeuwen" by Dr D J Uytterhoeven.

(i) "Mere Christianity, Jesus is God", C S Lewis, Fair Use.

5 THE COMING OF JESUS

(a) John M Redford, "Dei Verbum", Copyright 2011. Alive Publishing Ltd, Graphic House,124 City Road, Stoke-on-Trent ST4 2PH. With permission.

6 JESUS' MISSION STATEMENT

7 JESUS HEALS WITH A WORD

8 COR ET LUMEN CHRISTI COMMUNITY

Damian Stayne, Founder, High Field House, St John's Way, Chertsey.

9 WHAT DAMIAN HAS TO SAY

Interview by Christine Zwart for ReSource Magazine. With Permission from Ven. Kevin Roberts, Director.

10 CHARISMATIC RENEWAL AND GIFTS OF THE HOLY SPIRIT

(a) Smith Wigglesworth, "Greater Works", ISBN-13:978-0-88368-584-1, Printed in the USA, © 2000 by Whitaker House, 1030 Hunt Valley Circle, New Kensington, PA 15068. With Permission.
(b) The Toronto blessing; Johann Carol.org/updates/the-Toronto-blessing-what-it-is.gotquestions.org. Fair Use.

11 JACKIE'S STORY

(a) Wikipedia. Fair Use
(b) Jackie Pullinger, Christopher's Story, "Chasing the Dragon".
(c) ISBN 7980340908808, Copyright 1980. Published by Hodder Faith. 558 Words. Reproduced by permission of Hodder and Stoughton Limited.
(d) Jackie Pullinger, Winston's Rank in the 14K Triad, "Chasing the Dragon".
(e) ISBN 7980340908808, Copyright 1980. Published by Hodder Faith. 558 Words. Reproduced by permission of Hodder and Stoughton Limited.
(f) Jackie Pullinger, I sat in a cafe with a gang leader, "Chasing the Dragon". ISBN 7980340908808, Copyright 1980, Jackie Pullinger, Published by Hodder Faith. 558 Words. Reproduced by permission of Hodder and Stoughton Limited.

12 MULTIPLICATION OF LOAVES

(a) Excerpt from a Curate's Diary by Fr T Doyle, "Miracle of the Loaves". With Permission. Glendalough Prayer Centre, Co Wicklow, Eire

NOTES

13 THE POWER OF THE EUCHARIST

(a) Fr T Doyle, "Miracle of the eucharist at El Passo". With Permission.
(b) John Horvat, Head, Tradition, Family, Property Commission, "Second Miracle of the Eucharist". With permission.

14 THE RESURRECTION

(a) Roberts Liardon, Smith Wigglesworth is one of these men, Excerpt from "Gods General, Why some Succeeded and why some Failed?". With Permission.
(b) "Smith Wigglesworth", A Resurrection Miracle, A First Miracle, Greater Works. With Permission.
(c) "Smith Wigglesworth", A Resurrection Miracle, A Second Miracle, Greater Works. With Permission.

15 GUARDIAN ANGELS

(a) John Horvat, "Distance no Obstacle for Angels". With Permission
(b) John Horvat, "A Young Marine Saved from Attack". With Permission.
(c) Hope Price, "The Angel of Mons, Angels, True Stories of How they touch our Lives". Fair Use.

16 GHOSTS AND SPIRITS

(a) Investigation by the Catholic Church, Catholic Answers. www.Catholic.com Inc. Fair Use.
(b) Alison Morgan, "The Word on the Wind", Mozambique is Well Known for its Witchdoctors, With Permission

17 SATAN AND EXORCISM

   (a) "Bible Alive", January 2019. Fair Use.
   (b) Doreen Irvine, Satanists are very active in most countries…., From "Witchcraft to Christ" by, © Doreen Irvine, ISBN 9780854750726. Fair use.
   (c) The Film the Exorcist and Robbie Mannheim's Exorcism, Story by John Horvat. With Permission from the Author.
   (d) Two Powerful Testimonies, Exorcism by Dr Scott Peck, and Another Remarkable Story, Excerpted from Deliver us From Evil Spirits, 1995 by Francis MacNutt, Chosen Books, a Division of Baker Book House Company, POBOX 6287, Grand Rapids, MI49516-6287. With Permission from the Publishers.

18 HEAVEN, HELL AND REPENTANCE

19 APPARITIONS

   (a) Our Lady of Glastonbury, glastonburycommunity@cliftondiocese.com. Fair Use.
   (b) Walsingham, The History of Walsingham, Local Information Board.
   (c) Banneux, Belgium. www.marypages.com>banneuxbelgium. Fair Use.
   (d) The Lady of all Nations. www.divinemysteries.info.Fair Use
   (e) Also in Japan did our Lady Appear, www.com/Catholicism/library/messge-from-our-lady-of.Akita5167. Fair Use
   (f) Lourdes in the French Alps. Own Story.
   (g) Rue du Bac, Paris,

NOTES

www.chapelledenotredamedelamedaillemiraculeuse.com Fair Use

(h) Other Famous Apparitions, Our Lady of the Poor, Shrines of Our Lady in England by Ann Veil. Fair Use.

(i) The Apparitions in Fatima, John Horvat. With Permission

(j) Medjugorje in Croatia, The Marian Spring Centre. Fair Use https://mariancentre.org.uk>index_files.

(k) The Story of Wintershall, Beloved Grandchildren, by Ann Huttley. With Permission. admin@winternshall.org.uk

(l) Peter's Story, Letter from Peter. With Permission.

20 THE BIBLE

(a) The Bible Goodreads, www.goodreads.com, authors, Quotes by Mahatma Gandhi, Fair Use.

21 GREAT CONVERSIONS

(a) Conversion from a Prison Cell, Name Withheld.
(b) David's Story, An Extract from David Payne's Book, "Alive" ISBN 9y78-1-903623-34-3 (c) 2009 CREW TRUST. With Permission
(c) A Testimony about a Most Powerful Encounter with the Word of God, by Alastair Emblem. With Permission

22 FINDING FAITH

(a) Amazing Grace, by John Newton, Anglican Minister and Poet. 1725-1807.

Printed by Amazon Italia Logistica S.r.l.
Torrazza Piemonte (TO), Italy

WOMEN IN THE *Modern* BUSINESS WORLD

WOMEN IN THE *Modern* BUSINESS WORLD

We are now aiming to be everywhere with the Lobby app.

Find out more about Global Woman at:
globalwomanmagazine.com
Contact us at:
hello@globalwomanmagazine.com

WOMEN IN THE *Modern* BUSINESS WORLD

Our Aim

Our aim is to connect professional and business women around the world, and we are celebrating together, knowing that many of us may have come from different countries, different backgrounds and even being at different stages of life and our profession or business but we all have something in common: the drive and the passion to succeed in business or our chosen vocation.

Global Woman Club is a place for businesswomen, that helps them to build their confidence and belief that they can be successful in whatever they do. We help them build their brand and create awareness about their projects through our media platform.

Non-members can attend only once to see and feel the unique experience and then decide if wanting to join as a member.

We have created local communities by travelling and meeting women around the world, starting from London and then Paris, Amsterdam, Stockholm, Oslo, Vienna, Frankfurt, Brussels, Bucharest, Johannesburg South Africa, Los Angeles, Chicago, Dallas, New York, Nottingham and Birmingham UK, Dubai, Singapore, Manila, Albania, Kosovo, San Francisco, Cyprus, and Alicante.

Core Values

- We value diversity, justice, integrity, honesty, and to recognise our unique contribution
- We welcome all equally, and we encourage equality between women and men
- We promote the importance of being in a high level of consciousness and invest in their self development
- We value the gifts that each woman has and the opportunities that we have to collaborate. We value collaboration Vs Competition.
- We believe in women supporting other women and respecting each other.
- We value the evolution as a dynamic factor for positive change in our community.
- We are open to positive change and growth, respecting the voice of women.
- We welcome ideas and feedback from everyone, and at the same time we encourage women to recognise their power and claim it back.
- We motivate women to acknowledge their knowledge and empower themselves by the celebration of their gifts, talents and skills that they have.
- We strive to increase the sense of self-worth and self-confidence of every woman that is connected in our Global Woman community.

VISION

Connecting women locally, empowering them globally

Why, Mission, Aims

Supporting women's professional and personal development through education and training.

We aim to unite professional women around the world, regardless of their age, culture or race. To encourage them to stand in their power, invest in themselves and grow their skills and abilities by learning, and leadership development.

We do this by providing a safe, caring and supportive environment in which women can get support and services; take part in events, training and activities and become active in bringing about change for themselves and the society.

Education leads to empowerment. We provide women with access to a wide variety of information, knowledge and opportunities to implement them so they can make the right decisions.

WOMEN IN THE *Modern* BUSINESS WORLD

must learn to connect to build solid communities with a shared vision". This is what inspired me to start this campaign, which has the aim to raise more 'Global Awareness for Gender Equality' and the role of the women in the world. It has inspired me to start a movement with a new paradigm for women who are able and willing to actively contribute and make a difference to the planet and create a better world for all.

Women are usually the initiators when it comes to building peace in their communities – and now is the time to give them a voice; to help them speak from their inner spirit, their ability to feel empowered in many areas of life including wellbeing, spirituality and finance. Women have the capacity to share their dialogue with the world and contribute with their ideas about healing humanity's relationship with the planet.

In many diverse cultures, traditional stories speak about the changing of the ages. And in these stories it is always the feminine spirit, which brings about the transition and transformation to a new life. Power is to believe in togetherness, it is all about engaging with, and understanding the unique role that each of us has to offer in the world, while collaborating together to empower each other.

Those who believe in this vision of women empowerment join us and support us to make this journey fulfilled and inspiring.

WOMEN IN THE *Modern* BUSINESS WORLD

About Global Woman

Our Why

Today, women are having a powerful influence in the world, more than ever before, and bringing a more spiritual and nurturing presence to the planet.

In our view, power is to believe in togetherness, which is all about engaging with and understanding the unique role that each of us has to offer in the world, while collaborating together to empower each other. It is therefore time to think about, embrace and understand what this means for the world and realise that there is a genuine need to work together to change the old paradigms and become more involved in making a real difference.

At a time when the whole world is experiencing a huge humanitarian crisis, there is still time to create a new world paradigm based on conscious activism, financial empowerment and a spiritual moral compass.

Dr. Ervin Laszlo, in an exclusive interview for the Global Woman magazine said, "There is still a hope for humanity and in order to achieve a meaningful global impact, our leaders

WOMEN IN THE
Modern
BUSINESS
WORLD

Now that you have read this far, you may have realised that there were obstacles to overcome all along my way, but they were all worth it.

Dare to Dream

Be grateful and see the opportunity in every challenge. It is not the issue itself causing the result, it is the way you react to what comes your way during your journey. If you always get back on your feet, yet one more time, you will eventually succeed. Along with daring to dream goes the capability of not listening to the naysayers. Stay away from them. Who would have believed that I am writing a book in English? I wouldn't have, had I believed my English teacher. I am thinking of sending him a signed copy of my new book, once it is finished. What do you think? Last but not least, be aware of your own thoughts, they may sometimes be negative and in addition to that, not true.

I will leave you with one of my favourite sayings:

I am grateful for all the bad things that happened in my life, they made me to who I am today.

When you need support in creating your dream life and overcoming all your fears and obstacles, feel free to reach out to me. You can find me at my website: nicolebeissler.com Or feel free to connect via LinkedIn, Facebook and Instagram.

Nicole Beissler

The time was another good teacher, to have me throw away my limiting beliefs and just do what was needed. It was a very demanding, but also a very rewarding time. Working with the Spanish and Portuguese people totally served my values of encouraging and supporting others. My role was to help them go through the change smoothly. Obviously during a big transition, there was a lot of fear involved, such as:

"Will I lose my job?" "Am I good enough?"

"Is the way I used to do my work still valid?"

... and so on. All of these questions I knew very well for myself, and I also knew how to overcome them.

On the other hand, there were also a lot of expectations from the headquarter in the UK. We purchased the company for over 1.5 billion euros and the return of investment needed to be regained as quickly as possible. We had to establish plans and quite often the southern mentality did not match the one of the British. As a German, I was in between. But when you know your dream, and you can work towards it by living your values, it does not matter if you have long working hours. Nor if there are challenging and demanding tasks, as long as you reach your goal at the end.

The one-year relocation contract was extended for another six months, as it was clear that we still had a lot to do and while writing this chapter, I am in the middle of negotiating a new contract for the Head of Continuous Improvement role for Europe, with the home base in Spain.

WOMEN IN THE *Modern* BUSINESS WORLD

*Be courageous enough to reach for the stars,
eventually you will reach the moon.*

You have to take risks, if you want to be successful, and sometimes you may not know what the end result will look like. But ... if it was an easy decision, everyone would do it. A difficult decision will always be the one that takes you forward. Don't be afraid of tough choices, they are just a test for you if you really, with all your heart, want to achieve this dream.

The Win-Win Phone Call

After almost three years in my role as the Commercial Excellence Director, I got another phone call. The person who called me, knew me from my former company and offered me a job, which was indeed very close to my dream. It was a win-win situation. They were looking for someone who could lead the integration of the new Iberian company that we had just purchased. Being a strategic coach and a change expert, speaking Spanish and on top of that having a home base in Spain, made me the perfect fit. Even though I had no clue about the general merge and acquisition processes, or about the business of that division. The work had nothing to do with the work I was doing at that time, but knowing my work attitude and my capabilities, the head of the division was very convincing that I was the one.

Due to the fact that my long-term goal was to relocate permanently to Spain, it was the perfect match for me as well.

Nicole Beissler

My colleague was not really happy about my presentation, since he was part of the team, but I assured him that I would take all the risk. It was indeed risky. Our CEO from the United States was part of the meeting and it could well be that I would lose my job. A big risk, when your goal is to earn money and have a good position. Part of the risk was also the opportunity of gaining back the freedom of doing things the way I liked to, plus to constantly stop breaching my own values. Of course, it depends on what you want. In my case, I knew it was a chance for a change. Either the CEO would listen and think about my ideas of improving, or I would lose my job.

The luck was on my side, or the Universe listened again to the brave soul. A couple of weeks later I got a call from our European Commercial Director, to see if I would be interested in a strategic role for the whole division. It included not only Europe, it covered North America, Thailand, and Australia as well.

There I was, just a bold woman without a University degree, but with big dreams and ideas to change the world for the better. Suddenly I had become the Head of Commercial Excellence for an international company, and yet again I was asking myself; "Would I be able to fulfil this role?" My husband was very encouraging. He told me that they would not have asked me if they did not believe that I was the one. You may call me lucky, and believe me I sometimes thought that as well, "I am very lucky". However, the truth is:

to do, and I need to bring value to the company, which was not possible in that job. Again, I went back to searching and activating my head-hunter contacts. Eventually I landed a job in a UK based international company, as a Key Account Manager.

When I started, I was supposed to build up the customer base, as it had not been looked after very well. My predecessor had left more than a year ago and had taken some customers with him. What I found was, mildly said, a disaster. It took me a while to build the trust with the customers and I assured them that things had changed. Long working hours and overnight stays in hotels were my usual life again. Even though I changed in Peru, and I tried to live differently, we are who we are, and habits and beliefs are tempting to go back to. That is, if you are not careful and aware enough.

Back in the Corporate World

I mentioned earlier about the differences in the corporate world between women and men, and the biggest one is still, the salary. When I found out that my predecessor earned 20,000 Euros more, just because he was a man, I had had enough. It was shortly before the yearly European sales conference and we were supposed to prepare an overview about our customer accounts and the outlook for the next year. Usually this was every year, so the same boring stuff. Since I had had enough and there were many other things I did not agree with, I decided to be brave and highlight all the issues and concerns I had, and how we could change it for the better.

three months, than with my biological parents during my whole life.

Life is Changing

All the problems and issues I faced at that time back in Germany, suddenly became meaningless in the beauty of the Andes. I never faced so many shades of green in my life, combined with stunning buildings around the Plaza de Armas. It made me sit there for hours, just observing the Peruvians in their great colourful dresses. The most beautiful "dress" however, was their heartwarming smile. They never seem to lose it. I enjoyed the calmness and slowness of the Peruvian life, and when I returned home three months later to the craziness of Frankfurt's city centre, I straight away wanted to board the next plane to Peru. I missed my family, my new friends, the cute little toddlers, and moreover, this amazing landscape and the friendly people there. It took me a while to adapt again to our western life, but I was no longer the same as before.

A lot of things that were important for me before my stay in Peru, were no longer appealing to me, or of any interest. Money was no longer important to me, neither was my career, hence I decided to quit after only three months in my new role. My idea was to take a lower paid job, having more time for social work and my own social life. I wanted to give something back to society. Unfortunately, this turned out to be a big mistake. After only two months in the new company I was totally bored, and I realised that I am not an "eight to five person". My brain needs something of eight little bundles of joy. When I came in in the morning, they just woke up and the first action would be feeding them. From the moment I entered the orphanage until I left, there was no moment for myself. They needed my full attention, but it was so rewarding. They usually greeted me straight at the door, with either shaky steps or crawling. They tried to reach me and hugged my legs until I took them up in my arms. You can imagine it was quite difficult with eight of them.

The time in Peru taught me a lot. Not only the work in the orphanage, where you also hear the horrible stories. Stories of why the little ones are there, but also stories of the way of living. I met so many peaceful and happy people, even in the middle of nowhere. In our western way of thinking, we would call them poor, but they are much richer than you can imagine. They are so grateful for what they have, respecting nature, and living with the rhythm of it. In my family home, there was no heating system and being 3,400 meters above sea level, it could get very cold. The interesting part is, I was never cold. The warming atmosphere and the way they treated each other was so heartwarming, that I never had the feeling that I missed central heating. Well okay, when it came to washing my hair with cold water, it took me a while to not miss a hot shower.

You become very humble in a surrounding like this, appreciative, and I learned to concentrate more on my inner world. Instead of the outside world. My evenings were filled with long and intense conversations with my Peruvian family and I used to say that I spoke more profoundly with them in

NICOLE BEISSLER

the final result, but he never saw the trials as adversities, he even described it in an interview as, "There were no failures. I now know of 10,000+ ways on how to NOT make a lightbulb". Now, looking back, I can tell you, do not believe everything you think. It's more than likely to be wrong. My thoughts of fear and anxiety of what to expect in Peru, almost stopped me from going and I would have missed one of the best experiences in my life.

Arriving in Peru

I would have never met my long, lost "real family". Yes, I know, this may sound crazy, but when I arrived at the airport in Cusco and my Peruvian parents Sara and Abel were standing there with my name written on a big white paper, I knew I finally got home. They welcomed me into their life, as their long-lost daughter. There was no judgement, no negative words, the only thing I found was unconditional love and caring. When I went out to work in the morning – I was working in an orphanage – I was always reminded to wear a scarf. Funny, when you are 39 years old and someone is telling you what to wear and it never felt intimidating. It was always said with love and full of care.

My work in the orphanage was totally different from my normal job in the corporate world. It is so rewarding when you work with toddlers. They just show you straight away what they feel, and either they like you, or not. In my case, I took care

WOMEN IN THE *Modern* BUSINESS WORLD

God or the Universe, or any higher power, you may know that it always takes the side of the bravest souls. The ones who keep going and aren't letting go of their dreams by the first obstacle, will always receive support from the higher power. The moment I gave my notice, I received an offer from the other division in the company to join their sales team, after my return from the sabbatical.

My final destination was Cusco, the heart of Peru, in the middle of the Andes. I worked until the last day before my journey and I had no time to think of what to expect. Nor did I do any preparation work. When I was finally saying goodbye to my family and walking to the security control with a letter from my son in my hand, I realised that I didn't really know what to expect. I had no clue about Cusco, or even Peru. The only thing I knew was that Machu Picchu is there, and that it must be very impressive. When I was reading the very touching letter from my son, sitting at the gate, I started to sob. I did not care about the people around me, that was looking at me curiously. Suddenly I had that strange feeling, had I made a big mistake? I was on the edge of leaving the gate and going home, when I remembered the words of my friend. A friend who had said to me, "If you don't like it, you just board the plane and come home". Yes, I had made that decision to go, and at least I should give it a try.

Remembering the story about Thomas Alva Edison, and his development of the lightbulb, finally convinced me to board the plane. It took him more than ten thousand trials to get to

Nicole Beissler

The points I want to highlight are:

- Find something that your company also will benefit from (in my case: the language)
- Find a good time of the year, not in high season or at the end of the financial year
- Make sure you have an agreement with your colleagues for the handover of your workload
- Think carefully about the amount of time you want to stay away.

At first, three months sounds like a long time, but in my experience, I can tell you, it is over "on a whim". Good planning can also help when negotiating, it does not necessarily mean that your plan will succeed though. In my case, before I was able to sign the sabbatical contract, my boss was told by his boss that it would be better to convince me to stay. And have me move my plans to another year. This guy did not even know me, he had joined the company a couple of weeks earlier and even when my boss said I might resign, he refused to agree to the sabbatical.

The Sabbatical

Be aware, whenever you have a dream and you find obstacles in your way, it is just more proof. If your dream is big and important enough, you will overcome this. In my case I had the choice between risking my dream, and more over my health, or my job. I chose to quit. If you believe in

WOMEN IN THE *Modern* BUSINESS WORLD

I suffered from permanent headaches, which regularly resulted in migraines with vomiting. My digestive system was totally crazy, and I had the feeling that I needed to sleep all day long - and yet, it would still not be enough. My concentration level was very low, and I started to make mistakes and quite often, forgot to do things. My social life was almost non-existent, and if I went out to see friends, my only topic I could talk about was work. Because I had nothing else to say. After having collapsed twice, I finally agreed to see a doctor.

Luckily, I got a very good one, who recommended that I should take some time off for myself. The doctor told me that if I do not change my lifestyle, he could foresee that I would end up in a clinic on medication. However, it would still be possible to escape this horrifying future scenario and change something for the better. Before my body totally shut down and I couldn't control my actions anymore.

Rather than being on a sick leave, I asked the company for a three-month sabbatical. The idea of the sabbatical was that I would study Spanish, which would also be beneficial for the company, as one of my customers had the headquarters in Spain. I had always wanted to learn Spanish, but could never find the time, nor the energy to do it. If you ever think you need a break to do something else, a sabbatical is perfect for it. The negotiation process is quite easy if you prepare well beforehand.

Nicole Beissler

The list could be continued endlessly. The issue with limiting beliefs is that you'll find proof everywhere for your negative thinking, which is also known as self-fulfilling prophecy.

However, some of them were really true, and even in 2020, there is still a need to discuss the gender imbalance. And if you do not believe this, then ask yourself some questions. Do you earn the same amount of money as your male colleague? Is he working as hard as you are? And, what about the fact that women are more likely to stay home and look after the children than men are? Another list, and yes, I could go on and on. My point is, that if you want to be successful in the corporate world, you may have to work harder and be smarter than men. This is not about being a feminist, it just demonstrates that we still have an imbalance. But this does not mean that you do not have a chance to succeed. Dare to dream big!

My Body Cries Out

After six years of working endless hours and always trying to prove myself, I almost had a burnout. My body collapsed, and with the words of Ulrich Schaffer:

> *"Go ahead," said the soul to the body. "He doesn't listen to me. Maybe he listens to you." "I will get sick, then he will have time for you," made perfect sense to me.*

WOMEN IN THE *Modern* BUSINESS WORLD

Being a single mom was not always easy. It didn't really help either that, at that time, in my inner circle there were only stay at home moms who were showing me every day that I was not good enough. Clearly, I had support also from them, but quite often with a disapproving look at the watch, when yet again I was late to pick up my son. Being late was also a habit I thought I could not change, since I was always too late, and too lazy. What do you think, am I still too late or too lazy, or may I dare to say, that I was never either the one nor the other?

When I finally got an opportunity to work for an international company as a Key Account Manager, I felt for the first time in my life that I could really make it. In my wildest dreams, I could not have imagined that I would ever work in a men's world so successfully. It was the fault of a very good head-hunter, who obviously saw much more in me than I did in myself. He offered me a position in the automotive sector of an Australian company. A good salary, company car, bonus, and a home office – just perfect at that time. The first week that I started, all my limiting beliefs returned big time.

- I am not good enough.
- I do not have a University degree.
- I am not worth it.
- A man can do it better.
- It is a man's world, why should I succeed?
- My English is not good enough.
- There are others who are much better for this job.

Nicole Beissler

and included a lot of hard lessons. I want to encourage you to believe in yourself and do not listen to what others are telling you. Every time I took all my big steps, was actually when I didn't listen. But let me start from the beginning...

The Abusive Past

When I decided to leave my abusive childhood, at only eighteen years old, I was full of hope for a better future. But also full of limiting beliefs that I considered to be true. Being "not good enough" was one of them, and I guess you probably can relate to that in some way. But even if you are one of the lucky ones, not having this conditioning imprinted in your brain, I am sure that there are many others you would relate to. Later, when I had long left my abusive marriage, I read a sentence, which really hurt me:

You are only being treated the way you allow people to treat you.

Well, this means that I allowed myself to be treated like shit, that I allowed people to call me bad names, that I allowed my ex-husband to beat the hell out of me. That was a strong statement, but very true! When you lack self-esteem, you are not questioning the behaviours of others, you just take it, believing that you deserve it. The process of overcoming all this, started slowly while reading the enlightening book about dyslexia. If it is not true that I am stupid, what else might not be true? What other beliefs are no longer serving me, and what if I could really change my life to the better?

WOMEN IN THE *Modern* BUSINESS WORLD

This mantra changed one sunny day when I was sitting in my garden and reading a book. It was about how parents can support their child with dyslexia. Two weeks before I had had an appointment with the teacher of my little son. He was eight years old and already suffered in school. Mainly during the German lessons. His teacher, a young and enthusiastic lady, convinced me that I needed to get him tested. She thought that he showed all the traits of dyslexia. He was tested by a child psychiatrist, and she was right.

I was shocked and I tried to get all the information about it that I could find, back then in 1999. And there it was, clearly written, all the things I had faced in my life. All the "not good enough" traits and all the problems I had in school, suddenly made sense. I got myself tested and suddenly felt such a burden lift off my shoulders. I was not stupid, even better, I was extremely intelligent. I was just dyslexic.

It is something I dealt with all my adult life. I managed to cope with it and worked hard to climb the corporate ladder, but always with this feeling inside of not being good enough. Once this mega stone was lifted, I worked on my low self-esteem, and suddenly I sensed that I had advantages by mentioning that I have dyslexia. Standing by a whiteboard and writing, is now fun, rather than giving me the chills. I just say, "Hey, spell the word for me, you know I have dyslexia," and if it is a difficult one I love to say, "Oh, boy... you made it extra hard for me". Laughing, rather than criticising yourself is the best technique to overcome low self- esteem. But what now sounds like a piece of cake in overcoming, was really a long journey

Nicole Beissler

Do you know that they all have one thing in common? They were dyslexic, which means they may have had problems regarding reading or writing, or focusing on learning. For example, it might have been really difficult for them learning poems by heart, or other similar challenging activities.

Well, I never had any problems with reading. Actually, I loved reading. I was evidently slower when reading than others, but that wasn't a big problem. When it came to writing though, I was a disaster. My mom would call me stupid and said that I would never make it. Since I was used to it, it did not hurt that much. My English teacher once told me, "Look Nicole, English will never be something for you. It may be better for you to look for a job where you do not need English"! I was born and raised in Germany, so English is my second language. It is certainly true, over a very long time I had this limiting belief, that I will never be able to speak English.

Funnily enough, I am now working for a FTSE100 company based in London and leading a huge integration process in Iberia. I am also a LEAN Six Sigma Black Belt and have studied not only English but also Spanish, which is my third language. So, who said dyslexic people are stupid? We are creative in finding solutions, because we learn to deal with our lack of writing skills. Clearly, sometimes it leads to misunderstandings, as when I say to my husband "next, turn right", but I mean left. One more thing I am not good at. But I learned to deal with all of it, mostly during my years of lacking self-esteem. My mantra was, "I am not good enough, so I have to work harder".

CHAPTER 13

NICOLE BEISSLER

Dare to Dream and Succeed

When you hear names like Leonardo Da Vinci, Einstein, Winston Churchill, and Robbie Williams, you may think that they are a genius or have done some impressive work, that they are intelligent and knew what they were doing. You would probably not say, "What a stupid person, he will never make it".

Elizabeth Yang

- Shifting. You must learn to shift as life happens. Situations in life and people will test your patience at times, this is not a reason to give into madness, but rather a time to grow and remain calm. With your shifting and adapting, always lean towards what offers the most positive outcomes.

- Write Down Your Commitments. So it is truly clear, know what you are committed to and write it down. When things happen and they will, your response will be based on your commitment. Your commitment will remind you how to respond and help you manage your emotions.

- Be Responsible for Your Interpretation. Remember, you have a choice, and everything is a conversation. You are responsible for your own interpretation.

In conclusion, putting into practice all that I have learned is me being responsible. Taking hold of my responsibility has been a guide for how I navigate through my life. This has allowed me the opportunity to practice my skills instead of preaching them. In doing so I find fulfillment in being the Source.

are grateful for what you have already, it's hard to get more and be grateful.

Into the Future

The future is the next day, week, or month. For me, the future holds the sum of all that I have learned and my successes. This is what contributes to my fulfillment. Fulfillment is giving what you got, which is the sum of what is inside you. Giving material things are nice, but when you have given of yourself it is the ultimate gift to share with others. The gem I want readers to find in my words and my contribution to the world are the same thread that is weaved throughout this chapter. I want you to know that responsibility carries you through every life decision. When I am responsible, it makes me feel powerful and in control. Each day that I am positive, embracing my interpretation, being the source and responsible, I am contributing something to the whole of that which makes the future a second better than the past second.

My Top Tips

With the following tips, my hope is that you are reminded of the power you hold and become motivated in reaching beyond what is familiar. So you can experience the most fulfilling life ever.

Elizabeth Yang

say the getting is in your giving and giving is where you get the most reward. Life is not about getting everything just for you.

With all I was doing I had to think about what success was to me. It is different from fulfillment. Success to me is having what you have in addition to contentment with what you have. This is not to say that success does not include accomplishing all your goals, it is all that as well. It is stated among those who talk about success that there are seven areas that are considered successes when you accomplish them, they are:

- Career
- Making money
- Having a healthy family
- Having a healthy relationship with your spouse and children
- Engaging in a healthy and active lifestyle
- Involvement with community
- Vacationing and buying what you want

If you can accomplish any of these, it is important enjoying what you have, which defines success for me. You do not want to get into a position of always chasing the next thing without appreciating the present one. Take time to be satisfied with what you have. There are many examples of this that happen daily for some of us. One example is related to body image. Like a woman who wants to lose weight and tone up her body. The best way to do this is for her to love everything about herself first; the fat, the stretch marks, her shape. Then she can go and talk about her workout plan to improve. If you never when you end, it is the entire journey. My motto is live life to the fullest and do not waste a single millisecond.

I heard a good analogy that says, pretend life is an airplane that you are jumping out of with no parachute on, you know that you are going to hit the ground eventually but you can either close your eyes and be scared the whole way down or you can open your eyes and enjoy the view, maybe learn some flips going down. If other people are there with you, perhaps you could hold each other's hand while you fall. Everyone is facing the same fate; it really is about how you will experience the journey while you are in it. That made sense to me, so my search was not for one thing. My purpose is to intentionally enjoy every moment of my life with all the gifts it has to offer me.

Giving and Celebrating Success

While going about living your purpose, you function in a specific role. That role I feel comes from what flows out of you naturally, based on how you were influenced by your life experiences. Our experiences can either break us or move us to our full potential. My role simply put, is giving back. When I dissect it, it branches out into all the areas of my world where I give freely. I am there for my family and my children. Self-love is important too; I make sure I make time for the things I enjoy, like traveling and eating different kinds of foods. I try to do those things as often as I can between working. I also share my knowledge with my clients on their legal cases. The wise

Elizabeth Yang

with things they need to do, like have a partnership agreement in writing. We did not have that because my partner at the time said it was for people who did not trust each other. It does not matter how well you know the person or if they are family, business is business.

The Journey of My Life Purpose

I started off my legal career as an intellectual property attorney and then went through my own four- years divorce. This led me to family law. Having had the experience of working with a business partner, gave me the experience to feel confident branching out on my own, starting my own practice. I know firsthand how difficult a divorce can be, even when people agree. The severing of a relationship has its own unique hurt. In my law practice, I specialize in mediation. I feel that reaching some common ground is better than not. I also make myself available to my clients in their moments of anxiety.

I can now say that I would not be the person I am today without the experiences I had. My father's suicide, my four-year divorce period, and the problems my business partner caused, played a role in my personal development. About five or ten years ago I would ask myself what the purpose of life is. I was looking for one single goal to define its meaning. But after going through the transformation journey and doing a lot of personal self-development, I found that there is not just one purpose in life. Your life purpose is from when you are born to

WOMEN IN THE *Modern* BUSINESS WORLD

but I realized it would probably be better to just focus on my own practice than being tied up in a lawsuit with my business partner for a year or two. So, I just left and took a loss.

I decided to focus on the positive, I believed that what goes around comes around and karma will play out. Since then my law practice has grown significantly. From what I heard through the grapevine my ex business partner's employees were in a lawsuit with him. There are a lot of negative things going on with his business, that I am glad I am not involved in. It just goes to show if you let things go and be the bigger person, the universe will work things out. It never pays well to do someone wrong. You just live by your values and standards. I shifted my interpretation to mean something positive with this situation. I do not regret going into business with my business partner because I learned a lot and got some good experience. It was better to fail than to have never tried.

I saw starting my own practice as a challenge and an opportunity. A lot of people are indecisive about whether to do certain things. I say just do it and see what happens. I think people do not try because they are afraid of failing. But failing means learning something and that is what life is about, ups and downs and learning from mistakes. Imagine if life were just like a flat line, how boring would that be? There would be no excitement. You need the balance of challenges to keep you alert and make you feel alive. It raises the question: do we really fail at anything or are we just learning for the next opportunity? Because of what I learned with my business partner I can advise people who want to go into a business with a partner

Elizabeth Yang

the time married does not play a role in how much pain is felt, the severing that takes place still affects your emotions in a way that can't be fully explained even if you want the divorce.

Marriage is a union that has been around since the beginning of time. It has evolved for some into a more casual affair and for others it still holds the strong ties that bind a couple together forever. The times we live in today have so many options for couples who want to be together. Cultures and religion have their stand on the issue as well. It can be challenging to know what is good and acceptable.

During the process of my divorce, I learned something about myself and how to effectively communicate with others. In the end I was able to reach out to my ex and communicate my feelings. My desire was to heal. A lot had happened between us and we wanted the best for our children. Though we could not be together as a couple, we became friends. And that was the best ending possible for what had been a long fight to freedom for both of us. Yet, another example of how I became the Source.

Learning some hard lessons in business

In 2011, I started a law practice with a business partner I had met in law school. During our five-years span together, I felt disconnected with what was going on with the business. After continuing to grow apart, I finally made the tough decision to go my separate way. No longer in the business with my partner I started my own law practice. At that point I could have opened a lawsuit and worked to clear up the books,

WOMEN IN THE *Modern* BUSINESS WORLD

Four years to get a divorce is way too long and the stress of it was exhausting. Time was spent trying to plan the next move of how to keep everything in check. Instead we could have been communicating to reach an agreement. But we chose to fight because neither one of us had been taught a better way. I became certified in mediation because I wanted to help couples learn ways to communicate with each other. Communication, even in a divorce is not about who is right or wrong. It is about coming to an agreement. But, to do that, you must listen fully to what is being said, not to what is in your head.

We all have things in our story that cause us to feel or behave a certain way. Understanding emotional intelligence helps with the acceptance of self and the forgiveness process. It teaches you that forgiveness is not just for the other person, but for you to let go so you can move on in peace. I am not saying it is easy, but it is necessary. Another problem I realized that prolonged my divorce, was the competence level of the lawyers I engaged to help me. I went through five of them before I just gave up and wrote it myself. Papers were spread across my bedroom for a while as I learned how to best serve myself.

Every divorce case is a unique situation and should be treated that way. The best person to help is a lawyer who is knowledgeable about divorce through personal experience. They are more apt to handle your case as if it were their own. I think it is hard for a lawyer who has never experienced a custody battle to understand what to do for you. There is no template of one size fits all. The nuances are too unique for each case. Going through a divorce is no easy process. The length of

Elizabeth Yang

I was on the defense. I never expected the divorce to take as long as it did. Divorce is hard enough, so the extended waiting was not helpful. Our fight was over anything and everything; custody of the kids, alimony, assets and whatever else. I was hurt and I wanted to make him hurt too. So, I made things difficult and he pushed back each time with more difficulty. Our kids were young, but they could feel the tension between us. This went on for more than four years. After spending a ridiculous amount of money in attorney fees, for me it was $250,000 and for my ex it was $300,000, in addition I went through five lawyers before writing the divorce myself.

Conflict Resolution and Forgiveness

Amid all the chaos, the core problem presented itself. I had never learned how to resolve conflict. Divorce rates seem to be higher in California and with good reason. The movie stars seem to take advantage of the legal system in that way. But all that aside, a lack of education in conflict resolution is a problem that seems to be ignored or not considered as the culprit for the divorce rates. It was not until I attended a class on the topic of emotional intelligence that I realized the knowledge I was missing. My divorce was prolonged, partly because I had no clue how to communicate or resolve the conflict between me and my ex. No one teaches this in school at any level. Yet, it is where things fall apart in relationships. I had allowed my hurt to take control. I thought I was doing what it took to protect myself.

ago I came up with this airplane scenario as an interpretation concerning my father. When I get scared on a plane because of the turbulence, I just imagine my father holding the wing of the plane and God holding the other wing. I can then feel safe knowing they are keeping me safe. The interpretation is continuous.

My relationship with my dad continues day by day. I have a gratitude journal, where each day I list three things that I am thankful for. Last year I started writing that I am thankful for my dad and God every morning. To move on I had to forgive. I had to forgive my dad and myself. In my law practice I tell my clients they need to forgive the other person so they can move on. The main question I have learned to ask in interpretation is, "How is this serving me?" If the situation is not serving me in a positive way I shift to a different space. It is an ongoing journey.

My Four-Year Divorce

The longest I have been in a negative space was during the time of my divorce. At the time I did not have the question yet of "how is this serving me? I was just so angry that my ex made me a single parent, ruined our marriage by cheating and lying, that I was willing to spend my money making him miserable, instead of saving it for my kids college tuition. I was so stressed out, that it was not my client's paperwork scattered all over my bedroom, it was my divorce papers.

Elizabeth Yang

I knew for things to change I had to create something where I was responsible, not someone else. But this did not come easy. It took a continuous effort of learning self-awareness and putting energy in places that improve me. I had to become the Source. It is how I can make my relationship with my husband work today. He is not a bad boy and we have been together ten years now. The reality is my dad could have still been alive, and I could have still been picking these bad boys. I was the one creating the problem. I made up my mind that I was not going to blame it on my dad or my childhood. There were times I would talk to my dad in prayer and say, how could you do something so selfish to your two young kids and wife?. Then I had to ask how this is serving me. It did not serve me, it made me upset and angry. It was not the first time I had been in that space, so I knew not to linger long there, because I knew it did not serve me.

Interpretation

When I learned about interpretation, I saw how I could have viewed my past situation in a positive way. I could see how my mom stepped up and became both parents. She put so much energy into my brother and I, we would not be the people we are today if she had not stepped up in that way. If my father never died, we would not have had that experience. Concerning my father, I could choose to go through life with the interpretation of having an extra angel watching over me and my family, whenever I get scared I can say my father and God are working together to keep me safe. A couple years that support from my mom allowed me to be less distracted with not having a father figure in my life.

My Father's Suicide

At first, I did not really know what happened with my dad because my mom was sensitive about it. Chinese people are overly concerned about image, so my mom did not want anyone that was in our circle to know he had committed suicide. She never even told my brother and I until I was in my twenties, and in college. We had this thing in our house where we just knew not to ask questions, because deep down I knew if I asked questions it would stir up these deep emotions for my mother, so I just assumed he died from a car accident, cancer or something. I was never sure.

Not having my father in my life did affect me. I did not always understand the power of interpretation as I do today. So, I stumbled in the dark at times, and other times I just went with the flow of how I was feeling. At one point I was dating a lot of bad boys. They were smokers, cheaters, and party goers. I remember during one of my therapy sessions, my therapist asked me why I continued in the same pattern with these guys. Though I liked the adventure and intrigue of the so-called bad boy image, I did not hesitate to blame my behavior on not having a father figure in my life. I chose the negative interpretation of my situation. While feeling justified in my behavior, it just led to more situations of the same nature. It served no purpose in my life.

Elizabeth Yang

immediately. I could have accepted the victim role easily for the rest of my life, and there were times that I did. Thank goodness I did not stay there. Today, I know it is what separates those who are successful and those who are not.

The Beginning

I do not remember much about my early years growing up. I do know my mom was a stay at home mom, and she raised my brother and I in the traditional Chinese "tiger mom" way. Things changed for my family after my dad passed away. I was three years old at the time. My mom, who had never worked a day in her life, had to find a source of income so we would not be out in the streets. The food stamps and welfare we received helped to some degree. But I saw my mom step up to her responsibility in a very real, impressionable way. I imagine for her, at the time, she was probably just doing something to make ends meet. But when I look back today, I can see her providing an example for my brother and I of how to allow the tiger to rise within.

While caring for me and my brother, my mom also picked up some students from our school and started a little tutoring group in our home. That way she could watch us while she worked to earn some extra income. Her becoming an entrepreneur not only took care of us but allowed us to see a part of her that we might not have ever seen before, if my dad was still living. Since then her tutoring business has evolved into an education center called Monterey Park Education Center in California, where she is the owner, Principal and CEO. Having you improve, taking what lessons you learned moving forward. That is the power you have, even though a negative thing happened to you. You have the power to not let it happen again in the future.

It is also important for me to mention that the more responsibility you take on, the more powerful you are. But before you get excited about the power, know that with responsibility comes work. For this reason, some people choose not to have the responsibility because of the work it requires. Remember that everything is a choice and a conversation, so you get to decide what responsibility you will take on. Some people link blame and responsibility together, this then makes them defensive. There are also blind spots that are not always recognizable sometimes until after something has happened. Having the blind spots pointed out or questioned can also trigger a defensive response in some people who have not processed what happened or reached an understanding of their responsibility. Working through this is the path to understanding Source.

Shaped By My Past Experiences

The successes and lessons I have experienced stem from being raised by a "tiger mom" and from taking the time to engage in transforming myself into the best version possible. This is a continuous process that I look forward to every day. I currently reside in California. That is where my law firm is located. When I look back at the experiences that made the most impression on my life, three events came to my mind

Elizabeth Yang

ties in because if someone is Source, it means they accept 100 % responsibility. You are Source when you can say, "I am responsible for 100 % of things that happen to me in life". It is important in this part, that you do not allow yourself to think about fault or blame. The focus is on you as the individual to create change in your own life. I know we have been trained to blame others and focus on that, but the challenge I present is to only look at yourself with your eyes wide open.

Consider you are walking in the parking lot and you get robbed. For example, you may ask yourself, "How am I responsible for this?" This is where you are the source, that the interpretation comes through. After assessing the situation, you found some things that you could have done differently and that you could use in the future. This way of processing the information does not give place to self-pity or blaming others. It allows you the space to learn, grow, and move on. A few considerations you could glean from the situation may include not carrying five grocery bags and your purse barely hanging off your arm while trying to talk on the phone. Doing this allowed you to be less alert of your surroundings and you were not in the position to defend yourself.

Being responsible always starts with assessing the situation and seeing if there was something you could have done differently and taking notes for the future. You can either come from the interpretation of the victim or you can come from Source. Coming from Source puts the blame on you, but not in the sense of fault. It just gives you that power to not let the same thing happen in the future. Taking responsibility helps

Have you ever wondered how is it that the same things can happen to multiple people but based on each of their interpretation they can come out of it with completely different results? Two people can go through the same divorce and one person will never trust anyone again, while the other will marry nine more times. It is a powerful concept because it is all internal. And it provides us so much power to live once we realize everything is in our control.

Things can happen to us externally in society, the government, politics, the weather, basically everything that is out of our control, but the one thing we can control is our interpretation. If we can interpret things to serve and benefit ourselves, then we can create our lives just the way we want. More directly, if we can interpret life situations in a positive way that serves us, it does not matter what happens to us externally. Our decisions are based on how we interpret things internally. In that light we win every time in the present and future.

Source and Responsibility

By reading my story you will become familiar with the terms Source and Responsibility, as they relate to my interpretation. These two terms fit nicely with interpretation because they provide the substance for change. Source and responsibility are linked together to create new meaning and better results. When I write in my journal that "I am Source," I am referring to myself as the origin of which everything must be evaluated, assessed, filtered, and interpreted. Responsibility

Elizabeth Yang

foundational structures I live by today. Unfortunately, like many of us, I did not have this knowledge when I was toiling through some of my toughest hardships, yet my hardships paved the path to me having a better understanding of what it takes to live my very best life.

Meaning Making Machines

I have come to believe that humans are "meaning making machines." We add our own meanings and interpretations to everything! That is the reason why, "everything is a conversation". Even the statement itself is a conversation. Those who know will hear me say this often. It is no question that we can control our interpretation; it does not matter what happens externally. Interpretation is what happens internally. Since everything is a conversation, we get to choose how we interpret it. We can choose to see the negative situations in our life as very depressing, allowing them to bring us down, or we can see it as blessings in disguise.

The pandemic we are now facing globally, allows for some good examples of this way of thinking. For some people, Covid-19 has been or is seen as a negative. It has interrupted their normal routine of living and the intensity of being isolated has led some to depression, even to attempted suicide. Then there are those people who are having a whole other situation and interpretation about it. For them, the pandemic has presented even more opportunities for them than they had before the pandemic. Having the time to slow down and think, has allowed them to refresh old ideas and create new ones.

# CHAPTER 12

ELIZABETH YANG

The Power of Interpretation

"You can either come from Source or a victim mentality"

Life presents to us an array of ups and downs. I believe we all can agree that it is much easier to accept the ups than the downs. Through my journey of understanding the downs, I found myself questioning the ups as well. Was I as happy or content as I thought I was, at given moments? My search for the meaning of it all has led me to a few conclusions, which I would like to share with you, as they are the

Elona Lopari

I believe that women have many natural gifts and the potential that needs to be utilized, in order to make an impact. I absolutely believe that this is the time that we partner with our counterparts, our men, in creating better versions of ourselves, our families, communities and society as a whole. "The future is truly female". I am going to end with the lyrics of the Michael Jackson song "Man in the Mirror" that says, "If you want to make the world a better place, take a look at yourself, then make a change." This is where all magic and impact begins.

Website: elonaloparicoaching.com
Facebook & Instagram: elonaloparicoaching
Linkedin: Elona Lopari

could be utilized in helping them integrate in a new country after migrating there from Albania.

My work in my own community has been so rewarding, since I feel that it's helping to create a full circle moment for me. I am connecting my parent's past challenges of navigating in a new country with my purpose and contribution today, and I am well into the future of helping others in my own community do the same. This also contributes to making a difference in raising everyone's levels of consciousness. My strong emotional connection with my own community, and ultimately country, has helped me expand my ultimate vision of creating new platforms and opportunities to help even more people into the future. So my reason, my WHY, has taken on a different meaning after this discovery. I call it a double fulfillment, by helping others through my passion and I'm also helping my own community and country of origin.

In conclusion, my journey has been long and as I continue to evolve into the better version of myself, with each passing day, the journey is still in progress. I believe that my past has helped shape the person and character that I have today. Also, the struggles that my family or I have encountered, have helped fuel my fire and desire to not want to see others suffer. I want to turn all the hardships and blessings along the way as stepping stones to "build on", for the future that is being created. I want all the readers of this book to know that women need to rise, and position themselves in new leadership roles in society.

Elona Lopari

At this point, I started coaching female company executives for various companies, I really enjoyed it and the difference that I was making. Eventually, I started coaching women professionals, in the effort of slowly moving away from the corporate environment to everyday people. I also wanted to explore new environments besides corporate, which I was already comfortable with. I would help female professionals with their career, business and personal coaching, and specifically the mindset. It was through all my work with other people I had come to a greater realization. I was helping myself and others learn how to manage the brain, as creating and designing life on our own terms is the key to live a life of fulfillment and greater contribution. This is the skill that I am continuously focusing on and teaching today as well.

Reconnecting to my Origin

The Covid-19 pandemic hit the entire world around March 2020, starting in China. While the world was going through turmoil, I was attempting to stay focused and positive, despite what was happening. I came across certain Facebook group online communities, which Albanian women were a part of. Immediately after, an "aha light bulb" hit me, as when making the instant connection with my own nationality, the desire to help women from my own nationality was awakened. Ever since, I have been majorly involved with spreading awareness and helping Albanian women grow personally and professionally. While doing work in this community, I also discovered how my professional experience

WOMEN IN THE *Modern* BUSINESS WORLD

Looking and searching for answers, I started what I have come to understand now is, "A lifelong self-development journey of self-discovery into my life purpose". I always knew that I had many skills and experiences that I am grateful to have gained over the years. However, the struggle was that I wasn't sure how to utilize all of them. Also, I had my latest passion for personal development into a life of greater meaning and contribution, as I had already discovered that when I connected and helped others, that is where I felt the most happy and fulfilled.

Coaching as a Way of Life

Around this time, I was introduced to coaching as a new industry. I was almost immediately attracted to it, due to its connection of contributing and helping others and also utilizing my current skills and experience. Also, I was always attracted to helping others realize their truest human potential, since I was using similar skills in my corporate career in working with people and leadership. My special passion was talent development. So, then I started investing in many coaching programs and started following many well-known role models in this industry, such as Tony Robbins, Oprah, Lisa Nichols, and Les Brown.

The more I got immersed in this new industry, the more I was helping myself through many of my own limitations, holding me back from that next level of fulfillment that I was craving so much. This is how I got hooked.

Elona Lopari

and parallel to that, as I had said to my father, I had my first child. A beautiful daughter named Bianca, and less than three years later, I had my son named Elvin.

My Career Takes Off

Meanwhile, I continued to grow my career in the same company, and to my advantage, many growth opportunities were available. I was promoted numerous times, ranging from positions in the Human Resource department, to executive leadership roles. As years passed by, there was an important change within the large corporation that I was working for. It was bought out by another company. At this time, the culture of the company and the room for growth opportunities decreased.

When I realised this change, I started looking for and getting curious about something new. I wanted something that was going to continue to keep me growing, and that I could enjoy while utilizing all my current skills that I, at that point, had learned over a thirteen year period. In this transition time, I increasingly started to become more aware of what I felt missing inside of me and I was looking for new ways into exploring it. By cultural expectations, I had everything that most people could ever ask for, such as a successful career, a beautiful family, and the love of my life. However, there was something inside of me telling me that I was meant for something more, and I had outgrown my current career and I needed to follow that inner voice. Guiding me into what the next phase of my life was going to look like.

enjoying the business, marketing, and psychology classes that I was taking. This is where my interest in the world of business, leadership and psychology started.

University Degree, Love and Family

I was able to earn my bachelor's degree in three years, due to the possibility that I somehow felt internally, that by working hard I could achieve my degree faster and I could start my career, bearing in my mind that my father had said that I could do and be anything. I remember taking classes in winter and summer breaks, in order to finish earlier. Around this time, I also met my husband. It was through mutual friends that we got to know one another, and we started dating each other. When my family found out about the relationship, my father specifically wasn't very fond of the new relationship. He kept telling me that I was still too young and that being with someone that early on was somehow going to stop me from building a successful career.

So, I made him a promise then and said to him that that wasn't going to happen and that somehow I was always going to figure out a way to manage multiple responsibilities at the same time, growing my career while still raising a family. After all, this is what I had seen my mother do for all those years. Plus, I was also in a different country where I could be anything that I wanted to be. I continued to keep that promise and right after graduating from college, my first job was a management trainee at a large retail corporation. While starting my career

Elona Lopari

me that day, was that he told us that here you can do and be anything that you want to be. Not understanding at the time, but many years later, I realized what he meant.

Creating a New Life

We put down our suitcases in a rented basement, yet, still very happy and hopeful to start our new life in a new country. Our new life in the US progressed, we registered to attend school and all throughout I helped our parents the most, being the oldest child. They needed help in translating almost everything, since English was a language barrier for both my parents. I also remember at one point my parents delegated the family budgeting and paying of bills to me, since they had difficulties with the language. These early responsibilities came to help me grow up faster, and also shaped the character that I have today.

By this time, I also had started to work. I had my first teenage jobs as a babysitter, restaurant hostess and waitress, and so on. I also remember using the money I earned while working, to help my parents supplement the family bills. Then came the time when I finished High School and started college. My father had always told me, my brother and sister that he had worked hard to bring us here, and that we all had to finish college and earn a bachelor's degree, and then earning a master's degree was up to us. So, not questioning this early expectation, I started college and also continued to work while attending classes. I chose to major in Business Management and Finance, after thoroughly today. "Whatever I set my mind to, I can achieve." Certainly, my father showed his pride in my progress and started sharing my story with people he knew. I also remember this experience, as to be one of the times that I felt the most emotionally connected to my father.

Life Changing Times

Then, another event came into our lives, and it would change our lives for the better. At this time, I had just finished my first year of high school and was fifteen. My dad secured another visa, and this time it was for traveling to the United States. Staying persistent in his dream to have a better life, he took the leap once more and travelled alone towards the US, with the high hopes of bringing us all over to the US one day. This time he was successful. After less than two years, we also came over to the US. His dream of bringing his family over to another country with more opportunities had finally come true.

Our life in the US started, and I vividly remember my mom, brother and sister trying to imagine life here and trying to compare images we had seen on TV, or stories that our father had told us over the phone. When we landed at JFK Airport, we were very excited to reunite with our dad and were looking in awe at our surroundings and trying to imagine what this phase in our new life would look like. I remember the detail of a very noisy highway and people that looked so different, while our father shared stories of life here. One saying that stuck with

Elona Lopari

The Gift of Failing

On our way home, my father told me quietly of his decision to help me get my grades up in math. He was going to do so by helping tutor me in the subject, as math happened to be a subject that he was very confident in. I happily accepted, as I was also not feeling good about the struggles that I had been encountering with the subject, for quite some time by then. The tutoring sessions were going well at first, but shortly after, my dad was getting frustrated. He was trying to teach me how to solve math problems with the help of "a shorter version", with the intention of achieving faster improvements. Soon he realized that this approach was not working. He then changed his approach.

My father started helping me break down the problems to their root cause, so that I could understand how all the concepts connected together. We both noticed that this method started to work, and slowly I made progress. Feeling better about understanding the problem, I started practicing solving complex math problems after school. As soon as I came home, I would run and hide away on my side of the bunk bed that I shared with my sister. The days went by, and while practicing I noticed that I was making good progress.

It was a real improvement that my teacher was noticing as well, and that was also helping me increase my confidence and self-esteem. This was one of those few moments that left an everlasting impression on my self-belief, it also still serves me about missing him, by hearing his voice, we were thinking he was there with all of us. Then at about the three-year mark when the war was almost finished, my father returned back home from Germany due to the impossibility of securing permanent residence for all of us there.

My father returned happy to see all of us, but unhappy with the fact that his sacrifice of over three years of being away from home, ended with him coming back. He had not been able to provide a better life for all of us by moving to a new country. I felt that he took this as a personal defeat of letting us all down, and that took a toll on him. For the next few years thereafter, he struggled with re-finding himself in his career, by pursuing a few unsuccessful ventures in the pursuit of trying to build something new again...

There was a moment of meaningful impact for me at this time when my father returned from Germany. Due to the impact of what was going on in the country after the civil war, I had lost the focus and drive to continue my learnings in the subject of math, and at this time I was well into middle school. As a result, I was failing this subject. I remember my father coming to the parent-teacher conference and being told by my math teacher of my struggles with this subject. I remember seeing him disappointed, but also surprised of all the levels that I had dropped in math. This was hugely because I was overall a responsible kid doing well in all the other subjects, mainly the language and writing classes. Today I have found, this is still one of my strengths and favorite subjects.

Elona Lopari

My father encountered many challenges on the journey when traveling to Germany, where he had to cross the border since he wasn't allowed to go into the country any other way. He has told us he had to survive on a pack of cookies for over a week. Eventually he made it to Hanover in Germany, where he continued to attempt to find a place to live and a job to help him survive while not knowing anyone that could help him there. The entire time, he was also trying to figure out how to bring us over to Germany for a better life and greater opportunities, as this was no longer available in Albania, especially because of what was happening.

On the other side while in Albania, still surviving the daily ordeals of the civil war, I remember my mom trying to hold it together and protecting us from any harm. At this point we lived with my mom and grandmother. My mom worked in a bank and I remember her always working, while at the same time raising us with the help of my grandmother. I believe these were my early memories of a hard-working woman that handled many responsibilities at the same time, so very early on she was a strong role model for me. I believe my mom became a big influence in the way that growing up, I never questioned working while also taking care of a family.

My Father's Return

Meanwhile, back in Germany, I remember my dad sending us recorded audio cassettes in the mail that he had recorded himself, telling us stories of his journey in Germany. My siblings and I used to listen to them and feel better bullet that went through his eye and left him blindly impaired for the rest of his life. I remember my mom telling me that he had never seen her or her siblings due to his injury. He mainly recognized his children by the sound of their voice. So, my grandmother had to remain tough while she had to fulfill both roles of taking care of four children due to my grandfather's disability and his time mostly away from home. Her family left the village many years ago and moved to the city of Tirana thereafter. Tirana is also where my mom and dad met.

The Civil War

Years later, in the year of 1997, a rebellion happened that escalated to a Civil War in Albania, which was sparked by pyramid scheme of failures. The government was toppled and more than two thousand people were killed. I was thirteen at the time and remember people had secured weapons, were rioting, and destroying property and killing other people in the process. I also remember hearing gun shootings through my bedroom window and also watching news stories about people that were shot inside their homes. I firmly remember this being the most traumatic experience in my life thus far.

Around the same time, my father had secured a visitor's visa in order to travel to Germany. He chose to use this opportunity to give traveling to Germany a try and see what new opportunities would be available for him and us, especially because of what was happening in the country.

Elona Lopari

side, who also lived with us. The same grandmother helped, at one time or another, to raise most of the grandchildren of my aunt and uncle.

My Heritage

My father was born in a small village called Bulqize in Albania. He always spoke to me of his childhood being happy overall, but with lots of hard manual labor work involved, as he always attempted to help his family and siblings while his father was mostly away. His father was an official in World War II and visited them only as allowed, periodically, so as a result he did not have many memories of his father. I remember him telling me that he looked up to his father and missed him.

The village of Bulqize was the same place that I mostly remember visiting as a small child, in between school and summer breaks. I remember enjoying my time there because I got to be involved in many activities that would not otherwise be available in the city, such as milking a cow, ploughing the fields, planting a garden and feeding honey bees. For a child my age then, these activities were so much fun, and I hold them as memories of a happy childhood.

On the other hand, my mom was born in the city of Tirana. However, her family was also from the same village where my father was born, Bulqize. My mother's father was also a war official fighting in World War II, where he was injured by a

CHAPTER 11

ELONA LOPARI

Your Mess Is Your message - Use It to Do Good In The World!

I grew up in a small neighborhood in Tirana, Albania, where I hold dear a lot of memories of playing outside with friends, while reinventing very creative outdoor activities and games. It was a small, but very safe and loving community. I remember my parents working most of the day and my brother, sister and I were watched over by my grandmother on my father's

WOMEN IN THE *Modern* BUSINESS WORLD

businesses in Europe and Africa, while also taking into account social, environmental and economic factors. We need to create a world that is taken good care of and we need to provide hope for future generations.

You can contact me at Heliosinfinitas@gmail.com
and find out more at heliosinfinitas.com

Caroline Nijland

I always had this deep feeling of a mission in my life: helping vulnerable people to improve their living conditions, alleviate energy-related poverty and stimulate socio-economic development. It is unacceptable that still so many people in the twenty-first century are deprived of electricity. I have this fire that remains burning in my heart willing to change the world, combating injustice and inequalities in society. In that sense, my long life in Africa and the work of my parents has contributed strongly to this passion. It drives my energy and perseverance forward. My success code is working hard, supporting other people, staying true to yourself and being open minded towards other people's beliefs - and believe in what you want to achieve.

The transition needed to cope with climate change will require changes in many areas. This will raise questions and shake up today´s perceived ideas. It will lead to a questioning and remodeling of the current economic and social system. Citizen participation is essential to unite around this major project, which is the fight against climate change. This is a call to action. I invite each reader to take action and participate in existing climate actions and networks , or to create new movements and incorporate gradually in daily life actions towards a safer, secured and cleaner environment.

As environmental and social issues are a topic of my huge interest, I aspire to create a pool of female talent in the sustainable business sector, within five years. I would like to identify all those who have the profile to invest or accelerate the implementation of sustainable businesses or to manage these an individual. The countries of the world's population, with the largest footprint, are often least affected by the effects of climate change nowadays. While the countries that are already affected by those effects, often have a very small footprint. Eventually, if we do not intervene, that first part will face the consequences too. More extreme weather will result in more scarcity, climate refugees and wars.

As a privileged young person living in a country with many opportunities, I try to reduce my effect to limit the damage. I know that as a single person, I will not be able to solve this problem, but if I do not take responsibility, who will? I hope more people wake up and become aware that this is the time to change before it is too late."

Parting Words

I am visiting the field in Africa regularly, to see with my own eyes how we are advancing with our activities on site, and what real impact our activities have on people's lives. Moving in the field and meeting the people is the most beautiful part of my work, as one sees clearly how much electricity enhances the life of people. There are so many stories that move my colleagues and me in the field. During one of my visits I met an old woman, her exact age was not known, who was sick. She expressed her wish to get her house connected to a solar system. When she switched on the light for the first time, she could not stop her tears of joy. She had been hoping to experience this moment for a long time. Four weeks later she unfortunately passed away.

Caroline Nijland

very much interested in the topic of climate change. Below are some valuable thoughts shared by her.

"The most important thing that should happen in order to make the transition to a sustainable world, is that every individual should take responsibility for their own choices first. All pollution and emissions are eventually the result of our own choices. This is everyone's problem.

If you divide the total effect that we humans have on the planet, with all the influenced actions that we take, with the amount of people in this world, you will get the average effect per person. In a formula: Average effect per person × Number of people = Total effect

By 'effect' I mean among other things: Greenhouse gas emissions, land-use and the use of freshwater. If we want to achieve a society in which everybody has access to clean water, food and shelter, the total effect should decrease. According to the UN, the world's population will increase from almost 7.8 billion now, to 9.8 billion people in 2050. This means that we must lower the average effect per person.

Many people are not aware of the effect their choices have on the environment. Simple choices like what to eat, what stuff to buy and what not, what transportation to take, what bank, what insurance company, what energy company to choose and how to use that energy can make a difference. Even if you are not the prime minister, you can still make your contribution as the active participation of policymakers, regulators and companies. The process is possible and achievable, but it will require a massive orchestration by industry and governments to make it happen. But I can only repeat it, key, and part of the strategy being employed by countries such as Denmark, Sweden, Germany and African countries such as Mali and Morocco, is setting goals on energy transition, backed by targets and timelines. Transparent public-private partnerships with an emphasis on local content are also important. Governments and multinational corporations need the courage to break away from old models, to embrace new technology, and to loosen the reins of the state to allow the private sector and SME sector to be a partner in moving forward into this new world. Building partnerships across the countries and continents, gathering our forces and investing and acting are key to the success of the transition to a sustainable world. Isn't it an exciting decade that we are moving in?

Concerns about job losses in fossil fuel industries can be addressed by absorbing retrained workers into renewables with state support and incentives – an example shown by Germany, which is rapidly retreating from dirty fuel while preserving jobs.

Valuable Reflections from the Young Generation

Let me introduce Marlou Geraedts, an 18-year-old student at the University in Wageningen in The Netherlands. She is following the master's in environmental sciences, and is

Caroline Nijland

The International Energy Agency reminds us that Africa accounts for only 4% of global power supply, and in sub-Saharan Africa, people are suffering from frequent electricity disruptions. 600 million people in Sub-Saharan Africa are still reliant on charcoal, kerosene lamps, battery operated flashlights, wood and candles for their power needs. Energy demand is a key driver of rampant deforestation and roadside sales of charcoal are providing livelihoods to thousands of people. The growth of renewable energy is a potential game-changer for Africa but, given its needs, there is still a long way to go. Many countries still rely on fossil fuels for their baseload energy supply. Research shows that more than one hundred new power stations are planned in a dozen African countries, most of which will be coal or oil-fired.

I am working with many fantastic teams and the great support of multilateral organizations, such as the World Bank, EU, national governments in Africa and Europe, and corporate companies in Europe. We are working on initiating, implementing and operating small and big scale renewable energy initiatives in Africa, which will move the continent into a future characterised by new clean energy sources, driven by technology and innovations. Solar power and other non-grid options are being rolled out slowly across the continent, as the population continues to grow, and rapid urbanization is increasing the demand for energy.

The hope that technology alone will come riding to the rescue and deliver an energy transition is flawed. It requires world. First, show you are concerned with sustainability. Then act on it in your work and personal environment and share as much as possible through social media about what you are doing to contribute in your way with the resources and knowledge you have. Make sustainability topics part of the education of your children. Make the councils, local politics and your employer aware of the need for action towards a sustainable world. Visit meetings, conferences, and debates where you can be inspired by what others do.

Say no to the use of many toxic pesticides that are used in the agriculture sector, the many toxic substances used to clean or wash, and others that we also use in our houses. So many ecological alternatives do exist for cleaning and washing, but they have not been used at their full potential. Avoid plastic by buying alternative material that is less harmful for the environment. I believe that we will accelerate things in sustainability over the next five years. We can no longer put our heads in the sand. We must act together. There is much in the way of subsidies and financing available in the world, which allow you to realise initiatives with a focus on sustainability and climate change.

My Personal Contribution to a Sustainable World

"One of my most important goals is that we can enhance the lives of many vulnerable people on this planet".

Caroline Nijland

Secondly, the recent marches with young people all over the world showcased the urgency for climate action. The idealistic and capitalist worlds come together. Because when the Greta Thunbergs and the people with the most money talk about sustainability, it finally gets serious.

Thirdly, as having raised much subsidy for stimulating renewable energy projects in Africa, I noticed that still much of international public finance in African energy goes to fossil fuels, compared to just 18 percent to cleaner alternatives.

I also noticed that climate scepticism is less visible in the developing world, as they do not have much to lose, like other parts of the world where fossil fuel industry profits are a huge industry. Instead of supporting the developing world to reduce their CO2 emissions, cheap loans are provided for the export of fossil technology from Europe to the developing world. Instead, we can support the development world to move from fossil fuel to renewables, by helping them to invest in sustainable energy. We should be phasing out the use of fossil fuel, but the industry is fearful that all this knowledge, the infrastructure and resources, will become stranded assets. We have to think all the way about how we can reorganise society.

An Invitation to Engage

I would like to invite everyone to participate more actively in this transition. As citizens or small entrepreneurs, we can indeed contribute to the path towards a more sustainable climate change and strengthen the economy. These proposals will be proposed to the parliament or through referenda, without being filtered. This is an initiative, led by citizens, that could be set up in every country and that could enforce real transition.

Progress in Technology and Innovative Ideas

I see hopeful positive trends from past years. Firstly, many start-ups develop or support disruptive projects, capitalising on collective intelligence and strongly impacting society, in a process of better living. Many programs provide start-ups with access to the most advanced 3D design, modeling, simulation and visualization solutions, and a dedicated collaborative space in the cloud. All of these digital technological resources are enriched by a high-level mentoring program allowing start-ups to industrialise and internationalize their project and entrepreneurs are the engine of our economy. They are at the center of society that is changing rapidly. It is therefore necessary that they continue to innovate and make it more sustainable. Technological innovations, new competition, the energy transition, the food transition, the movement towards circular entrepreneurship: all of these are both threats and great opportunities for entrepreneurs. Let's think of opportunities to give innovative ideas a platform. There are already plenty of examples of companies making beautiful sustainable steps such as reducing or replacing plastic with other bio resources.

Caroline Nijland

The radical change in our way of thinking is not easy, as it conflicts with the system we have been living in for decades and that has shaped our mindsets and way of life. Should we not all reflect on our lifestyle and restructure it by looking at what we really need, and stop over consuming? Do we as citizens not all have a certain responsibility to challenge ourselves how we can contribute to "greening our way of living" and participate more to create a sustainable society?

We need to reduce emissions by more than 7% every year to limit the temperature increase to 1.5 °C. This means an unprecedented level or collaboration and transformation. Do we want to be the generation that grasps the possibilities and potential to make the impossible the possible? It would not be wise not to stimulate the economy without taking the green economy into consideration. If we proceed with business as usual, it only delivers limited economic growth for the future generations. It would be much wiser to invest in an alternative economy and to invest in the job market that will have to deliver different skills than we now have.

The Citizen's Convention for the Climate, an unprecedented democratic experience in France, aims to give voice to citizens to accelerate the fight against climate change. Its mandate is to define a series of measures to achieve a reduction of at least 40% of greenhouse gas emissions by 2030 (compared with 1990), in a spirit of social justice. The citizen committee that consisted of 150 citizens, selected randomly in France, submitted 148 proposals in June 2020 that should combat social injustice and

WOMEN IN THE *Modern* BUSINESS WORLD

We focus very much on reducing CO_2, but that remains a vague concept for the masses of people. Why not have real communication about what the benefits are of a better climate? Clean air and water, more biodiversity, energy bill down, better health… Capture the narrative of the story. This is good, and we need to be much better in telling the story of the future. We were always told what the benefits are of the coal and oil industry being beneficial for employment opportunities and the economy and that is why we poured in a lot of money.

As we mentioned about both topics, policies and communication, I like to refer to the concept of the thinking of Joyeeta Gupta, Professor of Environment and Law, who stipulates that we are in a huge health and ecological crisis. In fact, she says our GDP depends on natural resources. What do we prioritise? GDP, or do we instead prioritise our health, the environment and our societies? Does GDP reflect global health, well-being and happiness in the world? To what extent is GDP nowadays a useful concept for the way we govern our society. We have to undermine the concept of GDP and on the other hand we have to think how we can organise a society that focuses on well-being, social contacts, and enough food on the table. The radical change in our way of thinking is not easy, as it conflicts with the system we are living in since decades, and that has shaped our mindsets and way of life. Should we not all reflect on our lifestyle and restructure it by looking at what we really need, and stop over consuming? Do we, as citizens, not all have a certain responsibility to challenge ourselves on how we can contribute to "greening our way of living", and participate more to create a sustainable society?

Caroline Nijland

roofs being covered with photovoltaic panels, with electricity storage systems and intelligent networks optimising its use. In the basements, the heat and cold networks will recycle urban waste, biomethane, canal water, and geothermal energy. Large solar parks will have to supply the cities also with energy.

Citizens can indeed contribute to the transition to a sustainable world. We can think of changing our socio habits such as living in shared housing, such as colocation and intergenerational cohabitation. More and more women are thinking of sharing a house with other women where they can share the costs for living, nursing and medical care when they are reaching an older age. We are also seeing a proliferation of collaborative workspaces. We perceive an increase in the development of car sharing, carpooling, and telework.

Do we not all strive to zero or less air and water pollution, affordable and secured energy, smarter transport, high quality food? But why then do we not realise the need for immediate action. I notice many people around me not acting and thinking on ways to integrate sustainability in their daily life, while so many solutions already exist. Is it because there is no imminent risk, as it was the case with the coronavirus and that engendered a decision of governments to pour massive money to restore the economy? Is the communication around climate change and campaigns really effective and clear? Current campaigns about climate change showcase apocalyptic and horror scenarios of animals dying, sea rising and flooding in our lands, more forest fires etc. These campaigns are ineffective as they do not seem to move people to take action but instead people look away and it creates indifference. How can we communicate better about climate change?

it "Europe's man on the moon moment". Nothing similar has been attempted before, as the pattern of human progress since the industrial revolution has been one of relentless exploitation and despoilment of the natural world, filling the atmosphere with carbon and the seas with plastic.

Thirdly, as having raised much subsidy for stimulating renewable energy projects in Africa, I noticed that 5,000 billion euros is being poured each year as subsidies into the fossil industry. I also noticed that climate scepticism is less visible in the developing world, as they do not have much to lose like other parts of the world where fossil fuel industry profits are a huge industry. Instead of supporting the developing world to reduce their CO_2 emissions, cheap loans are provided for the export of fossil technology from Europe to the developing world. Instead, we can support the developing world to move from fossil fuel to renewables by helping them to invest in sustainable energy. We should be phasing out the use of fossil fuel but the industry fears that all this knowledge, the infrastructure and resources, will become stranded assets. We have to think all the way on how we can reorganise society.

Action Steps to Take

Many cities aim for carbon neutrality between 2030 and 2050. To achieve this, major changes will have to be made in the energy, transport and lifestyles of the inhabitants. To reach the goal, all the levers must be actuated. First, the local production of renewable energy with 20 to 40% of the

Caroline Nijland

Saharan Africa, I have learned that a transition from fossil fuel to more renewable energy can only take place when policies are lifted over the typical government elected periods. We need to invest in fundamental knowledge in the longer term. We need to build a world that is cleaner and fairer by incentivizing the energy transition through changes in social policies, land reform and transition to other materials, then there could be room for changes. Policy making needs long term goals and solutions - not short term - so an important shift has to be made. For governments, a real option is to encourage change through regulation and to provide tax breaks. In Norway, where no VAT is levied on electric cars, half of the newly registered cars are already electric. In the Netherlands there is no VAT levied on purchase of solar panels.

Secondly, governments and the industry should make clear and bold decisions to shift much of the allocated budgets for traditional economy to a sustainable economy that takes into account humans, environment and health. I was hopeful when the European Commission announced to invest much for greening Europe, the so-called Green Deal. The European Green Deal is the new growth strategy. According to recent figures, 1 trillion euros is needed in total for the Green Deal in the coming decade. The European Green Deal aims to transform the 27-EU country bloc from a high to a low-carbon economy, without reducing prosperity and while improving people's quality of life, through cleaner air and water, better health and a thriving natural world. If that sounds ambitious, it is. The European Commission president, Ursula von der Leyen, called

WOMEN IN THE
Modern
BUSINESS WORLD

A huge transition to "post-carbon" cities is necessary in a worsening climate context, where the days of heat waves are increasing, water resources are becoming scarce, air pollution is increasing and becoming unbearable in certain parts of the world. There are also increased floods, increasingly devastating storms, excess mortality of vulnerable and poor people, increased droughts that make certain parts of the world an unlivable place, and crop failures in millions of fields of small and medium farmers.

This list of consequences of climate change is alarming, all the more that the world, at least governments and big multinationals and citizens, do not seem to react too much. Awareness has a hard time landing in our minds. Thus, there is a real imperative for the ecological transition, the search for new energy production and technological solutions drives engineers and entrepreneurs around the world. Are we indeed aware of the climate urgency?

What is needed for a transition to a sustainable world?

We have just entered the ten most difficult, challenging decisive decades in the history of humanity. We have a huge and challenging task in front of us. What do we need to undertake?

Firstly, having worked for 25 years in the renewable energy sector and specifically in the rural electrification sector in Sub

Caroline Nijland

(savanna) in Brazil, the Amazon region, Southeast Asia and the Congo Basin and the Cape are crucial hotspots of biodiversity. A large part of the earth's surface is now intended for housing, agriculture, animal husbandry and forestry. In 2020, only 34% of all land is untouched or wild. Scientists think the oceans will have turned into underwater desert in less than 35 years. The world population is growing enormously and therefore more food is needed, especially protein. We are exhausting land and sea. Some other shivering facts are that seven million people yearly are affected by air pollution and 25% of all the diseases have ecological causes, such as water and food pollution. There were 18.8 million new disaster-related internal displacements recorded in 2017.

A quarter of the CO_2 emissions are the result of power generation and heating. "A strong political will can cut half of its consumption in half within ten years," Jonathan Foley, a Project Drawdown director, has said. Agriculture and forestry and land use also emit 25% CO_2 emissions. These are complex issues as the world population is expected to grow strongly from 7.8 billion in 2020 to 9.8 billion in mid-2050. So, the focus is on making agriculture even more intensive, and more food can be produced through the use of robots, genetically modified crops and big data. The rest of the disruptions come from industry, transport and buildings. Transport represents almost a quarter of Europe's greenhouse gas emissions, and is the main cause of air pollution in cities. A large challenge remains for the residual and tertiary houses to make them energy efficient and energy proof.

male colleagues in the sector. I was very successful in lobbying, networking, implementation of projects and partnerships and attracting finance, so that also helped to gain trust.

My work has been in many developing countries with complex factors, since there is hardly any infrastructure in place. There is much poverty, and it is difficult for people to realise their dreams, with limited or no available resources. With the support of many multilateral organisations and governments, my teams have introduced new technologies allowing the people to get access to electricity, to modern appliances and finance, thereby enhancing their lives.

I also support women in Africa to produce and sell their handmade sustainable indigo fabrics to Europe. I give free training for migrant women in Amersfoort and the suburbs of Paris, to set-up or grow their business with The Association Remarquables in Paris. My new business yourAcademy4growth is a global online platform for self-employed professionals with the goal to transfer and share skills and expertise, to grow their business through a large network of high-level experts.

A Sustainable World

I predict we are at the eve of a gradual transformation to a sustainable world. Only 15% of the land and 7% of the sea are currently protected. It is said that if we want to prevent any other species from being threatened, we must protect about 70% of the land surface against habitat loss. The cerrado

Caroline Nijland

on the board of the local companies as president and board member. I was also vice president of an international umbrella organisation for rural electrification in Brussels, the Alliance for Rural Electrification.

Since May 2018 I have been running my own business, Helios Infinitas, advising international companies, international organisations and the government how to advance energy access. As a consultant for GET.invest Finance Catalyst I also advise and support entrepreneurs in Africa to get access to finance, as they do not always have the same opportunities as us in Europe. Especially small and medium businesses do lack network and experience to access finances to start or scale-up a business. My time is also dedicated to coaching and advising a lot of young people in Europe and Africa that are interested in the field of renewable energies and rural electrification, or who would like to set up and run social enterprises. I am transferring my knowledge and expertise to allow them to develop themselves professionally and make them enthusiastic about the work of rural electrification, as there is still so much to undertake in the sector. It is very rewarding.

When I started my endeavour in the renewable energy sector in 1998 - specifically the rural electrification sector - I was practically one of the very few women in the sector. In some boards I was even the only female board member. By working hard, listening, willing to learn continuously, being patient, putting a lot of efforts in networking and being present in the field in Africa, I very quickly gained trust and confidence from my was not yet widely known and was not taken seriously as an alternative renewable energy source. He strongly believed in the benefits of electrification through solar energy, for the social and economic development of the rural and peri-urban areas in Africa.

Hence, soon after my studies and after a short professional detour in the education field, I quickly found my calling. From the year 1997 I gradually started to work in the field of renewable energy and specifically rural electrification, with the aim of supplying as many households, community services, and small and medium enterprises as possible, in the rural areas in Africa with electricity. All this with the help of decentralised, large solar power plants for entire villages and individual systems on household or community roofs.

Between 2007 and 2018 I was the director of the Foundation for Rural Energy Services (FRES) in Amsterdam, which was set up by one of the major energy companies in the Netherlands. During that period, I worked with a lot of passion and hard work - together with committed colleagues, to ensure that one million of people across six countries in Sub-Saharan Africa were connected to electricity by 2019. In addition to attracting funding from the World Bank, the EU, European and African governments and various international funds, I was also responsible for lobbying and negotiating with national governments to set up electricity companies, establishing concessions and partnerships, implementing the organisation's strategy, and following the progress of local operations. I was

Caroline Nijland

I have worked in the renewable energy sector for more than 25 years, connecting already one million people to solar electricity in rural areas in Africa. I have set up six renewable energy companies in Africa providing energy access to households, public institutions, health clinics, schools, and businesses. This has had a huge social and economic impact in rural areas. These companies provide direct employment to more than 300 staff and indirectly to 400 people.

I was born in The Netherlands. However, soon after I was born my parents moved with my sister, brother and me to Crete, where we lived for two years and then we moved to Cameroon where we were supposed to stay for two years, but instead we ended up staying for fifteen years. My father had a career in development cooperation in the agricultural sector. Later on, he combined it with a business in solar energy. He was the first pioneer in west Africa introducing solar energy to missionaries, churches and lodges in remote areas. We left Cameroon in 1987 and moved to Meaux in France, where I finished my high school. Later, I did my University studies in The Netherlands.

As a child I became very aware of the fact that 95% of people in Cameroon had no access to electricity. We had access to electricity in the capital city but with many interruptions, or blackouts. So, at sixteen-years-old, I left Africa with a strong awareness that there was a great need to support Cameroon and many other African countries with the necessary infrastructure. I have followed in my father's footsteps. He taught me the basics of solar energy since 1998, at a time when solar energy

CHAPTER 10

CAROLINE NIJLAND

What are the Ingredients of the Modern Business World?

I have a vision of a more sustainable world. A world where each of us can definitely contribute to make our world a better, cleaner and healthier world to live in. A world where we would pay more attention to the more and many vulnerable people, that are particularly affected by the climate change consequences. Unless we act now, our younger generations will inherit a huge task to make the transformation possible. Is that what we really want?

do with what we wear. When we are present and connected, we radiate presence, and this is attractive to all around us. Men love to serve us, so let them open the door, carry the shopping etc. However, if you want them to take the rubbish out, if you are not specific on timing, they will do it when they are ready, which may be hours later than you want. Communication is the key to all relationships.

Let´s Fulfil Our Dreams

Without the incredible practices I learnt and embodied from this work I would not be writing this chapter, I would not be an author, or speaker and I probably wouldn't be having the incredible experiences of travelling around the world. The only thing that is missing is another loving relationship. I'm now totally ready for it, but I'm not prepared to accept second best. I'm looking for a partner who can be a king to my queen, who I can explore and surrender with and have a sacred union with, on all levels.

We never know what tomorrow will bring. The only certainty we have in life is death, so please join me in living in the River of Life rather than a pond of mediocrity. Seize opportunities as they arise, be mindful and be in the now and don't forget to make health your number one priority.

I wish you a long, healthy and prosperous life where you get to fulfil your dreams. Find out more at pamlob.com

Pam Lob

trying to keep me safe. Heart IQ has taught me many things, but a couple of key ones are to find joy even in the darkest moments and to see there is nothing wrong with me! Yes, there may be some unpleasant experiences happening, but they are not who I am, they are just experiences occurring in that moment.

The Feminine and Masculine Essence

Alongside Heart IQ, the biggest transformations for me have occurred through the Art of Feminine Presence and working with its founder Rachael Jayne Groover. Partly from my upbringing, education, and health issues, I was very disconnected from my natural feminine essence. We all have both feminine and masculine essence, but we have one which is dominant and natural to us. This does not always go with gender. This work has transformed how I live. I now spend large parts of my day in feminine flow, rather than in the pushy, competitive driven masculine energy. The masculine gives to receive, whilst the feminine receives to give. When we are in our natural essence, life is easy and harmonious, we are each playing to our strengths. Yes, as women we can push a rock up a hill, but it stresses our body and stresses the males watching us. Men love to push the rocks up the hill, so let them get on with it and sit back and enjoy watching them.

Being feminine is not about make-up, fancy clothes and high heels. It's about being connected to our lower chakras, womb space (our powerhouse) and hips. Its energetic connection and attitude, and where we focus our attention, and has nothing to

WOMEN IN THE *Modern* BUSINESS WORLD

Heart IQ

Like many, I was excellent at hiding and not expressing emotion, and I could barely feel my energetic body. A huge turning point for me was when I started to train as a Heart Intelligence Coach, Heart IQ, with Christian Pankhurst. I learnt to connect with my body, to feel it and its subtle energies. To truly feel all my emotions and to let them run through me rather than suppressing them. Today if I am angry, I will own it and say, "I'm feeling angry right now because ….". I also love to have a temper tantrum, like a three-year-old. My inner child has such fun – I highly recommend them if you are in a safe space and can let rip. I challenge you not to laugh within a minute. If I want to cry, I cry no matter where I am. At first it was embarrassing but now it feels great and most people appreciate the authenticity and vulnerability.

At my first retreat I was overwhelmed by the love of everyone there. The unconditional love and non-judgemental approach blew my mind and my heart. From an exercise we did, I even had a heart orgasm and felt my heart and connection to all around me expand in a way I never thought possible.

To be whole, we need all our emotions, just like a rainbow needs all its colours to be a rainbow. I've learnt to pause and to feel my body, emotions, energy, and if my mind comes in with a story, to let it go and to tune into my intuition and what I really want right now. I've learnt to listen to my intuition and to trust it and discern when it's intuition or just my mind and ego

Pam Lob

might be harmful to another, so it's imperative you discover what is right for you, or you could be unwittingly adding to your bodies stress levels. Everything you do that is not in harmony with your body causes stress and stress is at the root of most disease. When I found the foods that were right for me, the excess weight I was carrying dropped away with ease. These were not major changes to my foods, just some minor tweaks. I don't believe in diets, I never have. I believe in healthy eating and a healthy lifestyle that gives you what YOU need. It's not about going without, depriving yourself, it's about moderation and honouring your body as the temple that it truly is.

We are energetic divine beings here on earth, having a physical experience. Modern western society focuses on the mind. Our educational and business systems have resulted in us becoming disconnected from our body and emotions, our natural sexual essence. A large number of people spend the day feeling guilty about the past they cannot change and worrying about a future that may never happen. We are told it is wrong to be angry, to cry, to express how we feel. When we suppress our emotions, they can go two ways. Firstly, is the pressure cooker effect: anger which is a healthy emotion can explode as rage, definitely not healthy for the person, or persons on the receiving end and sadness unexpressed can lead to depression. Secondly the emotions just get lodged in the cells, causing stress and damage which ultimately lead to disease. Many cancer patients find it very difficult to express emotions.

not being able to do anything to take away the pain and suffering, and intimacy can easily be forgotten.

All is exacerbated if you have young children and you don't have the strength or energy to meet all their needs. They may not only miss out on activities their friends are doing and family outings, but also can have implications on their long-term mental health. I know both my kids have had difficulties because of mine and Sandy's health problems and his subsequent death. There are also many children who have to grow up way too soon as they help care for a sick parent, or the loss of a parent.

I long for the day when health care is holistic and personalised, bringing the best of all modalities to do what is best for the patient. I am on a mission to teach people that prevention is better than cure, what optimal health looks like, and what they can do to obtain it so fewer families have to go through the heartache that we did.

Epigenetics, Energy and Divinity

What do I mean by holistic and personalised health? We are all unique, even identical twins. They may start out with the same genetic blueprint, but the environment affects how these genes are expressed – epigenetics - and this can result in very different health outcomes. What we require for optimal health is different for each of us. The first place most people focus on is food and exercise, but what is right for one,

Pam Lob

disease prevention, it falls well short, due to it concentrating on signs and symptoms, a one size fits all approach and the failure to address the causes of disease. Namely what we put into our bodies, both through diet, the air we breathe and our skin care products. They all affect our essential microbiome, environmental toxins, and stress of all kinds. The focus is on the physical body and if the mind comes into play at all, it's about mental illness, not mindset.

Mindset plays a huge part in outcomes. Sandy survived, and even managed to be at home, over the Christmas of 2004 through sheer determination. I have patients who were told they were dying still being with us years later, and others who were told they were cured but had given up on themselves died. No part of us works in isolation, everything is connected, which is why I love to take a holistic approach, and like the ancient traditions of Ayurveda and traditional Chinese medicine.

When your health is compromised it affects every aspect of your life. It is impossible or at least difficult to work to your full potential. If you are a business owner or live somewhere like in the USA where there is little social support and large medical bills, there are also huge financial implications. Even in the UK where we have excellent sickness benefits, it does not fully compensate you if you are off work for a long period. Then there are the implications for the family, as the ill health of one partner also affects the health of the other from the added stress, feeling of inadequacy and to practice what I preach and make my health my number one priority. As I've learnt to feel my body, emotions and energy, and to regularly tune into what and how I'm feeling, I'm quickly able to spot when things are going out of balance and to take action to rectify this.

A Holistic Approach

Take a good look at your life. Do you avoid feeling or dealing with a difficult situation by keeping busy, by running away? Where is your health and self-care in your list of priorities? How good are you at saying "no" to others demands, that don't resonate and saying "yes" to yourself? Be honest with yourself, as some of the answers you may not want to hear, the only person you will be letting down by not being truthful is yourself.

The signs that all is not well creep up slowly, and frequently go unnoticed, perhaps they are accepted as just part of ageing. By the time a doctor is able to diagnose a disease the damage is done, and it becomes harder to turn things around, but it's always possible. The body is incredible at repairing itself, if given the right things. Health is not just about the physical body, but also the mental, emotional, energetic, and spiritual.

Western medicine is all about 'sick care' and not 'health care'. I have come to see over the years, that they are poles apart. Western medicine is fabulous in an emergency. You can't fault it, but when it comes to dealing with chronic disease and

Pam Lob

of how awful I felt, or how much pain I was in. I was an expert at cover up and independence.

When Sandy was sick and in hospital for months at a time, I still rarely asked for help. I now see that not only was I doing myself a disservice, but I was also denying friends and family the gift of giving support and being part of our journey. I believed wrongly, if I accepted help I was being a burden, but what I was really doing was throwing a beautiful gift back at them. I will always be truly grateful to the friend who took me aside after Sandy died and told me what I was doing. I was mortified.

After Sandy died, I coped by always being busy, so I didn't have time to feel the pain. I was in the second half of my psychology degree with the Open University and added training to be a counsellor into the mix. I was also teaching the 'expert patient program' and was part of the team for a major project on end of life care, at the hospital where Sandy was treated. Plus, as if this wasn't enough, I started a network marketing business as well as trying to be a "Mum and Dad" to the kids. Just writing this list and remembering that time leaves me feeling totally exhausted.

I was on the brink of burnout and was saved by my counselling tutor who got me to take a long hard look at what I was doing and what it was doing to my health and the health of my family. I took a step back, reassessed, and walked away from several things. Over the years since, with quite a lot of trial and error. I have learnt to live a balanced life, to say no when things do not feel right and to take regular downtime. I attempt really knew what it was either, but he did refer me to a gynaecologist. The treatments were horrendous and gave me menopausal symptoms to add to the pain and fatigue. I came to the realisation that the western medical model of health certainly did not have all the answers.

I started on a journey of discovery into alternative, complementary and ancient medical and health traditions that continues to this day. A hysterectomy in 2001 finally removed the pain, but the fatigue and joys of menopause continued. It wasn't until I discovered personalised health in 2015 that I finally began to turn my health around. Then three years ago a friend introduced me to a unique breakthrough health technology that is native to the body. I am delighted to report I now have more energy than at any time in my adult life, and I feel and look as if I'm getting younger by the day.

Feeling the Pain

I have learnt many lessons along my journey into all aspects of health and wellbeing. A big one has been the importance of self-care and filling yourself up first. Like many people, especially women, I felt that putting my needs first was egotistical. Even on days when all I wanted to do was to curl up in bed with the pain, I would push myself through the day, caring for the kids, Sandy, the home, and supporting anyone and everyone in any way I could. If you asked me to do anything the answer was always, "Yes". Most people were totally unaware

Pam Lob

I knew prevention was important; not to smoke, keep alcohol to the minimum and to eat plenty of fresh fruit and vegetables. I would tell you I led a healthy lifestyle, and my health was excellent. Who was I kidding? I was in constant pain from a back injury I sustained from lifting a patient. I regularly took pain killers for this and always at the time of my menstruation for horrific period pain. I was told this was normal and to get on with life! Eh, no – it is not. Pain is always a sign something is wrong! Oh, I was also totally disconnected from my emotions and who I truly was as a woman.

An Unexpected Saviour

By my mid-thirties and with two young children, I was in constant pain for most of the month. I was exhausted all the time and often felt I was going crazy. I was told it was an irritable bowel. "You're a woman just put up with it". (That was from a female doctor. How dare she!). The doctors just gave me painkillers that made me drunk and hungover at the same time. Something I would not wish on my worst enemy. And to add insult to injury, they did nothing for the pain. Looking after two young kids was a daily challenge. In desperation I started to visit a reflexologist recommended by a friend. To say I was sceptical would be an understatement. How could tickling my feet do anything?

Maggie saved my life. She made all the symptoms I was experiencing bearable and suggested I had endometriosis. "Endo what?" was my first reaction. I don't think my doctor

I'm sure if you are reading this you are on the journey of change and self-improvement. You are one of the people who have seen the lockdown as an opportunity to take a look at your life and to see where and how things can be transformed for the better.

Creating a New Life

It is easy when we are busy and feeling well to take our health and our life for granted. This results in millions of people not getting the wake-up call until it is too late and they have been diagnosed with cancer, a chronic disease, or even worse, just dropped down dead. The lockdown for those who are ready has meant they finally have the time to take a step back, to rest, to feel and to tap into how they really want life to be like.

Health has always been part of my life. From the age of four, my dolls and teddy bears were always sick. At eight, I joined the British Red Cross Society and at seventeen left home to start my nurse training. I watched young men the same age as myself die from bone cancer. I saw the toll that ill health took on people and their families, but I was still brainwashed by the western model of health, that encourages us to believe the medical profession has all the answers. That a drug or surgery will solve the problem.

Pam Lob

Following the Breadcrumbs

As I write this, we are in unprecedented times, as much of the world is in lockdown and the death toll increases daily from the coronavirus. It feels like I have been in training for this time all my life. What exactly I should be doing is still not clear, but I just keep following the breadcrumbs that present themselves to me. Writing this chapter is one of these breadcrumbs!

My hope was that this virus would awaken more people to the fact we can't and shouldn't take our health for granted, as we never know what tomorrow will bring. However, many are still trying to run away from their feelings and fear by comfort eating, drinking copious amounts of alcohol and vegging out on Netflix. They are still believing they are invincible, and all will go back to normal. However, by the day their risk of disease is increasing. There is certainly going to be an increase in disease both mentally and physically due to the lockdown.

I wonder what it will take for people to wake up to the importance of putting their health first, as the risk of dying, or being seriously ill from the coronavirus, has not been enough for them to change their ways. I feel deeply frustrated by this, but I have also learnt throughout the years that I can't fix anyone, I can only make suggestions. Some people are just not ready to change and nothing I say or do will change them, but there are many who are ready.

have taken me around the world and given me an incredible multicultural group of friends. Many I now think of as family, and though thousands of miles apart connect regularly with. Today, every day I ask myself: "Did I love, did I matter, did I live today?" I do my best to make the most of every day, to grasp opportunities that present themselves to me and to make a difference to someone. I truly believe Sandy had to die for me to wake up and for me to teach others how to wake up also.

I had felt for years we would never get old together, I often had had the feeling he would die in a road traffic accident. I am glad instead we had a year to prepare, to grieve together. 2004 was a rollercoaster of a year, Sandy would spend a month at a time in hospital, three weeks at home and then it would all start again. At one time he went into remission, but this only lasted a couple of months. By far, the worst day of my life was the day we were told the cancer was back. I knew it was the beginning of the end. The feelings this day brought up, remained buried until two years ago when I was doing a writing retreat. Then I tapped into that day and the most incredible anger came up.

Back in 2005 I was unable to express anger. I went through an hour of letting the anger run through me, it was a temper tantrum on an epic scale, followed by minutes of sobbing uncontrollably and then half an hour of ecstatic dance. I knew I was being held by my friends around the world and felt safe enough to just go for it. It was as if a huge weight was lifted from me and I'm sure my health has also benefited from removing this stuck cellular memory.

Pam Lob

When I did my counselling training, I came across a model from a mother who had lost a child and for me was the relief someone else understood. I like to call it the "egg of grief". The egg yolk is the grief and rather than shrinking as in the stages of grief model it stays the same, but over time you build up more and more egg white protection and coping strategies, this protects from the triggers and allows you to move back into normal life quicker as well. I believe to the day we die there is always the potential to be triggered back into the egg yolk. What I've also learnt over the years, and this took some time, is to let the emotions flow. To not to suppress them in any way, this makes dealing with grief and loss less burdensome. In fact, easier, as what you resist persists!

As you can well imagine, life has not been the same since, not just from losing my beloved. In that intense 36 hours leading up to his death, I changed. Part of Sandy had merged with me and I frequently heard his words coming from my lips, a very bizarre experience. Fear of dying, flying, and stepping out of my comfort zone left me, and my buried spirituality and the intuitive powers I had as a child were reawakened.

Awakening

Fast forward fifteen years. Life is very different, who I am is very different, things have transformed beyond what I would have ever thought possible. Sandy is now so part of me it's seamless. It has been quite a journey and I would not change any of it. I have had the most incredible opportunities that

Suddenly at 5pm Sandy's breathing changed and within minutes stopped. His body finally let go of this life to the music of Chris Rea playing 'Heaven' and then immediately after 'Let me go' also by Chris Rea. Jenny and I, by now, were both standing gawping at the music player, more interested in the words it was emitting than what was happening in the bed. It had played a completely random selection of songs over the last 48 hours and now it played two by the same artist, one of Sandy's favourites and the words were more than pertinent to what was happening. Sandy always maintained he did not believe in god or heaven, so this felt like a very clear message that he had been mistaken. In this moment I did not feel sad, I just felt relief and total amazement.

The Nature of Grief

Part of me expected the world to stop, but of course it did not. Grief does weird and wonderful things to you. As a nurse, I learnt about the stages of grief denial, anger, guilt, bargaining, depression, and acceptance and believed it was a linear journey. This certainly was not my experience. I often went through a whole gamut of emotions in the matter of minutes, would act normally for a while and then, woosh, another whirlpool. At times I felt like I was going crazy. The number of spins gradually reduced over time, but even now I can be triggered back into it again, but it's usually only for seconds.

Pam Lob

Parting Ways

Sandy's body was shutting down bit by bit and he had lost the power of speech, but with the last of the energy left within him he locked eyes with me. For hours at a time we exchanged love, energy, and something beyond our comprehension. Throughout this time, we had music playing and Sandy had become very agitated when the batteries ran out on the speaker. My father dashed over to the hospital with replacements and calm was restored. His sister came and joined me, but Sandy and I kept returning to this deep connection and exchange, I could feel his energy blending with mine within me.

At some time in the early morning of the 10th January 2005 I dozed off, or at least I think this is what happened. I suddenly found myself chatting away with his parents. Both had died several years previously. It was as if they were alive and in the room with me, and we chatted for a while about what they were doing, and they finally turned away asking me to give their love to Jenny. I immediately woke, it was clear Sandy's soul had departed. There was nobody there! Yet his body breathed on as an empty shell for another 11 hours, it was as if he was waiting for something. As a nurse, I had seen many deaths before but never a soul leaving. It was weird, I did not feel sad, I really didn't feel anything but wonder. I felt I could not talk to Jenny about what I had witnessed, or what was happening. Instead Jenny and I sat and chatted across the bed, as if we were sitting at a cafe table, talking about mundane things. I even went for a chair massage with one of the holistic health teams as I didn't feel Sandy would depart whilst I was away.

CHAPTER 9

PAM LOB

The Meandering Road to Health and Transformation

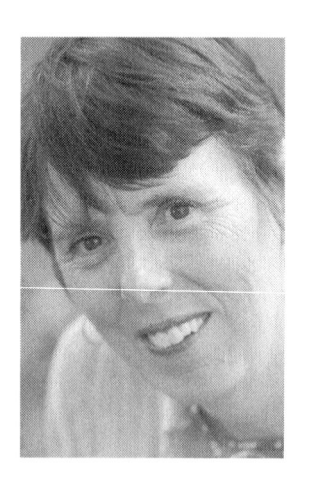

I'm sitting in a large hospital chair hand in hand with my beloved husband Sandy, who is lying propped up on pillows in the bed beside me. We have endured a rollercoaster of a year as he battled with leukaemia. I had come to terms over the last three weeks we were on borrowed time and it was running out...

Angela Soong

to guilt, shame, and judgement. I am here to promote that if you can overcome all this, your weakness will become your strength. You can build strength and help others by sharing your story, that we are all human. It is only when we realise this, that we can surrender to the emptiness, and it becomes essentially fullness. Then you will come to your real humanity and awaken your most powerful consciousness.

I wish every one of you all a happy and fulfilling life!

My Facebook videos will leave you with many interesting stories and the twist and turns of my life *journey so far, and also tips to take away. Please send me an email and I will add you to my Facebook community.* Angelasoong888@gmail.com

WOMEN IN THE *Modern* BUSINESS WORLD

I spent much more valuable time with them, with less distractions and cutting off phones and working in allocated slots. I teach them about life, educating them, creating memories that will last a lifetime. I didn't use to cook much, and I have now become a great chef. A way to anybody's heart is through the stomach. We never take our time together for granted.

My Future Vision. I am here to build fond memories with my children, my partner and all the lives of the people I touch. I want to make an impact, and this is the reason I am in existence. One day my dream is to build schools for deprived children, and settle with my wellness centre hospitality business in the Far East somewhere. The place where I shall call home will be with a beach, palm trees, healthy sweet fruits, and vegetables, which would fund the charity directly. I have just started to explore new opportunities, for after Covid-19.

Fixing your Happiness. If you are unhappy, it is not the external side you need to seek first. It is the internal you need to fix. No material things can give you long term contentment or fulfilment. Feel gratitude and practice this every day. The world is not so bleak when you can see so much beauty and goodness. Find your way to give back to the Universe, even if it's a prayer, a meditation, a regular blood donation, or food for the birds. These are examples of how I practice and also teach the kids.

The realities of life. Lastly, people only want to share their fairy tale. Seldom do we hear about people's reality; of pain, disappointment, failure, fear, betrayal, and disbeliefs, probably due

Angela Soong

change things. Hiding from the problems won't make them go away. Remember, bring your solutions to changing yourself! Don't expect others to change for you. And turn every rock to look for solutions, try different things before you make any decisions. At least you can tell yourself after committing to any decision that you have nothing to regret, because you have tried your best. Save what you can. Salvage what you can and when you have made a decision you must take full responsibility for the outcome.

How do you know you have made the right decision? With every decision you make in life, there is no right or wrong one. Take full responsibility for the decision you make and for making it RIGHT. Decisions can lead you down many pathways and create different outcomes. Make the decision RIGHT for you, and for the people around you.

Obstacles are opportunities. When I was separated, I had to leave the family house. Being apart from my children was the hardest at the beginning. It created emotional turmoil. Every night whilst I was settling in my new home I would be crying, missing them, not being able to read them their bedtime stories, a cuddle and kiss good night. However, acknowledging this, I became the best mother I ever could have been. My boys had my full attention when they were with me and have gotten both into the best grammar schools in the region. I am so proud of them. We have so much fun together and explore and experience many different countries of culture.

Self-love. If you cannot love yourself, how do you expect other people to love you? So, find time to take care of yourself, not just your loved ones.

Undo self-limiting beliefs by reversing what you say to yourself and continue to practice this. Start by looking at yourself in the mirror every morning and spend one-minute speaking out loud. Tell yourself all the positive things that are empowering you, the things you are or that you are going to become. For example: I am confident, beautiful, kind and forgiving. I am strong, powerful, and happy.... I am... I am… and I deserve. When you do that every morning, you must also believe in it. The brain knows no difference between reality and what you tell it, so then it becomes a self-fulfilling prophecy.

To write is to invite: better sleep. Start by journaling every day when you wake up or before going to bed. Write down all the good things that you have in your life and all the bad things that you would like to change. When you can't sleep, this will help you let go easier. Write all your thoughts down, whatever bothers you. It will feel like you have told somebody. Physical words on paper are the beginning of the healing process. First by acknowledging you have a problem, then by accepting it, you can then work out the roots and create a plan. You can throw away or destroy the paper after.

"Investigate your problems". Ask yourself how you can make subtle, small changes, by working backwards from the outcome you would like to achieve. To plan, you are being proactive to

Angela Soong

Culture. This is the community of people that we are surrounded by. They will always be talking about somebody else, but they don't help you. They only like to chit-chat and spread fire.

Don't live other people's expectations. If you do know somebody going for negativity, do not judge them. Don't just judge everybody's happiness based on what you see on the outside, because it is the truth behind closed doors that you do not know.

Never give up on yourself! Take one day at a time. Don't wait for negative things to happen to you, such as a health breakdown or falling into severe depression. It would be so hard to reverse. Many people have to go through self-destruction in many forms, such as turning to drugs or depressants to slow their minds down. There are other methods of physical self- harm. Yes, people are harming themselves with sharp objects or burning themselves with cigarette butts, so the bleeding and the pain became a form of relief for them. Alcohol is the most commonly used, but even worse, the effects of alcohol can cause accidents with road traffic, and it is a way of abusing a partner and the children.

The self-destruction is a cry out to gain self-awareness, even approval of others, wanting them to ask you, "What's wrong?" You are waiting for someone else to ask you, what's wrong? It might be too late by then. Don't wait for other people to validate that you have a problem. Acknowledging this as early as possible, that self-destructive behaviour, will show the direct link to your health problems. Including the mental and physical needs you have, waiting to be resolved by you. Don´t wait for someone to ask you what's wrong! You can only fix it if you want to.

- The need to rebalance: It is very hard to balance all sectors of your life to be successful. This includes health and fitness, financial, career, love relationship, spirituality, parenting, social activities, quality of your life, and beliefs. It is a struggle to spend more time and energy in one or two areas, and then the others are neglected. Therefore, it is a continuous balancing act, keeping all the plates spinning. For me, I focused on my career, money, and my children. Where energy goes, results flow. However, my level of EQ was very low when I separated. I had to study plenty of self- development material, working on myself instead of not just my multi million-pound portfolio projects. I am blessed to have met my present partner, who also taught me how to trust and fall in love again.

The reason I reveal the depth of the story is this…

Parents should only wish for the children's happiness, and support and love them. I needed my parents' support, as I had always supported them with their business and wealth creation, even though they don't see that. Instead they banned me from coming home. In fact, this was one of my biggest hurdles. But I was okay with it, I thought if I was going to die, that didn't not matter anymore.

Pride. Who is going to care when no one else is going to put bread on the table? It's only just speculation after all.

Angela Soong

Tips to improve on Relationships

From the experiences I have had I would like to share some tips to improve relationships.

- Learn to have open conversations. Open your eyes and look around, you will see everyone is looking down on their phones or electronic screens. It's so sad and although it changes lives and saves communication time, it also kills many relationships. Try to be more vigilant and mindful of how much time you and others in your life spend on consuming social media. Do you allow your children or partner to watch their iPads during family or dinner time?

- Don't let the excuse of a challenging relationship be that there is no time, such as "I had to work long hours!". Make the time. Love and affection can be based on the way you communicate with each other, the frequency and the intentional thought sent through a message or a video call are equally as valuable.

- Gain confidence to move forward by the "small wins of excellence". Maybe it is the small things that you don't care for or do well that people notice. That could be everything from making the bed in the morning, to making sure the dinner tastes better or self- caring more. This way you can build momentum and move to a bigger task and achieve your aspirations.

told me that I should not come to the city. I chuckled back, replying:

"Who do you think you guys are, the king and queen?

The answer was: "Never come back home again. You are not welcome, and your dad doesn't want to see you again".

Disclaimer

I do not wish to paint that I married a bad man. He was a good-hearted man, with no bad intentions, but our marriage never worked out. He has his own demons to conquer, after losing his dad in a car crash at the age of four. He had had a series of disconnection/communication relationship issues in the past, but love was blind at the time. I am sharing these insights to help you as the reader to perceive our relationship environment, and the challenges within a marriage, which some may resonate with. If he were a bad person, I would not have married him in the first place. I have no regrets of the past because this was a "purposeful relationship" and now the purpose had been fulfilled. No more negative energy will be given to the past. I have two beautiful boys who are the sunshine and soul of my life. No, at the present moment, I am so lucky as I have also found my other half. He is my soulmate and love, whom I liked to spend my days giggling and growing old together with.

Angela Soong

On top of that, the properties that I started investing in, they did not belong to me. They belonged to the bank, and I only put down a 25 % deposit. I imagined banks, or bailiffs, would come knocking on the door, I could see all sorts of worst-case scenarios I would leave behind if I didn't survive. I imagined what my family would say, like "You see, look what a mess your daughter has left behind"!

My pivotal point - Letting Go

When you have hit rock bottom, you cannot drop any more. There was something more scary than death, and that was leaving my children behind. You then kind of realise that "You know what, I am scared. I am really scared about disappointing my parents, I am scared of what other people are going to say about my next move, and how they are going to judge. But I don't really care anymore, and I cannot care about what other people think. Because my life is my life, and at the moment I don't even have control of it, never mind anything else. This is about my children's life. I need to be there for them and take care of them".

I decided it was time to let go and act not from selfishness, but to save the mother of my children. I needed to remove myself from this toxic environment. So, the separation process began, and all the worst calls and conversations came "falling in". I was prepared to defend myself and claim it was irreversible and that I would not regret it. There were threats and my parents even

WOMEN IN THE *Modern* BUSINESS WORLD

This happened at 2am in the morning when I was, as I usually did, working on my computer. I was sorting out my finances, covering my loans and credit card payments, financing all my ongoing refurbishments, and rebalancing my heavy debts. This incident did not just only happen once, it recurred several more times, and out of nowhere. I believe these symptoms are called anxiety attacks; they can reoccur any time without a need of emotional state to change. Why did they present themselves in my life? Well, I realise I had no control over my body. Even though I tried to "control my mind over matter", it was obviously unaligned, and my body did not follow my orders.

I got to a point where I thought I was going to die one day from these attacks. At one time I did blank out for, I don't know for sure how long. I needed it to stop, because what if I didn't get to open my eyes again next time? This was the wake-up call. I was not afraid of dying, but I was more afraid of leaving my two young children who still needed their mother. I feared what they would become without my guidance, love and support, and the trauma they would suffer, growing up without a mother. I knew my family was cold, and even worse, the family I had married into had no communication and showed little affection. This needed to change.

Angela Soong

also cold, egotistical, narcissistic and it was what I needed to accept. I am a woman of an ethnic minority, second class, not ever good enough, I am wrong, he is right, and I just needed to keep quiet. Therefore, there was no support from my own family, and I was trapped. Disempowering words kept echoing in me, but I only knew later that they were only other people's beliefs and values, installed in me, not my own.

So, the way I handled this, was to close down my emotions and my heart, and I didn't want to feel anything anymore. Was that the best way to deal with my pain? Was I in a depressed state? Well, I didn't even want to think about it or listen to my heart or soul. I wanted to portray that I had this perfect family, for my husband and my parents. My happiness and my marriage were not important. For many years I acted like an "Iron Lady" with no emotion, heart, or joy, and not letting anyone come close to my secret.

It felt Like DEATH had arrived

Until one day, when I had this pain in my chest. The pain was so strong, it felt like it clenched onto me, it was restricting my breathing and I dazed out. I dazed out for maybe 30-60 seconds and fell to the ground. I couldn't breathe because it was so painful. I didn't know what it was, but I wondered, could this be a heart attack or something? But then I got up and I carried on working, despite the shock of what I had experienced.

unhealthy. I knew that this type of relationship was not what I wanted to imprint into their memory, for years to come.

I switched OFF my emotions and decided to HIDE

I thought it was my fault and this was how life and my destiny was, so I must accept it. I was able to hide away from my unhappiness in my marriage, being in my home life. My sanity and joy was that I diverted all my energy and time through my work and children, so I did not allow myself to dwell into my emotions. To ease the burden of the situation, since I couldn´t make an impact on my marriage, I made different compartments. The one with the relationship/love/marriage/romance compartment would be locked away in darkness. Though I still was hoping, maybe I could be happy one day. I created and imagined a brick wall between us every time he walked in the house. I pretended he did not exist, so there would be no pain, feelings, reaction and expectations.

It worked and it was peaceful for a few years. I locked away my emotions and threw away the key. Because if you can't fix it anymore, it is time to give up and accept it, that's life. I thought my unhappiness, my unworthiness, and my reality of this was how my parents treated me. Being born to child slavery and the way my husband treated me was in this context too.

My father was a dominant figure, dominating my mother, and I had unconsciously attracted a man like my dad, who was

Angela Soong

change his mind or actions after all the discussions. I felt like I was already a bird captured in a cage, with nowhere to escape. We are traditional Chinese, like all the older generations. I had become a vase on the mantelpiece. We had had an expensive community wedding, we couldn't be allowed to disgrace our family. This was not just the marriage, it was about the connections of the family and the children, and how everyone was going to view us. Many Westerners do not understand this.

Women's roles would be to stand behind in the shadows, and just be supportive and quiet.

"Hush!" my dad would say, when he was on the phone, after acknowledging an argument that had broken out, from my mother-in-law calling my parents. "I want you to say sorry to your husband!" he shouted.

"But, but dad! I didn't do anything wrong; I am late from work because I have been working and on my business. The clients and staff required my attention, so I am late."

"I don't care, you are wrong, he is right, now apologise, and everything will be fine!"

I did not want any more arguments. At that point, attention and love was still there, but once silence broke out, this meant the love and expectations had dissolved. Although it became a quiet home again, the negative energy surrounding us in our home still vibed and I am sure the children and his mother felt it, even though it was invisible. The children grew up not knowing that their father was married to me, which seemed

WOMEN IN THE *Modern* BUSINESS WORLD

Before I was a full-time property investor and landlady, I had my own business as a technical skincare specialist. This was after I had worked with my teaching job. I realise I wasn't employable, and my entrepreneurial blood was always lingering. My expertise in my business was in modern technology, skin laser and other clinical techniques and chemical treatments. I also specialised in mole removal. During my marriage, I would come home and sometimes I would just like to discuss my day, certain events, and people that I've met.

However, he didn't want to listen to anything else, except demanding that my attention should only be with the children or family matters.

I would try to visit him at work, but he was not pleased with my presence and asked me to leave. There was no interaction with my friends, and he would hesitate to take me out. I really thought something was wrong with me, maybe I was not beautiful enough or good enough, as he did not want to be seen together with me. I would even encounter jokes and name calling, and it was humiliating in front of other people.

A bird in a cage

Realising I was trapped in this "wife titleship", unloved and unwanted, I felt really lonely and let down. I decided that if I could not change my partners perception, integrity and affection towards me, and my worth to my husband was deemed as such a low value, there was little more I could do to

ANGELA SOONG

had been. I wanted to know about his day, but he showed no interest. If I had something to say, I was only given every once in a while, ten seconds to speak, before he disappeared with his PJ's to take a shower. He paid no attention, nor did he respect my presence. Then, I would wait for him and ask him if I could spend some time watching a movie with him downstairs, as a couple, but his reply every time was;

"YOU, go to bed, I want to be left alone".

At this point, he would rather be in front of the flickering TV every night, and sleep on the couch, downstairs. This went on for years, so it became permanent that I slept with my children instead. I had stopped waiting for him to come home after work. It was useless talking to him, he took no notice or action, and did not see it was a problem. After all, I was married now, but the cracks in my heart appeared very quickly.

I had thought I could be married to my soulmate; my best friend, and we could share everything and our lives together. I thought we would be working as a team, naturally. There would be no yours or mine, but ours. And everything he would do, and I would do, would be part of building our family up together. But unfortunately, that was far from the truth. Even with my first property investment, I had collected the keys and arrived at the new house, all excited and ready to open the door together. However, when we arrived at the property, he and his mum decided to stay in the car. I never understood what that was about.

don't dare to put pictures of myself on social media. I am afraid of how the world sees me, judges me, for I am not living a true life. I didn't want to portray to people how great things are, when really they are not. I have come out of a marriage. My divorce has finally been settled. It has been three years now. And I don't want to hide anymore!"

The whole room was astounded and the tears I struggled to hold back came rolling down my cheeks. The other attendees gulped back their saliva, in empathising with my pain, streaming from my emotions and words. OMG! I had just publicly revealed and exposed the most intimate secret of my life. I was hiding, and, how had I been surviving this long without bringing it out? Why did I just share this information in public, to a bunch of strangers?

At that spur of the moment, I had just decided that I had had enough, and I needed to change and let go. It was kind of relieving, because I had held this secret for nearly a decade. I felt shameful, guilty, in pain and sadness, and fear of judgement. I needed to leave my past behind and that was the beginning of sharing my story.

Behind closed doors comes the darkness

Every night my husband would come back home, and I would wait for him, because he finished work very late in the hospitality business. I would hope he would spend a little time, catching up and talking to me, asking me how my day

Angela Soong

Unmasking the pain accidentally

The change in my life started happening when I attended a public speaking course. I had been a high school science teacher for five years after my graduation at university, and have a PGCE secondary teaching degree, specialising in Science. Teaching teenagers was something I had always been fond of and the ability to share knowledge, empower and help others is and always will be one of my core values.

My intention of choosing the subject was this: I would like to teach young people, teenagers and young adults, and those who are lost in the control of understanding finance, about the taboo subject of money, finance and entrepreneurship. After all, most of us have probably been to college or university, then been chucked out of the educational system to find a job and to do ... what? To make some money, of course. But for some reason if that was the ultimate goal, then what have they prepared us for, consuming this large chunk of our lives?"

However, at the introduction of all this, it actually didn't seem to turn out that way. For some reason, without thinking, I hesitated and said:
"Hello, my name is Angela Soong and actually, the reason I came here is because I... I... I don't want to hide anymore!"
Oh no, I have done it now. I´ve got to say more, as the silence grew.
"I have been hiding for over a decade. I have Facebook accounts, LinkedIn accounts, but I am not posting anything. I

work the children contributed to the family's wealth was not acknowledged or rewarded. Parents of this type of traditional background just expected it should be part of our existence. Why should they feel or show their children gratitude or worthiness? They believe that as they gave their children their life, they own it, and they are born to serve them. It could be a cultural thing or perhaps just my parents.

In my adult life, nothing has changed, I have given up on any expectation of support and encouragement from my parents. No matter what I do, I don't think they are ever proud of me. We cannot expect other people to change, we can only change ourselves, by changing the level of thinking. I know what type of parent I wanted to become for my children, and it is not the way that I was brought up.

I am full of love, touch, praise, playfulness, and communication. I had to self-teach myself to become that, as for many years I was this "cold iron lady", who showed no emotion or joy in my life, other than work. In fact, cuddling and bonding with my new bundle of joy, and playing with them, taught me how to be open and fun again, as I had lost my childhood.

I am telling you this because my message is to not wait for someone else's acknowledgement, approval, or support. If you want something to be different in your life, it may be you that needs to change. Don't look for it on the outside. Other people may never give you what you are seeking or even ever appreciate you with something as simple as a thank you.

Angela Soong

of the community were. We were embedded with being told self-limiting beliefs; "You are no good! You are not good enough! You are useless". Wasn't it more the fact that we were born female? Or how unfair it was that other children had a better education? They had never been made to work in their childhood life, they were instead given attention and investment in private schooling. If anything was done right in my family, it was the least expected of us.

On the contrary, I attended state schools and I was forced to work in the family takeout and restaurant food business, peeling and gutting out prawns. I was frying and packing mountains of prawn crackers, handling hot food inside the kitchen, until I was old enough to be seen working over the counter, serving customers and handling orders, money, and customer complaints. I had missed out on my childhood years and even more the time to study, and this started as early as four years old when we lived above the business.

No longer expecting support

I have always wanted my family to recognise me, be proud of me, say well done or get a thank you for committing to helping them, and being a part of contributing to their wealth. I am not whining that I have lost my childhood and teens, working for them every weekend, school holidays and being ready anytime ad hoc for a mere consecutive thirty years. It was what it was, and I didn't know any different and at least they are successful and wealthy. In my parents eyes, the who are immigrants, chased the opportunities of a better life when moving from Hong Kong. But the main thing is, there is a lot of ego that goes with pride. So, the communities here are traditional and only want to talk about pride, ego and "shiny, good things". Negative things spread like fire and destroy like fire. All because they care too much about what others think.

The things we do not want people to see or talk about, we brush under the carpet, not just with strangers, but within the family too. There are so many dysfunctional relationships out there, because of a lack of communication and understanding. We pretend it just does not exist. If, blatantly, you see your daughter not being happy for years in a marriage, it's better you don't ask, and it will all be alright.

So, it's all about the "gleam and shine", making sure you do not disgrace the family. So, to the females out there with similar backgrounds, if you relate to this, make sure you are only seen but never heard. Do not make any waves, and definitely don't answer back to your elders. Many people from the eastern part of the world will understand where I am coming from. I am probably brought up by an older generation's culture, in mindset and values, but certainly not all of these will be instilled upon my children.

Furthermore, my parents would never say kind words or encouraging words as I was growing up. They only liked to put me and my two sisters under comparison with how well educated, useful and proud, the children of other members

Angela Soong

Being just a few years old I even had to go to the hospital for playing too close to the stairs and accidentally falling off on numerous occasions. We were a burden to my parents, as they were workers for somebody else's business, and it was a privilege that they made space to keep our family together. My dad was the head chef, and my mum was an admin plus a food preparation assistant in the busy food takeout. My grandma would help out in the kitchen and tied me to her back when I was a toddler. I remember when she would kneel down to open the commercial oven, a massive gust of really hot air with the smell of the barbeque roasted meat, would blow into our faces, which was very overwhelming.

I was so lucky to be brought up by my grandmother, who was the most loving, kind, and generous woman, but she had suffered an enormous amount of adversity in her life. At an early age of four I was ready to work together with her, and that was my early programming engraved into my ethics. It meant that working is normal, and what life is about. Today I am no different, always moving one thousand miles per hour, full speed ahead. The guilt starts playing when I don't work.

My Heritage

Have you ever been judged, and have you had to live by other people's expectations? For me, being Chinese, I come from a very strong culture and it can be religious too. I am the first-born Chinese generation in the UK and my parents,

CHAPTER 8

ANGELA SOONG

Born Into Poverty

I lived under the stairs with my grandmother on the stair landing, because there was no other room for us to live in. Our room was made out of 'MFI' boards stacked together, that were removed during the daytime to reveal the bed where we were sleeping at night. That left us with enough play area of one to two square meters. I only played when everyone was working downstairs, because at night all the staff would be walking past us after work, passing the landing to reach their accommodation and using the shared bathroom.

Some Final Advice

1. Find a coach that will help you in soul searching from your feminine power
2. Work on your value and needs creed systems first as a foundation.
3. Trust your instinct and practice self-love.
4. Find yourself a network or tribe that supports your vision.
5. Grow constantly and upgrade your coaches to be in alignment with your journey.

Thank you to all my coaches and authors that came before me. That influenced my life in so many ways, and to my husband, who supported me on my journey!

You can reach out to me at dynamic-dental.co.uk for a 30 minutes virtual smile or confidence boost consultation.

MICHELLE WYNGAARD

selling toothpaste. Children die of malnutrition not famine. I also mentor and I am involved in coaching the parents of the sponsored kids of "Smartteens", through donations and some I also sponsor. They are mentored by a beautiful giving soul, a lady called Madine Tyson, and her small team in South Africa. They run a six weeks programme through smartteens.co.za making an impact in kids lives. Kids that would have been at the bottom of society, with no hope of a future in education, all over the world. We invest in their foundation of dreaming big and being the future entrepreneurs and leaders of tomorrow, and we inspire them to free themselves from a life of destitution. Donations are always welcome.

People that Influenced my Life and Recommended Books

- My mum
- Oprah Winfrey
- Mel Robbins
- Brene Brown
- Eckhart Tolle – The Power of Now
- Joe Dispenza - You Are The Placebo
- Wayne Dyer - Your Thoughts Are Not You
- Gay Hendricks - The Big Leap
- Simon Sinek - Find Your Why
- Robin Sharma – The 5am Club
- Lisa Nichols – No Matter What
- Napoleon Hill – Think and Grow Rich

WOMEN IN THE *Modern* BUSINESS WORLD

me giving advice that I use in my day to day problem-solving matters, at home or in my work life:

1. One has to set one's mind to a positive vibration to attract what you want in life.
2. You must have a strong belief that it can and will happen. If that desire is strong enough. your body responds to that thought. Just feel how you change in behaviour through that thought process, and programme this thought every day. Visualise it, so that it becomes real.
3. Life is like a camera, focus on the what's important, capture the good times, develop from the negatives and if things don't work out, you can take another shot.

So, here we are with the Covid-19 attack on the global economy; however, is this a curse or a blessing? I see it totally differently, a blessing in disguise to help everyone look within and reset the mind to default settings. To give us a chance to revive and restart from scratch and get rid of the old paradigm in preparation for the new world order. No longer do we have to respond to the old belief system, or modus of operation. You get a second chance to morph in alignment with your true self. Einstein said, "You cannot solve problems of today with yesterday's thinking and expect a different result".

The project I want to develop is to establish the "Find Your Voice Foundation", for underprivileged children in Cape Town. This will set them up for developing skills in confidence in public speaking. I support Force for Good, a business initiative donating nutritional meals to kids in the third world, through

Michelle Wyngaard

when we focus on the big picture. This overwhelms us, and we cave-in at the thought of being successful beyond our wildest dreams, instead denying ourselves of that wealth and happiness. "I am not deserving of it" are childhood wounds coming to the surface, or from past toxic relationships with others putting you down all the time, to the extent that you lose your self-worth. This sets our default pattern. We get so consumed with feeling unhappy, and wallowing in self- pity, that it becomes like a drug. The addiction is all that soothes us momentarily. The cycle repeats itself. I have to remind myself of why I am worthy of success.

Finally, the biggest thing I learnt is the power of our thoughts, the vibrational energy of the universe, and how it impacts on our thinking

My Contribution to the World

I believe today that the world is suffering, as people have lost their purpose. Therefore, I am out on a mission to help in healing it through mastering my skills and craft, being the best I can be at assisting people in transforming their mindset. Remember, your smile is the first and last thing that people remember you by. Why not invest in it wisely to realise its full potential. My mission is to transform one million smiles in my lifetime.

Here is a little something to use, when we find ourselves put to inaction, due to stress or worry. Try this, if you don't mind

everyone is prepared to change themselves.
- As long as I am alive, I want to be an instrument to help transform lives.
- Stay focused and become a master of your craft.
- Upgrade your peer group.
- Own your story.
- Be present and don't forget to have fun.

"Even the longest life is a really short ride". (Robin Sharma)

Your opinion of me is none of my business. Thank you for your opinion that you hold of me.

"Stop listening to the GOOP - good opinion of other people". (Peter Sage - my first step into self-development in 2016).

For the naysayers: *"One thing I don't understand about haters, they criticise my glory, but they don't know my story".* (Maya Angelou)

You must become a pro in your art, so you can break the rules and make it over again. The moment when you feel like giving up, is when you must keep going. I went on a journey of seeking the answers of how to resolve my doubts and fears of what success is about, in life and business.

Don't we sometimes self-sabotage ourselves and look back and wish we had taken the first step? The journey of a thousand miles starts with the first step. That for many of us is the hardest part. Why? My view is, and perhaps yours too, the fear sets in

MICHELLE WYNGAARD

- Fear is there to serve us not to harm us.
- Who is judging - you are the judge and interpreter as sender and receiver of the message - how others respond is not your business, how they respond is their business.
- Survival is to fit in and shut up, if we feel threatened, we adapt to the situation and environment. Why fit in if you can stand out?
- Surrender to success, not your fear.
- Other people's perception of me is not my reality, that is none of my business. It is a reflection of their reality only, so I am cool with that.

I love the inspirational story of Lisa Nichols:
"From broke to broken she rose like a phoenix from the ashes and reinvented herself".

- I am the director of how I want it to end, for better or worse, or the same at the end of the day; it's still my choice.
- I have no one to blame but me. Many times, we fall into the trap of the "it's someone
  else's fault" syndrome.
- Look in the mirror and see who that someone else is. Yes, it's YOU, that's what's missing in the picture.
- Let your message be bigger than your fear.
- Some people dream of success, others make it happen - which one are you?
- Sometimes you have to give up the good to fulfil the great vision you have inside of you.
- Everyone wants to change the world, but not

a book in a week and if the lights were out, I figured out if I opened the curtain to allow the street light to fall perfectly on my bedside against the wall, then I could hold my book up against the wall to finish the book. No wonder I ended up with spectacles at fourteen.

Success is not what reflects in numbers to me, nor how many accolades or awards you achieve, though it does satisfy the ego. For it is instead what you accomplish that is in alignment with your true purpose, once you realise your gift that you were born with to serve. Follow your spiritual path in life to help you find your way to serve from your highest purpose; as a result, the reward will follow.

Who you surround yourself with, is who you become, so make sure you are surrounding yourself with the right people. Do whatever it takes to find your inner genius. I encourage you to read or watch "The Big Leap" by Gay Hendricks. My special interest is to transform people's lives through rapid smile transformation, to help you find your inner smile and find your inner zone of genius, to ultimate fulfilment and happiness from the inside out.

My Collection of Life Lessons

Stop looking for yourself in others. What do I mean by this?

- Accept you for you, be comfortable with your perfect imperfections.

Michelle Wyngaard

for the whole week. So, here starts my revenge for the pain caused by one dentist that hurt me so much. Well I did cry afterwards, as he gave me no local anaesthetic to treat the infected socket. Guess what, I became the student he had to supervise. The rest is history. You never forget such an experience. Memory can be your friend or foe. We have to deal with aggressive responses to pain, as well. You learn as you go along. Unfortunately, we don't get taught these skills at university, these are life skills you have to prepare yourself through years of experience. Initially, it is daunting to be great at your chosen profession, but the people management skill comes with time. Looking back, I was a little entrepreneur at high school, and I found an opportunity to make business through selling items. My mum sewed and dad was a jeweller and repaired jewellery for the family. I asked him if he would be able to do this for the kids at school and the teachers. I had my little locket diary where I wrote all the names of my customers and charged a lot more than my dad's fee. I made three times the profit of what he charged me. I earned a lot of money then, at the age of fourteen, by selling anything that I could find. He asked how much I charged sometimes, I replied, "That is my business, not yours", grinning cheekily.

I again silently vowed that I wanted to work abroad. After having experienced the first dental congress in Brazil, my burning desire developed to leave Cape Town in search of a better future for my dental career. After a year in private practice, I found a small job advert for a dental associate to work on the east coast of England. I was usually a loner as a child, growing up with two younger brothers. I used to read ever thought about dentistry?" It was like a light bulb moment for me, when I gave it a quick thought and suddenly became excited at the idea. I made a comparison between the two and came to the conclusion: I don't have to work 24/7 with little social time for myself and be on call most of the time. I can use my creative ability working with my hands, and I would never be out of work. (Until the Covid-19 pandemic happened in March 2020). I do have an artistic side of me that I have not tapped into as much. That's it! I wanted to be a dentist instead. I could make people smile and alleviate them from pain. What a powerful skill that is to transform and make them free of pain.

When I was sixteen, I had a severe toothache, the kind that makes you not able to sleep, eat, let alone think clearly. Most patients now could relate to it, where access to dentists was very limited to emergencies only during the Covid-19 lockdown period. I implemented a virtual consultation platform immediately, to continue to triage patients for emergency advice. The benefit of belonging to self-development mastermind classes kept me ahead of the curve of change. I have great empathy, as I know what it is like to suffer from a severe toothache and you can't get immediate help. The pain is indescribable.

I eventually lost the tooth at sixteen. There was not much discussion about saving it, let alone affording root canal treatment. I ended up at the dental hospital with an infected socket, three days following the extraction of the tooth, which extended the pain period. I was on a soup diet through a straw

MICHELLE WYNGAARD

We do not realise the damage that our inner childhood wounds cause, which we burden ourselves with, carrying it into adulthood and repeatedly playing out the default patterns. It is important to show up as yourself, and be in alignment with your soul's purpose. You feel ultimate fulfilment to happiness, from the inside out. I applied for both medicine and dentistry. To earn some money, I did lots of holiday jobs toward my tuition fees. I did not want to burden my parents financially because I knew how costly the tuition fees were for dentistry in 1990. I applied and was successful in securing a bursary, which was privately sponsored from England.

Your Choices in Life and Career

My cousin's husband was a doctor at that time; he sat me down one day before final year high school exams. My mum had specifically asked him over to have a chat with me about career choices. I went through career guidance at high school, something we did to tease out what our future aspirations would be, based on our subject interest. It is not easy at that age, to figure out what you want in life, not everyone finds their direction. If you don't, then it's okay, things are just not in alignment for it to happen. However, my mum instilled in me that if you want something in life then go for it! Don't let money or the 'I can't afford it attitude", be an obstacle to achieve your dreams in life.

I was focused only on medicine, when my cousin's husband planted a new seed in my mind; he asked, "Michelle, have you my mother continually nurtured this desire. While still at primary school, a salesman came knocking on the door one day, selling a colourful set of A-Z medical encyclopaedias for children. Mum called me to peruse the collection and asked if I would like to own the set. It was quite expensive; however mum knew how much I loved reading medical books. She invested in what would be my first step into the medical world, at thirteen.

I immersed myself in reading it, from page to page, to the extent I became known as "the family junior doctor", using my acquired knowledge for the ailments of the family. It was her way of hoping that I would become a doctor. She had high hopes for me. It makes me laugh now, how they believed everything I told them. Thank goodness, they did not end up at the doctors after my amateur advice. I knew what I wanted to be at that stage already. I wanted to heal people. Sometimes we are not aware that we are on that journey already, of finding our purpose in life. Every day directs you in carving your path, without you realising it. Just trust the process, and your gut instinct or intuition.

Don't let others direct your destiny. When you look back you'll realise you should have listened to that inner voice. We go through childhood conditioning; it may be traumatic or moderate repeated behaviour that parents, teachers, siblings, friends, being bullied, lack of self-worth and confidence can suppress on who you truly are. I am fortunate, I did not go through any childhood trauma or bullying at school, and grew up in a loving, yet stern, environment and protection from my mother.

there to replenish you. No doubt there will be sacrifices to be made as part of your growth. It is up to you what you are prepared to give up for fulfilling your purpose, or else to live a life of regret to please others.

It is important to communicate your desire to do what your heart resonates with, instead of suppressing the dream that you know you were meant to fulfil. You will just know it. I see the mistakes as a series of lessons to overcome, tough as they may be at the time of experiencing them. There are times when you have self-doubt, sometimes tears, and then you brush yourself off and carry on, because the mission is so strong inside that nothing will stand in your way. You become more aware of finding what makes you get that inner joy, and find your true passion. Keep searching and don't settle for less, as you are saying no to your natural gift if you settle for less.

Early Skills Development, Primary and High School

My aunt worked at a doctor's surgery and realised I loved medical-related things, and I expressed at the age of thirteen, my wish to become a doctor one day. She gave me my first dental kit set and a thick anatomy textbook called 'Cunningham's Anatomy', which was twice the size of a telephone directory. I read it like a novel.

I mainly chose science-related subjects to qualify for university in the medical field. My skills stem from childhood;

Challenges in life ...
when life gives you lemons, make lemonade

As I developed in my early years of business, it was a big risk, in the recession of 2009, in applying for a business loan in an uncertain climate. I made many mistakes that cost me a lot of money. I struggled with numerous human resources and people management issues, and learnt not to wallow over it, maybe just for a few days. But I am aware that it was my ego coat that was hurt. When you become spiritually conscious, you catch yourself in the ego presence. When your calling knocks on the door, you can't ignore. Once that silent voice starts waking up and searching for your why, if you keep searching, it will find you. It is a deep subject that will need another book on its own.

No, I did not have the facts and performed my due diligence before I made my decisions, so as not to act on impulse and desperation if in a predicament. However, you learn from it, or you repeat the mistakes. If life keeps giving you a hard time, evaluate why you are going through the tough times. If you embrace it, you mature and enhance your self-confidence and belief, knowing you have overcome the obstacles.

There are always going to be highs and lows in life, as well as in business. It can sometimes be a lonely place. Find your tribe, belong to a network, as it reflects your net worth for support when you need it most. As the years progress, you realise you become stronger within yourself, but your support is always

Michelle Wyngaard

We are sometimes too consumed in the noise of life, the inner voice is silenced so much that we often find ourselves saying, "I should have listened to my instincts". A little tip: when life overwhelms, take time out and find a quiet space to think and reflect because this is when your creative ideas and solution of the day's problems pop up. We don't spend enough time out, to think. If we don't practice this, we function in paralysis by over-analysis. It's like running from a sabre tooth tiger every day, we cannot sustain this level of function. Stop to replenish your energy.

As females, we tend to act from a superwoman mode until we run out of steam, resulting in burnout. Our engines are not designed the same as men. Time management is so cliché in business. My best advice to women trying to make a success of your day, is to manage your energy. Something I learnt through my female coach support network. We do have to wear different hats on a daily basis for others. When do we stop to wear the hat that fits us, and be comfortable in it? Women have come a long way to find their respect in the business world and are becoming the new thought leaders. We have different energy levels than men, therefore understand when you are at your peak, then do the high-energy task and when you are low on energy, do the low energy tasks. When the business society expects you to imitate what men do, why do we have to fit in with this model? Don't, as physiologically, we are not the same in our hormones.

I loved listening to his stories of the war days. I did not enjoy history at school but remembered his stories, and one in particular, he kept telling about the colonel for whom he was the driver. One day the van he was driving with Colonel Montgomery was hit by a bomb and he had to run for cover. In the process, he covered the colonel with his body to protect him from the shrapnel, and instead he himself was shot in the chin by shrapnel, leaving an indent which I thought was just a natural feature of his cleft. He had the souvenir to prove it. He was brave and courageous to have lived to tell the tale, as they won the war in Egypt.

The Journey of Self-discovery – Be Still and Listen

Another lesson I learnt is not to be too egotistical and feel that we know it all, but to be humble. This is what my mum and grandmother taught me, so no matter who you become, always remember that. Today I still practise this lesson, and it has served me well on my journey in life and business. However, you have to keep a balance to not be a people pleaser, be humble and courteous, and make assertive decisions in business. You develop an awareness of when to use it. If you feel that you are in a weak position in dealing with negotiations, state your intentions clearly and if it is not a win-win, don't compromise and walk away from it. There is always something better installed, and most of all, trust your gut instinct; it is your guide.

Michelle Wyngaard

character, even in business. Those words were, and still are, so profound to me. I don't carry hatred in my heart, as it will only poison you for the days of your life. Let go and move on to learn the lesson of adversity, so that it can strengthen your mind and teach others this lesson. You waste your energy on the past and your future plans are not being realised, instead you can transfer your energy and time to make improvements.

We are faced with various challenges in our businesses on a daily basis. In my experience, if you face up to it, embrace it and find a way around the obstacles and you become bolder in weathering the next challenge. Focus on finding the solution, not the problem. If you avoid the issues, it will keep appearing; therefore, my advice is to embrace the lesson and ask for help and guidance from those who have been there already, to reduce the mistakes that you will make and the cost it will result in, for your business.

My grandmother lived in a village which had the backdrop of the iconic postcard view of Table Mountain, when you looked out of the front door. She was a strong and proud woman who worked hard all her life, raising 12 children and 13 grandchildren. She worked for the then president of South Africa, Mr JB Vorster, as a laundry lady. My grandfather fought in World War II in Egypt for England, as a very young lad. I am proud of him, and it afforded me the path to where I am currently, in England. He would be very proud of me, knowing that his efforts in contributing to the war brought me here.

issues with coloured folks, as long as you obeyed. The hatred stank on both sides of the divide – some of us survived to tell the truth. Never again, never again.

High school at the age of fourteen was challenging, during the riots and boycott period. We often had to run home to avoid being hit by rubber bullets, then eventually came the fall of the white supremacy. The youngest serving president of South Africa, FW de Klerk, realised that it was time to bring about change before civil unrest became uncontrollable, and ended apartheid. I had hopes for my future to make a better life for my family to thrive and partake in equal opportunities.

I had a chance to vote for the first time in my early twenties and applied to be one of the official voting facilitators in that year, while still at university. It was history in the making for all non-white South Africans. FREEDOM DAY 1994! Nelson Mandela, after twenty-seven years of being a political prisoner, was freed to become the first black president of South Africa. It was a joyous occasion for everyone in South Africa, to vote for the first time for equality and freedom. President de Klerk realised in 1994 that, "to do the right thing, is always the right thing", a philosophy I practice at work now.

Now, I recall a saying from Nelson Mandela which I use in my day to day personal and business life, "When someone has done you wrong, if you hold on to that thought then you will become the prisoner of your mind for the rest of your life, if you don't forgive those who harmed you". To have humility is an essential

Michelle Wyngaard

of who I am. It must have been hard for our parents to have lived through apartheid. Why did they accept this inequality? Why were we different? I kept asking these questions in my mind.

I thought, how will I free myself one day, from the shackles of my current situation? My freedom is the most valuable thing taken from me. To ensure that it will not be my future, I continued observing the dynamics of the apartheid and the effects it had on me, my family, and friends. I would not accept this segregation in life as my parents did. Recalling the past, still leaves painful memories in my heart and tears in my eyes, as I write today, when I think of the injustice of mankind. I forgive them, for they are not awakened to the spirit of love and kindness, and may have had repeated patterns of bad childhood conditioning. No one is born evil, but what makes us behave and act out our dark side of life to harm another. Why?

I discovered that we all have a choice and freewill in our mind, even though it is not exercised externally, due to living under those regimes who exercise their dark side on mankind, unto those who are vulnerable and subservient. Post-apartheid South Africa went through a healing process called the truth and reconciliation commission set up, to ask forgiveness for those who harmed you under the white regime. It was sad to hear the stories, however we forgave and moved on. During the riots, it was heart-wrenching and gruesome scenes seeing your loved ones tortured by police and traitors burned with tyres, shot, stabbed and locked up if caught on the streets beyond your curfew time, because you were black. There were less

WOMEN IN THE *Modern* BUSINESS WORLD

Conditioning of Belief and Value Systems

You question a lot as a child. I have a vivid recall of a train journey with my mother to my grandmother's house. It was fun to travel by train. We had a car, an old light blue Chevy, which my dad used for work mainly. I always looked forward to seeing my grandmother, as she spoiled me. I still miss her, and she played a significant role in my belief and value system. Her philosophy was, "It will always be ok, don't worry, tomorrow is another day." I digress, I must have been about six years old while standing on the station platform, dressed in my favourite orange coat with black buttons and furry black collar and cuffs and special "going out shoes".

I can still visualise the colour of the train, in the ugly military, maroon and yellow carriages and cold, mint green, hard plastic seats in third class. I begged my mum that I wanted to sit at the front, in a first-class carriage where the seats are upholstered, and no broken windows. Come to think of it, why was there not a second class then? At the entrance of the station looking up high, was a black and white sign which was directed with a white hand symbol, the index finger (like today's phone emoji), pointing to which side of the train we were not allowed to sit. Whites to the right and coloureds to the left. I asked mum:

"Why can't we sit in first class?" and all she replied in a calm voice was: "It is for white people; it is just the way it is, Michelle." The same with the buses. That day I silently promised myself that I would work very hard, get a good education and get a job so that I could afford the things that were denied to me because

Michelle Wyngaard

it despite the financial constraints I faced. My parents could not support me on this venture, however my mum said: "If you want to go then I will help you fundraise". I did it!

My biggest regret was when we hosted the congress for the first time in 1994, when the inauguration of President Nelson Mandela took place. We invited him to be the special guest at our opening ceremony in Cape Town, which he accepted and honoured to attend. A few of the planning committee students were chosen at random to sit at the host table for the evening gala dinner. Guess who was absent to get some lunch as she could not wait for the hat draw to take place when her name was pulled first out of the hat? Yes, gutted forever. Lesson of patience learnt that day. They forfeited my turn as I was absent. I encourage you to watch the inauguration on YouTube and feel the energy of history in the making. It still gives me chills of inspiration when I watch it. Forgiveness was brought, and united our country.

I was quite sporty and quite good with my grades throughout school, and I enjoyed learning. Even to this day, I seek to find new skills that will empower me on my journey of finding my true passion in life, in order to serve mankind. The journey of discovery starts from the day you set foot on earth, and you are meant to make a difference in this world. Now you ask, but how do you know your purpose? Let's hold that thought, for now, I will tell you later.

first year was hard to adapt to when you were eighteen, set for six years of study.

Dentistry is a tough course; you need tenacity and determination to become a confident communicator. It was an honour for our dental faculty to be elected to host, for what was to become, for the first time ever, a post-apartheid South African international dental event. I was in fourth year then and it was the first international association of dental congresses and young dentists worldwide, which was chosen to be held in Cape Town. We were overjoyed with the news. I connected with so many international students, who became friends, and through this experience, it inspired me to plan my future to work abroad.

The economy in South Africa was going downhill at the time and I saw no future in my career. One of our final year students was chosen as the president for that year in 1994. In my fourth year in 1995, I went to São Paulo and Rio de Janeiro in Brazil, representing our university at the international dental congress. I transferred the chain and gavel to the new president, elected in Brazil, as our president could not attend due to writing final exams. It was terrific, both events were memorable, especially as it was on my twenty fourth birthday that I left the shores of Cape Town for my virgin flight to Brazil. Through my fundraising efforts and funding from the university towards the cost, I could afford my dream to become true. Looking back, I now realised how bold I was, going to a foreign country for the first time as a senior student. With just a belief that I could do

MICHELLE WYNGAARD

what I may be one day. You could call me a bit of a daydreamer. Despite living in such a beautiful country to foreigners, one would be oblivious to the depth of race inequality, and at that age, we were just happy kids who loved to play. Being unaware of anything different, for a dominantly Christian country, the political climate contradicted biblical teachings.

Does apartheid exist in the bible? I thought to myself. As children we accepted this as the norm, as usually you dared not question or challenge the regime for fear of being locked up. We were not allowed certain privileges, like going to restaurants, individual shops or going swimming in certain parts of the beaches, public swimming pools or parks. Making friends with the white children was forbidden, let alone going to the "white" schools, as we called it. We used to stand at a distance and watch the other kids enjoying the facilities.

My Education Journey and Accomplishments

Little did I know the impact apartheid would have on my life and education going forward. Segregation in education left a scar on my mind. No wonder that I am so driven to assist and form a non-profit organisation, *Global Growth Success with Smartteens and LSA in South Africa,* and have it go global. It is being formed as I write, to help all children from the age of 12 to 18, to teach them leadership, and entrepreneurial and life skills that set them up for life. I have fond memories of my school and university days, though. My university years afforded me to discover my confidence. The

the many talents that she has been blessed with". What talent! "Mr Lewis, do you know something I don't know?", I thought, with a cheeky grimace smile.

I was not very confident in high school. I was an observer of people and learnt by watching their behaviour in human interactions. My family called me a bookworm, reading all that I could. Head always stuck in a book. Back in the day, having a library card was like a special ticket to go socialising, as an excuse to meet your friends after school, like a hangout place. I saw it as my escapism in the knowledge world.

My mother was very strict and ensured that I focused on studying. As a child, I thought that doctors were superheroes in their white coats with stethoscopes, and nurses in those days wore navy capes and white hoods. That image left an impression on me. Both the nurses and doctors were very respectful of the matron. She wore a maroon cape and wore a pristine white uniform with several lapels on her shoulders demonstrating her seniority in the ward. You would not have a hair out of place with her around. So here I am writing this chapter, with gratitude towards the doctors and nurses that saved my life. I could not walk for what seemed like half of that year, but it was more likely three months, according to my mum. I was sent to a convalescent home to strengthen my legs, which delayed my start for prep school. I eventually caught up at the age of seven.

I was a happy, quiet, shy little girl who was quite content, though very much kept to herself, and I loved to dream about

Michelle Wyngaard

Kensington, in South Africa. At that time childhood diseases were quite common, and yes, I was one of them who contracted bacterial meningitis in January of that year. It happened so fast, one day I was fine, then the next day I started with unusual pain in my legs, which caused me to limp and develop symptoms of confusion, deliriousness, and with sensitivity to light. I told my mum my legs felt funny and they hurt. Next thing I knew, I was rushed to the local doctors who immediately said, "Take her to the Red Cross Children's Hospital", which was to become my new home for a while.

I woke up half groggy with a plaster cast on both my limbs, with just my toes exposed on my left leg and the other half leg exposed from the knee down. I looked like an Egyptian mummy from the waist down. The doctors said, had my parents not acted promptly I would not have made it. I think back now to why I always did love the hospital environment. It never scared me. I was fascinated about it all, which sparked my interest in the medical field.

I could not see myself doing anything else but heal people; it just felt in alignment with my soul. I did think of becoming a dietician, anything to do with nutrition, or an archaeologist, because of my love for geography. I was an ace in this subject. But I did not see a long-term future in it, instead perhaps, I could travel the world searching for old treasures. Don't talk about maths, I hated it but did reasonably well in it. My high school teacher remarked in my final report that, "Michelle could do so much better if only she hides her modesty and shows more of

CHAPTER 7

MICHELLE WYNGAARD

Trust Your Inner Voice to Reveal Your True Self and Step Into Your Genius

"Our greatest fear is also our own greatness"
(Nelson Mandela)

How It All Began ...

It was the beginning of 1976; I nearly died that year. I turned five years old that winter of July. I still recall vividly as a little girl, growing up and living in the apartheid years in the natural, beautiful, and scenic coastline of Cape Town, in a suburban town called

WOMEN IN THE *Modern* BUSINESS WORLD

You are also warmly welcome to check our website for more detailed information: generationphi.com

And feel free to contact us for any questions or comments as we absolutely love to share our vision:

info@generationphi.com

Inga Phoenix Kokalevská

women, educators, speakers, leaders of different initiatives, representatives of social projects, and all who want to step forward, cannot be overestimated, and is to contribute to the creation of our interconnected future, where the center of the focus will not be an individual, but society as a whole.

How you can get engaged and work with us

We created a movement **Generation Φ**, dedicated to giving support, mentorship and collaboration opportunities to the new generation of leaders. To support our vision with a strategic program that will help bring it into life in a natural, though conscious way, we founded **a Generation Φ Academy for Transformational Leaders** - an innovative *educational platform* that offers its community members trainings on transformational leadership in combination with psychological literacy, and helps them directly integrate that knowledge into their professional fields. Our goal is to build a learning and action oriented network of solutions driven leaders and offer them a platform for interdisciplinary collaborative work, so they can address the needs of the new era more effectively.

Those who want to become a member of our community, get regular content on inspirational transformational leadership, collaborate on interdisciplinary common projects with people who share the same vision, and take an active part in shaping the future, are very cordially invited to join our *private Facebook group* **Generation Φ Tribe**.

market and will be defining the direction of the economy. This generation completely differs from the previous ones and brings new values to our society. If we want to interact with those young people on a new level, we need to understand what the new era, that has just started, is about. Those companies that will rethink their communication language with the new generation, in accordance with the values of the new era, and will integrate the concept of transformational leadership into their corporate culture, offering psychological and leadership trainings, and high-level mentoring to their teams, will be pioneers of change. But just under one condition - if they approach their clients and teams, and create services and products with the intention to contribute for the good of the society as a whole. And if they create an ecosystem of healthy collaborations, a space for deeper interconnection of shared visions, instead of a competitive environment.

No matter what your cultural or professional background is, whether you come from a business, non-profit or public sector, if you're a part of a well-established organization, or planning a start-up-together with you, we want to build societies, institutions, companies, communities of the future, offering you an innovative view for the existing "operating models" and helping you develop services and products that reflect the needs of the new era.

Let's open a dialog and think out of the current box to create a meaningful future. Our future. With you. For all of us and our children. Therefore, the role of mothers, business

Inga Phoenix Kokalevská

Women Are Creators of the Future

As a mother, woman, global citizen and caring human being, I have a dream for our children living in a more conscious, selfless world. My role as a woman is to raise awareness of other women that we, mothers, like nobody else are motivated to ensure a better future for the next generation. It's our natural desire. And it also means that we are capable of that like no one else. We should just realize that we have that power to shape the world and directly influence the evolution of humanity, by raising the new generation. The future of humanity will look exactly the same way we are raising our children now.

If you want your children to live in a better world, we should start working together on the change that is needed now, more than ever before. A community is stronger than an individual or a family. No person can survive by him/herself, especially in the times we are facing now, so the quality of young people's lives will be dependent on the quality of their cooperation with each other. It's our main responsibility as mothers to teach our children and lead them by example how to live a happy life with other people. Let's start using more "we" than "I", seeing the world as a smart, interconnected system created by nature, where we, humans, are interdependent cells of one body. Nature is the source of everything, and everything is part of nature, and is therefore part of the whole. Thus, ALL the children are ours.

We should also realize that the new generation we're talking about in this chapter has just recently started entering the job society, and the key to understanding the meaning of life is in fulfilling that role. The most fulfilled and happy life that will leave a legacy and will be imprinted in the evolution of humanity is the one lived in serving others with your unique talent. Leave your print in the soul of humanity.

• Every person is born with his or her specific desires and a set of qualities that cover those desires. Your thoughts are the results of your deepest desires. You can only imagine what you unconsciously long for. And nature provided you with specific skills that can help you fulfill those desires. It means you can achieve whatever you want and live a fulfilled life.

• You can only discover yourself through discovering other people, by focusing on their true needs. You can't change another person's behavior but you can realize and correct this behavior in yourself. By doing this, you justify the other the way you justify yourself. And you feel empathy, compassion and love to that person the way you feel love to yourself. You can only correct the other in yourself, which will leave a print in the evolution of humanity and help change the world.

• Be a phoenix who consciously chose to live at a new level, by serving others, giving to them and inspiring them with your story of transformation. Step out from the dark and choose light. You came to this world to help connect it, by discovering a higher purpose of creation and helping others with it.

Inga Phoenix Kokalevská

that freedom of choice which will bring a peaceful smile to your face and light you up from the inside out. And you'll become an authentic leader people will love to follow.

- Choose LIGHT. In every moment of our life, we have that freedom of choice - mastering the situation as a giver, or being its victim as a receiver. We can't choose time and environment to be born into. But we can choose the intention which we're going to live our life with, receiving or giving. And that's the only freedom we have. Turn each challenge into a blessing and let your story inspire other people.

- Realize your intention to receive and change it for the intention to give. The highest fulfillment of human potential is when a person receives with pleasure and gratitude everything that is given to him, in order to serve others. He or she shines with joy and gives this light to others.

- Joy is a reflection of good deeds. People who shine from the inside out are those who chose to live in giving, no matter what obstacles they had to overcome, they don't feel life wasn't fair to them. You can be truly happy and fulfilled only by serving other people. A true transformation will bring light into your life and to those around you. You're meant to live an awaken, conscious, enlightened, blissful life.

- There is a higher purpose behind the fact that we're all unlike, with different needs and talents. Your task is to discover this purpose. Each person has a unique role in our

WOMEN IN THE
Modern
BUSINESS
WORLD

- The highest energy is given to the one who wants to give. The more you give, the bigger influence you have. Real power is not about domination. It's naturally given to the person who is determined to dedicate his life to his tribe. Imagine, the world is your company. If it profits, you profit. If someone in your company is not happy, not progressing, or not at the right place, then you and the whole company are not profiting. So make your company work at its best.

- True leaders are givers. They unite their tribe by giving them a higher purpose and a mission that is bigger than any individual profit. They take them to a better future where they can jointly improve their lives, discover their true purpose and grow to their fullest potential, and inspire them to start giving to other people. They put the needs of the tribe before their own and serve them the best they can - not for improving their social or financial status but because they are true leaders who live their life for their tribe.

- No fear, just LOVE. Be fearless - give love instead of acting out of fear. Know yourself and love other people. Be a next generation leader who won't divide the world by spreading out animosity and manipulating with people's fear. Be the one who will help transform the world to the light and therefore save and connect it. Be a channel of light.

- Let's make GIVING the sexiest currency in the world. Receiving is limited, giving is endless. There is no competition in giving. And that will set you free. Choose

Inga Phoenix Kokalevská

- Have a mission that is bigger than yourself, build a team whom you give a higher purpose in life, create a movement that brings light into other people's lives. Individualism, a lone wolf, 'one man show', Superman, Wonder Woman - it's so yesterday. Only a strong community of people who are on a common mission and collaborate on a higher level can have a really big impact in today's world. Become a pioneer, an agent for change. Be a leader of the new generation.

- We are ONE. We can't live and survive without other people, we're interdependent. One body with 7.8 billion cells. If one cell breaks down, others may follow, and if they start to fight against each other, we have an autoimmune disease. If you lose, nobody will win in the end. Your pain is my pain. If I hurt you, I hurt myself first. If so many people are in fear and frustration, the whole humanity is paralyzed by fear and frustration and can't move forward.

- UNITY in diversity. We all have different desires, needs and talents. Nature created us that way, so we as humanity can cover more tasks from different areas of life. A tricky part is to realize a higher purpose behind that, and to make a conscious, free choice to collaborate with other people for something bigger than any individual goals. The new era needs a new generation of leaders who will help others discover a higher purpose behind those differences. Transformational leaders who will inspire society for change towards a conscious choice to act selflessly. Be one of those who will help bring humanity to a common mission.

character, interests, nation, religion, and they will provide you with job opportunities themselves, looking forward to working with you?

• you can build deep emotional relationships in the era of virtual reality, instead of feeling lonely and socially alienated?

• you can build a dream team of highly driven people who will be motivated to work on a common mission?

• to overcome any challenges and always stand up again, even in the hardest times?

• to stay on track in the rapidly changing world, no matter what the external circumstances are?

• to keep performing great quality, fair and valuable work in the world of overnight businesses, fast-food entertainment and self-proclaimed gurus?

Here are some principles from our concept of transformational leadership that you can apply in your daily life. They will guide you on your journey and won't let you fall, no matter what challenges you'll be going through:

• Life has a bigger vision for you. Live with a purpose, and leave a legacy by impacting other people's lives. Help those who need you more than you need your privacy, rest and comfort zone. Choose a path not because it's easy, but because it's hard. Next level happens out of your comfort zone. A leader's personality is measured by the extent of challenges he is willing to face for other people. He doesn't let his personal limits prevent him from serving his tribe.

authorities, economic experts, scientific elite, tech tycoons, but now more than ever we need transformational leaders. Agents of change, who will connect them all under the same mission, that in the end will connect the whole world.

Learn the Principles of Transformational Leadership to Live a Meaningful Life

Do you want to know how...

- the concept of transformational leadership can help you raise to a higher level of consciousness and transmit to a more selfless attitude to life?
- it can make you a better leader and parent and give you direction on your daily journey towards a truly fulfilled and blessed life?
- to find peace and joy in cooperation with people, instead of being constantly stressed from competition?
- to act authentically out of love and compassion, and not reactively out of fear?
- you can feel a high level of energy, instead of pain of accumulated frustrations?
- you can discover a higher meaning of life in today's world that is focused on material values, and live a meaningful life?
- you can gain strong psychological immunity, which is a main foundation for physical immunity, and be not afraid of your future?
- you can become attractive for people of any kind of

WOMEN IN THE *Modern* BUSINESS WORLD

Young people need new leaders who will empower them with a strong, positive vision of the future, give them a higher meaning and a deeper sense of belonging, also showing direction and leading them to the light. We need leaders who will build bridges between generations and create fruitful cross-generation projects and partnerships. We need great communicators who will help people orientate themselves in the new era without stress and panic, who will encouragingly articulate the message that any social crisis and disintegrated society is here for showing us the opportunity to unite on a higher level.

The world needs new transformational leaders who will unite and become role models of unity. Who will connect society by leading others to realization that we are all one, and will be transmitting this vision of reality to the new generation. We need leaders who will set new standards and trends, proclaiming giving and compassion as new values. Who will teach young people psychological literacy - how to understand other people's needs, get along with them synergistically, and work together towards outcomes that are good for humanity as a whole.

We need a new generation of transformational leaders who will start building a global network and collaborating on an interdisciplinary level, throughout all cultural, social and professional environments. Who will, with the help of leading experts from various industries, develop strategic, game-changing action plans and implement them. We have political

Inga Phoenix Kokalevská

Our Vision for Humanity

Our main occupation as society should now be saving our civilization through transformation of its current values, resulting in unity. We should start investing in our future by raising a new generation of leaders. Developing people, instead of growing financial wealth and mass production that nature doesn't actually need. It's necessary that we, humans, switch our mindset from "how to make a living out of each other" to taking our time to explore why we are here, what is our role in this world, what is the meaning of life, and how to cooperate with other people for the common good.

World leaders must finally stop investing in security operations and proliferation, and instead start collaborating strategically and systematically on interdisciplinary, cross-country initiatives for ensuring global peace. The next step is to become one world, one nation, one soul. Otherwise, we'll be facing various forms of calls for actions, such as viruses, till we finally get the message.

The urge for responsible cooperation among individuals and states will be the main moving force of the new era which will lead society to discovering the higher purpose of life, and giving will be the main currency. So the skill of getting along with people synergistically will be the most essential and required skill of all.

But it surely does contribute to a bigger mental, emotional and social gap between people, and supports the idea of unequal living standards, and as a result of this, even bigger collective frustrations, envy and hate arise. Core values that stand behind those formulations divide us, and don't empower us for a common vision. They no longer meet society's new needs and won't take us to the new era that has actually already begun. So, we can indeed "stay behind" mentally, but in this case it happens if we keep following this out-of-date value system.

Let us again refer to Thomas Reid's words in his Essays on the Intellectual Powers of Man, "The strength of the chain is determined by that of the weakest link, for if they give away, the whole falls to pieces, and the weight supported by it falls to the ground."

In other words, the strength of a group, community or society, is in its realization that all its members are interdependent, and if one of them falls, it will lead to the fall of the whole. And how society approaches its weakest, helpless members, such as children, orphans, single mothers, the elderly, abandoned, sick, disabled and deprived, is a reflection of the level of its evolution. True leaders don't long for domination, they make it their mission to save the group and make it strong by uniting it and protecting its weakest members. They don't teach individuals how to achieve personal success and win, they teach them how to collaborate on a common vision and succeed together as a group.

Inga Phoenix Kokalevská

Society lost its ability to see reality for what it is as our ever growing egoism totally distorts it. On the one hand, this brings forth fast-food, shallow pseudo-psychological trends, easily formed opinions, and thousands of overnight life coaches, social media influencers and "thought leaders". On the other hand, moving so far away from the source pushes the new generation, now more than ever, to start searching for the true, higher meaning of life.

Creating Healthy Core Values

Since the breakout of COVID-19, we have witnessed so many well-established and newly born online marketers, business and life coaches, success trainers, consultants, and all possible influencers of the information age, flooding social media and email boxes with messages. A very common one would look like, "If you want to ´win´ in those ´unprecedented times´ and not ´stay behind´ while ´others are waiting´, you should sign up for the generous offer that will last ´just a few hours´, otherwise you'll be ´regretting´ it forever, and you should ´act fast´ since ´the price will go up soon´".

In our humble opinion, those formulations might cause an even bigger panic as they create an illusion that we live in very uncertain times, and if you don't use the opportunity to earn more money you'll stay behind, while the others will grow. This philosophy, "Be the first, take what you can and win", doesn't contribute to the unity of our humanity, to the formation of a mindset that puts other people and the collective good first.

meaning in life. Secure higher salaries for teachers and medical workers to attract more qualified and dedicated people to those professions.

So many young people who are talented and can be fulfilled as teachers, social workers, nurses or physicians, choose to study business and finance instead. But what if society needs them more in another way - for finding healthy, engaging, creative and innovative ways on how to communicate with the young generation, and inspire them to live a more conscious, responsible and selfless life? Perception of financial wealth as a measure of wellbeing has been dictating the following trend in society, "If you want to be rich and happy, don't go to school as it won't teach you how to earn money". But this philosophy won't make the young generation truly happy, it won't stop growing mass depressions and suicidal thoughts by youth, it won't solve accumulated collective frustrations and the threat of armed conflicts and wars. We believe this rhetoric is so much a thing of the past. Let's move on and step into the inevitable new era.

All basic needs of all people would be covered if each nation would start investing in fulfilling them, instead of dedicating huge amounts of resources into security initiatives. If nuclear superpowers start distributing all that money they invested to build their nuclear arsenal rather for saving the new generation and ensuring weaker links of society, there will be no need of armed conflicts and wars, since the new generation will be raised based on the values of synergistic cooperation, with no hate and envy.

dissatisfaction, since receiving is always limited to external conditions. They will be truly happy as giving is limitless and brings deeper, lasting fulfillment. While teaching children financial literacy is fine, as they can later take better care of their families, psychological, emotional, social and spiritual literacy is much more essential, as it teaches them how to be happy by being responsible not just for themselves, but also by living their life in service to other people.

Action Needed from Authorities and World Leaders

What can world leaders and governments start doing to save the new generation? They can set new trends and examples to follow, where the new heroes are those who give more to other people. The ones who save lives and devote their time for making our world a better place to live in for everybody. To compare with current role models like Hollywood actors, models, sportsmen, social media influencers and the financial elite.

What else can the authorities do? Invest in better quality education and health systems, making them accessible for everybody. Make innovative methods in psychology and leadership (not management but leadership, the way we define it in this chapter) part of a school program, in order to teach children how to understand other people and cooperate with them. Integrate discussions about spirituality into the educational system, to help avoid depressions and suicidal thoughts by those children who question and can't find

Investing in the New Generation

It's all achievable if we now join forces and go through this process of transformation together. The most logical, though still neglected, way to strategically approach the future is to start investing in the new generation. What can we do as parents? First of all, stop for a while and take some serious time to discover who we are and who our children are, so we don't raise them by our own desires and needs. We should realize that everybody is different and has his or her unique role in our society, so we can complement each other by contributing to the whole with our innate talents. And if we learn how to fulfill our own role in society and to live to our true potential, we would also create a healthier and happier environment for our children. It's essential to raise them through true love, acceptance and appreciation for who they really are, instead of through our own frustrations and fears.

What else can we do? Spend more quality time with children, talk to them, and build strong emotional bonds, read classical books that cultivate their sense of compassion and create desire to undertake heroic deeds for saving those in need. Teach them how to be happy and fulfilled by sharing with others, by helping women, children and the elderly, and by feeling compassion for socially weaker and disabled. They will grow up into emotionally healthy, conscious, caring, compassionate and giving adults, who will feel responsible for our planet. They won't be driven by a desire to have more and dominate over other people, which leads to a feeling of constant

Inga Phoenix Kokalevská

growth but cause great harm. A real, deep joy comes from fulfillment of our social role that serves as a force for good. So, isn't it about time to understand that a fundamental change of our mindset and values, that will transform society's status quo, is inevitable? We're at the crossroads where humanity will have to choose its direction before it's too late. The faster we act, the bigger disasters we can avoid.

To be able to cure, which means not only to survive, but leave a legacy for the next generation, first of all, we as humanity have to identify very clearly the problem we're facing and clarify the status quo for ourselves. We need to describe all the manifestations (symptoms) of today's world and come with the right diagnosis. We have to find out the reasons why we got sick, the source of this social crisis (as the biggest threat to human species are not the viruses, but self-destruction of humanity resulted from our growing egoism and frustrations). The next step is to create the best healing strategy - getting clear on what must be done in order to move to the next stage of evolution. And to ensure lasting results, we need to empower our actions with a strong, positive vision of the future, so that everybody can see the meaning in change, and engage and connect for co-creating a new status quo.

for a limited perception as a "higher purpose". We call it, "I was born free and can do whatever I want!" More and more, behind the concept of "democracy", we actually hide our egoistic desire to do whatever we want for our personal good, to dominate financially and socially over other people and compete with them. We're like those little children on a playground who don't want to share and just long for taking other children's toys. Greed is driving our constantly growing desire to consume more, to buy more, to see more, to have more than others, to achieve more than others, and to be faster than others.

Time for a Change

In fact, recent events show that it's not possible to continue this road any more, it's unbearable and no longer sustainable for humanity. Our values brought us to the current position, the coronavirus only represented a catalyst for change. More than ever before, since WWII, every single human being should deeply realize that no one can survive alone. No financial wealth, life on a private island or personal success will secure the future for him and his children, if the rest of the world falls. We need to cooperate with other people to ensure that the civilization will survive. Viruses are here to stay, till we finally get the message that there is no future for the next generation without our collaborative work for a common good.

It's time for our society to grow up. Those infantile, egoistic substitutes for true happiness, like overconsumption, shallow entertainment or fast-food books, don't contribute to collective

Inga Phoenix Kokalevská

the world, himself and other people as it is, as he perceives all through his own frustrations. And there, those flashes of pleasure become the only reality for him, the standard and the norm, since our psyche naturally tends to pleasure, defending itself from pain. So, he doesn't want to see that he is an alcoholic since this recognition would force him to deal with his pain and look for its true causes. But there are only two ways for him: either starting healing his deepest source of trouble by finding a solution and working daily towards lasting change, or after having identified his true pain, refusing to do anything with it, which will bring him into even deeper frustration.

Doesn't this resemble exactly the crossroads where we as humanity are now? We're going through a fundamental social transformation pushed by force - like unconscious, unwise children - towards transition from a selfish to a selfless attitude to life. Just as the addicted patient, we didn't realize we were sick, and that we had to choose life-supporting behavior over our growing addiction. COVID-19 pushed us to a collective delirium, taking away all addictions of the modern Western civilization: excessive shopping, travelling, drinking and eating. And we think we're in pain without all those "goodies", calling for "going back to normal" and resisting needed change, even though our current lifestyle is destructive from a long-term perspective.

We don't want to sacrifice our individual joy for other people, our country, the common good of the whole society, and not at all for something so abstract and incomprehensible

WOMEN IN THE *Modern* BUSINESS WORLD

For the last seven decades, material wealth has been the leading value of our society. The COVID-19 pandemic, acting as a social transformer, accelerated the beginning of a new era where social status won't be defined by financial success any more, nor will economic trends be driven by consumerism. We shouldn't primarily worry about the economic crisis, as the economy is always a consequence of human activities and is based on our current needs and values. Instead, let's redefine our values and choose the direction in which we'll be focusing on our resources. We as humanity need to choose a path that will bring us to a better future for us all. We should support that vision with new values that will help us unite rather than separate from each other, we should invest in people and not in property, find time for the new generation and not for excessive consumption. Our egoistic attitude to life has led us to the point where we're now. In the days of a technologically advanced civilization, we're facing a very fundamental question about its survival, and what we should do to save it.

Pain as a Catalyst

A metaphorical comparison for our situation would be an alcoholic who was used to drinking for many, many years, which brought him short flashes of pleasure and long, dark, painful times of even deeper frustration. Instead of seeing his life's purpose in doing something meaningful for society, he was satisfying his psychological needs and compensating fulfillment of his desires in a very primitive way, lying in oblivion. Over the time, losing the ability to see reality,

Inga Phoenix Kokalevská

people, offering support and mentorship, and motivate them to jointly achieve more than they thought was possible. They give a lot to others, that's why people trust them and naturally follow them.

The world is ready now more than ever before for a new generation of transformational leaders. Why do we think so? The COVID-19 pandemic shook up the status quo across all areas of social, political and economic life of today's society. Some people might still wish the world would go back to its settings before the virus, calling it "back to normal", but let's have a closer look on what this "normality" actually means. Have we as humanity been moving towards a better future for the next generations and a higher level of evolution? Or have we been increasingly focusing on "receiving" for ourselves, and not "giving" to others?

In fact, it became a social norm to concentrate mainly on our personal everyday needs and fulfill them in a pretty basic way, with no desire to look further and beyond our current individual enjoyment. Like constantly looking for entertaining experiences, such as travelling, shopping and browsing social media for hours, instead of creating emotionally healthy and safe environments for families, local communities or our country. Also showing off external beauty, with selfies, instead of cultivating our inner beauty. We've been consuming goods of all kinds the same way as emotions, people, relationships and nature, instead of spending time educating children and building a better, more conscious future for them.

I explored different paths in life in an attempt to find where I can serve with my most authentic self and light a fire in other people, as I was looking for a soul-enriching fulfillment. I wanted to inspire others to see that no matter what happens in your life, it all is here to serve a higher purpose, to offer you the option of making a conscious choice of correction. There is no greater joy for me than seeing people light up from the inside out when they discover their true purpose and find a powerful motivation to change for a happier tomorrow. Or even better: when they make someone else's tomorrow brighter than today.

Raising a New Generation of Transformational Leaders

What is the concept of transformational leadership and what qualities should transformational leaders have? Without going too much into the theory of this leadership style, let's for the purpose of my sharing, look at some main definitions of transformational leaders presented by researchers.

Transformational leaders have a strong, positive vision of the future. They identify the needed change and work closely with their teams, encouraging the team members to challenge the status quo and inspire them for a vision that goes far beyond their self-interests for the collective good. They explore new ways of doing things and empower others to experience the same passion. They help members of their group grow and are always open to collaboration. They deeply care about their

Inga Phoenix Kokalevská

Only after I had chosen the spiritual path and studied psychoanalysis, was I able to start seeing reality - people, world events and any situation – systemically, which means seeing it as a whole, by deducing a cause-effect relationship. Thanks to my great teachers and four decades of my personal life lessons, experiences and knowledge, I was able to describe the situation we're in now as a society, and anticipate necessary strategies for change. Life has been preparing me for something I had to grow up to, which required a transformative inner work and answering fundamental life questions, rather than a diploma or a certain career path.

The Idea is Born

I came with the idea of *transformational leadership,* the way it's defined in this chapter - as a concept when a person consciously chooses altruism and helps others consciously transform towards selflessness. It involves raising a new generation of leaders as the best strategy for change in society's status quo. I formulated a clear vision, developed a strategy, and defined the characteristics of transformational leaders.

I'm blessed to have people who got passionate about this joint mission, and are now members of my team. Therefore, further in this chapter, I'll write "we" referring to our collaborative work. We make it our mission to inspire and support a new generation of transformational leaders for creating a new society based on selfless values and unity.

do differently, what was my true purpose, why I came to this world, and what life was really about. I became aware that each obstacle was here to be a great teacher on my journey towards becoming a better human being, each time giving me the freedom of choice - what I was going to do with it?

While working with people from various professional, social and cultural environments, I found out that it was the human element that stands behind everything. The quality of any relationship and human performance, or sense of fulfillment, both in personal and work areas of life, is always directly dependent on a person's sense of belonging and fulfillment of his/her psychological needs. But I realized that what fulfilled one person, didn't make much sense to another one. So, how can we collaborate with people, work in teams, get the best of them, and mentor and lead them to progress, if we don't know what best motivates each of them?

I saw the most famous life coaches working with their audience, and I realized they didn't deal with psychological differences between people but tried to fit their own experience and universalized knowledge for everyone. I wanted to get educated to extend and deepen my understanding of people, myself, the specifics of the human psyche, and differences in the way of our thinking, and this led me to study psychoanalysis. I was blessed to find the best teachers and the most innovative method of modern applied psychology, which today enables me to address people's true needs very effectively.

Inga Phoenix Kokalevská

free hands in their several projects. They saw my energy and passion for working with people's potential and making them grow. In a short time, as part of a crisis leadership approach, I reformed their branches in several countries by rebuilding a whole system, training managers and putting together teams, setting new goals, introducing new strategies, and improving overall results and key performance indicators.

I worked with about thirty teams in eight countries and trained them in diverse fields in over one thousand hours, including leadership training for managers. I helped open new branches, passed the whole concept and values of the brand to new business leaders, and set up processes between the parent company and its franchises. I worked hard to deliver the best results I could, and I left the company at the moment when I realized that my role there was completed. I've learned in life that thinking what we can give and not receive, being determined, stepping out of our comfort zone, staying on track through any challenges, helping other people grow, playing full out, and being able to give up our benefits and certainty at the moment when we see that we won't give our best, is what makes our life dignified.

Opening Up to a More Conscious Life

Searching for a meaningful existence led me to the inner crisis that pushed me towards a more conscious reflection of my life, what I had and hadn't done, and where my unconscious attitude brought me. I wondered what I could

WOMEN IN THE *Modern* BUSINESS WORLD

lecturing for university students in Germany, I found a passion for working with the young generation and inspiring them to think critically. I developed my own way of teaching where I stimulated students' interest in different topics and engaged them in discussions, taking on the role of a moderator. I found it highly important and rewarding to spend time with the new generation, being able to give them fresh perspectives, explore new ways together, and enjoy their progress.

My interest in the U.S. - Russia relations, and seeing their potential improvement as one of the key factors for ensuring global peace, brought me to work as an intern in the think-tank East West Institute in New York. I was monitoring the so-called "reset", the new strategic relationship based on mutual trust and cooperation between two new country leaders, and was involved in such initiatives as preventive diplomacy, nonproliferation issues and the New START Treaty. I had a chance to advise on the selection of business, public and intellectual leaders for the Global Leadership Consortium, and participate in high-level expert dialogues. This enabled me to gain complexity in problem solving and also to see the growing need for filling in the gap in cross-country and cross-sector collaboration.

Life has always been for me a continuous opportunity to learn new things. I didn't look for a career, I looked for a mission where I could serve my best and make the change. And though I've never seen myself as an employee in a corporate world, I was given a great chance by a business company that gave me

Inga Phoenix Kokalevská

Awakening a Passion

In my teenage years, I found a passion for languages, philosophy, psychology and international relations, and later got my master's degree in Russian philology and Slavic Studies. I became a member of a unique PhD program that functioned like an interdisciplinary "hub" of young enthusiastic scholars, who worked on the same topic under the mentorship of leading experts from different fields. There, I learned how to work in a team contributing to a common idea while using various perspectives and methods.

Though my PhD thesis had an innovative approach in the field of leadership and gender studies, I didn't finish it, since I deeply realized that I didn't want to analyze the past but was passionate about creating the future. I just got a strong feeling that writing about something that wasn't any longer in my power to change and what wouldn't improve anybody's life, wasn't in line with who I truly was. I loved to work with people and see the results of our cooperation, but I didn't have enough patience to spend hours and hours in libraries.

At the same time, I feel very grateful that being in the academic community in Germany, Austria and the U.S. allowed me to be a member of prominent educational and research institutions, like the UC Berkeley, University of Vienna, Harvard, University of Chicago, Stanford, and Columbia University. I had the opportunity to learn from great intellectual brains on how to challenge the status quo with philosophical questions. While also had to forgive my whole family for washing their hands of the situation, because I always felt that I was mentally strong enough to stand up for others and not expect others to do the same for me. Moreover, at that same time, I remember telling my mother how grateful I was that my life was wonderful, while I saw so many others suffer.

I never felt spite towards my stepfather or any of my "tough teachers", as I felt that they were unhappy and didn't know what they were doing. Coming from a challenging family background, that stretched me and pushed me to grow and rise above any obstacles that were determined by the social environment I was born into, taught me great lessons of mercy and forgiveness. I saw life in its diverse manifestations. As I now understand, it was part of my journey to experience different facets of life, so I could better understand people from various social backgrounds and life situations, and serve them more authentically.

I protected my little sister during family storms, and spent time with my great-grandmother, listening to her life stories while she was sitting at home alone during her last years of life. I was there for my stepfather's father, who was losing his vision, to make it easier for him to integrate more smoothly into a new life in a foreign country, and helped secure a pension for him as well as my grandparents. Those deep relationships with people based on love and compassion, together with my loyal school friendships, the right guidance from our class teacher and reading great books, taught me more about life than any theoretical leadership training would do.

Inga Phoenix Kokalevská

My Early Journey

When I was a child and somebody would ask me who I wanted to become, I couldn't exactly define the profession, it just didn't exist in my mind back then. I loved to read books about heroic and mercy deeds, especially of female heroines who, together with their gangs, were saving the weak and helpless and helping the common good. I was dreaming about saving people too.

I was born in Russia to a Czech-Russian mother and a Georgian father. I spent my childhood between Russia and Georgia before my family moved to the Czech Republic. My multicultural background, knowledge of four languages, and frequent moving at a young age prepared me for a cosmopolitan life in different countries and an openness to the many-sided world. I grew up to be an independent and kind of mature kid, who was used to taking responsibility for myself and other people. I was raised by my grandparents until I was three, spending my days with a nanny. When I was five, I would stay at home by myself or go shopping and to a laundromat while my mother was at work. At eight, I flew alone by plane and was commuting alone to school, daily changing buses and subway, for an hour long trip.

By the age of twelve I made a mature decision to do the right things and not do things rightly, and take responsibility for my decisions when I made my choice against my stepfather's will. I paid a tough price for my decision, but never regretted it. I

CHAPTER 6

INGA PHOENIX KOKALEVSKÁ

Raising a New Generation of Transformational Leaders

> The strength of the chain is determined by that of the weakest link, for if they give away, the whole falls to pieces, and the weight supported by it falls to the ground. (Thomas Reid, Essays on the Intellectual Powers of Man, 1785)

Maaike Driessen Laverman

We all need to support and empower each other to shine and share our gifts with the world! We are made of energy, let's use it!

You can reach me at I4PE.com, or by email to maaikedl@gmail.com

Or if you want more tips, please check my LinkedIn page and YouTube channel.

Enjoy living your Blueprint

Wishing you many Bright & Sparkling Days

Love Maaike

decided to start challenging myself by being more visible on social media. An example of welcoming the challenge and using it to grow.

I believe that my 'adult and kids kit' fit perfectly into a sustainable lifestyle because all you need is your physical body, and the knowledge that I am sharing with you. Reducing stress, remaining focused and re-balancing your energy is always at your fingertips with the 'tips and tricks' that I have learned, as well as the ancient wisdoms that I 'borrowed' along the way.

When we live the life we are born to live, we are 'in FLOW', life is effortless, work is effortless, your mission is aligned with a higher plan, with your blueprint.

When you contribute your unique gifts in service to the world, energy is plentiful and you experience that glowing feeling of fulfilment, knowing you are on the right path and living your full potential. You attract the right people at the right time, and this is what I want for everyone! That is why I developed this kit and methodology. Helping other women find their blueprint in the modern business world is a blessing. I would be honored to help make your business also your calling.

My dream is that everyone has access to these tools to develop positive mindsets, embracing their challenges as opportunities to grow and using the tools and passing them on to their friends and family, but also to their children, grandchildren even great grandchildren, so that future generations also maintain balance and live their blueprints.

Maaike Driessen Laverman

personal level too. My kit for children is also close to my heart and offers a way of empowering the next generation so they can avoid making the same mistakes we did, and teach them they can achieve whatever they want and be whoever they want to be.

Dreaming a Mission for the Future

Success is liking yourself,
Liking what you do,
and liking how you do it
(Maya Angelou)

Parting Words

During times of crisis in our lives, when fears are high, economic stability precarious, or when staying at home/working from home and social distancing becomes a 'new norm', the future can be more uncertain than ever. It's challenging health wise, not just physically, but perhaps more importantly mentally and emotionally as well.

I am writing this during the Covid-19 pandemic in the Netherlands and I was thinking … What can I do to contribute? So, I started filming a few of Maaike's one-minute morning tips on, for example, how to boost your immune system. This pandemic is frightening, and fear lowers our immune systems hence we need to learn how to upgrade them. Sharing this made me feel I was part of the solution and I felt less helpless. I also

WOMEN IN THE *Modern* BUSINESS WORLD

My method allows you to have all the knowledge you need to reprogram yourself, and re- balance your food intake and energy levels. It helps you understand how often you need to move; it even helps with tips to improve the quality of your sleep and how to "release" pain.

Furthermore, it helps you take full advantage of which colors to wear, eat or even drink and how these colors can best support you.

Next to my work as a teacher, coach, mentor, therapist, and the work I do developing the kits, I am proud of my two new courses. Their main topics are stress, sleep, and energy management. As mentioned earlier, you can use my tools anytime, anyplace!

Transforming Lives

I believe we are all here to make a positive impact on the world from our own set of unique gifts, abilities, skills, and experience. My mission is to empower women to access and live their blueprint, and clearing out past obstacles along the way. Energy needs to flow. When stuck, emotions cause stress which can lead to burnout. My gift to the world is to teach people how to regulate their energy, so they can become a better version of themselves, every day.

As I said before, many women in the modern business world want to be 'it all': a good mom, wife, daughter, sister, friend and employee or boss. My tools can be life-changing and enable you to indeed do it all and feel satisfied and fulfilled on a

Maaike Driessen Laverman

on sleeping medication in the Netherlands. I follow my heart in all I do and I'm so happy that the tools for kids from 4-12 years old are now taught in Dutch and international schools, showing children ways to improve their focus and learning, their eating and sleeping and regulating in general their energy. You are never too young to learn and I hope to avoid a lot of the mistakes we make.

My work for children, now taught in schools, was inspired by Confucius who says:

> *f you have a plan for one year, plant rice*
> *If you have a plan for 10 years, plant a tree*
> *If you have a plan for 100 years, educate children*

It is so important to me that children also learn to live their lives according to their blueprints, thereby increasing their self-esteem and living their colorful lives with joy, purpose, and fun! They invariably become the best versions of themselves.

The MAAILA Method

After many discussions with teachers, students, coaches, and clients, I decided to integrate my experience and knowledge into a sustainable practice which became the MAAILA Method. This method helps you become and live the best version of yourself. With learning how to operate in alignment with your individual needs and making the correct choices.

unveil recurring themes. This is so empowering. The great news is that once we no longer take those unhelpful paths, no matter the previous hardships, we can start anew with the mindset needed to live life according to our blueprint. Time to live YOUR life, and not the one imprinted on you by others!

The result? After reprogramming, people will ask what you have done because your energy will be different, and more in a flow. You will be able to live your life according to your blueprint and, therefore, be better able to serve the world in your own unique way. You will enjoy a feeling of focus, of being true to yourself and giving back to the world.

Energy Survival Kits

As mentioned previously, helping parents with severely ill children is an empowering way for me to make sense of all the pain and anguish, and I have designed a kit edition specially tailored to parents of severely ill children. Knowing firsthand their pain, struggles and challenges, I feel privileged to be able to support and empower them so they can be there for the sick child, but also for their other children and loved ones. This lies very close to my heart. The slogan "put on your oxygen mask first, before you help others" is so true for them. I strongly believe self-care is the only way to go through all these extremely painful times. Not to underestimate your friendships and doing things which give you energy!

All children are dear to my heart and I was shocked to find out for example how many children under the age of ten are

Maaike Driessen Laverman

nutritional, mental, and emotional sides of the person. A touch for health balance can be life changing, I'll never forget my first session over twenty-seven years ago. I have suffered from migraines from the age of thirteen, as did my aunt and grandfather and one of my children. The sessions involved modern chiropractic; osteopathy combined with TCM (Traditional Chinese Medicine). I gained a totally different point of view, which changed my reaction to migraines. I now handle them better and have learned to recognize the pre-warning signs.

If you are looking to develop yourself or be more aware of what your body or mind is telling you, this is the best thing for you! Forty-two muscles are tested, bringing you the awareness to connect the dots yourself and clear out your personal blind spots. I have developed different tools that I strengthen my clients with.

Coaching and Reprogramming

As a teacher and therapist, I have been working and teaching for many years, helping people reprogram the less resourceful patterns and old coping mechanisms of the conscious and subconscious mind. These patterns and mechanisms may have made sense at one stage but may now be holding you back. Reprogramming the subconscious mind helps people deal with all kinds of issues, including self-talk and awareness levels. As you become more aware, you will recognize your blind spots and by 'connecting the dots' you

You are the colors you choose

There is no doubt about it, and it holds true at every level, be it:
- Physically - food & drinks
- Mentally - what is my advantage/marketing
- Emotionally - how I react to colors

Spiritually - gaining awareness of which colors to wear in any given situation and why Helping clients make healthy and colorful choices gets me out of bed in the morning!

After the color therapy I started studying "Touch for Health", because it could make me even more independent, and I was longing for that. From now on, a part of my health would be in my hands!

The Magical Side of Touch for Health & Kinesiology

Here I learned just to wonder, literally without any judgments. It was one of the greatest gifts I ever received in my life. I started to practice it, and it became one of the major changes in my life. To live with this awareness.

Touch for Health, part one of kinesiology, is a simple and truly holistic system of health care. It combines western and Traditional Chinese Medicine and provides the tools to become happy, healthy, and whole, by looking at the structural,

Maaike Driessen Laverman

eat and drink, those in our environment, or the colors we wear. Do you know, for example, what colors to eat during times of stress and how they support your immune system?

One of the most important things I try to share with mothers is, let your child decide which colors he or she wishes to wear because their choice of color supports their whole system, as well as their self-esteem. Similarly, this kind of information can be extremely helpful when you are hiring people for a job, i.e. seeing what colors they wear, or which foods with colors they choose to eat. It can even be eye-opening for yourself when you notice what colors, food, and fabrics you turn to during stressful times. I, for example, turn to pink for self-acceptance. I'm wondering - what colors do you wear in a particular process? There are always times you're more attracted by a color than in another time, or process. Awareness on the colors you're choosing to wear is always interesting when you want to know or understand yourself better. What do the colors you refuse to wear will tell you? Especially when you have the same colors you don't like as your mom or grannie.

I deeply believe there is an ancient wisdom inside each of us which is aware of the colors we need on a subconscious level.

I knew what I wanted but had no clue where to start. I wanted to be independent and realized I needed to "go back to school" and start studying again. To gain independence and know how I could support myself, in parallel to what a doctor can do for me should I become ill. I ended up studying all kinds of different methods which could improve my self-care. I love studying, and It felt like I was feeding my inner child all the time. There was hardly anything which could have made me happier! That deep joyful feeling of happiness made me start developing myself in many different ways. By being independent, I mean you need nothing else than yourself and all your heart desires, knowing that everything is already inside of you. You only have to find it! You can have self-care at the tip of your fingertips.

I have come to understand that support is essential, actually acknowledging you need help and daring to ask for it as well. This can be from an independent perspective and it is a strength! Your life will be different. My first action after my illness was to go to a nutritionist and color therapist. Witnessing the results I got from this amazing session, I decided to study those topics myself.

Color Therapy

Every day I am grateful for having learnt this. The knowledge is amazing and influenced my life in so many ways. Healing with color is the oldest therapy in the world and was often passed on from generation to generation, on all continents. Colors tell you so much more than you can possibly imagine and strongly influence how we feel; be it the colors we

Maaike Driessen Laverman

The Importance of Being Independent and Authentic

Wisdom begins with wonder (Socrates)

I find it fascinating to observe how I communicate with myself, see myself and also how I support myself. I wanted to understand how I could become more independent on a physical, emotional, mental, and energetic level and this is where my work begins! When observing your patterns, it's always good to look at the timeframe in which you started using this coping mechanism, how old you were and what the advantage was of doing it this way. When we get older, advantages sometimes become disadvantages.

I'm wondering, are you aware of your patterns? Not only yours but also your moms, grannies and great-grannies? In what kind of way were they independent or authentic and living their blueprints? When I started comparing their patterns with mine it was really interesting to notice how they managed their challenges and how I manage mine. How their belief systems worked and how mine do. It brought me a lot more clarity on who, what, where, and why I started using these copings mechanisms and patterns. Of course, there are a lot of differences between generations but also a lot of similarities when it comes to patterns. The big idea behind it is that we are all here to live our full potential, what I call your blueprint.

your mental, emotional, and physical wellbeing. Through my tools I try to raise your awareness before you encounter serious health issues or a potential burnout, so you can use the tools to 'readjust' what life throws at you. One of my tips is to be aware of what your soul food is. What gives you energy, what makes you feel so happy that time flies when you're doing it and you have a smile on your face all day?

What happens when you smile? Your system thinks you are happy, which leads your system to release endorphins. When you smile every day, your life flows and you can handle challenges better. You are more grateful for what life offers, you can transform your negative ideas and thoughts into ones that make you feel happier. Once you are aware of this, you can change your perspective and look at things in a completely different way. I strongly believe this will make a significant difference in your life as it boosts self-care and nutritional choices, as well as create more positive thoughts and self-talk. The list is endless, and all these aspects of life are crucial. Maybe you don't even know what you are missing, but believe me, once it is there, life is so much more enjoyable, and you will have much more fun.

Maaike Driessen Laverman

Go Where Your Flow Takes You

As I began to use and combine the tools that my courses, students, friends and coaches taught me, I noticed that I was sleeping better, I was feeling better, I was coping with stress better, I had more energy, I even changed the way I was talking to myself. I learned to listen to my needs and balance them.

When you do this, your life will be in a 'flow' as you recognize challenges, opportunities, and possibilities. You listen and act on what your gut is telling you, knowing that this is your best guide. It is easy to create everything that needs to be created; it almost looks like the world is giving it to you! You will attract precisely the right people at just the right moment and be grateful for it. It feels like magic! All these things are just happening to you, sometimes even before you even know you need or want them. You will enjoy everything you are doing so much that time flies when you are working. When things are not going according to plan, you are able to examine them from a different perspective: e.g. how do these people challenge me and what can I learn from it? Transforming setbacks and obstacles into opportunities to learn and grow.

For most of us - businesswomen in particular - we are less aware of living our blueprint than the effects of NOT living it. Think of effects such as anxiety, frustration, the feeling you were meant for something else or that you are stuck in the proverbial hamster wheel. All of these have a huge impact on

For me it is crucial that I help those around me, but also teach these skills so that our children, grandchildren, and great grandchildren lead better lives as well, with less stress. Fully knowing how to balance themselves.

Birthing a Business from Pain

My business was born out of my own pain. And so was 'Your Energy Survival kit' and 'Your Easy Learning and Living Kids kit'. For me it was such a liberating and gratifying experience to make something good and powerful out of my anguish and pain. I am ready to teach this incredible self-care kit to the world and will not rest until I do.

As a businesswoman today, I see so many women struggling with the same issues I did, i.e. the constraints of society and family, the needing to be 'it all', the desire to succeed, the fear of not being 'seen or heard' and the anxiety that can lead to poor sleep and inadequate self- care. Does this ring a bell? See what you need! This helped me learn to operate in alignment with my needs and make the correct choices, which were leading me to improve my health and well-being, better relationships, and fulfillment in my professional life. Creating the life I wanted.

Maaike Driessen Laverman

Energizing You

When my daughter was in the hospital, I was studying and working as an entrepreneur, and was in definite need of getting more sleep. However, even though my body was exhausted, I was unable to sleep. I used to lie awake for hours at night because of the stress I felt never left me. It was then that I began to look into ways of naturally improving the quality of my sleep, as I did not wish to become dependent on medication. I knew that sleep was imperative to regenerate my body and detox my brain. This idea scared me... what would happen if my body failed to regenerate and detox my brain during all those sleepless nights?

Thanks to the many courses I took, I started to combine and create exercises to ENERGIZE myself and raise my life force. I realized the exercises had to be easy to do, take only a few minutes of time, and be applicable anytime, anyplace and without anybody noticing. I succeeded and saw how powerfully they worked. All I needed were my own two hands!

People around me noticed that I had a great deal of energy despite the draining situation I was in, and they asked if I could teach them how I did it. This then inspired me to create and teach the "Your Energy Survival Kit". My personal journey became my mission.

A mission to help people boost their energy, lower their stress levels, and regain crucial balance within just a few minutes, to enable life to flow more freely, to fully live our unique blueprint.

help my daughter, I needed to be strong. I went to my study and looked at all the courses I had taken, the books I had read and finally understood what they mean by saying those words during the safety speech on an airplane, "In the event of a loss of oxygen, place your own mask on first, before helping others".

What helped me was making taking care of myself a priority. The tougher the situation, the more you need to do this. I began practicing this for myself and I must admit, it made a big difference, as I gradually regained control of my life. Below are seven tips that I practice daily.

My 7 Steps to Feel Good

- Do your self-care exercises every day
- Eat and drink (smoothies) of as many different natural colors as you can
- Be aware of negative thoughts, and rephrase them in a positive way
- Follow your passion, live your blueprint, and most importantly impress yourself!
- Be aware of the ultimate significance of your life
- Believe in yourself and in your dignity
- Treat everybody with respect and value what they can teach you
- Keep your heels, head, and standards high
- Be grateful, show wonder and smile a lot

Try it, you have nothing to lose!

Maaike Driessen Laverman

The Second Wake-Up Call

My second wake-up call involved one of my children who became severely ill and had to fight for her life. She lived in a hospital for several years, as it was impossible to give her exactly what she needed at home. The very real fear of losing my child is indescribable… When she was at home, I lay awake all night, every night, terrified of missing any possible sign and desperately wanting to support her in every way I could. Sometimes we found her lying on the bathroom floor unconscious. It took us a while to get her back and I cannot tell you how much FEAR I experienced during that "endless" time, feeling so alone in the middle of the night. I prayed, firstly that she would stay with us, secondly, I prayed a lot for my beautiful daughter to be well one day, so that she too may live the life of her dreams, and feel both happy and fulfilled.

An important part of having a seriously ill child within the family, is that your life is totally controlled by the illness. On the one hand, you feel desperate and helpless in the face of her pain, and on the other, you feel terribly guilty for having so little time for the other children still living at home. They are also entitled to a "normal" life, with as much support, love, and attention as they need, which means that it is often difficult to take proper care of yourself.

As a mother, our maternal instinct to protect is very strong and, for me, that meant endless phone calls and talks with doctors, specialized therapists, and the school. I realized that in order to achieve it. It became clear to me that I had to look inside myself and stop being fearful of what others would think about me or my life. I realized that what someone else thinks about you says more about them than it does about you! This was such a relief that I decided to live to my full potential, regardless of what others thought about me.

Do you recognize this? Are you aware of running patterns that no longer serve you or do you feel you have much more to give? Life is energy and when we ignore or run away from our issues, we are holding our energy back and it often turns against us. How wonderful would it be to live our life's blueprint by allowing our energy to flow effortlessly, in line with our unique set of skills, abilities, and our life mission? Overcoming your toughest challenges and seeing them as worthwhile life lessons, contributes to your experiencing the miracle of living life according to your own blueprint.

In 2009, I began a course, and it was the best decision I ever made because what I learned produced significant changes in my life. My self-esteem grew tremendously, I felt more confident, and happy - as well as more in charge of my own life! I became a color therapist, Health and Wellness Coach, Mentor and Teacher, and a Touch for Health Instructor, which means teaching how to activate the self-healing system of the body. And, most importantly, I became a better mother. This also inspired me to develop the Kids´ kit, which you will read about further on.

Maaike Driessen Laverman

The First Wake-Up Call

My first wake-up call came in 2008. Two of my vital organs were severely compromised and I found myself fighting for my life to become healthy again. The idea of maybe not surviving or being able to raise my three beautiful children, filled me with an incredible sense of sadness, powerlessness, and anger. I felt like screaming. The thought that somebody else would take care of MY kids made me cry for days. I cannot even begin to express how it felt. There are so many things you want to teach them as a mother, in order to prepare them for the big world. It is perhaps, as mothers, our biggest fear is to not be able to be there to love, protect, support, and hug our children. Unable to celebrate their victories like graduation, or milestones like weddings or the birth of grandchildren. Who will be there to celebrate all these special moments with them? Thinking about all of this led me to fight as hard as I could.

Looking at the enormous effort and hard work the doctors and nurses put into caring for me, I also realized that I needed to take responsibility for my own life too. I needed to take better care of myself, not only physically but emotionally, mentally, and spiritually as well. It was clear that I needed to make some changes, including creating a healthy way of managing my feelings – both good and bad – so as to not allow them to negatively impact so much of my life.

I thought of this a lot while I was in the hospital and started making a 'pros and cons' list of what I wanted and how to they make as being who we are, and we start developing coping mechanisms at a conscious, or subconscious, level.

Let me start my story…

Allow me to share a few of the coping mechanisms that I picked up during my upbringing, to bring even more light to these phenomena. My parents divorced when I was only four years old, which was quite rare back then in the Netherlands. At times I would not be invited to some of my friends' homes, as I was the child of divorcees. I felt left out and sad, for there was nothing I could do about it, and it did not change who I was. You can imagine my joy when I finally did feel welcome somewhere! I think this was when I began to develop a strong sense of gratefulness. Both my father and mother were in new relationships and busy with their own lives, and my siblings and I had to try and fit in somehow. As a result, I became a 'people pleaser', from a young age and for a long time.

My mother was always working, so other people took care of us children instead. They did a great job, but I missed my mother when I got home from school. To fill the emptiness I felt inside, I often brought many friends home. I realized that I wanted something different for my own children and instead I devoted myself completely to my family. It took my 2008 health scare for me to realize that my 'pleasing mechanisms' had taken over to such an extent that I was barely aware of my own existence, and very far from living my blueprint and unleashing my full potential.

Maaike Driessen Laverman

The Most Authentic You

For most people, a BLUEPRINT is the A to B plan to achieve their goal. For me it's different. I see a blueprint as YOU, you at your most authentic. The unique YOU, with all your talents and gifts, added to your personality and your life's mission, your contribution to making the world a better place. This blueprint means leading the life you were meant to live. When everything is aligned and 'in flow', there is less room for frustration, stress or burnout and more room for a life of fulfilment and success.

Why is this particularly important for businesswomen? Because of the added stress, time constraints, ambitions and fears we tend to carry with us. We often feel we need to be 'it all'; successful in business, fit, well groomed, sociable, as well as often having to care for spouses, partners and/or children.

Overcoming Obstacles and Challenges

The journey to live your blueprint isn't always a straight line, perfect, or even in the "right" direction. Our paths to awakening are filled with missteps, lessons to learn and suffering. According to Vickey Wall, founder of the widely admired Aura Soma Color Therapy, our limiting beliefs often start accumulating when we are young and do not yet have a well-formed opinion of our own. Nor a knowledge of the world and therefore, we take on the judgments and comments of those we trust, such as parents and teachers. We accept the judgments

CHAPTER 5

MAAIKE DRIESSEN LAVERMAN

Changing the Perception of a Blueprint

"When We Overcome our Biggest Challenges, We Experience the Miracle of Living According to Our Blueprint"

My life story is a journey that consists of many experiences, challenges, courses, and research, and it has led me to dedicate my life to helping others live according to their blueprint. I discovered the consequences of not living my blueprint the hard way. Many years ago, I became very ill and was almost staring death in the face.

WOMEN IN THE *Modern* BUSINESS WORLD

Be different than everyone else and keep moving forward. Being different is good as it means you are unique and special, and you really are. Even though I have been preparing myself for years with knowledge and new skills, I know that my time to shine has come. I have been on the sidelines of the game, but with everything that is happening, the time has come to get in the game and move forward to the path of a legendary life. Every day that you wake up is a new day filled with new blessings, new opportunities and new possibilities, a kind of rebirth. Every day start with different thoughts, and create a new atmosphere in your mind to bring about what you truly desire and appreciate. Start designing your life, your business, your lifestyle from the inside out. Give wings to your dreams and create the life you deserve. I don't know what the future may hold but the truth is that our lives will never be the same as a new digital era has just begun. Every day make conscious efforts to take some action, and do something positive and productive towards your goals and dreams. Shift your consciousness, advance confidently, follow your dreams and meet "Success", because success is waiting for you.

"The time has come to accept and embrace exactly who you are and exactly where you are today. Truly love yourself and realize deeply that you have great worth. Then decide and commit to heal past wounds, to do your best and to improve yourself for yourself at your own pace every day from now on." (Doe Zantamata).

You can find me at motivated-women.com

Lisseth Barrios

My Pursuit to Happiness and Fulfillment

At this moment, I have many projects on the go, but for now I need to focus on one project at a time. As entrepreneurs, we have many things on our plate at the same time and we want to conquer the world, but as the saying goes: 'You cannot eat an elephant in one bite ', so I am employing small changes on a continual basis in order to add up to big impact. It's about focusing on the small details in order to make my workflow more efficient.

To be a successful entrepreneur, you need to learn new skills, adapt to any changes and think like a winner. When you adapt easily to change, your brain becomes used to it and it is ready for progress on any challenge. The important thing to remember here is to avoid the comfort zone, as that is a dangerous place to be if you want to pursue happiness and fulfillment. If sometimes you feel uncomfortable, that is a very good thing as it means your mind is ready for some challenges. All you need to do is crave growth, happiness and fulfillment. You can only achieve what you put your mind to, but it has to start with motivation and action to do it. Every day try the things that worry or frightens you the most. Train yourself to get out of your comfort zone on a daily or weekly basis. Keep persevering at them until you get better at what you do, and you won't be afraid any longer.

Those people lost their motivation. Without it, they have no fuel to continue their journey, so they stop in the middle of the road. They end up waiting on the sidelines, watching life go by. They get stuck in their comfort zones and they think they have no other choice but to live out the rest of their lives in misery.

The one-million-dollar question is: How to get out of your comfort zone? Fear is real and it is the success enemy number one. Fear stops you from achieving anything in life, fear makes people sick, fear keeps you far from your dreams, fear shortens your life, fear closes your mouth when you want to speak. Fear is what makes people accomplish so little and enjoy little in life. The antidote to fear is confidence. It's time to gain back your confidence and move on with your life to the next level you have been wanting to. We are all important in life and we all have different goals and dreams. In order to achieve your goals and dreams, you first need to understand and find your true life's purpose. The time has come to discover the real You, to embrace your greatness and calling, and to make your life a masterpiece. You deserve the happiness you have been searching for, the fulfillment and freedom that will make your dreams come true.

LISSETH BARRIOS

Why do you want to be happy? Who are you doing all these things for? For yourself or for someone dear to your heart? Use these as a motivation to stay on track. Try to surround yourself with positive people and stay away from negative people, who will tell you that you're never going to amount to anything else, or who will simply suck your energy like 'energy vampires'. If you get trapped within a circle of negativity, you will find it extremely difficult to succeed in anything.

Learn to establish boundaries and listen to your heart and gut feeling, but under no circumstance give up on your dreams. Fight for your dreams! Establish milestones and celebrate even the smallest wins. These are going to help sustain you and encourage you to continue doing your best. Don't be afraid of failing, either. Treat failures as your friends and learn from your mistakes. It's going to show you the path you need to take to be happy and successful in life. In today's society, we learn to treat failures as something negative, but if you think about it, they are also part of our success. When we fail at something, we learn the lesson and get back up again.

Why is motivation the key to happiness and success? It's so easy to say we want to be happy and successful but getting there takes so much more than just saying it out loud. You need to take action, too. Taking action is where most people fail. They start off brimming with enthusiasm. They will plan out how they are going to become successful and happy, but along the way, they will realize it's too much work, so they stop and forget all about their dreams, and they end up unsuccessful and unhappy.

Why do some women strive for more and others don't? There is no exact reason for why one person wants to endure the hardships of moving forward, and some others quit at the first obstacle they encounter. Everyone will work differently from different perspectives and tactics to get to the top and it won't be the same for everyone. Yet by being kind, lending a helping hand or being a supportive friend or coach, you will earn another friend, a client, a customer or a person who will follow you on social media. As women, we are worth much more than we think. We all deserve a better life and if you look closely enough there are signs everywhere that will help you uncover the next steps to take towards your personal fulfillment. Don't waste another moment being miserable, go for what you want and fight for your dreams, as they were given to you for a reason. If necessary, ask for help but don't give up, start living a better life today!

Motivation to Keep Moving Forward

We all need motivation to do anything we want to achieve, whether it's going to the gym, doing certain tasks, waking up on the right foot or just starting a new project. The only question now is how to get your motivation back. Motivation can be classified into: Intrinsic, and extrinsic motivation. Intrinsic motivation is that fire burning within you, while extrinsic motivation are external factors that will motivate you to get off your feet, like rewards and punishment. Never forget your "Why." Why do you want to be successful?

Lisseth Barrios

for one, but a couple of training and coaching courses with mentors that are helping me achieve my dreams, and push my limits to reach what I have been craving for. When you have an inspiration as powerful as the one embedded inside of me, there is no room for doubt.

My time has come to shine, meeting new people, have lots of fun and travel the world. Step by step, I moved along my path and for every bump in the road or every cloud I saw, there was a silver lining and rainbow waiting to be seen. Change is happening for me and I made the decision to commit to my dreams and move with confidence towards them. The key to release resistance and realize your dreams is to believe that you are powerful, that the Universe is on your side and that you can accomplish anything your heart desires when you truly believe and think big.

As a Coach, I want to inspire women to get their confidence back and take action. As a Coach, I constantly motivate myself because when I do, I propel myself further. Motivation is what propels you. There is no going back once you make a decision and motivation is what takes you closer to your dreams. What everyone wants is to see how high they can go and where they find a place they can proudly fit into. That was me, trying to fit in like a piece in a giant puzzle. I was chasing the opportunities in life, but I decided that I didn't want to do that anymore. I want opportunities to chase me instead, and not the other way around. I won many silent battles as I went through my journey and I will win many more because I am strong, dedicated and committed.

WOMEN IN THE *Modern* BUSINESS WORLD

Releasing Resistance and Making Change Happen

Our path is often unknown, unexpected and unpredictable but we learn along our journey. Each moment of our life is a gift, and we cannot respect the gift of life if we live in fear and negativity. In any situation that we are living, it's important to be positive and take any challenge as a lesson. For years, I have been preparing myself, studying and getting ready to accomplish and reach my dreams. However, something has stopped me and that is F.E.A.R. (False Evidence Appearing Real). A couple of years ago I took some training to prepare myself to be on a stage. How to be a public speaker and be in front of hundreds, maybe thousands, of people is something that I wanted to do for a long time. However, even practicing being in front of the camera to film myself in my house is scary, as I am an introverted person. Even though I am a Health, Life and Business Coach, I want to touch the lives of many people, make an impact and leave a legacy.

For such a long time, limiting beliefs, fears and negativity block the success I have been waiting for. I understand that the path to my dreams has been difficult, but it doesn't have to be that way. I am the one who is in the way of achieving my dreams. The Universe likes speed and it rewards people that take action. Well, this year, 2020 is a big year for me. Even though we went through this pandemic situation worldwide, even though I was laid off from a job that I had, and even though I am currently unemployed, I started my business and I signed up not only

LISSETH BARRIOS

to our inner voice in order to find it. To some, it's easier than for others to hear the calling of destiny, for some it's a little bit harder. Life gives us many surprises and unfolds in amazing ways. What is important is to keep in mind that success comes in different forms and shapes and that sometimes it's so different from what we expect, but it still happens in magical ways. Never give up and always be ready when opportunities knock on your door. In the movie, I learnt about the *'Law of Attraction',* and its magical and powerful ways of working. I started applying those principles into my life and even though I didn't always manifest what I truly wanted, I manifested the experiences that I needed at that time.

Modern research demonstrates that what you think, you attract, like a magnet. The reality is that most people think about what they do not want, instead of focusing on what they truly desire. Unlocking the life of your dreams begins by aligning yourself with the higher energies, having clarity about what you truly desire and finding your purpose in life. With you knowing this, you transform, empower and move forward with confidence to live the life you have always dreamed of. If there is something I learnt over the years and through the experiences I had, is to have a warrior's mentality. Let your mind transcend limitations and your consciousness expand in every direction because you will find a great and wonderful world at the end of the rainbow.

WOMEN IN THE *Modern* BUSINESS WORLD

Today, I can say that it's important to have the courage to heal and to surrender. When things don't work out your way and obstacles show up, let it go. We all have those moments when we want to give up, but that's when you need to stay focused on the big picture, believe in yourself and pray to God - or a Higher Source, whatever way you may call it.

For years I have been reading books on self-development and how to empower myself. I have learnt that our mind is everything. What you think shapes your life because your thoughts shape your behavior, which indirectly controls the way your life unfolds. There is magic in thinking big. The more you stay positive and think big, the more you will vibrate at a higher energy level. You will be amazed at what you attract after you start believing in what you deserve. Your thoughts change your life in unexpected ways, and they have the fuel that transform your life by using daily affirmations. Well, that's exactly what helped me move forward when I was in negative and challenging situations. As women, we can be a little emotional sometimes, but that's when you need to be stronger and determined for the next move. We all go through those challenges in life, it's up to us to rewire our brain, as our thoughts empower our words, which shape our reality.

A friend recommended that I watch the movie 'The Secret', which I did, and I even bought the CD and watched it again and again until the message sank in. That movie is the masterpiece that also changed my life. I realized that as humans we all have dreams, goals and therefore we work to accomplish them. We all wonder, 'What is our purpose in life?' and we try to listen

Lisseth Barrios

own a hotel. Before getting my hotel, however, I am ready to get in the real estate game again but this time with experience, knowledge, contacts and confidence of doing the real deal to my advantage.

Transcending Limitations

After the passing of my mother and the stress that I went through of being a landlord, I detached myself a bit from everything and everyone for a while. I shut down to meditate and refocus. Eckhart Tolle's books: *'The Power of Now'* and *'A New Earth'* changed my life. I was able to let go of emotional attachments to the situations and move on with my life. After I thought everything was settling in and getting ready to heal, another situation showed up. In September 2018, my house was hit by a tornado. Material damages in my house, no roof for months, uprooted trees and some cut in half, BBQs blown away with the wind and many other damages from the natural disaster that totally took us by surprise. I could even see the stars from my bedroom.

During the winter months at minus 25 degrees Celsius, it was cold and hard to take, but we moved along. We had to take quick showers as it was freezing in the house. The positive side to this is that:

1. We were safe and sound, so no injuries.
2. I didn't take it too personally, as I decided to go with the flow.

The first week I cried a lot but then, I became stronger.

My Real Estate Adventure

In 2007, when I became a landlord, I learned a lot about being in the business, dealing with tenants, doing renovations, hiring and firing people and much more. Besides collecting rents, I was maintaining the property, doing some renovations and inspections in the units in order for the property to be in compliance with the city building and security codes. Most of the renovations were done on the weekends and after all the time I spent doing the work, I had to have my construction boots as well as my toolbox. In order to save some money, my husband and I worked on different projects such as painting, fixing units, basement renovations, grass cutting and much more. It happened that I evicted some bad tenants and I even went to Court in order to have the eviction notices from the Court house. Occasionally, I had to call the police in order to go in the units, as tenants were not cooperating. When I think about it, my real estate adventure was very challenging. At first, I had a property manager, inspector and other maintenance people and I even tried to hire my power team, but for some reason I had to learn the hard way, because dealing with them was challenging too.

Today, I accept everything that happened as business experience because it made me stronger. As the saying goes: 'What doesn't kill you makes you stronger'. I made all the mistakes that a new landlord can make and even if it costs me money, energy and time, I can say that I am ready to do it again. In fact, I think that everything happened for a reason because one of my big dreams to accomplish in a very near future is to

Lisseth Barrios

'Angels On A Mission' reached over 250,000 fans. Yes 250,000! I couldn't believe it, and for the first time I knew what it really meant to go viral. It was less than a second that I pressed the 'sent' button and everyone was liking and sharing my posts. Some people approached me, and they wanted to purchase my page because of the visibility that I was having, but I told them that it wasn't for sale. Short time after that, someone scammed my page and 'poof' it disappeared. Then, I noticed that people were copying me. There were over twenty-one other 'Angels On A Mission' pages and groups with my name when I stopped counting.

I reported the situation to Facebook, but of course they didn't do anything about it. I was so sad but there was nothing I could do. I was almost going to give up and not write anymore, but I put myself together again and then re-open other Facebook pages and groups. I lost some followers but the real ones found me again. I guess we all have a special and unique way of expressing ourselves that people like or don't like. To this day, I continue to write every day on different pages and groups that I created such as 'Angels On A Mission Movement', 'Angels On A Mission III', 'Angels On A Mission Group', 'Motivated-Women Group and 'Motivated-Women' page to inspire people from every corner of the planet. In total I have over 52,000 followers, reading my daily posts on Facebook and Instagram but whether I have one like or one thousand likes, I am happy to be able to touch one person's heart every day.

pretty well, in today's society, the first thing when they force you to stop working is prescribing medication. Well, even though the doctor recommended a bunch of medication that made me sleep and feel relaxed, I decided not to take any of the recommended medication. I always like to go on the natural side of things with the least pills and medication.

The magical secret that took me out of depression was going to the gym and thinking positive. I admit that it wasn't always easy, but we are more powerful than we think. At that time, I wasn't only going to the gym, I was also going to my aqua-fit classes which I loved, I was reading positive books and messages from spiritual teachers. When I was at home, I was dancing, trying to work on my mind and reading positive quotes. I tried to spend as much time as possible in nature. Mother Nature has such healing energies on us, when we take time to connect with her.

'Angels On A Mission'

Following my mother's passing, I created a page on Facebook called 'Angels On A Mission' to inspire myself to go on with my life. Why that title? Because I believe that we are all Earth angels changing and touching someone's life at the perfect time, not before and not after, but at the precise time. I was writing daily posts. Shortly after, I noticed that some friends were reading my posts. Then, they were sharing my posts and then more people were liking my page.

Lisseth Barrios

you are going, what you want to accomplish and to keep on track with your goals.

Grieving and a New Way of Life

On August 8, 2006 my mother passed away at the age of 57. She didn't even have time to retire. She went to the hospital on a Thursday and the following Tuesday she passed away. It was a shock to me and my family, but we managed to accept it as there was no other way around. As you may know, losing a loved one is always hard, and it destabilizes you in a very big way. After this life-changing moment, I tried to keep my family together and not only being a super-mom, but trying to be a loving and caring daughter to my father and continue with the family's traditions for the first year, by trying to fulfill my mother's role. However, I couldn't keep up thinking about everyone else's needs before mine, giving time and energy to others and not thinking about myself. On top of that, I didn't even take the necessary time to grieve, so this situation took me straight to depression. I wasn't crying the way I wanted to, as if I was starting, just like the domino effect, my family was going to start crying too.

While in depression, and for the first time in my life, I was forced to take care of myself and put myself in the list of priorities. As women, we tend to put ourselves at the end of the list. During that time, however, and in order to get back on track as soon as possible, I focused on myself and I meditated. I was working out and putting my energy on the things that matter most, trying to avoid stressful situations. As you know more than ever before. That's when you realize that it's a MUST to control your thoughts and to not let them control you.

During the course of life, we all face plenty of unpleasant, embarrassing and discouraging situations, and believe me, I have been through those a couple of times. However, unsuccessful and successful people react differently and in opposite ways to the situations they faced. Successful people specialize and focus on positive thoughts, and unsuccessful people stay in their 'victim' mentality and replaying their unpleasant situations over and over again in their minds. To boost your confidence, recall pleasant and positive thoughts, positive experiences, count your blessings and recall good things that happen every day. When facing critical moments in life, I always took action that gave me better options, seeking abundance and avoiding limitations.

While I was growing spiritually and mentally, I felt more confident, more effective and more successful. I was so excited that I was on the road to success and achievements, and to this day I am still traveling on the road of success. Not only am I working as a *Life, Health and Business Coach,* but I am working and shaping myself as well. I cannot help others achieve something that I cannot achieve for myself. In fact, while searching and learning, I have found that most successful people never rely on luck, but on being prepared for opportunities. One of the main components to set up for success is to have a plan. We all need to write our plan. Just as Brian Tracy said: "A genius without a road map will get lost in any country.". As an entrepreneur, you must have a plan in order to know where

Lisseth Barrios

for a couple of years, my entrepreneurial journey started by doing network marketing and many other business ventures. I went from being a beauty consultant to a health specialist in different companies and an independent travel agent. I was so determined to succeed that I was always following the rainbow of opportunities. However, I learnt that not everything that shines is gold. It always cost me money to join those companies and time spent learning the components of the company I was representing. I always had the illusion that I was going to be the next millionaire… but I gave up on network marketing after all the try outs. I had to work hard to move up the multi-level ladder. I achieved some wins, but I also experienced some failures. The good thing about being in business is that whether you win or lose, you always have to take in the lesson and keep moving forward. As one of my mentors said: 'Don't take things too personally as the important lesson is to keep going no matter the circumstance'.

In today's society and as we move to the digital era, we are more and more subject to the *'shiny object **syndrome**'.* Always promising that we will get rich quick, but unless you devote yourself 200%, it's not happening for everyone and not overnight. Well, I must admit I got the *'shiny object syndrome'*, and it's not my fault. If you notice, we are always bombarded with publicity on the internet, newspapers, television, and while we drive there are signs everywhere, at all times. Being able to focus is becoming quite challenging, as there is an infusion of media controlling our need to keep consuming and consuming. As an entrepreneur, I know we have to keep learning and updating our skills, but the focus time is limited and precious

wasn't always easy to do what I did, but my determination and desire to succeed was more powerful.

While in the learning curve, I came across Robert Kiyosaki's book series of *"Rich Dad, Poor Dad °* and other works of his. The books and some online training were a real eye opener for me, as I learned that there is a way to escape the 'rat race' and my goal was to become an entrepreneur and to own real estate. Those were the rules, the big guys were playing to become rich and to be savvy with taxes, so I got in the game as well. In 2004 I bought my first piece of real estate and then in 2007 another one. In the meantime, I also invested as a passive investor in other projects. I attended seminars, webinars, meetings, conferences and tele-conferences but I was on a continued learning curve. Of course, I was doing that while still educating my son, helping him at school and pushing him with extra-curricular activities such as swimming, football and karate classes. As most mothers would understand, we are super-moms and always multitasking even when we are exhausted mentally and physically. Sometimes, I was so exhausted that I fell asleep while reading a bedtime story to my son.

Entrepreneurial Mindset

When I got out of the University, I started working for a company but deep down, I knew that it was just temporary, in order to pay the bills and prepare for what I really wanted – financial freedom. While I kept my full-time job

Lisseth Barrios

graduated as a translator, but I knew it wasn't enough for me as I wanted more. I had a true desire to live my life the way I wanted to, no matter what. I have always been passionate about teaching and inspiring others and traveling the world at the same time. I spent a couple of years chasing the corporate dream, working my way up through high-paying jobs across a diverse range of industries. Working for someone else really taught me important lessons about what works and what doesn't from different perspectives. I knew inside me that I had entrepreneurial wings and that it was up to me to make the next big move. To my professional titles, I am adding online entrepreneur, investor and coach, but let's start from the beginning, as my journey began far away from where I am today.

Starting a New Life

In 2001, I moved to Ottawa, in Ontario, Canada with my young son. This is Canada's capital region, located two hours away from Montreal, where my family and friends reside. I left my comfort zone to begin a new venture. As a single mom, I was starting a new life. I encountered some challenges in my new city, but new doors opened up for me and great opportunities showed up as well. At that time, I joined a real estate group where I met real estate investors and made new contacts that later changed my life. I took some real estate courses, and because I was by myself in Ottawa, I was taking my son to meetings and conferences, as I didn't really have the resources to pay a daycare on the weekends or evenings. It

WOMEN IN THE
Modern
BUSINESS
WORLD

CHAPTER 4

LISSETH BARRIOS

A Woman Creating Momentum For An Exciting Life

"Too often we underestimate the power of a touch, a smile, a kind word, a listening ear, an honest compliment, or thesmallest act of caring, all of which have the potential to turn a life around."
(Leo Buscaglia)

I was born in Guatemala City, Central America but I grew up in Montreal, QC, Canada, where my parents had settled after immigrating to Canada. My parents worked hard to raise three children and even though language was an issue at the beginning, we managed to speak Spanish, French and English fluently. At the age of 23 I

When we go through limit situations of intense darkness and despair, the practice of entering into the silence within gives us the ability to call forth GRACE, to help us surrender to Someone bigger than us who loves us totally and completely. We begin to see that surrender does not mean giving up. It simply means trusting that He will take care of us. Even if we do not understand why, our hearts know that His love will carry us through. Light enters our wounds and magically, fragments of pain are gathered in time into a loving wholeness.

Take Wing and Fly

For me, there is no fulfillment greater than witnessing people entrusted to our care, find their roots, take wing and fly. Uncovering the light of their souls so they can truly shine, knowing that we have somehow fanned the flames of their desire to give back to the world, is priceless.

Through it all, gratitude so tenderly expressed is enough reward. John said it so beautifully: "For being mother and friend, for listening to our deepest hurts and wildest dreams, while keeping us safe and assuring us that all will be well, thank you."

over two thousand people. He no longer rides a motorbike. He now has his Kyani dream car. But for Russ, more than all these and the monthly seven-digit income, what fills his heart with unspeakable joy is the knowledge that he has added value to many lives. I always say that every dollar you earn in Kyani, means you have helped a life become better. The more money you make simply means you have blessed many more lives.

The Sacred Space

One of the most important life lessons I learned as a mother and corporate leader is the need to regularly take time off from the busyness of every day by going to the sacred space within and finding rest in the love of God. Wayne Muller, in his book Sabbath: Finding Rest, Renewal and Delight in our Busy Lives said, "If busyness can become a kind of violence, Sabbath time, effortless, nourishing rest can invite a healing of this violence." When we consecrate a time to listen to the still small voice within, "we remember the root of inner wisdom that makes work fruitful."

From these exquisite moments of silence and stillness, creativity and inspiration flow. Questions are answered, what we need comes to us with ease. Nourished by GRACE and pure love, we find ourselves staying true to who we are and being who we are meant to be. Somehow the silence of our hearts flows to our eyes, so we begin to see what is beautiful in other hearts. It flows to our lips, so we speak only words of kindness. It flows to our hands so we always reach out to another in love.

WOMEN IN THE *Modern* BUSINESS WORLD

Back in Davao, with pockets still empty and just a burning desire to succeed, Russ sold eggs and iced water to neighbors, so he can treat his prospects to biscuits and cheap instant coffee. He borrowed money to buy a motorcycle so he could move about. The downside of this was that he had two accidents while driving through the rain on the bumpy country roads. But GRIT kept Russ going. The vision of living the life of his dreams burned like an unquenchable flame in his mind and heart.

One stormy night, Russ took shelter in a huge sewer pipe and braced himself to endure the revolting stench from the open canal. It was not his lucky day, because ten meters away, a security guard kept firing at his direction. He probably thought Russ was a robber hiding in the sewer. Frozen in fear, the gunshots ringing in his ears, Russ wept silent tears and whispered a prayer to God to save him. After two hours, he slowly crept out of his hiding place, pushed the motorbike for some distance and drove home. It was one of the longest nights of his life. He said the thought of dying stayed in his mind the whole time. He said what gave him strength were the words of comfort and inspiration whenever we had the chance to talk about his dream of a better life through Kyani.

What Bethany Hamilton, the professional surfer who survived a shark attack, said is true: "Courage doesn't mean you never get afraid. Courage simply means you don't let the fear stop you." Russ became Blue Diamond last November 2019. GRACE flowed. Only in his thirties, he was able to grow his network of happy and loyal users of the Kyani products to

Kate Bellosillo

"While we can't bring back their lives, we can honor the lives of Kirk and his family members by continuing the legacy they left behind and that is to give generously so other lives can be blessed."

Russ

One young man took my challenge to heart. Russ grew up in a rustic barrio in Davao, a province in southern Philippines. He worked as a fast-food service crew while studying and then landed a corporate job in Manila. Blinded by the city lights, he got in deep credit card debt, was kicked out of his rented condominium and spent one week secretly sleeping in his workplace.

I first met Russ at the reception area of the Kyani Philippines office. He stood out from among the crowd of business partners and guests because he kept chugging down glass after glass of water from the dispenser. When asked why, he smiled and said it gave him the strength to walk for one and a half hours home to a tiny, rented apartment outside the city. He had no money for the bus or cab fare.

When he received his salary, Russ used the money for his monthly rent to purchase his first pack of Kyani food supplements that cost $150 at that time. He had to hide from his landlady by leaving the apartment at dawn and going home close to midnight. He was able to pay her when his next salary came. By then, he had resigned from work and decided to do the Kyani business full time.

WOMEN IN THE
Modern
BUSINESS WORLD

What I found most admirable about Kirk was not only his tenacity but his humility amidst success and his infectious desire to give back to the world. Together, with founders Carl Taylor and brother Jim, he put up Kyani Caring Hands to dedicate time and resources to poor communities in need of help and hope.

The most memorable Caring Hands day happened in 2016 when 17,000 meals were provided to poor, malnourished children in the slums of Tondo, Payatas and other depressed areas in the Philippines. Kirk, Carl and their lovely wives Rebecca and Linda spearheaded the activity that drew thousands of smiles, as the children happily feasted on steamed rice and crispy potato croquettes made from the Taylor farm's nutritious Potato Packs. When Kirk found out that a feeding station in Payatas (a former garbage dumpsite) was supposed to be closed because they had no kitchen and toilet facilities, he donated funds for their construction and supported the feeding program for an entire year.

"Kyani Caring Hands is only part of what we do, it's all of who we are," Kirk said.

Around Thanksgiving Day in 2019, Kirk and eight family members died in a plane crash. A deep sadness enveloped all of Kyani. I felt Rebecca's anguish at the loss of Kirk and her sons. They were definitely gone too soon. In these difficult times, GRACE gave me the GRIT to rally everyone in Kyani Philippines, to stay the course as one of the top ten performing markets out of sixty countries in the world. I urged them on.

Kate Bellosillo

As a young boy he and his brother Jim would help out in the gas station, which was their family business. He was there every day, right after school. In one of those seemingly ordinary days, Kirk overheard his father in a serious conversation with someone who was offering to buy out their gas station business. Kirk's father kindly refused because he said it was a legacy for his children. The man pointed out that there was no way they could compete with him because he had more than ten gas stations while the Hansens only had one. Despite the veiled threat, the older Hansen refused to give in. Hearing all of this, the young Kirk promised himself he will work very hard to help his father grow their business. This resolve stayed in his mind and heart, it woke him up every single day excited to give all not only to the business, but to life.

Fifteen years later, that same man came back and asked the older Hansen to buy out what was left of his gas stations. By then the Hansens had grown their business to a successful gas station chain that combined the attraction of convenience stores. After fifteen long years, GRACE came and brought with it victory for Kirk who has turned a huge challenge into drive, passion and perseverance, to make things better for his family. Kirk said:

"We do not win by hoping and wishing, or planning and preparing. We win by doing. The knowledge, the skills, the experience will come as you apply passionate, intentionally focused action. Begin creating your legacy today, and stay with it the rest of your life. Go, just do it."

WOMEN IN THE
Modern
BUSINESS WORLD

Kyani was founded in 2007 by "the Hansen and Taylor families who came from humble beginnings, but achieved enormous success through hard work and innovation. The Hansens turned a small petroleum company into one of the largest independent distributorships in the United States. The Taylor family transformed three acres and a horse into one of the largest potato farming and cattle operations in Idaho." When these two families discovered the incredible properties of the wild Alaskan blueberry and the wild Alaskan sockeye salmon, they knew they had the chance to create powerful nature-based products that could enhance the health of millions of people throughout the world. Kyani was born.

Kirk

We would gather at the headquarters in Idaho Falls for our annual general managers summit. In one of those conferences, I still remember with great clarity that moment when Kirk Hansen, Chairman of the Board, asked:

"What wakes you up every day excited about life?"

His question totally caught all of us off guard. The pockets of conversation died down, until a compelling silence filled the room. Kirk must have been in his early forties at that time. Known for his astute business acumen and keen mind, that day I came to see the GRIT that was so much a part of him. With a sparkle in his eyes, his voice rich with passion, Kirk began to share his story.

Kate Bellosillo

Later on, she spread her wings and joined Shopee, an online selling site, as brand incubation manager for toys and baby's stuff. But there was a restlessness in her heart, a gentle stirring in her soul that only found peace when she finally decided to heed the call of the academy. She went back to MINT where she was promoted as Director of Students Services, a position she holds to this day. At 26 years old, she finds unfathomable joy in touching young lives and helping them discover their gifts. Chrissie's passion for music continues to find expression in producing jingles and creative content for corporate clients. In college, her life purpose was to change the world with her music. Now it is to connect people, so together they can do great things. Discovering her life purpose at such as young age and living it every single day is truly GRACE.

Kyani

We bring to the workplace who we are. Our purpose, our soul print, which includes the values we hold dear, our dreams, our greatness. We cannot be who we are not. Authenticity is crucial for leadership, whether we are a parent, a student, a public servant, a civic, business or corporate leader. I saw myself being drawn by GRACE to a company that resonated with my being. Kyani is a global company with a presence in over sixty countries all over the world. When I was chosen to be country manager for the Philippines, deep within I knew it was more than just a corporate job. I was answering the call to make Filipino lives better with its leading edge nutritional supplements and a unique business opportunity that allows ordinary people to build extraordinary lives.

guitar with agility and soul. She found other music smart friends and played beautiful music with them. If in the past, learning was such a bore, it was now fun. Music changed her life.

GRIT gave me the endurance to accompany Chrissie in this journey of self-discovery. We went through tough times because it seemed like it was just the two of us against the world. When many had given up on her, I held on to the spark I had glimpsed in her soul, that bit of light that was flickering in all its beauty. With all the love in my heart, I cupped that light in my hands to shield it from the wind and nurtured that spark until it burst into a glorious flame that lit up our world. The discovery that she was music smart was truly GRACE. But it was GRIT that gave her the boldness to walk that path. She was not fazed by the people who judged her as a slow learner. She had her music that allowed her to express the voice of her soul and to connect deeply with people in unimaginable ways.

Chrissie took up Music Business Management at the Meridian International College (MINT) where she met amazing friends Rizza, Jam and Juice. Together they put up Chimichangas, a pop- rock indie band that featured their original compositions. After graduation, life with the band took a backseat when MINT hired her to be its admissions manager. Chrissie was not only music smart, she was self-smart, meaning very confident and highly motivated. She was also people smart, someone who is able to influence the opinions and actions of others. With her smarts, Chrissie slipped with ease into her new role of transforming young lives. GRACE was flowing.

Kate Bellosillo

their standards of a good student. When she was Grade 4, her homeroom teacher anxiously reported to me that Chrissie was not paying attention in class, did not do her daily assignments and failed to submit her projects. When I asked Chrissie why, her answer was simply:

"I'm bored, mom."

She barely made it through the year. But the president of the school, a kindhearted and intuitive lady said:

"Chrissie is not the problem. Find a school whose learning style fits her personality."

Grit together with Grace

My search brought me to a Multiple Intelligence School that adapted Howard Gardner's theory on the eight different types of intelligences that were called the 8 smarts:

Logical/mathematical (logic smart)
Linguistic (word smart)
Musical (music smart)
Spatial (picture smart)
Bodily kinesthetic (body smart)
Naturalist (nature smart)
Interpersonal (people smart)
Intrapersonal (self-smart)

We discovered that Chrissie was music smart, someone who is able to discern sounds, their pitch, tone, rhythm, and timbre. Chrissie found joyful expression in music that led her to play the

WOMEN IN THE *Modern* BUSINESS WORLD

"Your daughter is climbing the trees with her friend."
I detected some amount of exasperation there.
"I'm afraid they might fall and hurt themselves," she said.
I apologized profusely and assured her I will tell Chrissie to stop doing that. On my way out of the classroom I looked out to the school grounds and noticed the trees weren't really too high. I saw Chrissie and her best friend sitting on one of the branches. They were merrily dangling their feet, totally oblivious to the possibility of falling some six feet to the ground.

When Chrissie heard me calling her name, she nimbly crawled down, and ran towards me, her face flushed with excitement.
"Hi mom! You met teacher?" she asked with pure innocence.
"Yes, I did. She asked me to tell you to stop climbing the trees. She's afraid you will fall and hurt yourself."
I knelt and tenderly held her in my arms. Then I reluctantly pulled away and asked:
"Why, Chrissie? Why do you have to do that?"
She looked at me, flashed her most enchanting smile and said:
"Mom, have you seen what the world is like from up there?"

This moment was truly GRACE. I had come face to face with a heart so pure, it saw the world with eyes filled with awe and wonder. To me, Chrissie was an old soul, someone wise beyond her years. She seemed to have an innate reverence for all of creation and a deep knowingness that life is beautiful.

Most of the adults in the academe could not understand Chrissie's curiosity, boundless energy and excitement. To them she was a problem because she did not conform to

Kate Bellosillo

"Teacher is afraid you will get hurt. Can you please just stay in the classroom during recess?" "But mom," she protested, "who will feed them? They will get hungry and die!"

"Chrissie, I'm sure they have a mommy cat who will take care of them," I firmly said.

She stayed away for two days. After that, the teacher reported that Chrissie was back feeding the kittens. I brought this parenting concern to prayer, to the silence deep within, hoping to find a solution.

One day, the household was in an uproar. Chrissie's nanny was bitten by a stray cat. I shouted instructions to the driver to rush her to the emergency room of a nearby hospital to have anti- rabies shots. Quietly watching all of the ruckus around her, Chrissie pulled me aside and whispered:

"Mom, what's rabies?"

I looked at her straight in the eye and with all the bravado I could muster said: "Rabies is a kind of germ that enters your body when a cat bites you. It travels through your blood to the brain. When it gets there, you can die."

Her eyes opened wide in horror.

"Really? Oh my, remember the little kittens in my school? I think they are old enough to take care of themselves."

GRACE came and solved the kitten problem.

Two months later, I was called to another parent-teacher conference. With a sinking feeling, I gingerly asked Chrissie's homeroom teacher what the problem was.

WOMEN IN THE *Modern* BUSINESS WORLD

Chrissie

I am often asked how I am able to raise eight lovely and accomplished children. My answer would always be: "I simply love them to excellence."

Chrissie was the eighth child, the darling of the family. From the start, I knew she was different, like an old soul that was plucked from eternity and planted in our homes to bless our lives with so much joy and delight. One day, when she was in nursery school, the teacher called me for a conference. I was so excited because I thought my daughter was going to get a medal or an award. To my dismay, I found out that she was playing with the kittens at the construction site of the new building. The teacher was afraid she would get hurt. She asked me to talk to Chrissie and tell her to stop.

"Teacher said you were playing with the kittens on the construction site", I admonished her. "Yes mom," she replied confidently, "because they are newborn kittens and no one takes care of them."

Chrissie would fill her old milk bottles with fresh milk and feed the little kittens at break time. She would gently hold the nipples of the bottles close to the kittens' tiny mouths and would squeal with delight as they sucked hungrily at the warm milk.

Kate Bellosillo

twinkling brightly. For the first time in a long time, he said: "I feel good! I'm ready to go back to school."

Like magic, the experience of that deep, restful sleep began to happen every night. John was back to his usual bright and bubbly self. Once again GRACE came, like a radiant Easter morning where everything is kissed by the gentle light of the sun, bringing with it the promise of a new day, a new life.

There are moments John would reflect on his kidnapping experience and still ask God, "Why me?" To this day, he still does not know why. So, he started to change the question to "What lesson do I need to learn so I can contribute to make this world a better place?" His unending search for answers brought him to the field of education. At 34 years old, John is the head of Dual Transformation Management of IPeople Inc. under the Ayala and Yuchengco group of companies, which manages seven schools. He is involved in providing quality education to students across all classes of society and preparing them for meaningful careers after graduation. He is also head of Strategic Planning of the National Teachers College which focuses on providing affordable and quality education for aspiring teachers and education leaders. John's life purpose is to uplift the lives of people through education. He believes that by molding teachers, he can contribute to the collective effort to touch the lives of thousands more. GRACE has made it possible for him to see the shadows of the past with new eyes and from them, gather goodness, meaning and light.

surgery was being ripped open as indescribable pain coursed through me. But GRIT stayed with me.

Night after night, week after week, month after month, I held my son in my arms, assuring him that he is safe, that this too shall pass. In one of those nights when I was holding him close, he whispered:
"I'm so afraid mom. When will this fear go away?"
I tried to hold back my tears, and in a very gentle but firm voice I said:
"I don't know John. One thing is certain. There is someone greater than your fear and that is God."

Angela Lee Duckworth said GRIT is "passion and perseverance for long term goals." It means doing what needs to be done, day in and day out, every week, every month, every year. Because life is a marathon and not a sprint.

GRIT accompanied me in this journey through the dark night. It stayed with me until the God of silence was awakened, and the darkness had become a holy darkness and the night a blessed night.

Grace returns

A friend had introduced me to a magnetic bed, designed with advanced Japanese technology that was supposed to relax John and help him sleep better. True enough, he slept straight through the first night and woke up refreshed, his eyes once again. Cheryl Richardson, author of The Unmistakable Touch of Grace, said grace comes from the Latin word gratia, which means favor, or thanks. She went on to say that in Christian terms grace is "the infinite love, mercy, favor and goodwill shown by God to humankind." She said it is a kind of spiritual intelligence, a form of energy that comes from the Divine Source. This energy is available to us as we need it, like abundance on demand. I understood what she meant, that when we connect with and trust this Higher Power to lead us, the universe conspires to give us our heart's desires.

Grit

I thought when I had my sons back, everything would be all right. But John, the little one, had lost his youthful spark. His usual lively chatter was replaced with a fearful silence. He refused to sleep because of the terrible nightmares that he was being taken again. Just when I thought the dark night was over, an even deeper darkness had set in. Night after night, John would weep uncontrollably, his frail body trembling in fear. All I could do was hold him close, hoping that a mother's embrace could drive the fear away.

Then GRIT came. It sprung from somewhere deep within, called forth by GRACE. It came, with a boldness that gave me the strength to be with John in all those nights when sleep was so elusive, and the dawn seemed so far away. I had just given birth to my eighth child Chrissie by Caesarian section. Every time I held John in my arms, I felt as if the wound from that soul. I wept until there were no more tears. I ached for the dark night to end. I felt like I was being swept into an abyss of pain and despair. In my grief, there was only silence. But somehow, this silence led me back to that sacred space deep within, a place no fear or pain seemed to reach. As I entered this place in the deepest part of me, a sea of calmness bathed my soul and filled me with comfort and joy, healing and strength.

There I found solace and peace

Finally, morning came. That voice called again, reminding me of the money. He ended the call with a threat not to tell the police, or the boys will be killed. After that, every time the phone rang, a sharp pain would stab at my heart. I had to put up a strong front as I negotiated for my sons being released. It was not easy to navigate unfamiliar waters, as I asked the voice on the other end of the line to whittle down the ransom demand and show proof that my sons were still alive. It took us nine days to raise the money. As soon as we paid the ransom, the boys were released unharmed. They were home at last! That was truly grace.

Grace

GRACE came, like a glorious river of fire melting away the darkness, bringing with it power, healing and light. It made me see that dark nights were not forever. As certain as the dawn, the glory of a far greater love will come shining through. And everything would be beautiful in our lives

Kate Bellosillo

John and Paolo

I distinctly remember that early morning 26 years ago. My two sons had disappeared.

John was 8, Paolo was 13. They were on their way to school when a car crashed into them. The driver was forced to stop. Suddenly, heavily armed men jumped out of the other car, abducted the boys and took them to a safe house outside the city.

The Philippines at that time was gripped by a rash of kidnap for ransom incidents. The newspapers were filled with stories of the ordeal of the victims and their families. It was something I just read about. It never dawned on me that it could happen to my family too.

A wave of fear, horror and anguish swept over me when I answered that first phone call. The voice was cold and demanding.

"We have your sons. If you want to get them back alive, give us 10 million Philippines pesos, cash."

The nightmare began

The first night was one of the longest nights of my life. I remembered sitting in the darkness, crying my heart out to God, waiting for the blanket of fear to be lifted from my

WOMEN IN THE *Modern* BUSINESS WORLD

In those precious moments of silence and solitude, as I discovered my true self, I began to see that every person is unique, and we are in this world for a reason. My life purpose also became very clear to me. That is, to love and nurture people to greatness.

Sally

My eldest daughter Sally was a very sickly child. Barely a month old, she had surgery for hernia twice and was always in and out of the hospital for all the childhood diseases. I was a young mother then and the challenge of taking care of a sickly first born was overwhelming. Especially when she asked me: "If Jesus loves me, why am I always getting sick?" Unable to answer, I would just hold her close to my heart, hoping that my love would ease away her doubts and fears. In those difficult times, I found refuge in that sacred space, deep within where I just surrendered all to Him and trusted that all will soon be well. Over time, Sally regained her health, became a top-notch soccer player in her teenage years, graduated college with honors and is now shining as CEO of her own film company.

Little did I know that life has a way of preparing us for greater things and putting out signs to show us if we are on the right track. In my case, the lessons came with suffering so intense and grief so deep.

Kate Bellosillo

The Greater Being

Even as a young child, I knew there was a Greater Being who watched over me. A kind, grandfather type whose quiet, gentle presence made me feel safe. Others call him Buddha, Allah, the One. I call him God. Over the years, my friendship with Him grew. From the time my little heart desired to be a teacher, to the time I became a mother and had all eight children, one after another. I would spend quiet moments with Him in the silence of my heart, where no words, no thoughts were needed. All I had to do was to be silent and still, and be present to the great Presence who is pure love. Somehow, He entered my life so surreptitiously, He is closer to me than my own breath, and nearer to me than my own heart. In Him, I found infinite goodness, mercy without limits, and incomprehensible love.

Knowing everything about me that no one else has discovered, He has given me a heart that has tasted love at its kindest. It is this experience of love that wakes me up every day, excited about life and the myriad of surprises waiting for me as the day unfolds. For me, everything is a pure gift. The sunlight that warms our hearts, the leaves dancing in the wind, the joyful singing of the birds, the flowers in full bloom, the gentle breeze, the sound of my children's laughter, the tender embrace of the people we love. Everything and every moment is magical because it is touched with love. We are all expressions of that infinite love.

WOMEN IN THE *Modern* BUSINESS WORLD

CHAPTER 3

KATE BELLOSILLO

Rising with Grit and Grace

From Mother of Eight to CEO

I have always believed that there are no accidents in life. That by some divine design, the One who holds eternity in the palm of his hands, allowed our paths to cross. We are here, at this moment in time for a purpose. To allow the heart to speak to the heart. And in the baring of the soul, find comfort in the knowledge that we are not alone.

Laura Götz

business. Because I love my wonderful husband, we work every day to bring joy into the life of the other, and know that children will join our family when the time is right. Not a day goes by without taking a couple of minutes to reconnect with the other women and me and make sure that whatever action I take will be to serve my true purpose in life, inspire others to be the real versions of themselves.

Sharing my story

I love stories and as a writer myself I know the impact they have on people. With my honest share about the most painful moments in my life, I want to let women know that they are not alone when silently going through the same experiences. What I advise is to take action even faster, before the breakdown, depression, or burnout occurs. I have learnt the hard way that putting myself first was not selfish at all, but vital for others as well. Now my family can enjoy a happy me and my patients and clients profit from a well-balanced and energised professional.

It was my pleasure to share my story and I would love to hear from the women who felt touched by it. Feel free to contact me, I am always happy to meet others on their journey to self-love, self-discovery and self-healing.

Stay happy and healthy.

Website: thisisyourpotential.com

WOMEN IN THE *Modern* BUSINESS WORLD

In order to be happy every day of our lives, I believe we should be constantly connected to the 7 women that guide our actions and reactions, so we can please them all at the same time. In order to do that, we have to get to know all of them, hear what they have to say, integrate all of that into our being.

When I was in my dark place (stage 4 and 5), I felt lost, disconnected to the past version of myself (stage 1,2 and 3), because I did not honor her, that rebellious girl who used to fight for her beliefs. I muted her voice, but she kept fighting inside of me, fuelling my discontent. There was no light in my future because I never actually planned for the future. Others did get a job, get married, have kids, retire in fifty years and die. I sat down with the little rebellious girl and a vague version of my future self (stage 6 and 7) and asked them what they wanted. The girl said she wanted to be able to express herself the way she felt like it, to do whatever felt right for her and change the world for the better. The future woman agreed and in that moment, I could see her clearly, with a smile on her face. I promised I was going to honour them both from here on out. I was going to love myself and live every day according to my rules.

By awakening the seven women inside of me, I activated my full potential to experience happiness. Now, instead of pleasing everybody else, I am pleasing these seven beautiful parts of me, which I cherish and adore.

The new me could not work in the previous setting for much longer, so I decided to change jobs and focus on my own

Laura Götz

I still keep working on mine, depending on the inner work progress that I am continuously making.

The Femindipity method works with the 7 developmental stages of the woman:

- Little girl
- Pubertarian girl
- Early womanhood
- Motherhood
- Adult womanhood
- Menopausal woman
- Senior womanhood

Each stage has a number of milestones, but I extracted the most relevant for our global development:

- Gender association
- Menstruation
- Sex
- Pregnancy
- Life-purpose
- Atonement
- Legacy

need and can get help. They do not challenge the social system which has failed them over and over again. They don't question whether or not they deserve more than what the environment has provided for them. They comply with the status quo of feeling unhappy with no apparent reason, just like their mothers before them.

If I hadn't had my breakdown, I would have never questioned what was wrong with me. It felt like a time-out from the Universe, to really stop and see the world around me. Stop and think. Just take a break from it all. So, I am thankful for the hell I went through mentally and emotionally. I finally catered to my roots and now I feel more energised and alive than ever.

Awaken the dormant female potential

Our female potential is the source of unlimited happiness. Allowing ourselves to truly live like women will open the gates to a fulfilled life. This means accepting our femininity on the three levels: body, soul/heart and mind.

The *Femindipity* method uses various techniques to uncover any blockages that prevent a woman from letting herself be happy: introspective journeys, theta healing, timeline, color and inner child therapy. I even developed an exercise called Stop-n-Go, with which women can speed up the process of recognizing, accepting and thus healing a certain problem. Every session is customised to my clients' needs and at the end of the first meeting each woman gets her personalized chart.

Laura Götz

Never had I thought that all my problems are connected to my own image of femininity and what a woman was supposed to be and act. I neglected my female body. I suppressed my female emotions. Whatever I did was to take decisions based on what others have told me I needed to do, in order to fit into the mold that they have created for me. With *Femindipity*, not only did I heal old wounds, but I also allowed the real me to express herself boldly and freely.

The Happiness Tree

Remember the list I made of things that were supposed to make me happy? While working on myself, I made an analogy with a tree.

In life, we run to this *Happiness Tree* and pluck the fruit of our hard work but forget to dig deep and tend to our roots. That is why, somewhere along the way, we don't feel happy, even though we should. Some call it depression. Some, a form of midlife crisis. Whatever we call it, it is a symptom of personal unfulfillment. This happens to men too, but women have this illness engraved into their DNA, because of thousands of years of undeniable patriarchal oppression. Even today, *femininity* is seen more as an external, rather than an internal trait.

Women are taught to neglect their true selves and seek outside approval at all times. They need to look the part and care for others. Their "self" has no priority and gets lost along the way. The majority of women don't even know that they

Diana, not only shared my values but also my favorite colour: PINK. To us, it represents femininity, sorority, gracefulness, mindfulness, peace.

Femininity and Serendipity

When I began my journey to self-discovery, I asked myself WHO am I. Because it was too complicated to answer, I rephrased and asked WHAT am I. The gynecologist in me replied: you are a woman. That answer blew my mind because I realized that was the first step in accepting me for me. I had to love myself as a woman, even though this status has caused me so much pain in the past. Because I had all the theoretical knowledge and had personally treated thousands of other women, I made a list of what a woman was: physical traits, emotional traits, known stereotypes, hormonal pattern, and so on. I scientifically dissected my body, mind and soul and looked at what was missing, what was out of line, what had been neglected. It was so that I learned to literally love every piece of me, even the broken and ugly parts.

Retracing my steps, I structured my findings to develop an easy-to-understand self-healing technique. Because my burnout sent me on the amazing journey which led to this discovery, I named my method *Femindipity*. It was through serendipity that I have found the true potential of my femininity.

Laura Götz

After I have learned to love myself, I made peace with everything that hurt me. Changing perspectives helped me realize how many great lessons I have learned from my experiences and that I have acquired unique tools to support my mission.

My patients taught me that there is a great need for psychosomatic care in medicine. That they need more than a clinical, pill-prescribing doctor. I felt it on my own skin, how a holistic treatment does wonders on not only the human body, but also mind and soul. The research that I carried out for myself helped me crystallize my own conclusions about self-love and the power behind that. On the premise of **If I understand it, I can also teach** it I developed my own therapy programme, designed for women.

I strongly believe that once you discover who you really are and what drives you forward, you can tailor the Universe around YOUR needs with incredible ease! After finishing the programme, I want women to awe at the incredible person waiting for them at the end of their journey! I know how emotional I was as I saw the real me, as I hugged myself for the very first time and told myself how wonderful and strong I was!

This is your potential was born after a mentoring session with Mirela. She asked me "Why just a book? Make a whole life around your dream!" That is how I started coaching, got my NLP certificate and found a partner to join forces with, in order to create an extraordinary experience for women. My partner, completely different from the creative arts. I kept writing and even published my fantasy books with dragons. During my dark moments, this was actually my only light of hope. Looking back, my characters have said out loud what I was afraid to admit: *I have been living the life others had designed for me. When will I be free?*

Accepting me for me is accepting that writing is a big part of who I am and that it makes me happy. It might not be as lucrative as medicine, but money doesn't buy happiness, a saying that I have just recently admitted to myself to be true. What I truly want with writing is to send my message out there, to help people with my words, to make a difference. Before my transformation, I did not see myself as a non-fiction author. Now, I have dozens of titles on my mind and many big plans! The first on my list is my own self-healing book, where I detail all the steps I took to get out of the dark place in my mind.

My wonderful life blueprint is pink

Mirela asked me: What is your mission and your vision? I could not give an answer right away, but now I know it.

I want to help women unearth negative beliefs and counter productive behaviours that keep them from reaching their full potential, because I want to live in a world where women can act unapologetically like their true selves!

thinking about quitting, she advised me to take it slow, think about it and try to work on it. I did not care for that advice that night, but she ended up saving my marriage.

I made a list of strengths and skills. I wrote down what I wanted in life and what I did not. I developed my own strategies on dismantling limiting beliefs. I changed perspectives. I adopted positive attitudes and habits.

One day, my husband and I were getting ready for bed when he told me: "I love you so much and I am so happy to have you in my life!". I then realised we hadn't fought in a while. Actually, our life had been quite harmonious. In a couple of weeks, while I focused on discovering myself and allowing myself to be happy, the tension between us vanished on its own. I was glowing from the inside and this positive energy influenced both my life at home and at my job, where I felt like I and the work that I did had meaning again.

In a couple of months, my life had changed completely, and my future looked brighter than ever. I had an amazing man by my side and have managed to see for myself the beauty that he had long seen inside of me.

A dream of books and dragons

My childhood dream was to become a writer. But since the career is not always lucrative, my parents encouraged me to follow medicine, a field I also loved, but

We all talk about self-love with such ease but never really imagine how hard it is to actually reach the state where we can actually do that. I was determined to figure out what self-love was all about because I promised myself to never allow myself to fall into that very dark place again. For the very first time in my life, I put myself first. In fact, I was the only one in the equation. The only factor to determine. I was going to make my life all about me, as much as I could afford it. I soon circled back to the same question as before: Who am I?

Taking action leads to miracles

A feeling of excitement took over me when I started the journey to discover myself, the person I was supposed to love unconditionally. I started taking action. Bought books, watched seminars, and dared to think about a glorious future. One thing I knew for sure: I was going to do what I wanted, how and when I wanted it. The era of the true-to-herself Laura had begun.

When I found out that Mirela Sula, the founder of Global Woman, was coming to talk in Frankfurt, I bought my first ever ticket to a breakfast meeting and drove all the way from Cologne. The experience was eye-opening. So many women there who faced similar challenges, who had been through pain, like I did, but continued to fight for their dreams. That evening I had a private chat with Mirela. She saw right through me, told me my strengths and motivated me to take more action. When I mentioned I also have problems in my marriage, and was

Laura Götz

The hard talks with myself

Why am I not happy?

*W*ho is *"I"*? Such a strange question to ask anybody. Such a difficult question to answer. I struggled with this for months, feeling lost and more disconnected with myself than ever before. I felt ashamed of what I was going through and could not speak about it with others.

Romanians don't have burnouts. They work till they drop! Romanians don't have depression. They are just sad!

I did this to myself. I am an awful person! My thoughts turned me into a negative person. My future seemed gloomy. My work felt like torture most of the time and I wanted to quit. My relationship with my husband had gotten so awful, I was threatening him every day with a divorce. Fleeing my problems always felt like the easiest way to go. What I had did not make me happy so I should look for a new life, reinvent myself, reinvent a new and happy me! That will make me happy!

Of course, I had tried to seek help. After a couple of months, I reached out for a psychotherapist, but the waiting list was too long. So, I googled phrases to heal myself. *What does one need to be happy?* The answer is written everywhere: "The secret to being happy is loving yourself. You are all you need."

five minutes. I did what doctors are supposed to do: prioritise patients and duties. With every minute that passed, I could feel IT coming. Nobody cared that I was running out of breath, everybody else's problem was more important. No bathroom breaks, no food, no water, I was on autopilot. I could not feel myself; my soul was not part of whatever was happening with my body. After managing the urgent matters, after ten hours of an uninterrupted marathon, one of my bosses drags me aside and yells at me because I have failed to do what she felt was important. Nothing else mattered to her, not my effort, not the other patients and problems I have taken care of. I did not matter.

Who did not matter? The Doctor? The German Laura? The I-have-to-prove-myself Laura?

They tell you how it feels like. You hear it being so metaphorically described by patients in the mental clinics. It is tearing me up inside! Take a piece of paper and slowly rip it in half. That is close to what a breakdown feels like. My mind turned blank and there was only anger. Anger at those who have wronged me. Anger at me for not speaking up more for myself, for letting others dictate what I should do and how I should do it! What is the point anyway? I was never going to be good enough!

Laura Götz

A year into my marriage, my husband and I started having fights. Now I trace it all back to his burn-out and depression, but then we were both clueless to what was mentally happening tous. Since he also fantasised about having the perfect family, we agreed to start trying. The sex helped our marriage for another year. But every month my period came, we both felt disappointed. I blamed myself. When the results of the fertility clinic showed the problem was with him, both our worlds fell apart. He needed acute therapy. Left alone while he was in the clinic, I saw him as the sole cause of my unhappiness. To me, one thing became clear in my mind: my marriage was over.

The moment my life turned grey

Every day I felt like I was running, never finding the time to take a break and breathe, and I was getting more tired by the day.

Who am I, if not the girl who was programmed to give her best to prove herself to everybody else? A burn-out was thus a foreseeable event in my lifetime. I knew I was at risk, as doctors working long hours are. I even recognized symptoms of anxiety and depression in me. But I will still be fine, the drive was there. A couple of weeks before THE THING, I felt it instinctively: my car was running low on gas. The blinkers were on and everything, but I ignored them, because what is the worst that could happen?

One day, we had so many patients, I was overwhelmed. My superiors hanged me out to dry. My phone rang every

However, being a great doctor was not enough for my colleagues and bosses. They did not approve of loud opinionated Laura, not even in Germany. It was bad enough that I was a woman, I was always a foreigner. Trying to please everyone around me, I remember scolding myself in the mirror for being a bad person. I tried my best to stay in the lines others defined for me. Then came a time when my life seemed perfect in the eyes of society: I was a doctor, a German-approved version of Laura and a good wife to my husband.

I had checked everything on my list. People told me that my life seemed perfect. So why was I not happy? I thought the problem was my list. It was too short. So, I added more items on it, thinking that was going to make me happy.

The crack in my perfect life

I started a medical blog in Romanian. In three years, I had helped hundreds of thousands of women through my content, and I answered over ten thousand questions free of charge. The experience made me into a better doctor and the **likes** and **hearts** on Facebook felt like tiny sparks of happiness. But it was not enough. I needed something else.

Every day I witnessed how a baby enriched the life of families at work. My Facebook timeline was filled with my friend's maternity photos. So, I began to think that a baby's smile was the magical ingredient to my happiness problem. Just like the fairytale goes.

Laura Götz

The world is not black and white

Do good in school, become a doctor, move to a better country, get married: this is what I thought I needed to be happy. This is how I structured my life, as an easy to-do list. Add all the points and the end result is HAPPINESS.

That is how I also saw medicine, as something highly structured. The patient presents with pain, if it is appendicitis we operate, if it is a headache, a painkiller will suffice. Quickly after I had started working as a resident doctor in Obstetrics-Gynecology, my dream specialty, I came to the realisation that I was playing the role of a psychotherapist more often than not. Most women came to the hospital not because of organic ailments, but because of psychosomatic disorders: anxiety, depression, fears about pregnancy and birth, postnatal maladaptation. That was why, when the opportunity arose, I picked up a course on Psychosomatic Medicine so I can become a better physician.

Almost every patient that I ever treated received from me various doses of psychosomatic or psychotherapeutic care, be it in the ER, delivery room or ICU. Patients thanked me and told me that I was very good at my job. This motivation drove me to work more, give more of my time and soul to my job. At one point I was pushing 80-hours weeks. I was happy serving people but when I was working, I was the Doctor, not Laura.

Listen to mother

My mother was the first in her family to go to University. She got in as first on the list and graduated as the top of her class. She fell in love, got married, had kids and kept working to support my father and raise her daughters. The perfect Romanian wife. Because she was rarely at home, working up to twelve hours a day, I raised myself with books and took care of the household and my sister. Seeing her come home, tired but with food and gifts, was the highlight of my day. I wanted to make her proud and make her see that I am doing as much as she does for our family. These days, she cries when she remembers not being there for us as much as we would have needed her. But I believe she did the best she could and managed to raise not one, but two doctors. In my time of need, she was there. Supported me through all my projects. She was and is my rock, my number one fan and my best advisor.

Now that I am grown up, I don't need my mother to tell me how to live my life. However, the two lessons she taught me when I was a little girl, guide me to this day.

1. Be independent! Learn and work as much as you can, so you can stay on your own two feet. If a man you live with hits you, you should always be able to pack your bags and leave!

2. Find a man with whom you can work with. Money comes and goes! There will be good times and there will be bad times, but with a partner with whom you can grow, you can build a home, a family, a future.

my true story, the "whys, the whens, the whats and the hows", to my incredible journey of self-healing, creating a wonderful life by my rules and setting up a business in alignment with my true self.

No country for loud girls

I was born in Romania right after the communist regime fell. Growing up as a girl in a conservative country which was just discovering freedom of speech, feminism and all the gifts a lot of people take for granted was not easy. In this culture, obtaining respect as a woman is difficult, since your clothes value more to public opinion than your words. The double standard mentality led to me being discriminated against during my upbringing years. I was bullied because I was "the nerdy girl". I have been shown my place, because I was rebellious and spoke up against matters, I thought to be wrong. I have been criticised for talking too much and too loudly. Girls were supposed to play nice and stay quiet, while boys faced almost no punishment. No matter how much I tried to prove, in my own way, that I was in fact, a good girl, the Romanian society never truly accepted me. Looking back, I have learned to control my frustration and anger towards the adults who consistently attempted to break my wings.

In my heart, I always felt that I did not belong in Romania, so moving abroad was the natural thing for me to do after graduating from University. I had fallen in love with a German during my one year of studying abroad, therefore Cologne became my new home.

WOMEN IN THE
Modern
BUSINESS
WORLD

CHAPTER

2

LAURA GÖTZ

Choose to be the hero in your life story!

"You are never too old to set a new goal or to dream a new dream".
(C.S.Lewis)

My life was never a fairytale, even if it felt like one for the better part of it. Playing the role of the warm-hearted princess who pleased everybody, finding Prince Charming, planning to buy a house with the white picket fence and raise a fabulous family - this was the fairytale that dragged me into depression and caused my burnout. Let me share you

Carla Sridevi Cohen

What have I done since that climb? I launched the Women's Health Revolution to help 100,000 women heal over the next two years. Thus far, I have helped over 5,000 people get healthy.

I am coaching and growing a community of powerful women to reach their fullest potential. Individuals and corporations hire me to lead workshops for emotional intelligence, brain profiles, stress reduction, meditation, conscious communication, breathwork, healing and essential oils. In addition to my hands-on healing practice and online courses, I have built a successful essential oils business; wrote and contributed to three books and have accumulated 20+ certifications in a variety of healing modalities, including, Unlocking Emotional Intelligence and Brain Profiling. In 2020, I was honored with the Exceptional Global Woman Award.

"Life is a series of natural and spontaneous changes. Don't resist them - that only creates sorrow. Let reality be reality. Let things flow naturally forward in whatever way they like."
(Lao Tzu)

Has my story resonated with you? Connect with me
at: Carla@womenshealthrevolution.com
Website: womenshealthrevolution.com

continue to become a better human being. More compassionate, and wiser. For nearly thirty years, a big part of my path has been service for a global humanitarian organization called Embracing the World. For many years, I couldn't help myself from putting the organization first. I've had to train myself to shift my focus to my business.

Being mindful and intentional in my business has created a positive explosion of growth. With each passing month, and year, I am more and more happy. I continue to improve and grow my businesses. I am now coaching, training, and healing online, and am happy to say I find it very rewarding in addition to my hands-on healing practice.

My path totally changed direction when I left Hollywood. Although I accidentally became a healer, I had to intentionally learn how to be a successful businesswoman. The best growth happens with the best coaches. The mountain was one of my best coaches, even though it coached me in silence. A not so silent coach, a rare jewel and catalyst I've been fortunate to work with, is Mirela Sula, the founder of Global Woman. What makes her special is how she pours so much heart into every woman she mentors.

Everyone needs multiple streams of income and the world is filled with opportunities. It is more important now than ever, that women create a strong economic foundation for themselves, so they are not in fear of poverty in their old age. The world is changing, the economy is changing. During the pandemic of 2020, many people lost jobs in the blink of an eye.

Carla Sridevi Cohen

You probably remember my mom being against my trip. Well, it wasn't the first time we butted heads on my exotic adventures. To her credit though, after I returned, she said, "I don't know what happened to you over there, but you changed. I can't put words to it, but it was clearly good for you". I never shared with her how sick I got in India.

The journey up the mountain was really about overcoming my negative mental conditioning and moving past my perception of physical and emotional limitations I was holding onto. In a circumstance like this, there is no one to blame, there is no one to rescue you, there is no retreat, there is only going forward and ultimately, once you've put in the effort, surrendering to the outcome.

There are many parallels in my story with anyone building a business or embarking on a spiritual journey. We cannot let the obstacles define us or defeat us. Similarly, as an entrepreneur, I have faced many obstacles on my journey. I can say without a doubt that no matter how much any of them looked like they came from the outside; they all ultimately came down to some obstacle in my mind.

With each small victory, we shave away at the doubt, the fear, the limitations and ultimately, we can choose to land on our feet or stop before the last 2,000 yards. We always have choice… and choice is a choice. The lessons from the trip and the mountain continue to gift me on my path forward as an entrepreneur. As I remove obstacles from my mind, my business grows, and I the divine. There was no mistake. It was worth every cut, every scrape, and every setback.

The lessons I experienced from climbing Mt. Kailash are still with me. I had never been pushed to my limits until that climb. I experienced many physical obstacles, but the real takeaway was what I learned about my mind. Going from "I can't do this" to "this isn't so bad" to "what have I gotten myself into" to "I can't do this" to "I am gonna do this" to "I have to do this" to " I did it".

India took me apart and re-constructed me. The trip was a constant reminder about will over circumstance. Working with the rocks in the river was a transformative experience. The trip taught me new and different ways to get my needs met. It forced me to trust my gut more. It showed me how I could overcome seemingly insurmountable obstacles. It also gave me multiple tangible experiences of the ecstasy of the divine.

When I came back to the US, I was very silent inside and although everyone wanted to hear about my trip, I did not feel like talking. After a month or so at home, I saw our home differently. It reminded me too much of the cave I spent time in at the Ashram. I sanded and meticulously filled every crack in every wall. I painted on happier paint, redid the floors, and replaced the floorboards. All the crazy sanding and patching I did was a physical manifestation of me putting myself back together again. The process gave me time to contemplate and process my experiences. On a deep level, I knew I had somehow reclaimed a piece of my soul on that trip.

Carla Sridevi Cohen

My "encourager" and I switched roles more than once. I encouraged her, she encouraged me. Our hands were dirty, our knees were scraped, and we were sweaty and uncomfortable. We could not eat or drink because the Sherpas said so. It was tough. We did this for seventeen hours. Seventeen hours of ten steps forward and sliding back seven. Grabbing the sides of the mountain with our bare hands. Crying, whining, wondering what we were thinking.

When we reached the top, we were told to remove our shoes. The mountain was covered in burs and rocks, but it was considered holy. It would be disrespectful to walk with shoes on holy ground.

I could see tridents, signs of Shiva off in the distance, as well as a kind of makeshift tent. I could feel the holy man from where I stood. He must have been over two thousand yards away. I had no resistance left. I was empty. I had no thoughts. My exhaustion had left me silent inside. I removed my shoes. The woman who had been my encourager, sat down on the ground, defeated. She would not remove her shoes. She no longer cared whether she met the Holy man and got his blessing. She was exhausted and broken.

I got as close to his tent as I could. I had brought some gifts for him, which I left at his door. He started singing and praying. I felt myself being transported somewhere else. I was overcome with love and peace. I remember I cried, but this time the tears were those of gratitude. I knew that I had been in the presence of

WOMEN IN THE *Modern* BUSINESS WORLD

There was no life to be found, but then at some point, we passed by a few huts. Without warning, and very quickly, we were surrounded by hundreds of Indian children who were looking for candy and wanting us to take their picture. My camera was on the fritz, but I had been warned and had brought Jolly Rancher watermelon candy from the states. They fully appreciated the candy and squealed with delight. The throng followed us for a while, until they got bored or were called home.

It seemed like forever, before we were actually gaining altitude. We finally reached a clearing. I looked up and said to the Sherpas, "This doesn't seem so bad, is that the mountain there?" I had pointed to a lower mountain in the distance. "Oh no, not that mountain missy. <u>That Mountain</u>". I almost fell over. That mountain was at least five times higher than the one I was pointing at and we had already done a fair amount of climbing. It was too late to turn back. I was in the middle of nowhere. There was nothing to do but go forward.

When we reached our actual mountain, it was mostly shale. For every ten steps forward, we slid back seven. It was defeating and exhausting. I remember crying. I also was sure I would never make it to the top. One of the women just kept urging me on. "You came all this way. You have to have to go to the top." I would climb for an hour or two, cry for a while, then go through the same process all over again.

Carla Sridevi Cohen

Every morning, I would climb the 108 steps down to the Ganges and bathe in the sacred icy water. During the day, I helped build a rock wall to protect the temple on the other side of the ravine from the monsoons. I had never touched rocks that felt so alive. It was hard labor, but I actually enjoyed myself. We did our laundry in the river and hung it on the bushes to dry in the afternoon sun. I had very little appetite for Ashram food and rarely ate a meal. I lived on these cookies that were like an Indian version of an Oreo. I had very little excess weight on me then, but my Oreo diet easily helped me drop another ten pounds. Luckily, I met some lovely Italians who had their own café and made me scrumptious food to eat whenever their deliveries arrived with Italian friends.

Stay On The Path, Wild Tigers

I had heard rumors about a renunciant hermit, turned Saint, who was living on top of Mt. Kailash. He supposedly never came out of his tent but had this amazing impact on people. Some of the Sherpas heard of our interest in meeting him and offered to lead a group of us up the mountain to get his blessing. I had no idea what I was in for.

We started really early, before dawn with strict instructions that we do not eat or drink unless given permission. The altitude was a big factor, and they did not want us to get sick. The hike started out gentle enough. We waded across the river, through fields of wheat and dry arid land. The cool morning gave way to some pretty strong afternoon sun. The path was dirty and dusty. They warned us to stay on the path for fear of wild tigers.

Throughout all of this, I continued with breathing practices and bodywork to gently release old thoughts and emotions with different coaches. I studied both Vivation and Rebirthing. It turned out the woman behind the conscious breath movement in Los Angeles was very connected to Babaji. It all started to come full circle. By this time, I was also coming out more as a healer and had started traveling to different cities and countries to offer healing sessions and teach.

I finally received the letter inviting me to travel to India with the group. I had no idea what awaited me there, but as I said earlier, I felt a compulsion to go. After New Delhi, we traveled north toward Uttar Pradesh. From Haldwani, a rickety bus up a narrow winding hold-your-breath road to the Ashram. The Ashram itself is deep in the Himalayas, very near the source of the Ganges River. The last few miles for entry meant wading through a raging river or hiking down a steep hillside with donkeys and Sherpas. We did the hike. As we carefully navigated our way down the slope, I couldn't help but notice an army of wild monkeys along the opposite side of the ravine checking us out.

The dorm was like a cave. It was dark and cold. Spots were first come, first serve, so I grabbed the first bed closest to the door. I liked the airflow and there were some natural shelves where I could put my stuff. It also felt a little more private. Later on, I found out that I had picked the bed directly beneath Babaji's room. Undeniably, the most energetically charged location in the ashram; this led to some very intense experiences.

CARLA SRIDEVI COHEN

medicine clinic. That place became my lab. I used all of my tools, including essential oils to help people who didn't believe in any of this "alternative" stuff to heal. I ended up having a two-months waiting list.

Babaji and a letter to India

I was a good healer, but not the best businesswoman. Like many healers I wrestled with what I should or shouldn't charge. I spent thousands of hours to develop my skills and well over $30,000, but never focused on how to run a business. I wanted to make money, but my focus was really on helping people and I had trouble reconciling the two, often giving more than what I felt okay receiving.

A man who identified himself as Babaji started appearing to me and teaching me in dreams. They were very real. I would wake up with full recall. I actively sought out information on him and found out he had died twelve years before he revealed himself to me.

Clearly a doorway had opened to another part of me. I was even hearing Sanskrit songs in my dreams and meditation. I met some people, who knew some people, who found out a group was going to his Ashram in the Himalayas. I knew I had to go whenever the next opportunity came up and I knew I needed a guide. From what I had heard, the Ashram was deep in the Himalayas and impossible to get to, unless you had a connection.

WOMEN IN THE *Modern* BUSINESS WORLD

I started seeing things on people's bodies that I had no words for. Instinctively, I knew they were blocks. I had a rapid expansion of psychic abilities and no resources to help me make sense of what I was experiencing. Again, I had to do my own research and started consuming any book that could help me get some understanding of my new awareness.

I was a corporate girl who had been thrust into another world entirely. More teachers seemed to appear out of nowhere. I met a Lakota Indian Chief who invited me to multiple sweat lodges and schooled me in native American healing. I remember climbing… no crawling, out the tent and collapsing face down in the dirt. How dignified! He unceremoniously threw a bucket of cold water on me to bring me round.

I met an extremely amazing psychic body language expert, named Patrick, and apprenticed with him and another exceptional bodyworker, Don. Don looked like a beer brawler and a sailor, but his hands were magic; they felt like they encompassed the world when he touched me. I studied intensely with him and he was the first to publicly endorse my healing work. I dove deep into tons of breathwork, energy work, Myofascial release, Pranic healing, Cranial Sacral, and even some Rolfing. I studied some Chinese medicine and plant medicine.

I wanted to be able to work in more traditional settings, so I set myself on a course to learn anatomy, massage, sports medicine, and a deep dive into essential oils. Before I finished my course of study, I was invited to audition my work at a sports

Carla Sridevi Cohen

I settled onto her massage table and she put her hands on me. Almost immediately, she ordered me to get off the massage table. She told me that I was a very powerful healer and that my problem was that I had no idea how to control my energy. We switched positions, she got on the table, and my apprenticeship began. I paid her and worked on her. This went on for a couple of years. I also did distance readings and healings on her clients for her. What a gig for her, right?

In the meantime, I was spotted by a very well-known local psychic at the shop where I had met the Tarot Reader. Charlene owned and operated the Cosmic Academy of Healing Arts, a modern-day Hogwarts for promising healers and psychics. She saw my potential and invited me into her spiritual practitioner certification course. She took a particular interest in developing my skills and routinely quizzed me on different things to stretch and test my psychic abilities. I worked my way through courses in distance healing, psychic self-defense, crystals, ESP, psychometry, energy clearing, Tarot and more. I honestly wish I had written down the names of some of the talent who showed up there. That place was a magnet and a light for the gifted.

As I continued with my meditation practice, I started to have some things happen that I couldn't explain. My teacher said not to make anything important that happened. That was the only advice I received. He never warned me about anything, and he was not reachable.

When we did my initiation into TM and Vaughn recited the lineage of the gurus, I knew it. Not like I could recite it, but I knew it. I immediately took to the practice and have not missed a day of meditation since. This was over thirty years ago. I initially felt like someone had just helped me clear the cobwebs out of my mind and body. Every time I did TM it was a different experience, but the constant was the feeling of having my house swept clean.

A Modern Day Hogwarts

One night, the meditators needed a place to practice, so we offered our home. The first person over the threshold was a very old meditator. She looked me in the eyes with great conviction and said, "This is the home of a very powerful healer". I was a little taken aback but didn't respond. I had no way to mentally process what she was saying to me, nor did I have any context.

Within a week of that experience, I felt a little better and had heard there was a psychic fair not too far away. I had a Tarot reading done and the woman said, "Oh, you have been sick for a really long time. What you need is energy balancing." I was at the point where if someone had told me to click my heels together, whistle a tune, and dance a jig to heal; I would have done it. I asked what energy balancing was. She said she could not explain, but that it costs $50. I had no money. I mean no money for anything. That night, someone gave me a check for $50. I was on the phone the next day booking my session.

Carla Sridevi Cohen

was enough to really mess with my head and my confidence. Suddenly, the reality I thought was true... that I had based my life on, was gone.

I spent two years and a ton of money going to all kinds of healing professionals, alternative doctors, bodyworkers, massage, chiropractors, acupuncturists and more. I had shots injected in me of vitamins - and God knows what else - to help me. When I could stay awake, I studied nutrition and books on natural healing. I read tons of metaphysical books. My mom and dad came over quite often during the day to help. I was so weak I could not walk from the bedroom to the bathroom in our tiny 800 square foot house without help. I remember laying in a chaise lounge in a sleepy haze under the giant elm in our backyard, staring up at the umbrella of leaves, wondering if I would wake up from this horrible dream.

On one of the days where I felt a little better, my neighbor happened to mention that she was going to check out a Transcendental Meditation Introduction. I invited myself to go with her. I was moved by the experience and wanted to sign up. Remember though, it had been two years of zero income from my end. The TM practitioner/trainer, Vaughn, quoted the price and I just looked at him. I wanted this, he saw that in me, but I also could not pay. He must have asked me in four or five ways if I could afford it, but I could not offer him anything in the moment. He looked me straight in the eyes and told me he felt compelled to teach me. I knew it was true and I knew I was supposed to learn TM. We agreed that when I had money, I would send it to him.

WOMEN IN THE *Modern* BUSINESS WORLD

My "come to Jesus" moment

My normal habit of sitting and reading on my sofa at work, turned into short naps, and then longer naps. I was running out of juice and had no idea I was about to hit a wall. It got so bad, I had to quit. At the same time, they were about to fire me.

I went to the doctors for answers. They ran tests on every part of me, testing every liquid in my body and probing every orifice. The doctors were not sure exactly what was going on. My brain started to feel foggy. I had an elevated white blood cell count and constant fever. All I could do was sleep. They threw out terms like Epstein Barr, CFS, and Lyme Disease, but the tests were never conclusive. They asked me if I was depressed, I said I wasn't. Regardless, they sent me home with antidepressants and told me I would just have to sleep until this cleared up.

I remember taking one of the antidepressants and getting very depressed. I was trying to fix my hair and collapsed on top of the toilet, too weak to lift my hands over my head. I threw the rest of the pills out and have not done another antibiotic or over the counter medication since.

This was my "come to Jesus" moment. My doctors could not fix me. My parents could not help me. I had been the main wage earner in my marriage for twelve years. I no longer could trust my body to do what I wanted. That single thing, right there,

CARLA SRIDEVI COHEN

I really loved my new boss. He was super sharp, and we had fun collaborating. I had been working for him for about seven months, when the owners of our company fired him and asked me to take over. They offered me a change in title, but no raise. I was uncomfortable taking my friend's position, but I could not afford to quit. I literally called him and asked his permission to take the job. He encouraged me to stay. He knew I was in no position to leave.

My hours grew with my responsibilities. In addition to supervising and training a small team of readers - the people who read and analyze stories - I had my own books, scripts, and treatments to read, analyze and fix. I was also packaging talent with the more promising projects. In order to stay afloat, I found myself putting in at least seventy hours a week. I was working more hours for less money. I packed some boxes and fully intended to quit, but as I was leaving, they offered me a raise, so I stayed.

I was making nowhere near what my male counterpart had made, but, by now, I had started to wise up to the fact that the money and recognition issues I had encountered throughout my career in public relations and in development were more an indication of the institutionalized chauvinism in Hollywood, than a reflection of my personal value. Hollywood was a man's world. Between the crazy long hours, constant striving, financial pressures, and lack of encouragement from a male dominated industry, I was feeling exhausted most of the time. Our office was toxic. My bosses routinely did drugs that wafted down the hallway. How was I supposed to conduct business?

physique and routinely touted the benefits of a 5am workout routine. He was also a long-time friend of John Wayne.

Andy liked the sound of his own voice and would roam the hallways reciting lines from John Wayne movies. He was also constantly giving mixed signals. On the one hand, he encouraged me to read scripts, develop story ideas and actively seek out books that might be good for movies. He seemed to encourage me to come out professionally as a story developer. On the other hand, culturally he was a typical Greek man. He treated me like his daughter, but also sprinkled on a fair amount of chauvinism. Unsolicited, he had a tendency to comment regularly and sometimes unfavorably on my hair, my weight, or my appearance. At that time, I was a size 6, but I thought I was fat. I look back now and think, what was I thinking?

When I worked for him, he promised me that if any of the movies I helped develop eventually went to production, I would receive payment. I believed him. Imagine my surprise and disappointment when I saw one of the movies that I helped him develop on TV with no credit to me and no payment.

I was looking for something and didn't know what, so I took a course at UCLA night school on the history of Hollywood. The paper I turned in for my final got me an A+ and an offer to get me an interview. A friend of the teacher's was looking for a development person to help the new Head of Development at a production company. We hit it off and I was hired.

Carla Sridevi Cohen

A Kept Woman

I started looking for a new cause and was contacted by a temp agency about a permanent job. It was an unorthodox interview. We met at a Jewish deli to chat. She hired me on the spot. I started the next day at Lorimar/MGM Studios as an assistant for the woman in charge of Cable Movie Development. Cable movies were still fairly new as a genre.

The problem was the company was not doing well. Our billionaire founder was into some sketchy stuff and eventually was convicted of tax fraud. Our company had a couple of hits like War Games and Mr. Mom, but the winds were changing, and our production company was about to get kicked off the lot. When my boss' contract ended, she kept me on a retainer for months. Sometimes I worked and sometimes I didn't. She didn't want me hired by someone else, so she took me off the market. I was a kept woman. Occasionally, I helped out one of her producer or director friends.

We hopped around at a few studios, finally landing a home at Twentieth Century Fox. When her contract ended, a year later, she was escorted off the lot by security. It was the way things were done, but it was humiliating, and my heart bled for her. A different producer, who had seen me at work for her, didn't even wait for the body to get cold. He solicited me to come work for him before I could blink. Andy was a proud American Greek man, a good writer, albeit old fashioned, but he was considered a successful producer. He was proud of his revolt when his job was given to a guy who was rumored to sort through office trash cans at night and knew nothing about our clients. The company wanted me to stay on and help the new guy. I was insulted. With two feet out the door, a powerhouse female publicist approached me to work with her and I accepted. I stayed with her for a little over a year. She was Hollywood royalty.

We represented the only 4-star Michelin restaurant in LA, L'Hermitage, Finlandia Vodka, Pottery Barn, Richard Zanuck, Irwin Winkler, Lee Rich, Bud Yorkin and Arnold Kopelson.

I mostly handled the corporate clients and she focused on the talent. I felt especially blessed to work with L'Hermitage. I was a foodie and Patrick, the Chef/Owner was always very appreciative of my work and my palate. After hours, he would make me special meals and treat me to expensive wines I could not afford. Some were $2,000 a bottle. We would sit and sip golden nectar and chat. It was amazing. My palate was forever spoiled. I was heartbroken when he decided to call it quits and joined Physicians Without Borders.

I enjoyed my clients and my boss. Ronni was fun, smart, and never censored her mouth. She truly was a woman I admired. Regardless, when I was offered a Vice President's slot at another firm, I took it. I did not stay long. I realized public relations was not my life's dream - I had developed an immunity to fawning over celebrities.

Carla Sridevi Cohen

Jim felt my talent was wasted at AFI and encouraged me to apply with one of his friends at Rogers and Cowan, the largest and most prestigious PR firm at the time. I ended up getting hired and placed with the man who had a reputation for being the most difficult of all of the publicists. He literally had a revolving door of assistants, and because of it, everyone was afraid to work for him. Everyone warned me that his assistants lasted no more than a couple of weeks. He was gorgeous, smart, and a hard worker; he was also the only black man at the firm. He worked harder than his white counterparts because he had to, in order to survive in an all-white firm. He was a perfectionist because he didn't want any excuse getting in the way of his success.

I learned to craft publicity campaigns, news releases and actively handled clients. Ramon was a good but tough teacher. He treated me like an equal, and I was a willing student. I also really loved the work, so I ended up working with him for a couple of years. Our firm, Rogers and Cowan had everyone who was anyone at that time. Our team handled Bette Midler, George Benson, Vanessa Williams, Herb Alpert, Peaches and Herb, Ashford and Simpson, Michael Jackson, Priscilla Presley, Lola Falana, Ann-Margret, Lionel Ritchie, the Commodores, the Bee Gees and so many more. My boss and I shouldered seventeen clients, more than any other publicists at the firm.

My boss realized he had gone as far as he was going to go at R&C, so he eventually left. Everyone thought I would be promoted to take over his/our clients. There was nearly a

WOMEN IN THE *Modern* BUSINESS WORLD

We worked in the old Doheny mansion. It was a gorgeous place to spend my days. Home to the Doheny family for nearly sixty years, the Doheny Mansion was built in 1899. The grounds and gardens were magnificent. The mansion is as grand as it sounds - Romantic Revivalist on the outside and dripping with opulence on the inside. I loved the energy that permeated the place – ghosts of a golden era; the grandeur of the endless shiny black and white marble floors, the long staircase and ceilings that went on for days.

The mansion's layout was perfect for film shoots and a party, so I took it on myself to organize their first ever Christmas party. I worked for two bosses, the Faculty Head, and the Director in charge of the Independent Filmmaker Program and Directing Workshop for Women. I found my niche there helping write grant proposals for funding. I also met a few directors who went on to become quite famous.

While at AFI, I befriended an older man who handled their public relations, Jim Powers. He would tell me stories of the golden era of Hollywood and he literally knew where all the bodies were buried. Jim had connections at every major studio and knew people at the most important Hollywood publications, like the Hollywood Reporter and Daily Variety. He had personal relationships with some of the most famous and infamous gossip columnists like George Christy, Hedda Hopper and Louella Parsons. He was a true gentleman, very giving and caring. To my knowledge, he did not have any kids, and I think he got a real kick out of mentoring me.

Carla Sridevi Cohen

I was happiest when I traveled. By the time I was seventeen, I had camped more times than I can remember, been across the United States several times, traveled to Europe and spent time living in Cusco, Peru and Newcastle, England. When I met my husband, I warned him about my gypsy spirit, and he knew what he was getting into.

I went to college but never felt like I found my calling until I was introduced to Sociology. I became a Sociology major on a bet. I enjoyed hanging out with my teachers and the postgraduates. It was a progressive culture, and I enjoyed it. The Graduates students and Faculty thought I belonged there, and they encouraged me to attend postgraduate courses even though I was an undergraduate. I just could not see myself staying on for a PhD for four more years, so I would teach.

Hollywood's Golden Nectar

My husband wanted Hollywood and I didn't know what I wanted, so we moved back up to Los Angeles. The first job I landed was at the American Film Institute (AFI). Frankly, it was a miracle. I had none of the qualifications, but the two women doing the interview liked me and promised to train me. The pay was good, and I instantly fell in with the people who worked there.

WOMEN IN THE *Modern* BUSINESS WORLD

Most of my life, I felt a little displaced, like I didn't quite fit in. I had been skipped forward twice in school and, after starting in one high school, was transferred to a new one that opened. Our new school was the first school where they bussed in black people to achieve integration. That was not a problem for me, but the skipping grades was. My friends were always older than me and I lost some good friends and some dreams I had when I had to change High Schools. I was very attached to the school I was at and was looking forward to tryouts as a Highlander dancer - the dancers were featured like cheerleaders at all of the football games. I didn't want to skip grades again; it had already happened to me in junior high. In the end, the adults decided I would jump forward again for my own good.

In high school, I would sometimes wear clothes from other countries. No one batted an eye at my odd antics. For me, it was a way to express myself. An Indian girlfriend of mine used to lend me her saris. She was gorgeous and I wanted to look like her. Somehow, I had a Kimono type outfit and matching Geisha sandals that I also remember wearing.

I joined the newspaper and the choir because I liked singing and journalism. I hung out with the smart girls, drama majors, geeky techno-nerds, and other journalists. I regret I never thought about learning to act. My friend Morgan, who was a drama major, always seemed so confident, mysterious, and interesting. I had friends but I felt awkward socially.

Carla Sridevi Cohen

about me getting health insurance. I was not going to spend money on that, so ultimately, she bought health insurance for me and reluctantly wished me well.

A Narrow Escape

After twenty-four hours in Delhi, I was still acclimating. When the rest of our group arrived, we all went for a day of shopping, some decent food, and a stretch. Much as I wanted to explore New Delhi, I was feeling off. My sense was that I needed to get more rest. The woman who organized the trip was not too happy with me, but she flagged a cabby down, told him where to take me, and ordered me to get in. As we sped through the crowded streets of Delhi, he started asking me some very odd invasive questions. I grew more and more agitated and started to feel like his intentions were not good.

I had heard stories of Western women being abducted into sex trafficking. My gut was tightening, telling me I wasn't safe. I am not normally a fearful person, but my right and left brain went to war in those moments. Logically, I had very little money on me, and was not clear where I was. My gut was now yelling at me, "get out!". We stopped at a stop light; my survival instincts kicked into high gear. I jumped out the cab into the middle of a chaotic, crowded intersection, horns honking, cars without lanes and people everywhere. I successfully signal another driver and miraculously make my way safely back to the hotel. Lesson one, right or wrong, trust your gut.

WOMEN IN THE
Modern
BUSINESS WORLD

My travel partner pulls down her blankets to reveal a layer of crumbs. I don't dare touch the blankets on the bed. Our trip organizer, whom we are scheduled to meet, is delayed somewhere in the Gulf due to a storm. It is very late. There is no way to change rooms. I am a good traveler and pretty flexible, but this is way beyond any idea of bad I had ever experienced. We are too afraid and ill prepared to strike out on our own, so we stay. Welcome to India!

There is a note for us in an envelope, advising us to hunker down in our rooms for our own safety, and keep the doors locked. I lay my plastic poncho over the bed to protect me from potential bed bugs; climb into my clean sleeping bag and do my best to crash. Sometime during the night, someone jiggles our door and tries to get in. I am blasted out of bed the next morning by the sounds of Muslim prayers blaring over loudspeakers directly into our room from the mosque next door. What had I gotten myself into?

Yes, I felt called to India. It was an overwhelming urge to find something I felt I was missing. I couldn't articulate what I was feeling at the time, but I just knew that I knew that I had to go.

I was already married, I had already spent two years in bed, sick from something they never could truly nail. My husband supported my choice to go. My mom, who had taken care of me during my two-year bout of sickness, was understandably against me going. I remember us fighting. She was adamant

Carla Sridevi Cohen

Literally sixty or so people are screaming at once at the arriving passengers; holding signs with names, trying to hustle naive Westerners into their cab for too much money or trying to locate their assigned fair. It is utter chaos. The air is humid. I am exhausted, scared and exhilarated at the same time.

We flag down a cabbie and are thrown into the bargaining process on price. This guy seems decent enough, so we hop in, not realizing the hinge on his trunk is not closing properly. There are horns blaring, minicabs, bicycles, cars all driving in random directions – there don't seem to be lanes for coming and going. As we make our way through the crowded Indian streets to our hotel, I hear pounding from the rear. The trunk, where my luggage is stuffed, has sprung completely open and is percussing on my suitcase. I cross my fingers, hoping my bag makes it to the hotel with us.

All I want is a clean bed and a hot shower. In my head, I am not expecting American, but I am expecting clean and decent. We are supposed to meet our group here. The place is called Hotel Ranjit. It should have been named Hotel Rancid. The room is a total shock. I knew this was a budget trip, but I had no idea we were talking about a dilapidated slum.

The floors are one big red concrete slab. There is nothing separating the floor between the bathroom and the bedroom. The pipes in the room are rusted and clogged. The bath towels are badly stained. My roommate showers first and, as she finishes water leaches into the sleeping room floor.

WOMEN IN THE *Modern* BUSINESS WORLD

It has been close to two days of flying and I am relieved when we finally hit the heavily potholed tarmac of Indira Gandhi International Airport in New Delhi. Clearly, I am no longer in the USA; there is no one even trying to stop the wave of anarchy that sweeps through the plane. We are still moving, nowhere near the gate. Unfastened seat belts dangle en masse down the aisle, as the plane continues to roll. Nearly everyone stands up, fighting for space and pulling down their luggage over everyone else's heads. If it wasn't so dangerous, it would be funny.

I finally get off the plane. Stiff and swollen from sitting too long, I am struck by how challenging and healing it is to simply walk down the hallway toward customs. After being jostled about by the passengers who were making a mad grab for their luggage, I am still a bit on guard from my earlier encounter with the sex hungry man; all of my senses are on hyper-alert. Not too happily, we carry our luggage down an escalator that isn't working and wait for an elevator. After we help a man get into the elevator with his luggage, another man lets the elevator doors close in our face and hijacks it downstairs.

From a lengthy and tedious process with immigration, we miraculously find our way to the receiving area. My senses have no idea what awaits them. First my nose is overloaded, then my ears. There are multiple aromas - curry, fabric softener, carnations, urine, and foul body odor, mixed with cigarette fumes, garlic, stale incense, motorcycle exhaust, horrid hair product smells and cheap perfume. People are hanging over the railing, trying to get our attention. Everyone is yelling.

Carla Sridevi Cohen

we can disembark outside the terminal. Our feet slide on the icy stairs while our faces are kissed by a soft leisurely burst of snowflakes. The crisp, cold air is a relief after so many hours of sucking in stale air on the plane. Even though it is wickedly cold outside, I don't bother to put on my jacket. I just have time to get a fresh salad and some cheese before my next flight to India. Frankfurt is a lovely place for a layover. My last stop in a clean orderly world before I enter the chaotic, exotic, and mysterious land known as India.

I climb through the doorway of the next plane and am struck by the fact that most of the passengers are male - heads covered with turbans - predominantly Sikh. There are very few women on this flight and even fewer Westerners. I smile at the Sikh man sitting next to me, and he counters my smile by soliciting me for sex instead of having a polite conversation. Really? This is not the first time I have encountered a man in a foreign country who thinks that ALL Western women just can't wait to have sex. I quickly approached the flight attendant to rescue me to another seat. After that man's lascivious advances, I suddenly crave a shower.

I end up in a row of empty seats very far away; a place I can relax without fear of molestation. Across the aisle, a soldier is fast asleep before the wheels are up. He's out the entire flight. I had never seen someone who was so adept at sleeping through the worst turbulence I had ever experienced. Somehow, miraculously, I connect with Kate, another woman who is part of my group.

CHAPTER 1

CARLA SRIDEVI COHEN

Will Over Circumstance: Rising From The Ashes

From Hollywood to Healer

> "No one saves us but ourselves. No one can and no one may. We ourselves must walk the path."
> Buddha

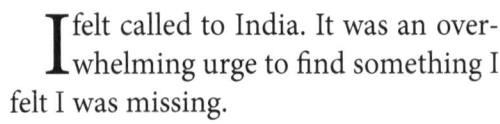

January 9, 1993

I felt called to India. It was an overwhelming urge to find something I felt I was missing.

After nearly a full day of flying, from LA to Frankfurt, we arrive. A rolling staircase is brought out to the plane so

WOMEN IN THE *Modern* BUSINESS WORLD

By the time you finish this book, you will know what you really want and how can you turn your gifts into a successful global business. You never know how strong you are until being strong is the only choice you have.

I am both privileged and inspired to introduce you with these outstanding women who wrote not just a chapter of the book, but a new chapter for many women who will follow their path to succeeded. As Winston Churchill would say:

"We make the living by what we get but we make our life by what we give"

Mirela Sula
Founder of Global Woman

thought leader, can create in your own life to strengthen your business and your brand on a global scale.

"Women of the Modern Business World" will stir you to find clarity and creativity on multiple levels, so you can return to your projects from a place of deep presence and renewed imagination and create your leadership path in your home country. You'll gain insights into how to grow your business and leave here feeling empowered. These women have not only shared their wisdom with us but also they have invested so much energy to bring their stores as real and authentic to you. And you know, everything that we do takes energy, and if we want to be successful it takes even more, time and investment. You need to have a reason and a vision of something you're truly passionate about, where you are serving more than yourself. This will give you energy, and will keep you going regardless of any obstacles you hit along the way.

These chapters from thirteen different women around the world will remind you to be hungry and learn everyday. To benefit from our experiences and not be scared to face new challenges in life. To see, to feel, by taking carefully calculated steps and follow our own intuition. We need to have the attitude to fight hard for the things we want and always be hungry and search for more. We should not stop seeking the place where we feel good and make sure our roots are firmly planted there. Life will bind us up in its arms and then we should squeeze it hard with our whole self and love it as long as we breathe.

WOMEN IN THE *Modern* BUSINESS WORLD

This book is designed for the Global Woman leaders who bring revolutionary ideas to the table, in order to give women a voice and the place they deserve.

You are reading this book because you have a mission, a vision bigger than yourself, something you want to outlast you. This is what inspires you to keep going and gives you hope during the dark zones, to see the light at the end of the tunnel, when it feels like nothing is working and you've given it your all. As you read this book, written by exceptional women, you will find not only their stories but also the lessons they learned by working so hard and believing in something beyond them, even when there was nothing left inside. They show us that you have to keep the faith and believe that you can find something more. That's the place where women as heroes sit, the celebrities of the new era.

As you read these chapters, written from women who come from different cultures, backgrounds and all walks of life, you can see how we are all are creating a new movement together, opening a new path that many have only dreamed of. In this dynamic and rapidly changing community, I have met so many women who know that the constant and never ending improvement is the only way to succeed.

This book is intended to give you the tools that we need to grow, stimulate and achieve the success that you want. The main focus of this book project is on how to optimise and maximise the impact that you as a woman in business, entrepreneur, and

WOMEN IN THE *Modern* BUSINESS WORLD

Let's Go to Your Bigger Future Where Women are the New Celebrities

Foreword by Mirela Sula

It's not what you do – it is how you do it
It's not what you see – it is how you look at it
It's not how your life is – it is how you live it
Unknown

When I started the Global Woman movement it was very important for me to see the full picture of my vision, and this is what inspired me to call women with an entrepreneurial mind to share their stories. This is how everything started, "where the local meets the global" and we all learn how to think outside of the box and women become the heroes of our time.

Acknowledgements

I would like to give special thanks to the following people who have been a huge inspiration in my personal and professional development that has also been instrumental in the growth of Global Woman, with a club membership community network, online members platform, Academy with 200+ videos of informative and educational content, four magazines, and this being the ninth book published by Global Woman.

Veronica Tan
Kim Kiyosaki
Tony Robbins
Ervin Laszlo

Thank you also to my amazing team, past and present, without whom none of this would have been possible.

MIRELA SULA
Founder/CEO Global Woman

Women in the Modern Business World

Editor's note: While some general rules have been applied, you will experience different writing styles in each chapter and either in American English or British English spelling. While a whole chapter will be in one or the other, we have not adopted one rule for the whole book, to reflect the global nature of the writers.

WOMEN IN THE *Modern* BUSINESS WORLD

Chapter 12
Elizabeth Yang
The Power of
Interpretation
page 253

Chapter 13
Nicole Beissler
Dare to Dream
and Succeed
page 271

WOMEN IN THE
Modern
BUSINESS
WORLD

CHAPTER 8
Angela Soong
Born Into Poverty

page 179

CHAPTER 9
Pam Lob
The Meandering Road to
Health and Transformation
page 201

CHAPTER 10
Caroline Nijland
What are the Ingredients
of the Modern Business World?
page 218

CHAPTER 11
Elona Lopari
Your Mess is Your Message -
Use It to Do Good In The World!
page 239

WOMEN IN THE
Modern
BUSINESS
WORLD

CHAPTER 4
Lisseth Barrios
A Woman Creating
Momentum For An Exciting Life
page 82

CHAPTER 5
Maaike Driessen Laverman
Changing the
Perception of a Blueprint
page 102

CHAPTER 6
Inga Phoenix Kokalevská
Raising a New Generation of
Transformational Leaders
page 123

CHAPTER 7
Michelle Wyngaard
Trust Your Inner Voice to Reveal Your
True Self and Step Into Your Genius
page 154

WOMEN IN THE
Modern
BUSINESS
WORLD

Table of Contents

Acknowledgements 10
A word from the publisher, Mirela Sula...............11

CHAPTER 1
Carla Sridevi Cohen
Will Over Circumstance:
Rising From The Ashes
page 15

CHAPTER 2
Laura Götz
Choose to Be The
Hero In Your Life Story!
page 43

CHAPTER 3
Kate Bellosillo
Rising With
Grit and Grace
page 61

WOMEN IN THE *Modern* BUSINESS WORLD

Publisher: GW Publishing
Prepared by: Kicki Pallin
Editor: Trevor Clarke
Art Design: Nevila Samarxhi

E-mail: hello@globalwomanmagazine.com
Web: globalwomanmagazine.com

GW PUBLISHING

London UK, 2020

WOMEN IN THE *Modern* BUSINESS WORLD

"A BLUEPRINT ON HOW TO LEAD YOURSELF TO A BETTER LIFE"

WOMEN IN THE *Modern* BUSINESS WORLD

WOMEN IN
Modern
BUSINESS
W